fushigi yûgi™

The Mysterious Play
VOL. 16: ASSASSIN

Story & Art By
YUU WATASE

FUSHIGI YÛGI
THE MYSTERIOUS PLAY
VOL. 16: ASSASSIN
SHÔJO EDITION

STORY AND ART BY YUU WATASE

Editor's Note: At the author's request, the spelling of Ms. Watase's first name has been changed from "Yû," as it has appeared on previous VIZ publications, to "Yuu."

English Adaptation/William Flanagan
Touch-up & Lettering/Bill Spicer
Touch-up Assistance/Walden Wong
Design/Hidemi Sahara
Editor/Frances E. Wall

Managing Editor/Annette Roman
Director of Production/Noboru Watanabe
Vice President of Publishing/Alvin Lu
Sr. Director of Acquisitions/Rika Inouye
Vice President of Sales & Marketing/Liza Coppola
Publisher/Hyoe Narita

Printed in Canada

Published by VIZ Media, LLC
P.O. Box 77010
San Francisco, CA 94107

Shôjo Edition
10 9 8 7 6 5 4 3 2 1
First printing, September 2005

www.viz.com
store.viz.com

CONTENTS

STORY THUS FAR

In the winter of her third year of middle school, Miaka was whisked away into the pages of a mysterious old book called *THE UNIVERSE OF THE FOUR GODS* and began a dual existence as an ordinary schoolgirl in modern Japan and a priestess of the god Suzaku in a fictional version of ancient China. Miaka fell in love with Tamahome, one of the Celestial Warriors of Suzaku responsible for the protection of the priestess. Miaka's best friend Yui was also sucked into the world of the book and became the priestess of Seiryu, the bitter enemy of Suzaku and Miaka. After clashing repeatedly with the corrupt and vengeful Seiryu Celestial Warriors, Miaka summoned Suzaku and vanquished her enemies, reconciled with Yui, and saved the earth from destruction. In the end, Suzaku granted Miaka one impossible wish: for Tamahome to be reborn as a human in the real world so that the two lovers would never again be separated.

Miaka enters Yotsubadai High School and plans to settle into a normal life with her beloved Tamahome, who is now named Taka Sukunami. But Suzaku returns to give Miaka a new mission: She must re-enter *THE UNIVERSE OF THE FOUR GODS* and find seven special stones that contain Taka's memories from his former life as Tamahome…or her soulmate could disappear forever! After explaining this new task, Suzaku takes up residence in Miaka's watch, and with the help of the reunited Warriors of Suzaku, Miaka and Taka are able to recover three of the stones. But a demon-god named Tenkô keeps terrorizing Miaka and Taka and says he will stop at nothing to thwart their quest! One of Tenkô's servants, Lian, who is posing as an exchange student at Miaka's school, seems able to hypnotize all the students and he uses this power to attack Miaka and to take over the student council. Now, Tenkô has invaded the world of the book as well as the real world, and Taka's future seems to be in grave peril….

THE UNIVERSE OF THE FOUR GODS is based on ancient Chinese legend, but Japanese pronunciation of Chinese names differs slightly from their Chinese equivalents. Here is a short glossary of the Japanese pronunciation of the Chinese names in this graphic novel:

CHINESE	JAPANESE	PERSON OR PLACE	MEANING
Feng-Qi	Hôki	Empress	Phoenix Beauty
Mang-Chen	Bôshin	Crown Prince	Spreading Dawn
Shi-Hang Lian	Shigyo Ren	Transfer student	Worship-Journey Collect
Yang	Yô	A monster clan	Illness
Lian-Fang	Renhô	A monster	Collect Beauty
Lu-Hou	Rokô	Nuriko's brother	Backbone Lord
Liu-Chuan	Ryûen	Nuriko's given name	Willowy Beauty
Mei-Song	Miisû	A monster	Demon on High
Hong-Nan	Konan	Southern Kingdom	Crimson South
Rong-Yang	Eiyô	The Capital	Glorious Heaven
Bei-Jia	Hokkan	Northern Kingdom	Armored North
Lai Lai	Nyan Nyan	A demigod	Nanny
Tai Yi-Jun	Taiitsukun	An Oracle	Preeminent Person
Daichi-san	Daikyokuzan	A mountain	Greatest Mountain

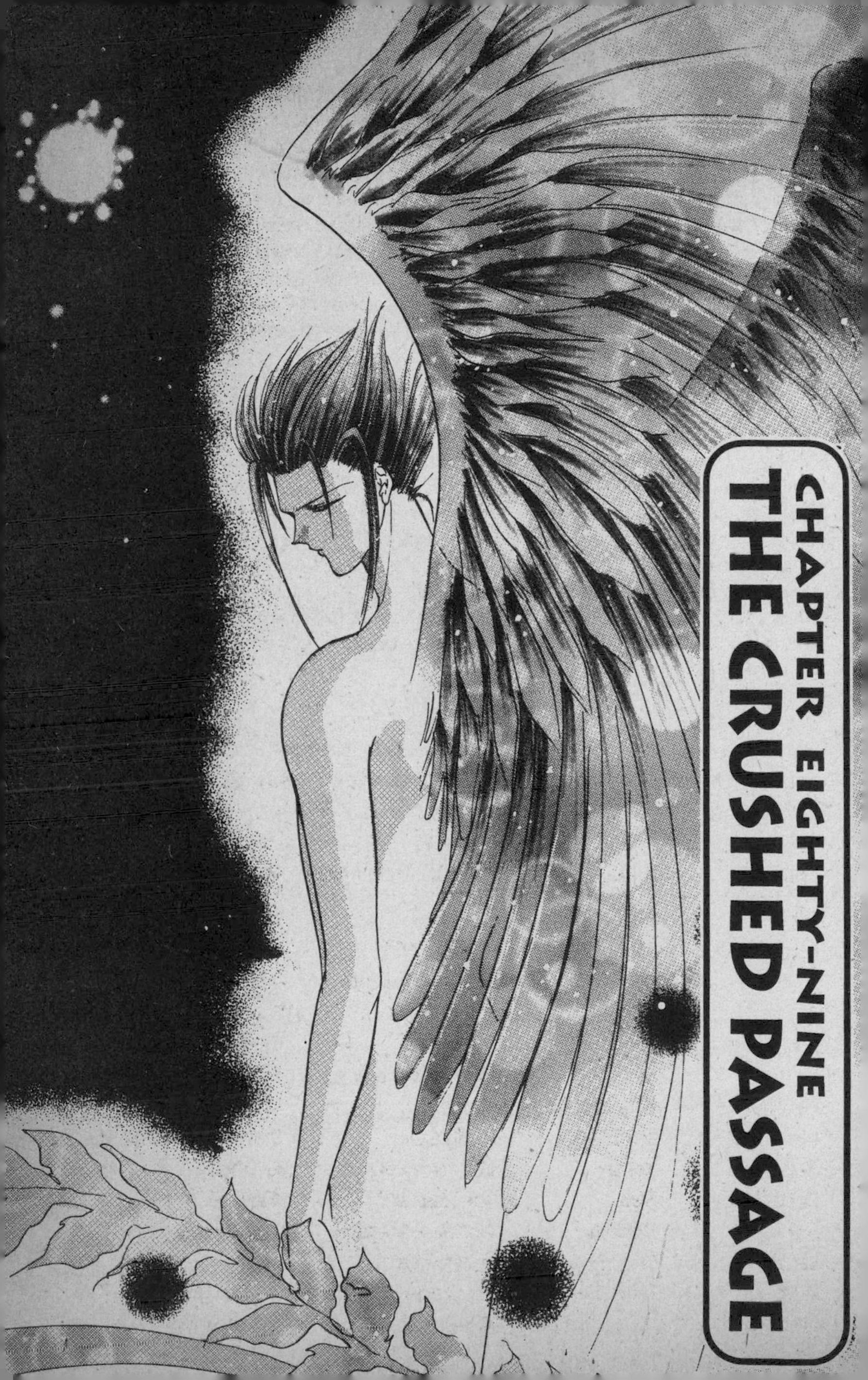
CHAPTER EIGHTY-NINE
THE CRUSHED PASSAGE

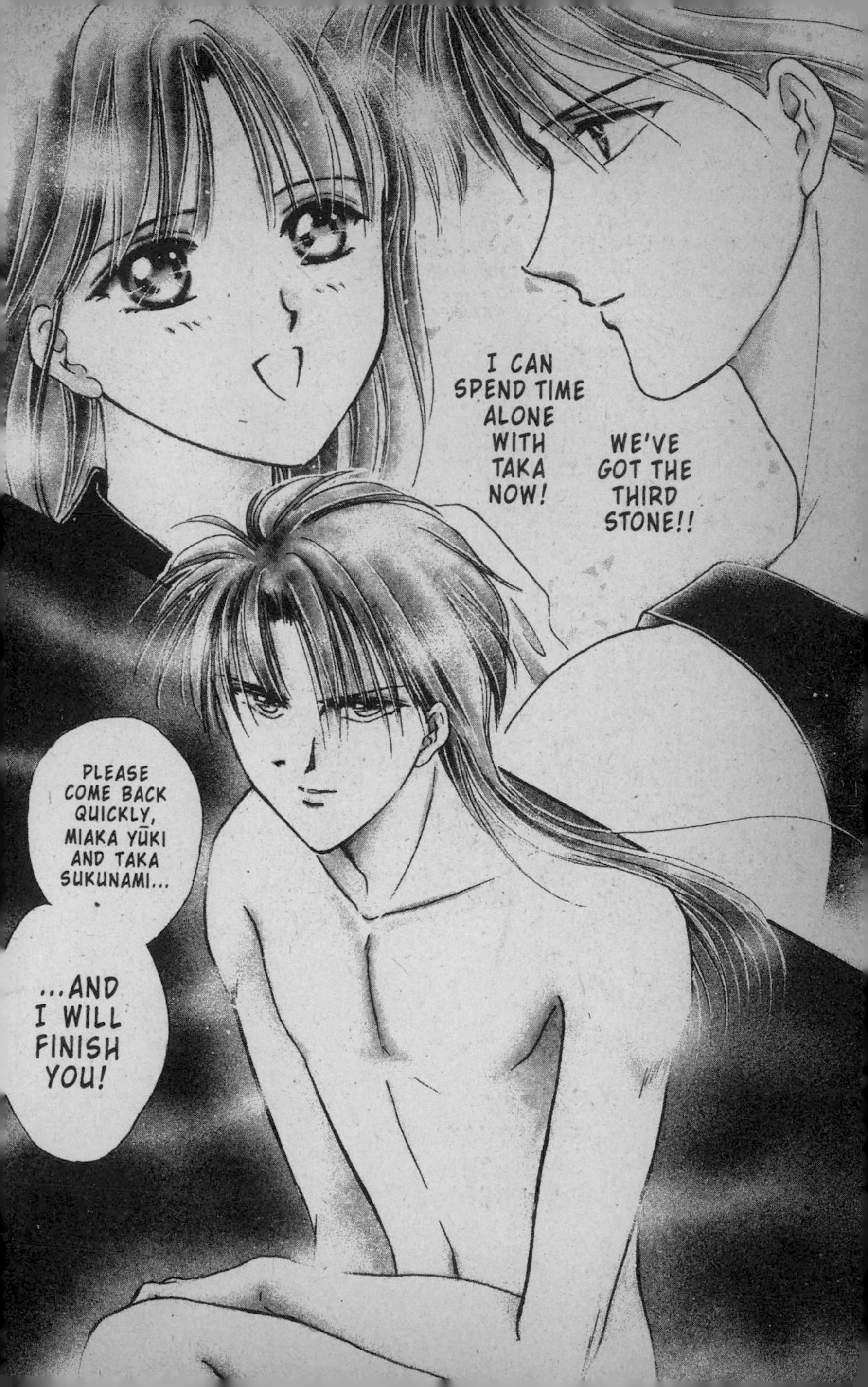
WE'VE GOT THE THIRD STONE!!
I CAN SPEND TIME ALONE WITH TAKA NOW!
PLEASE COME BACK QUICKLY, MIAKA YŪKI AND TAKA SUKUNAMI...
...AND I WILL FINISH YOU!

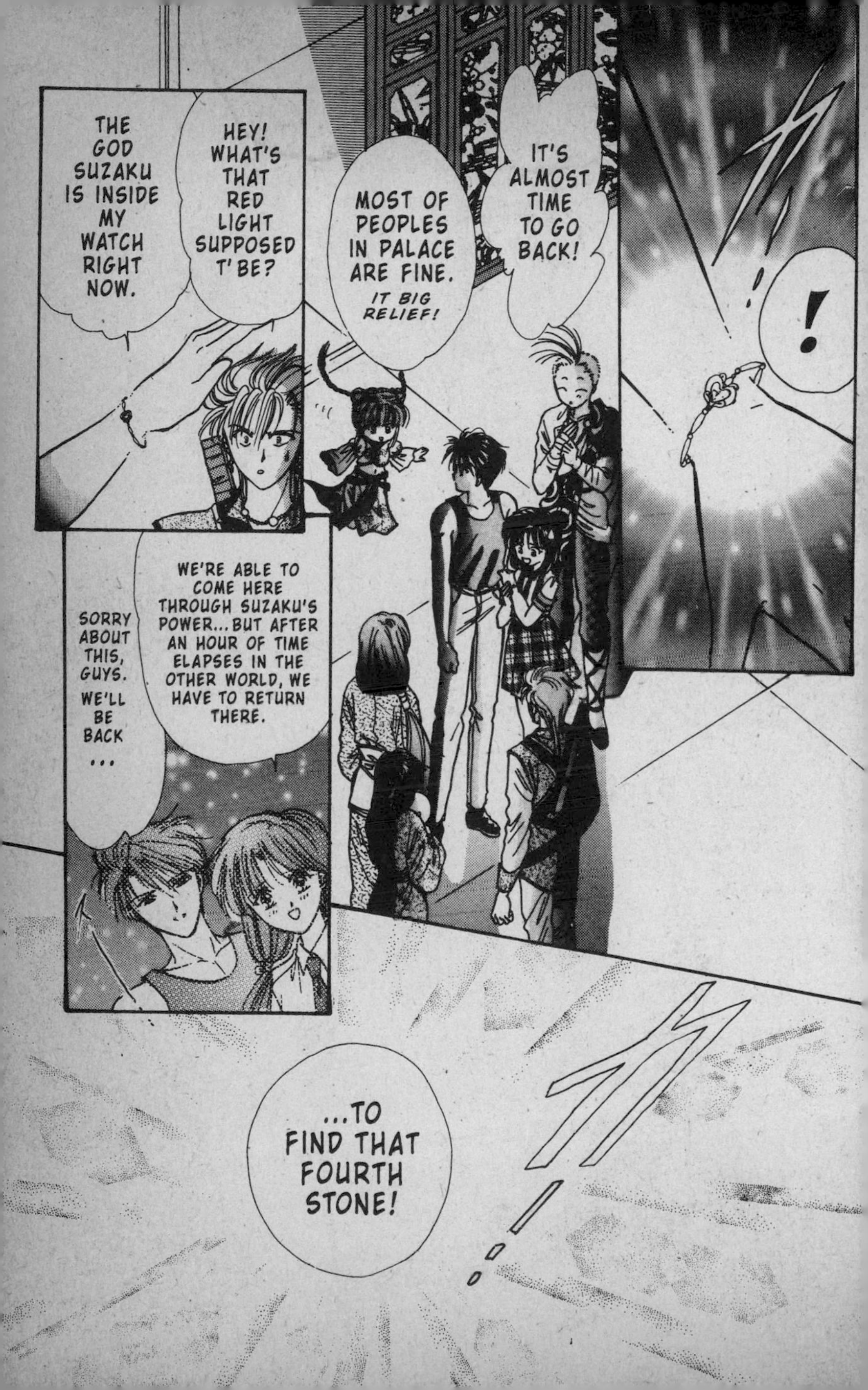
!
IT'S ALMOST TIME TO GO BACK!
MOST OF PEOPLES IN PALACE ARE FINE. IT BIG RELIEF!
HEY! WHAT'S THAT RED LIGHT SUPPOSED T' BE?
THE GOD SUZAKU IS INSIDE MY WATCH RIGHT NOW.
WE'RE ABLE TO COME HERE THROUGH SUZAKU'S POWER... BUT AFTER AN HOUR OF TIME ELAPSES IN THE OTHER WORLD, WE HAVE TO RETURN THERE.
SORRY ABOUT THIS, GUYS. WE'LL BE BACK ...
...TO FIND THAT FOURTH STONE!

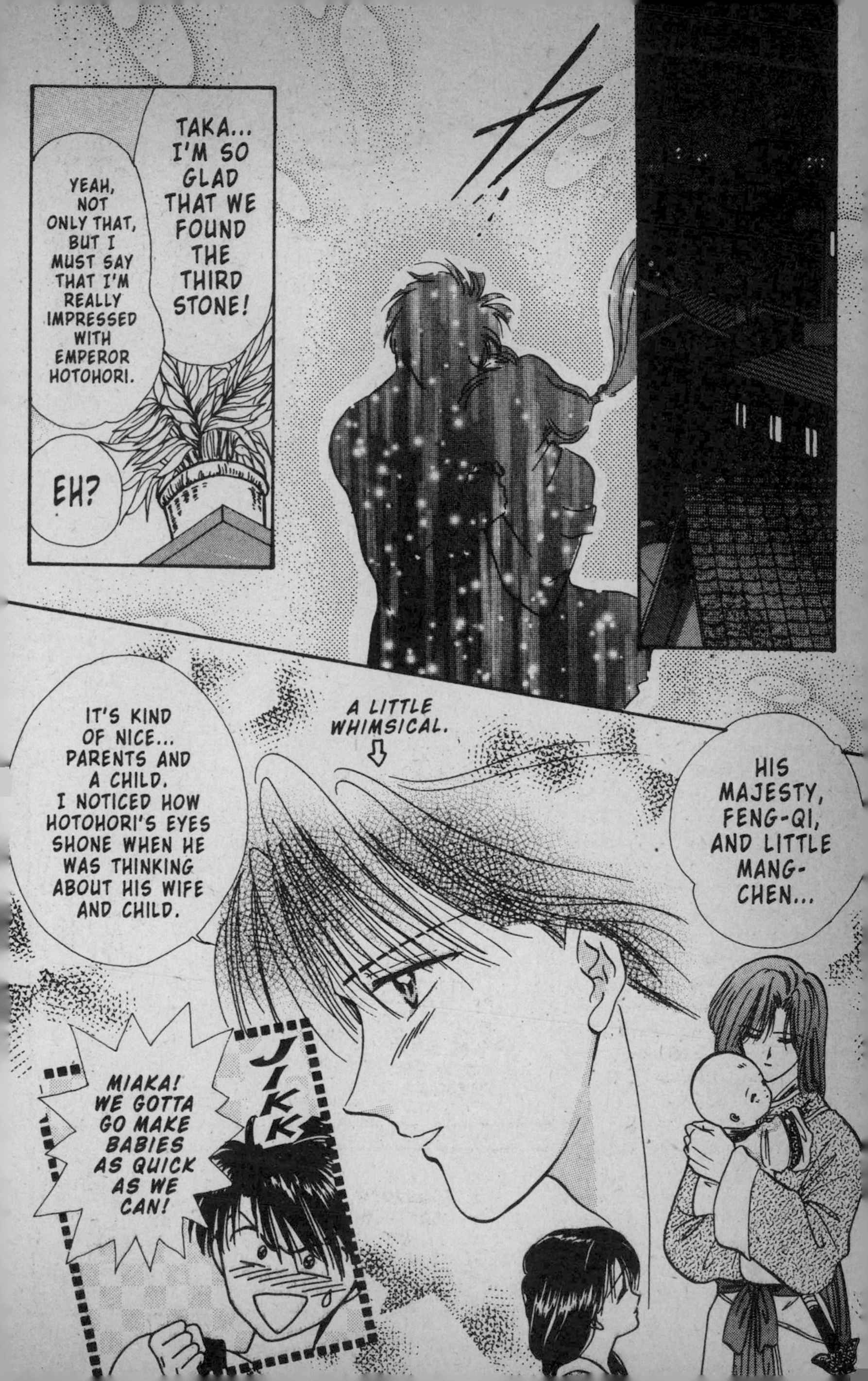
TAKA... I'M SO GLAD THAT WE FOUND THE THIRD STONE!
YEAH, NOT ONLY THAT, BUT I MUST SAY THAT I'M REALLY IMPRESSED WITH EMPEROR HOTOHORI.
EH?
HIS MAJESTY, FENG-QI, AND LITTLE MANG-CHEN...
A LITTLE WHIMSICAL.
IT'S KIND OF NICE... PARENTS AND A CHILD. I NOTICED HOW HOTOHORI'S EYES SHONE WHEN HE WAS THINKING ABOUT HIS WIFE AND CHILD.
JIKK
MIAKA! WE GOTTA GO MAKE BABIES AS QUICK AS WE CAN!

I was so surprised that we're already on Volume 16! Yay! That's normal for shōjo manga, but for shōjo manga, it's like...whoa! Yay! Ha! What am I talking about!? Hello everybody, this is Watase. In the background, the soundtrack for Miaka and the Seven Warriors is playing. But this isn't a CD. It's a tape where we've put a whole bunch of music from a variety of sources recorded off of CD. I'm lonely for my TV! By the way, have you picked up all nine of the "Character Vocal Collection" CDs yet? Watase loves them all!! The lyrics are great...the music is wonderful! Everything about them! ✿ ☺ I think it would be great if they were collected somehow! A CD box set would be just fantastic!

Now, to continue the story about the Taiwan signing... It ended without incident. (Oh, yeah! I received quite a lot of hand-arranged bouquets!) There were some other things that made for ⇦ fond memories, too.
I was invited to the home of Mr. Xie, a movie director. The interior design of his home was amazing! It was such a clever use of limited space! He lives in an old, traditional Chinese home, and I learned so much! I also got some tea out of the deal! ☺ The president of Daran Publishing was kind enough to give me a seal that he received from Mr. Xie. I was shocked! It's a seal that was made by an artisan named Yù from the Ch'ing (Manchu) dynasty, and usually only serious collectors of cultural objects own stuff like it! It's really valuable! ☺ So right now I'm keeping it very safe! Oh, also Daran Publishing took me to their offices to see how they do things. Everybody was smiling, and I really felt at home!

I got several soundtracks from the animation company! ♪ I also received six famous Taiwanese CDs!

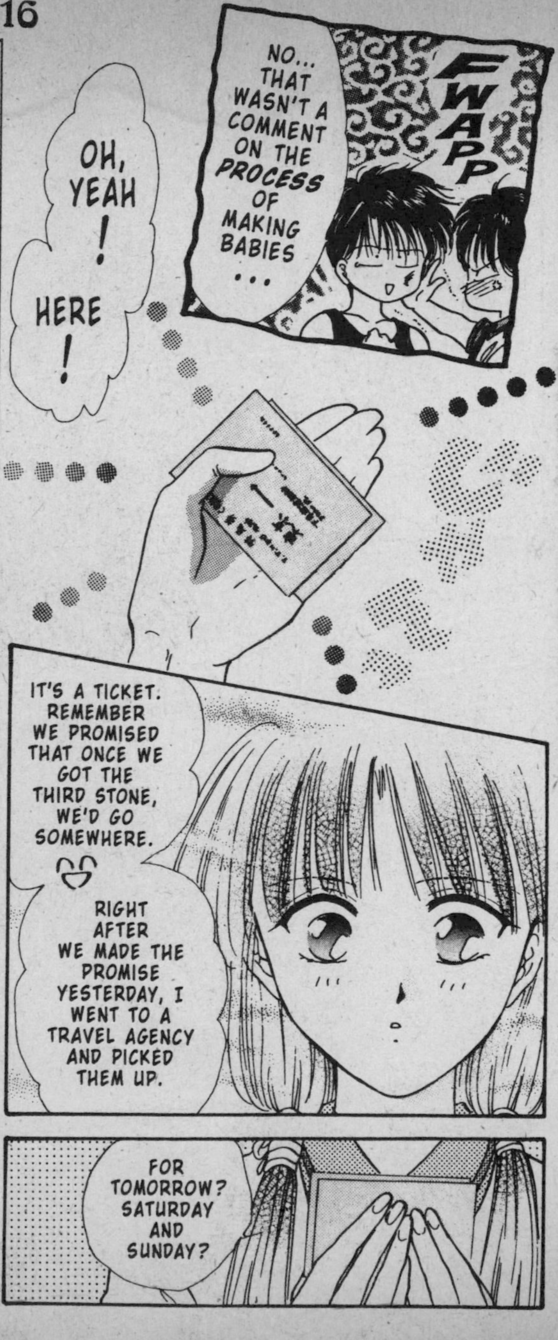
FWAPP
NO... THAT WASN'T A COMMENT ON THE PROCESS OF MAKING BABIES...
OH, YEAH! HERE!
IT'S A TICKET. REMEMBER WE PROMISED THAT ONCE WE GOT THE THIRD STONE, WE'D GO SOMEWHERE.
RIGHT AFTER WE MADE THE PROMISE YESTERDAY, I WENT TO A TRAVEL AGENCY AND PICKED THEM UP.
FOR TOMORROW? SATURDAY AND SUNDAY?

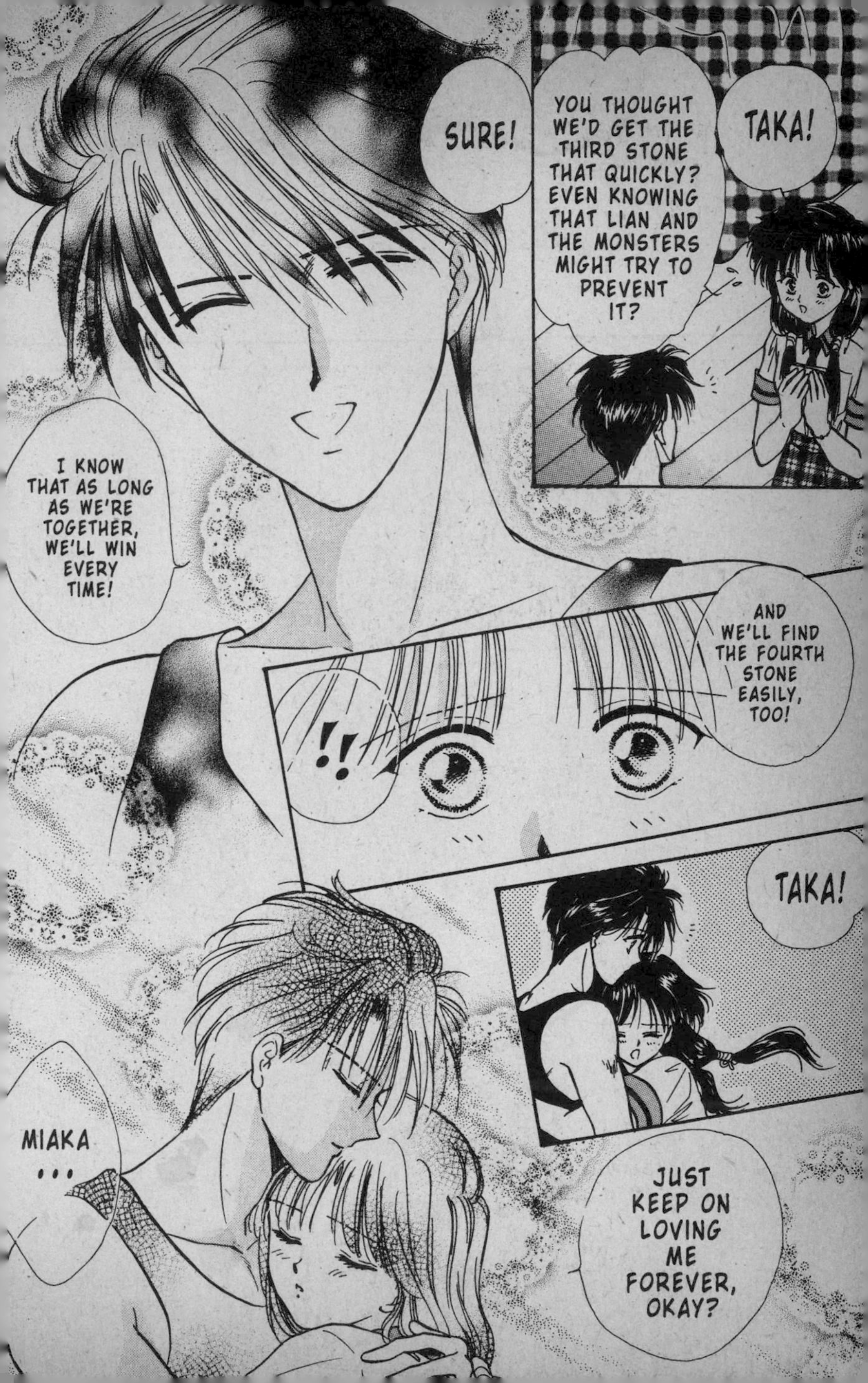
TAKA!
YOU THOUGHT WE'D GET THE THIRD STONE THAT QUICKLY? EVEN KNOWING THAT LIAN AND THE MONSTERS MIGHT TRY TO PREVENT IT?
SURE!
I KNOW THAT AS LONG AS WE'RE TOGETHER, WE'LL WIN EVERY TIME!
AND WE'LL FIND THE FOURTH STONE EASILY, TOO!
!!
TAKA!
JUST KEEP ON LOVING ME FOREVER, OKAY?
MIAKA...

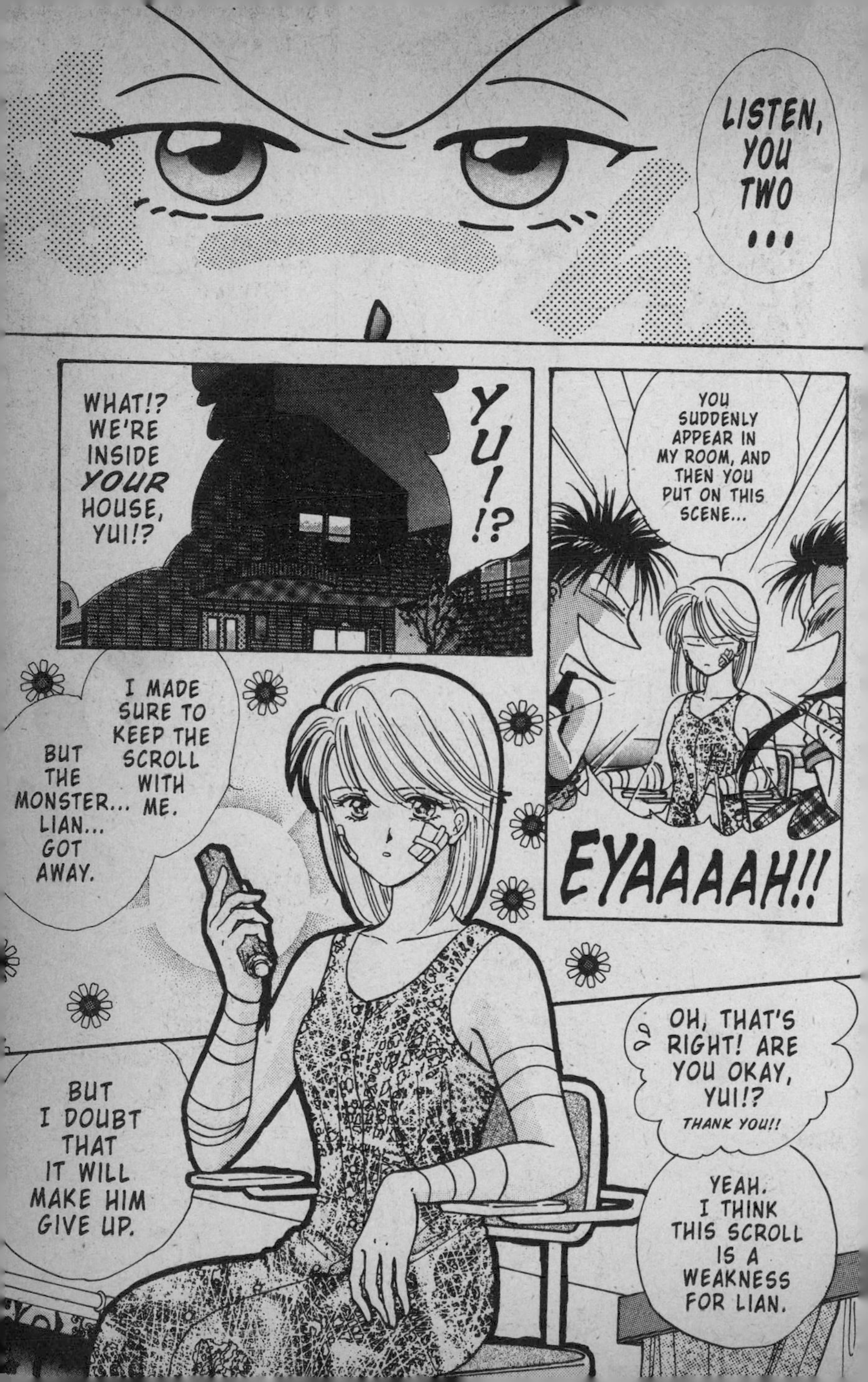
LISTEN, YOU TWO...
YOU SUDDENLY APPEAR IN MY ROOM, AND THEN YOU PUT ON THIS SCENE...
EYAAAAH!!
YUI!?
WHAT!? WE'RE INSIDE *YOUR* HOUSE, YUI!?
I MADE SURE TO KEEP THE SCROLL WITH ME.
BUT THE MONSTER... LIAN... GOT AWAY.
OH, THAT'S RIGHT! ARE YOU OKAY, YUI!?
THANK YOU!!
YEAH. I THINK THIS SCROLL IS A WEAKNESS FOR LIAN.
BUT I DOUBT THAT IT WILL MAKE HIM GIVE UP.

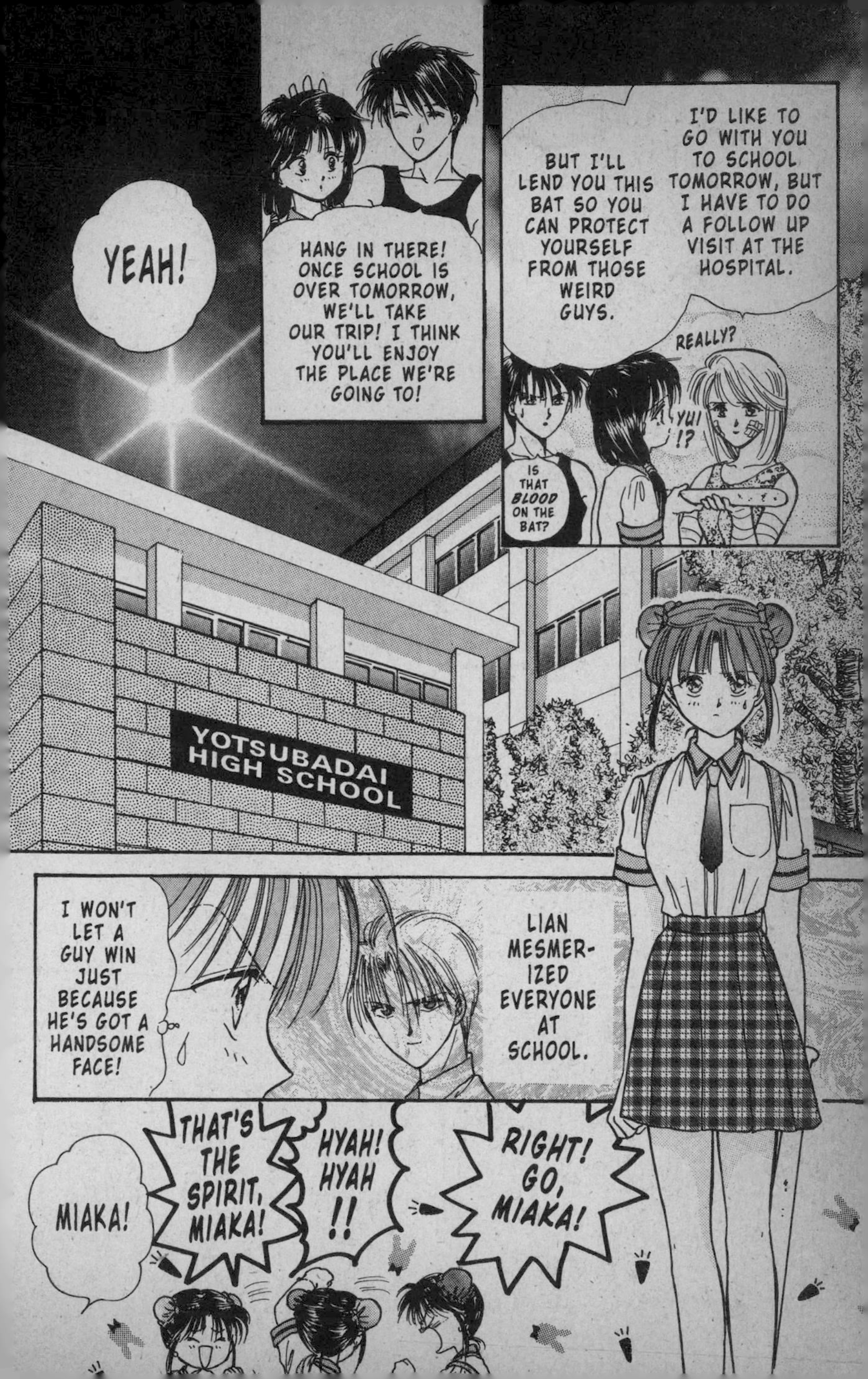
I'D LIKE TO GO WITH YOU TO SCHOOL TOMORROW, BUT I HAVE TO DO A FOLLOW UP VISIT AT THE HOSPITAL.
BUT I'LL LEND YOU THIS BAT SO YOU CAN PROTECT YOURSELF FROM THOSE WEIRD GUYS.
REALLY?
YUI !?
IS THAT *BLOOD* ON THE BAT?
HANG IN THERE! ONCE SCHOOL IS OVER TOMORROW, WE'LL TAKE OUR TRIP! I THINK YOU'LL ENJOY THE PLACE WE'RE GOING TO!
YEAH!
YOTSUBADAI HIGH SCHOOL
LIAN MESMER-IZED EVERYONE AT SCHOOL.
I WON'T LET A GUY WIN JUST BECAUSE HE'S GOT A HANDSOME FACE!
RIGHT! GO, MIAKA!
HYAH! HYAH !!
THAT'S THE SPIRIT, MIAKA!
MIAKA!

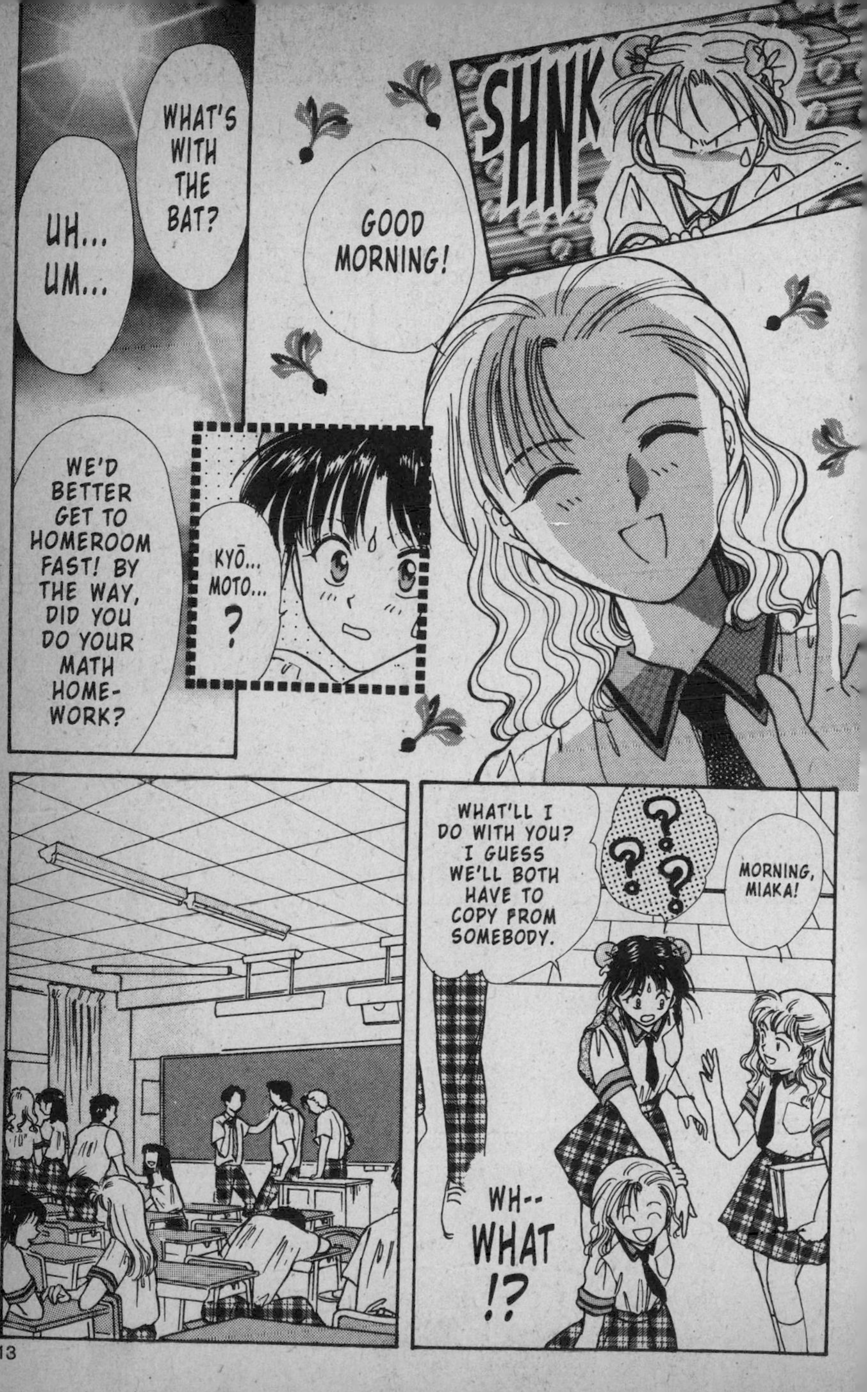
SHNK
GOOD MORNING!
WHAT'S WITH THE BAT?
UH... UM...
KYŌ... MOTO... ?
WE'D BETTER GET TO HOMEROOM FAST! BY THE WAY, DID YOU DO YOUR MATH HOME-WORK?
MORNING, MIAKA!
WHAT'LL I DO WITH YOU? I GUESS WE'LL BOTH HAVE TO COPY FROM SOMEBODY.
WH-- WHAT !?

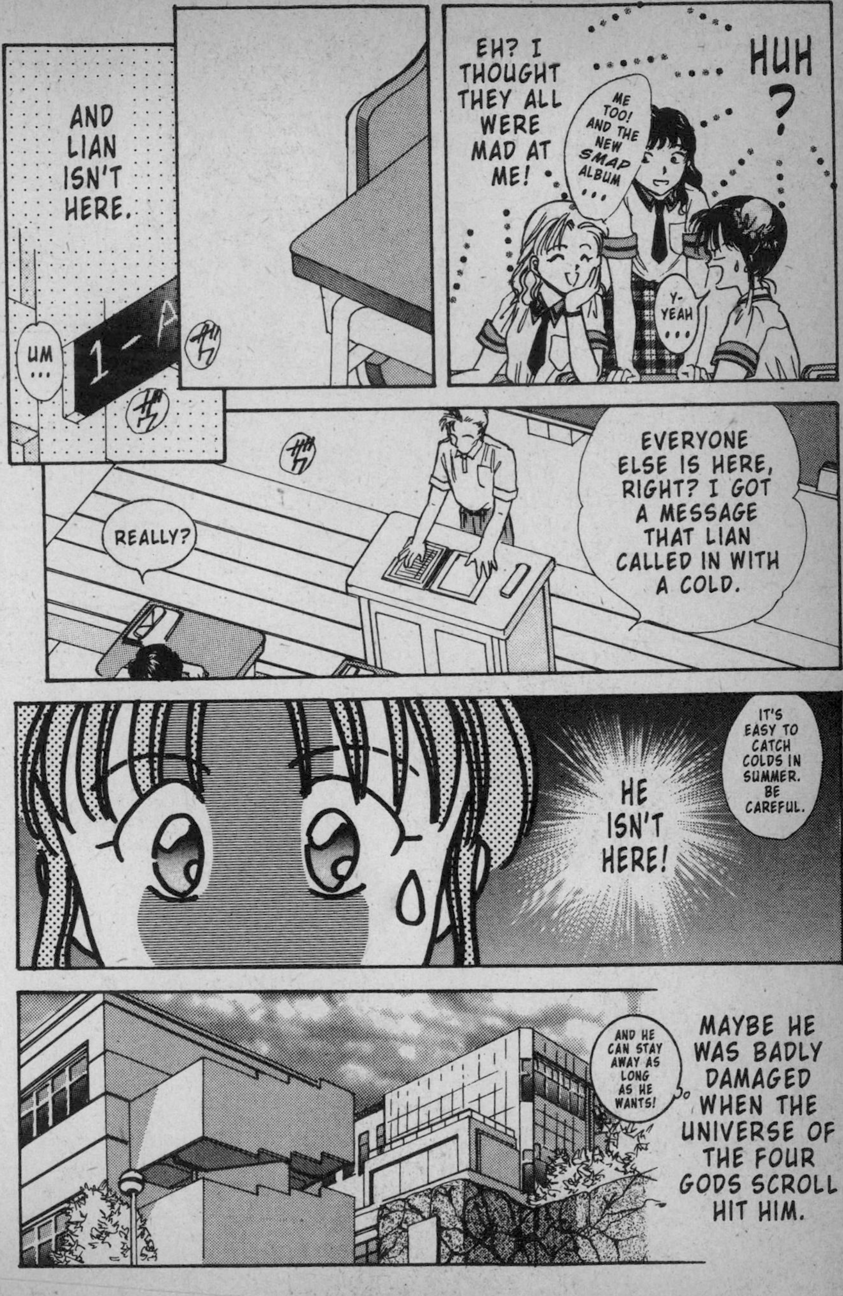
HUH ?
EH? I THOUGHT THEY ALL WERE MAD AT ME!
ME TOO! AND THE NEW SMAP ALBUM ...
Y-YEAH ...
AND LIAN ISN'T HERE.
1-A
UM ...
EVERYONE ELSE IS HERE, RIGHT? I GOT A MESSAGE THAT LIAN CALLED IN WITH A COLD.
REALLY?
IT'S EASY TO CATCH COLDS IN SUMMER. BE CAREFUL.
HE ISN'T HERE!
MAYBE HE WAS BADLY DAMAGED WHEN THE UNIVERSE OF THE FOUR GODS SCROLL HIT HIM.
AND HE CAN STAY AWAY AS LONG AS HE WANTS!

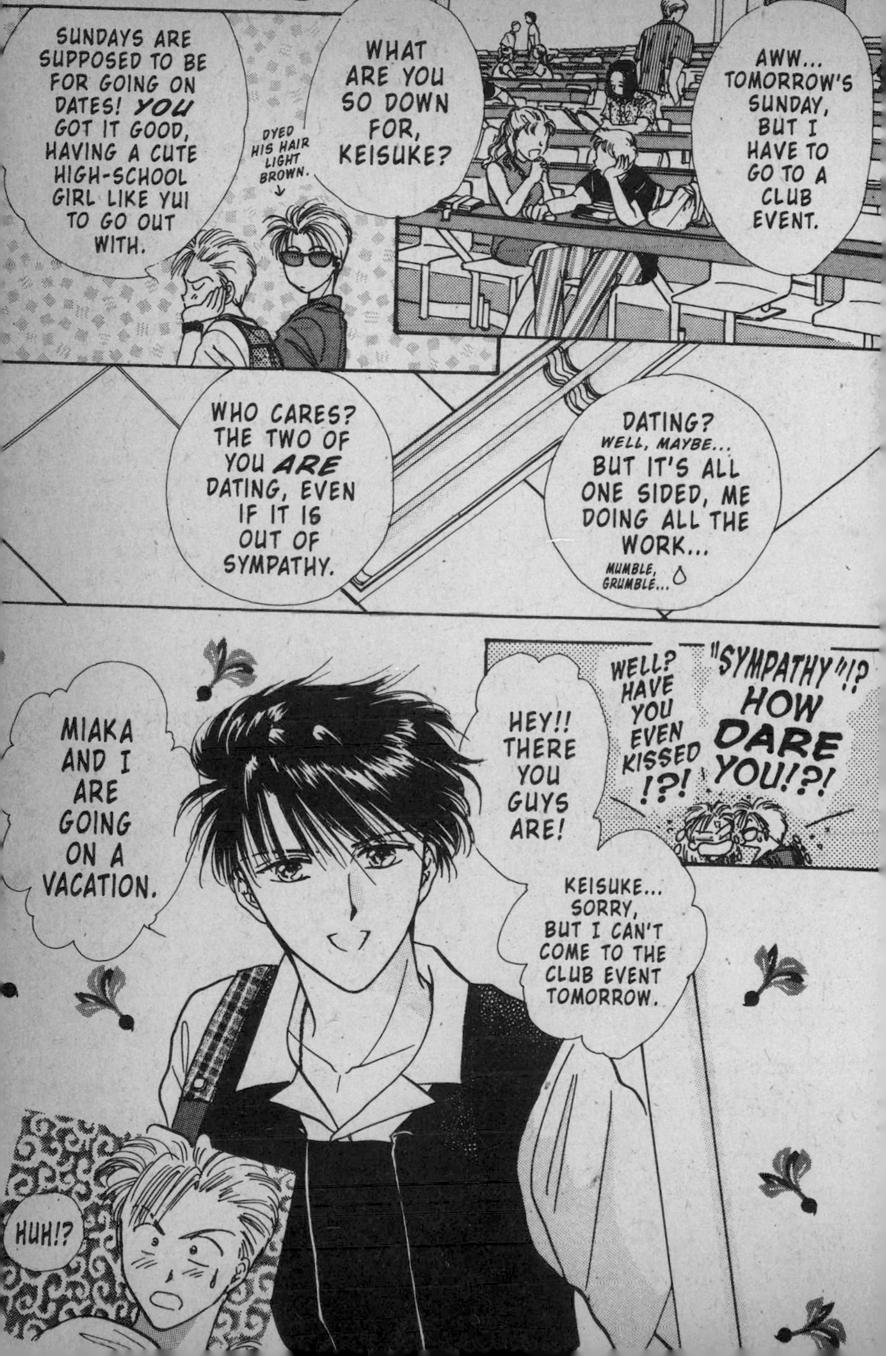
AWW... TOMORROW'S SUNDAY, BUT I HAVE TO GO TO A CLUB EVENT.
WHAT ARE YOU SO DOWN FOR, KEISUKE?
DYED HIS HAIR LIGHT BROWN.
SUNDAYS ARE SUPPOSED TO BE FOR GOING ON DATES! YOU GOT IT GOOD, HAVING A CUTE HIGH-SCHOOL GIRL LIKE YUI TO GO OUT WITH.
DATING? WELL, MAYBE... BUT IT'S ALL ONE SIDED, ME DOING ALL THE WORK... MUMBLE, GRUMBLE...
WHO CARES? THE TWO OF YOU ARE DATING, EVEN IF IT IS OUT OF SYMPATHY.
"SYMPATHY"!? HOW DARE YOU!?!
WELL? HAVE YOU EVEN KISSED !?!
HEY!! THERE YOU GUYS ARE!
KEISUKE... SORRY, BUT I CAN'T COME TO THE CLUB EVENT TOMORROW.
MIAKA AND I ARE GOING ON A VACATION.
HUH!?

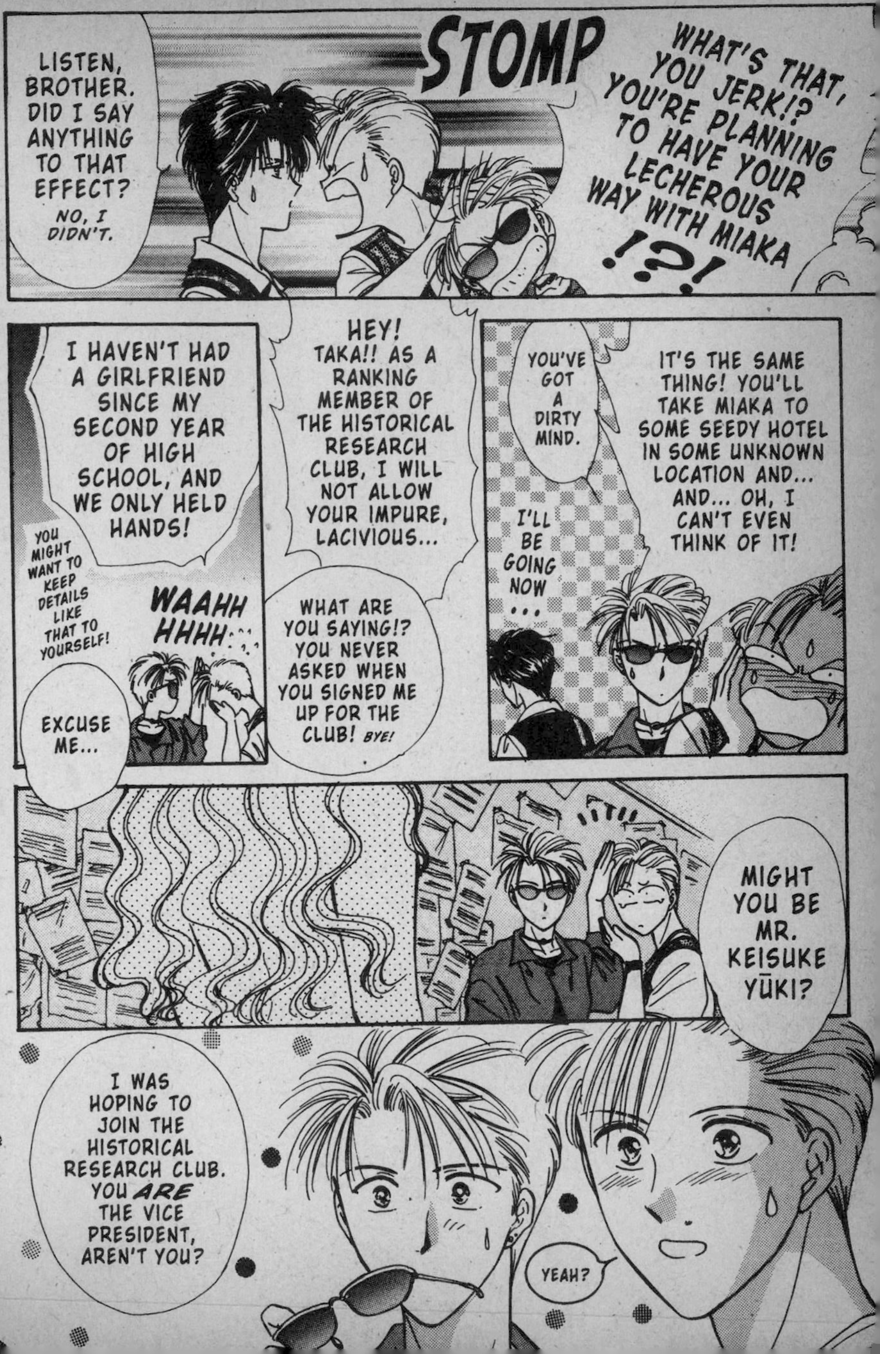
WHAT'S THAT, YOU JERK!? YOU'RE PLANNING TO HAVE YOUR LECHEROUS WAY WITH MIAKA !?!
STOMP
LISTEN, BROTHER. DID I SAY ANYTHING TO THAT EFFECT?
NO, I DIDN'T.
IT'S THE SAME THING! YOU'LL TAKE MIAKA TO SOME SEEDY HOTEL IN SOME UNKNOWN LOCATION AND... AND... OH, I CAN'T EVEN THINK OF IT!
YOU'VE GOT A DIRTY MIND.
I'LL BE GOING NOW...
HEY! TAKA!! AS A RANKING MEMBER OF THE HISTORICAL RESEARCH CLUB, I WILL NOT ALLOW YOUR IMPURE, LACIVIOUS...
WHAT ARE YOU SAYING!? YOU NEVER ASKED WHEN YOU SIGNED ME UP FOR THE CLUB!
BYE!
I HAVEN'T HAD A GIRLFRIEND SINCE MY SECOND YEAR OF HIGH SCHOOL, AND WE ONLY HELD HANDS!
YOU MIGHT WANT TO KEEP DETAILS LIKE THAT TO YOURSELF!
WAAHH HHHH
EXCUSE ME...
MIGHT YOU BE MR. KEISUKE YŪKI?
YEAH?
I WAS HOPING TO JOIN THE HISTORICAL RESEARCH CLUB. YOU *ARE* THE VICE PRESIDENT, AREN'T YOU?

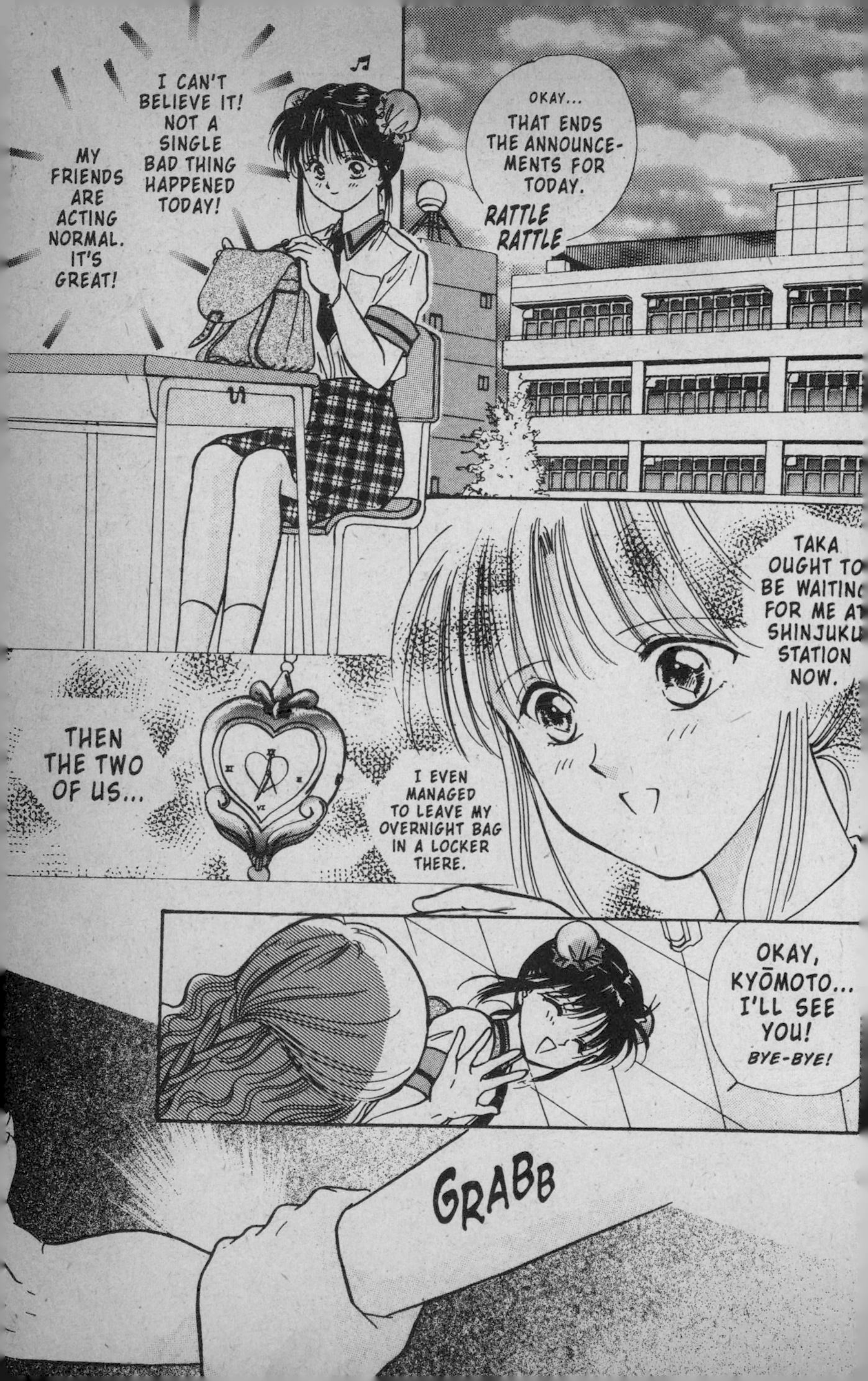

OKAY... THAT ENDS THE ANNOUNCEMENTS FOR TODAY.
RATTLE RATTLE
I CAN'T BELIEVE IT! NOT A SINGLE BAD THING HAPPENED TODAY!
MY FRIENDS ARE ACTING NORMAL. IT'S GREAT!
TAKA OUGHT TO BE WAITING FOR ME AT SHINJUKU STATION NOW.
I EVEN MANAGED TO LEAVE MY OVERNIGHT BAG IN A LOCKER THERE.
THEN THE TWO OF US...
OKAY, KYŌMOTO... I'LL SEE YOU! BYE-BYE!
GRABB

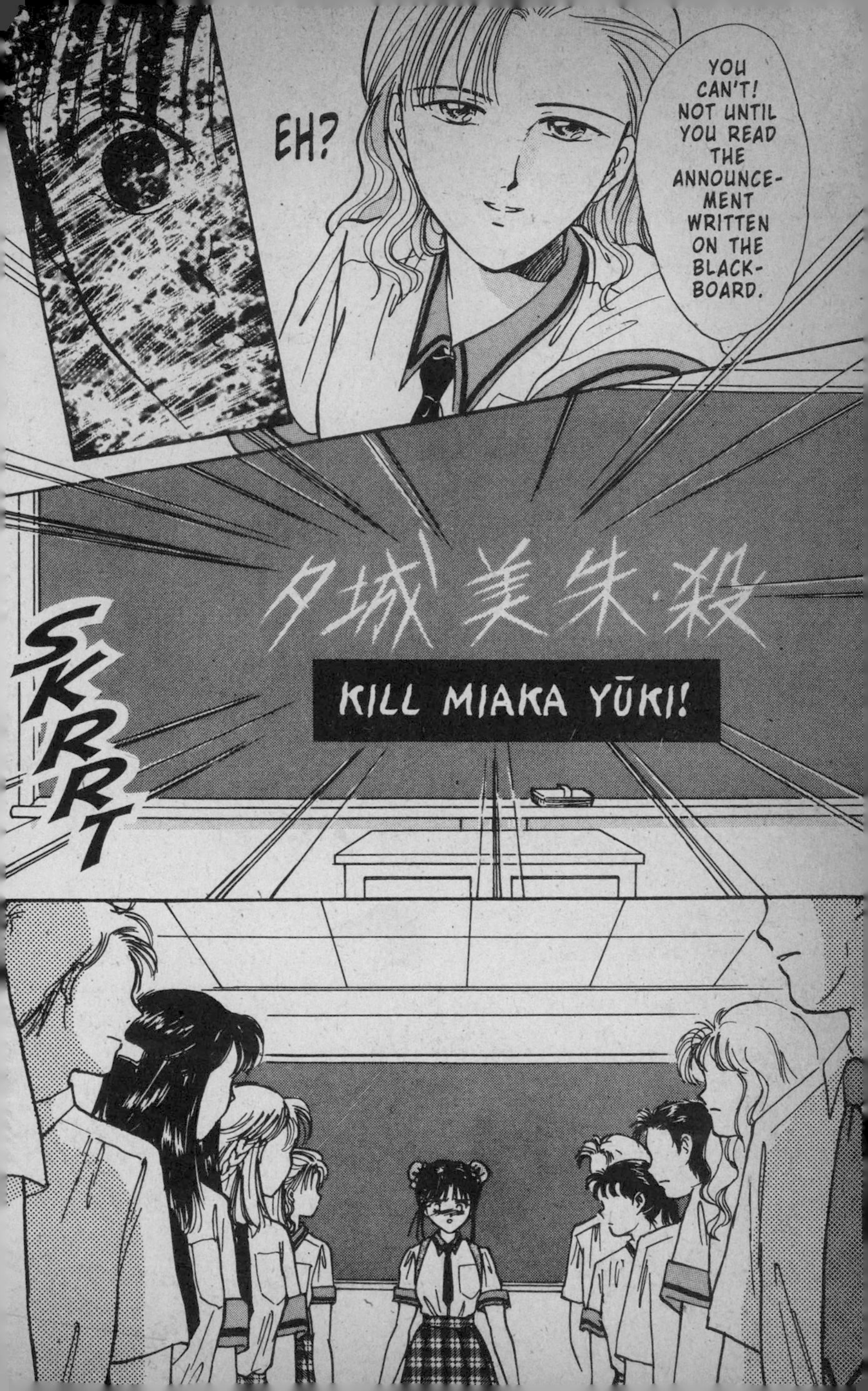
YOU CAN'T! NOT UNTIL YOU READ THE ANNOUNCEMENT WRITTEN ON THE BLACKBOARD.
EH?
夕城美朱・殺
KILL MIAKA YŪKI!
SKRRT

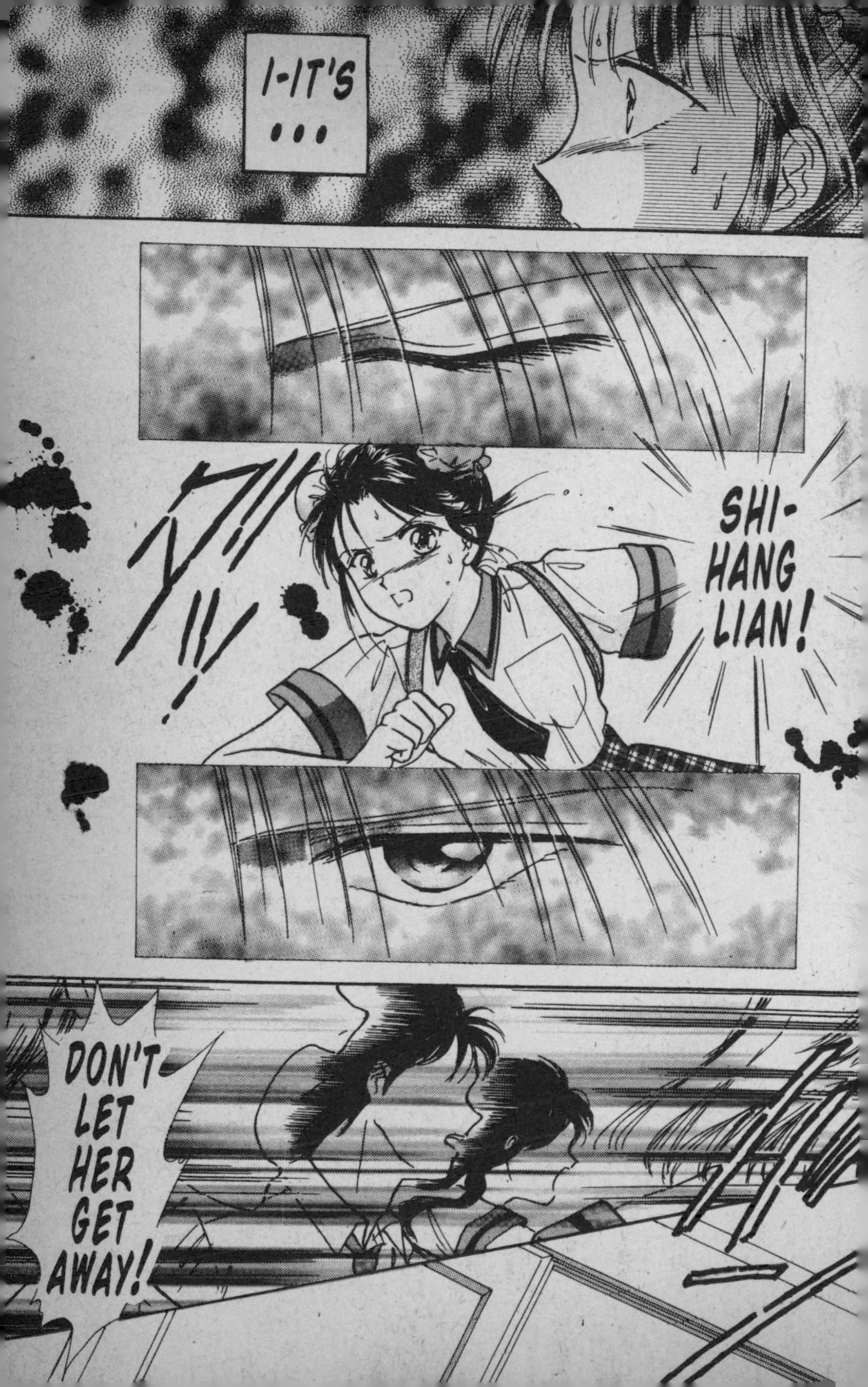
I-IT'S ...
SHI-HANG LIAN!
DON'T LET HER GET AWAY!

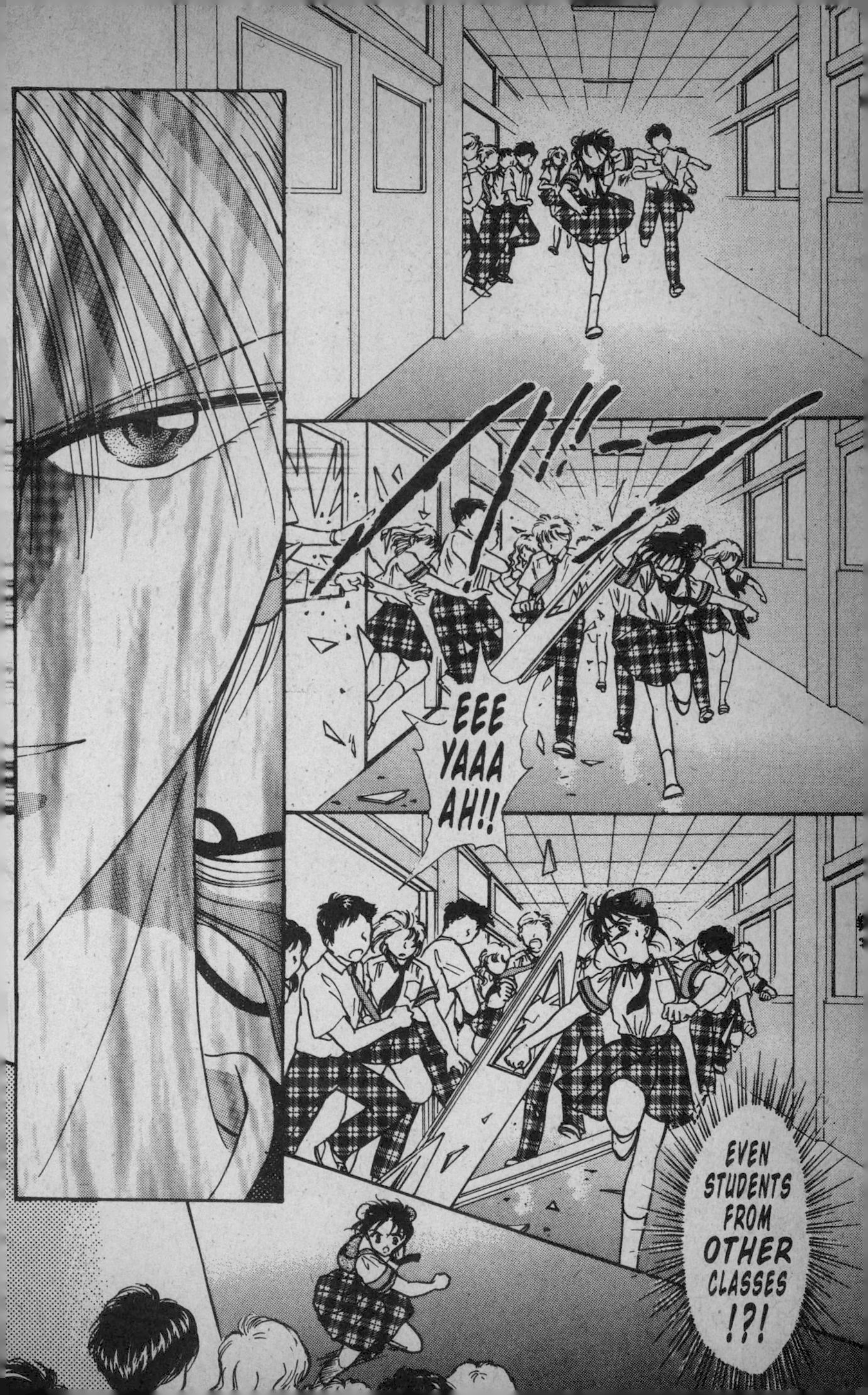
EEE YAAA AH!!
EVEN STUDENTS FROM OTHER CLASSES !?!

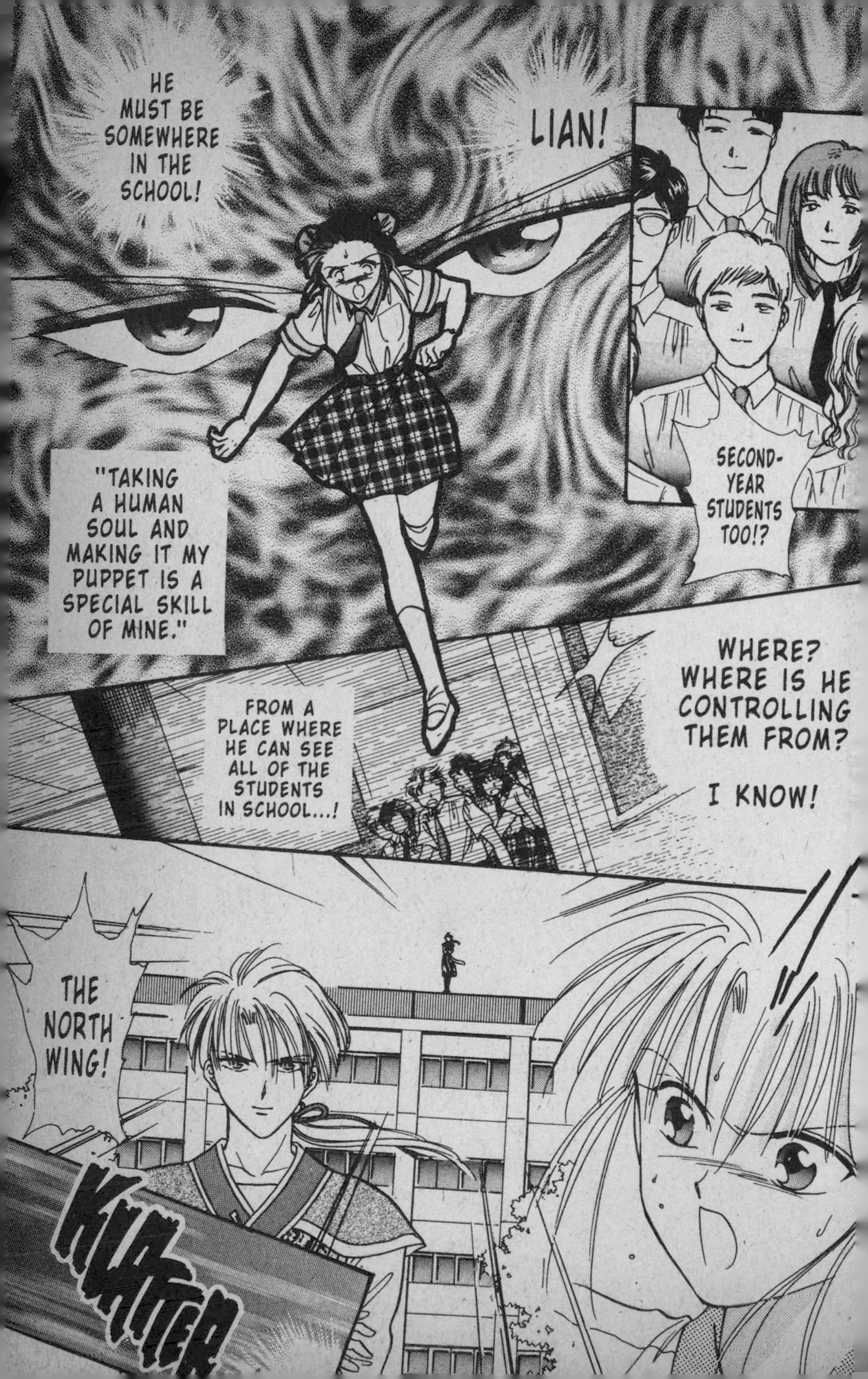
SECOND-YEAR STUDENTS TOO!?
LIAN!
HE MUST BE SOMEWHERE IN THE SCHOOL!
"TAKING A HUMAN SOUL AND MAKING IT MY PUPPET IS A SPECIAL SKILL OF MINE."
WHERE? WHERE IS HE CONTROLLING THEM FROM?
I KNOW!
FROM A PLACE WHERE HE CAN SEE ALL OF THE STUDENTS IN SCHOOL...!
THE NORTH WING!

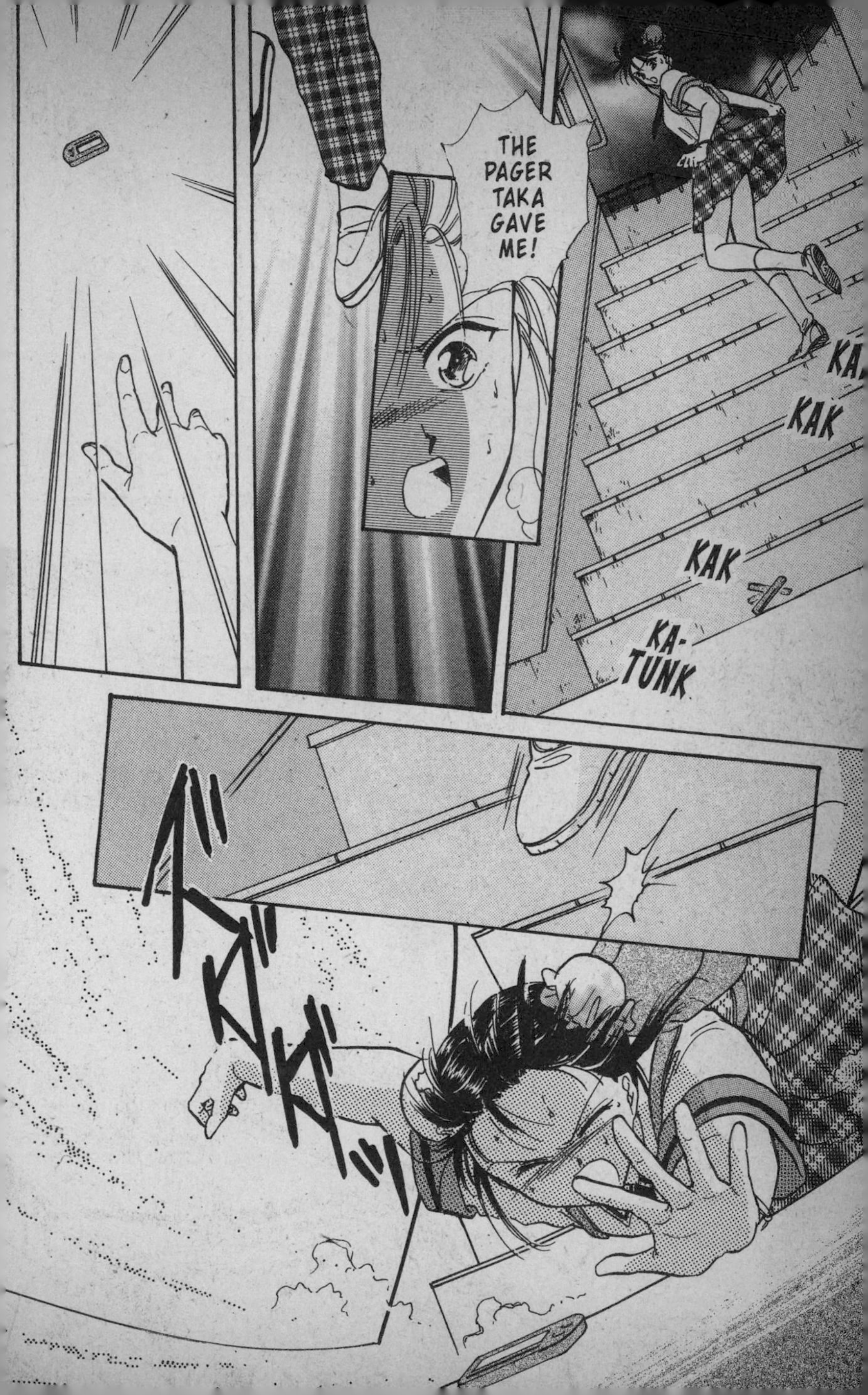

KA
KAK
KAK
KA-TUNK
THE PAGER TAKA GAVE ME!

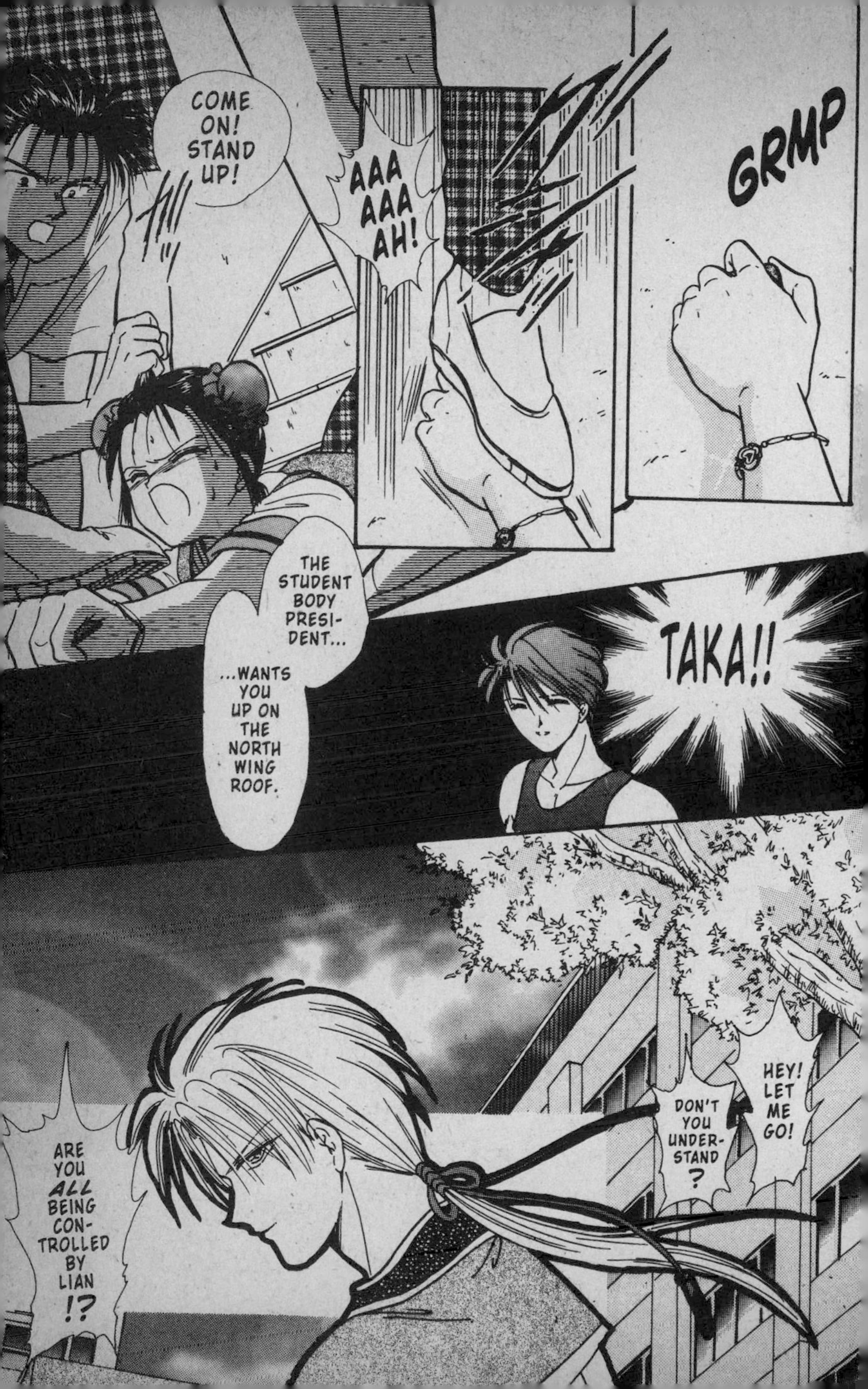
GRMP
AAA AAA AH!
COME ON! STAND UP!
THE STUDENT BODY PRESIDENT...
...WANTS YOU UP ON THE NORTH WING ROOF.
TAKA!!
HEY! LET ME GO!
DON'T YOU UNDERSTAND?
ARE YOU ALL BEING CONTROLLED BY LIAN!?

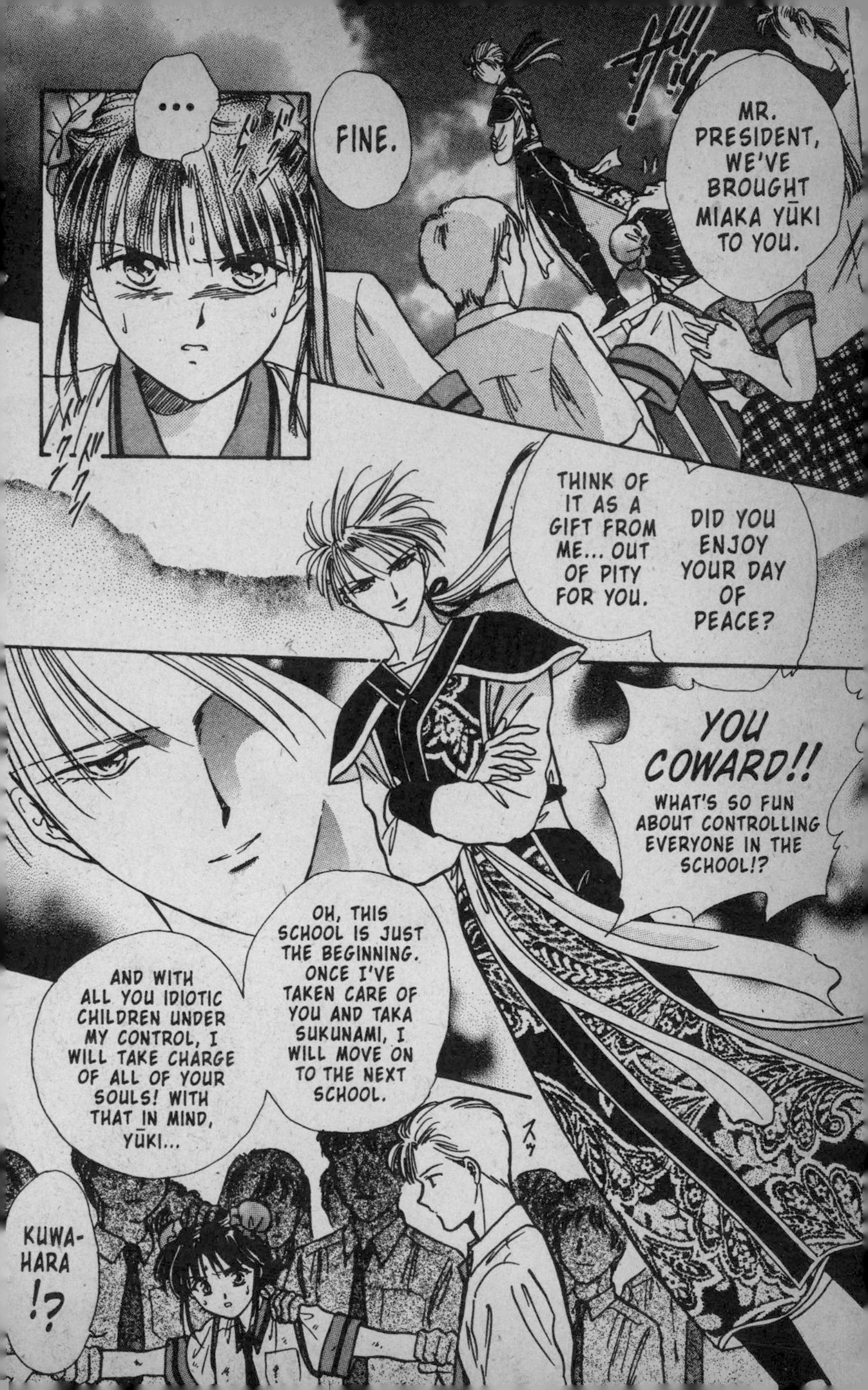

MR. PRESIDENT, WE'VE BROUGHT MIAKA YŪKI TO YOU.
FINE.
...
DID YOU ENJOY YOUR DAY OF PEACE?
THINK OF IT AS A GIFT FROM ME... OUT OF PITY FOR YOU.
YOU COWARD!!
WHAT'S SO FUN ABOUT CONTROLLING EVERYONE IN THE SCHOOL!?
OH, THIS SCHOOL IS JUST THE BEGINNING. ONCE I'VE TAKEN CARE OF YOU AND TAKA SUKUNAMI, I WILL MOVE ON TO THE NEXT SCHOOL.
AND WITH ALL YOU IDIOTIC CHILDREN UNDER MY CONTROL, I WILL TAKE CHARGE OF ALL OF YOUR SOULS! WITH THAT IN MIND, YŪKI...
KUWA-HARA !?

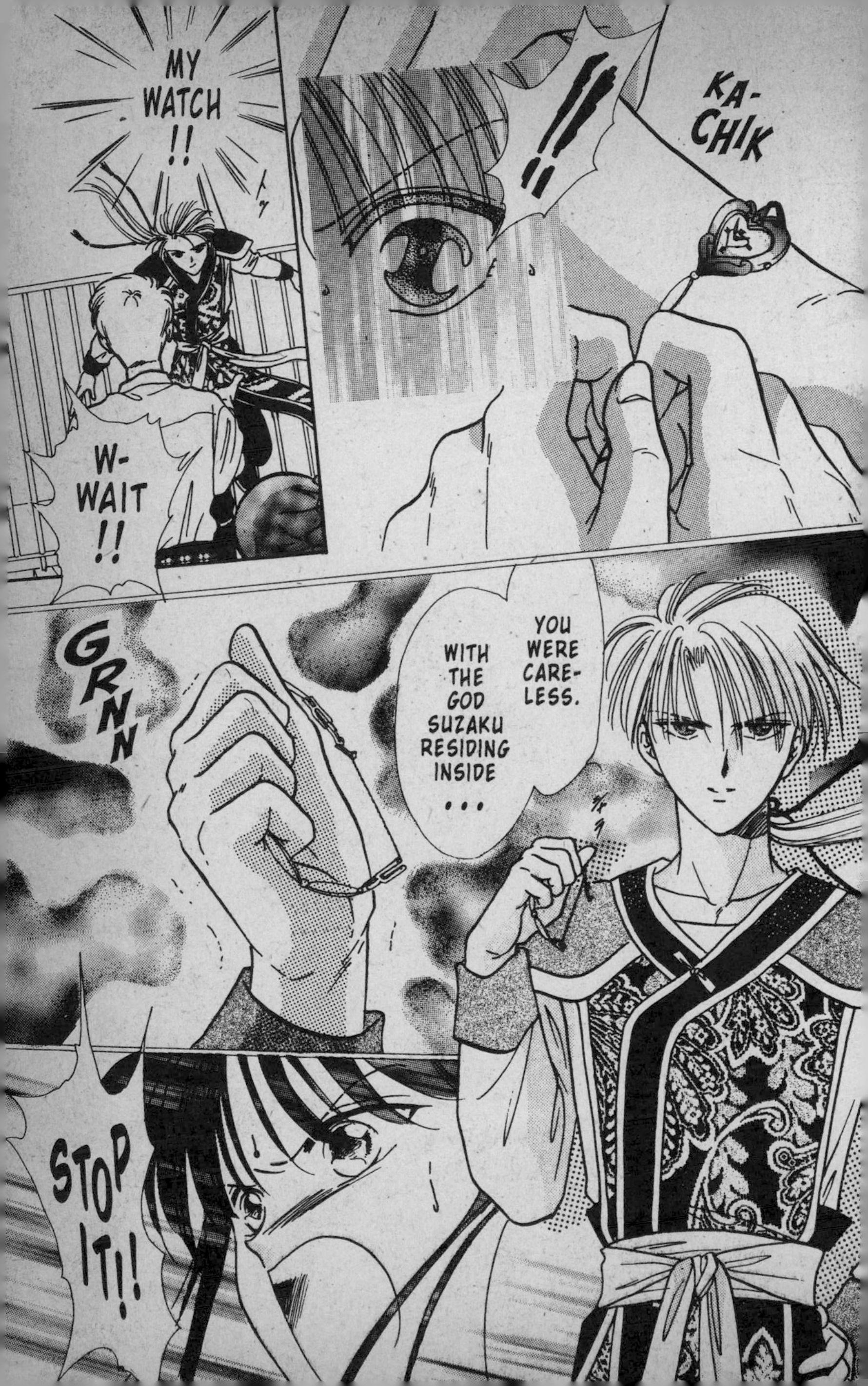
KA-CHIK
!!
MY WATCH !!
W-WAIT !!
YOU WERE CARELESS.
WITH THE GOD SUZAKU RESIDING INSIDE ...
GRNN
STOP IT!!

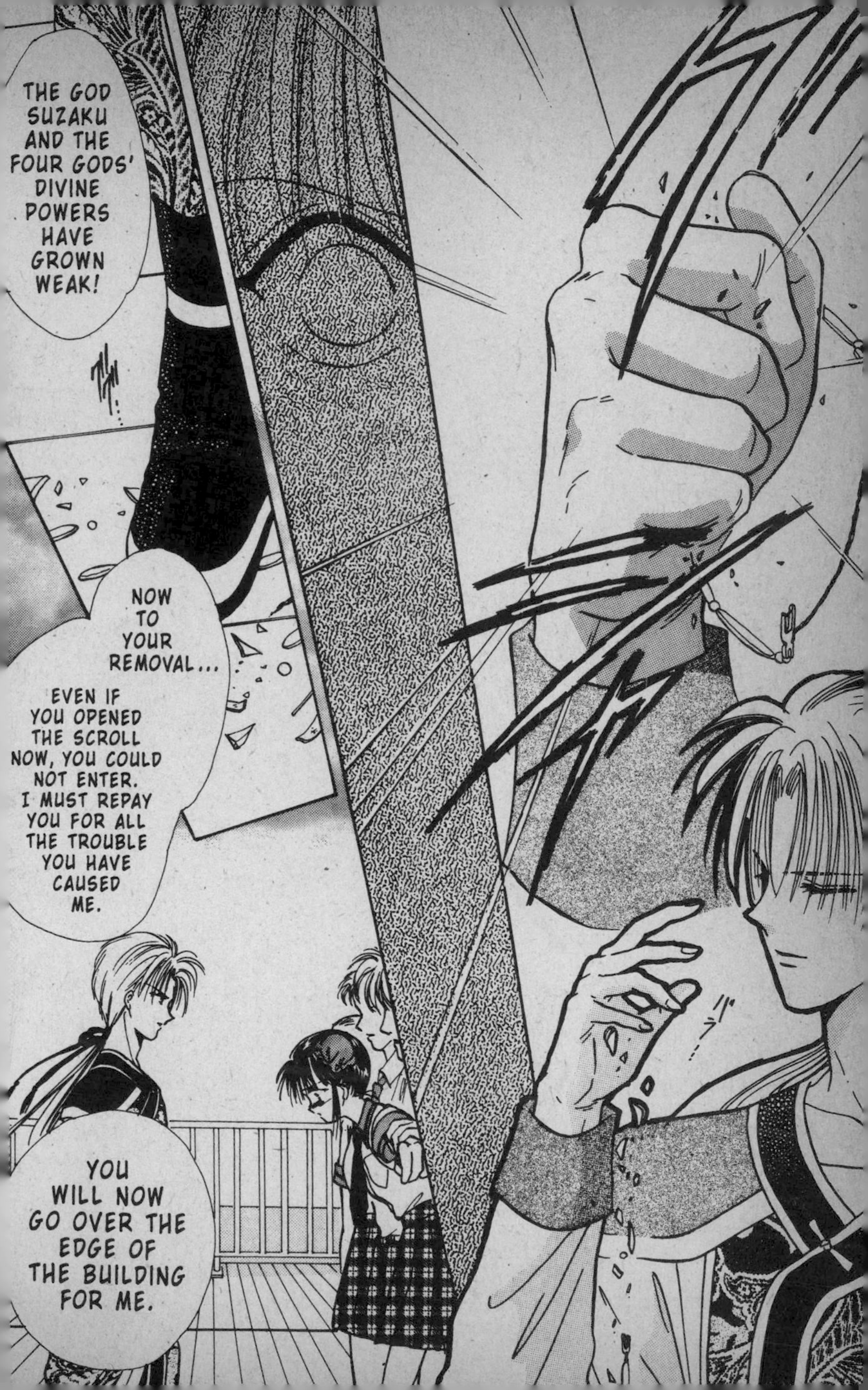
THE GOD SUZAKU AND THE FOUR GODS' DIVINE POWERS HAVE GROWN WEAK!
NOW TO YOUR REMOVAL... EVEN IF YOU OPENED THE SCROLL NOW, YOU COULD NOT ENTER. I MUST REPAY YOU FOR ALL THE TROUBLE YOU HAVE CAUSED ME.
YOU WILL NOW GO OVER THE EDGE OF THE BUILDING FOR ME.

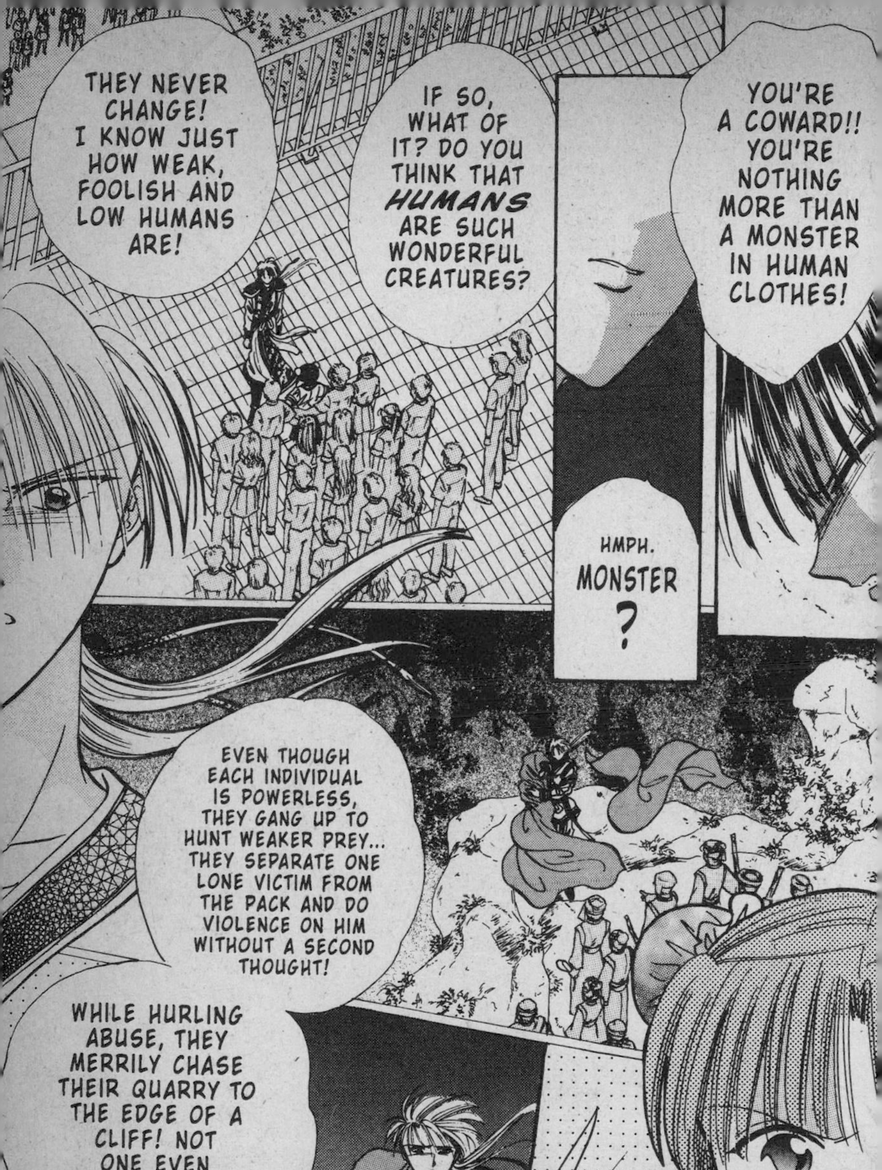

YOU'RE A COWARD!! YOU'RE NOTHING MORE THAN A MONSTER IN HUMAN CLOTHES!
HMPH. MONSTER ?
IF SO, WHAT OF IT? DO YOU THINK THAT *HUMANS* ARE SUCH WONDERFUL CREATURES?
THEY NEVER CHANGE! I KNOW JUST HOW WEAK, FOOLISH AND LOW HUMANS ARE!
EVEN THOUGH EACH INDIVIDUAL IS POWERLESS, THEY GANG UP TO HUNT WEAKER PREY... THEY SEPARATE ONE LONE VICTIM FROM THE PACK AND DO VIOLENCE ON HIM WITHOUT A SECOND THOUGHT!
WHILE HURLING ABUSE, THEY MERRILY CHASE THEIR QUARRY TO THE EDGE OF A CLIFF! NOT ONE EVEN CONSIDERS THE FEELINGS OF THEIR PREY!
!?

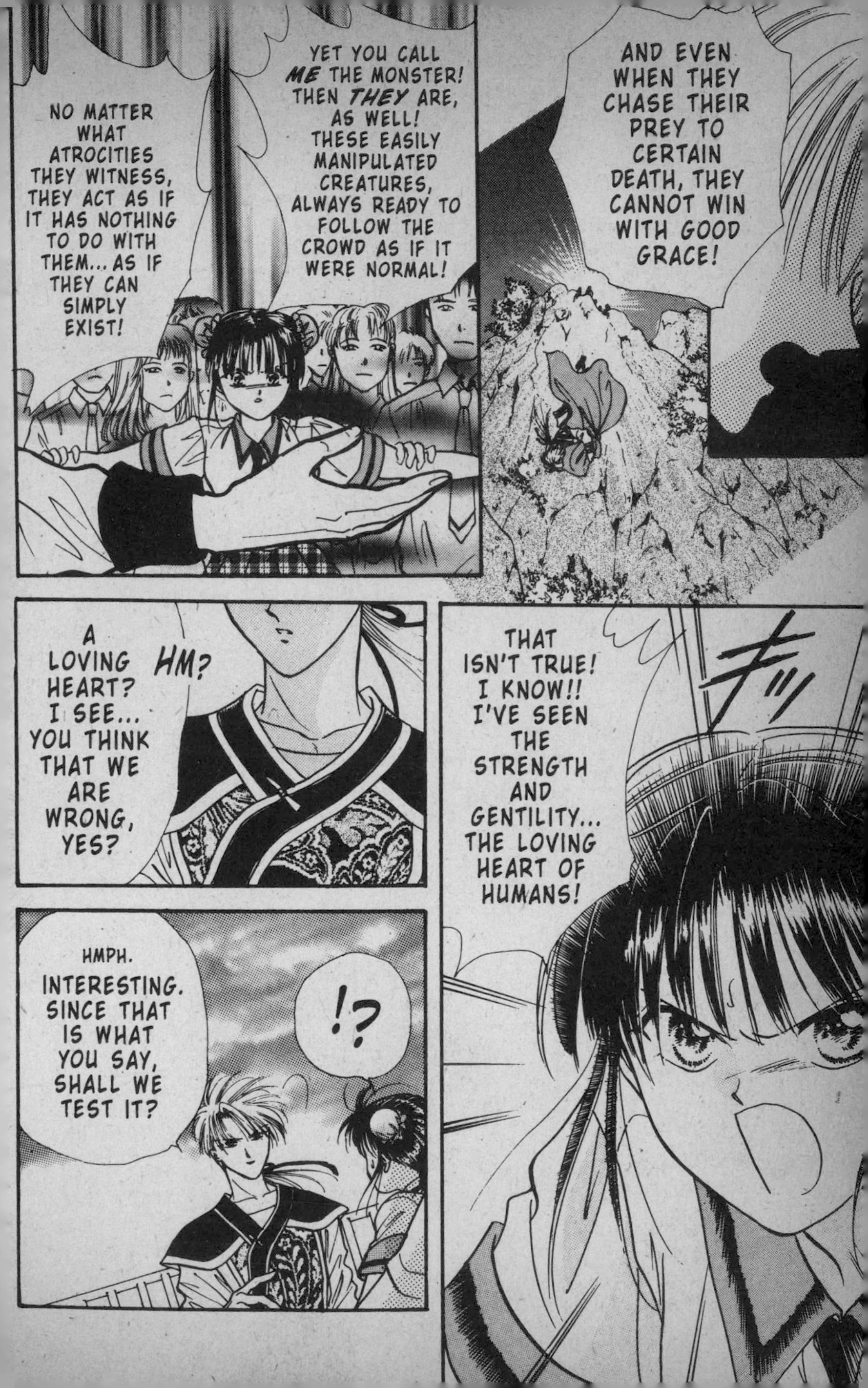
AND EVEN WHEN THEY CHASE THEIR PREY TO CERTAIN DEATH, THEY CANNOT WIN WITH GOOD GRACE!
YET YOU CALL *ME* THE MONSTER! THEN *THEY* ARE, AS WELL! THESE EASILY MANIPULATED CREATURES, ALWAYS READY TO FOLLOW THE CROWD AS IF IT WERE NORMAL!
NO MATTER WHAT ATROCITIES THEY WITNESS, THEY ACT AS IF IT HAS NOTHING TO DO WITH THEM... AS IF THEY CAN SIMPLY EXIST!
キッ
THAT ISN'T TRUE! I KNOW!! I'VE SEEN THE STRENGTH AND GENTILITY... THE LOVING HEART OF HUMANS!
HM?
A LOVING HEART? I SEE... YOU THINK THAT WE ARE WRONG, YES?
HMPH. INTERESTING. SINCE THAT IS WHAT YOU SAY, SHALL WE TEST IT?
!?

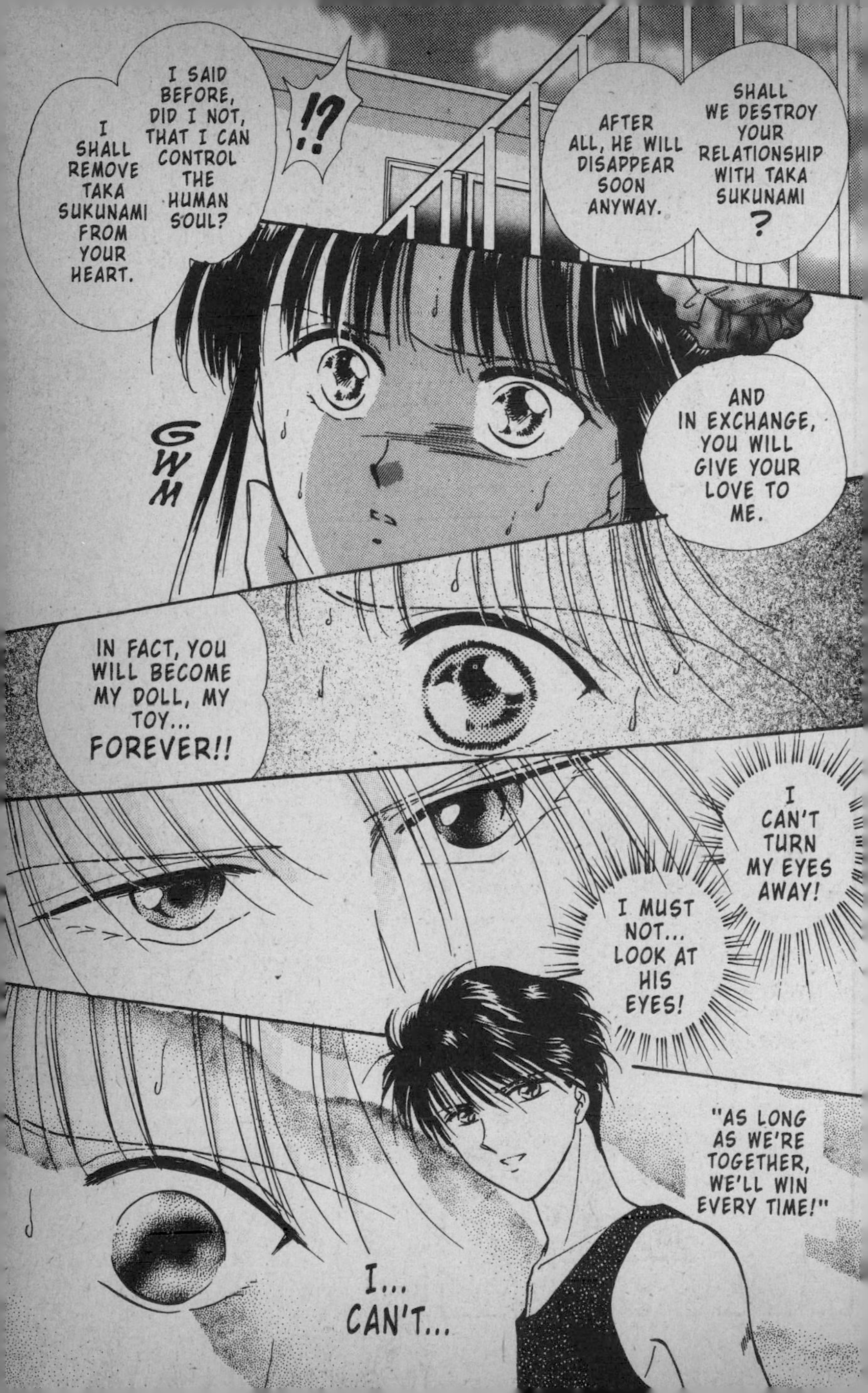

SHALL WE DESTROY YOUR RELATIONSHIP WITH TAKA SUKUNAMI?
AFTER ALL, HE WILL DISAPPEAR SOON ANYWAY.
!?
I SAID BEFORE, DID I NOT, THAT I CAN CONTROL THE HUMAN SOUL?
I SHALL REMOVE TAKA SUKUNAMI FROM YOUR HEART.
AND IN EXCHANGE, YOU WILL GIVE YOUR LOVE TO ME.
GWM
IN FACT, YOU WILL BECOME MY DOLL, MY TOY... FOREVER!!
I CAN'T TURN MY EYES AWAY!
I MUST NOT... LOOK AT HIS EYES!
"AS LONG AS WE'RE TOGETHER, WE'LL WIN EVERY TIME!"
I... CAN'T...

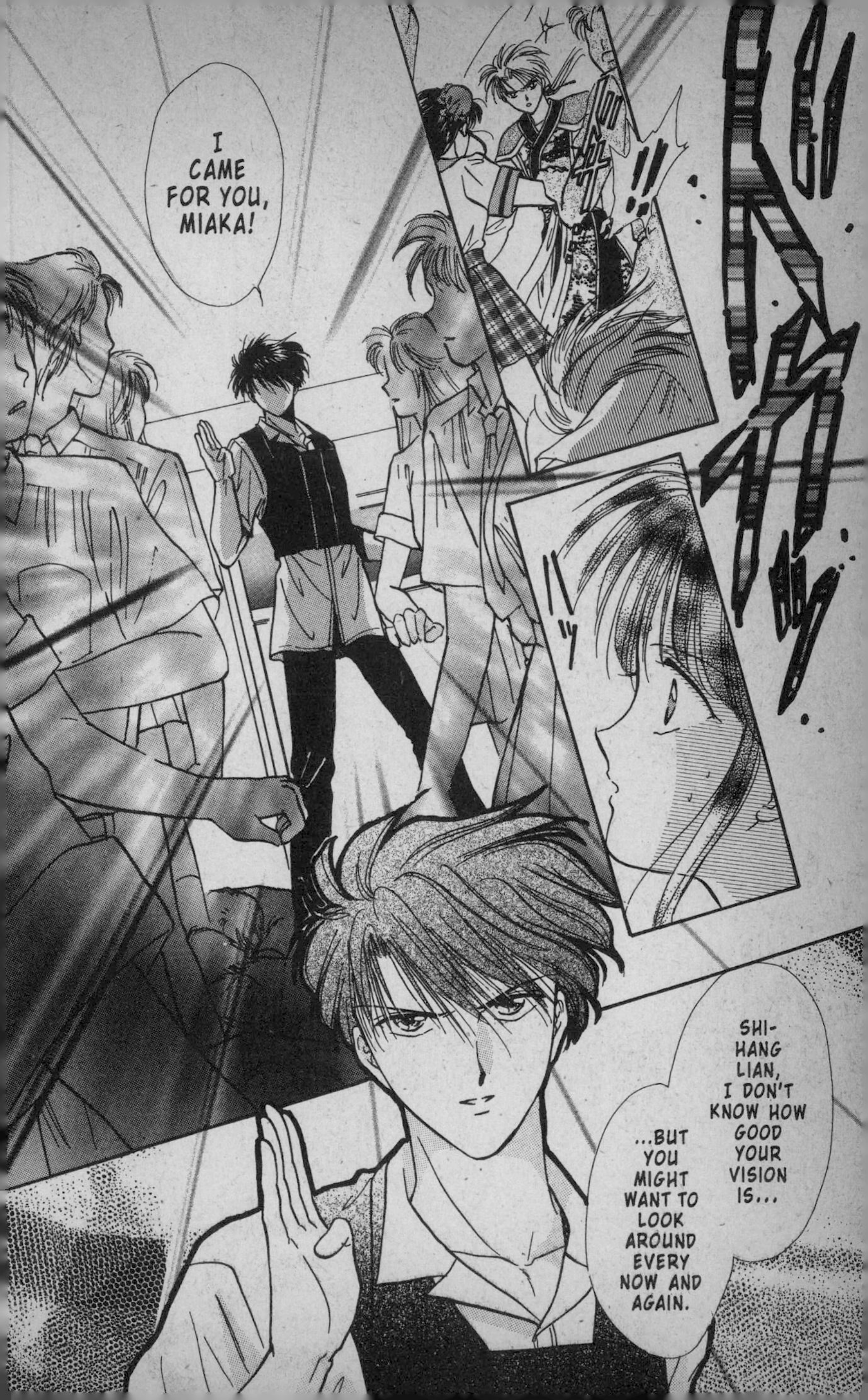
I CAME FOR YOU, MIAKA!
SHI-HANG LIAN, I DON'T KNOW HOW GOOD YOUR VISION IS...
...BUT YOU MIGHT WANT TO LOOK AROUND EVERY NOW AND AGAIN.

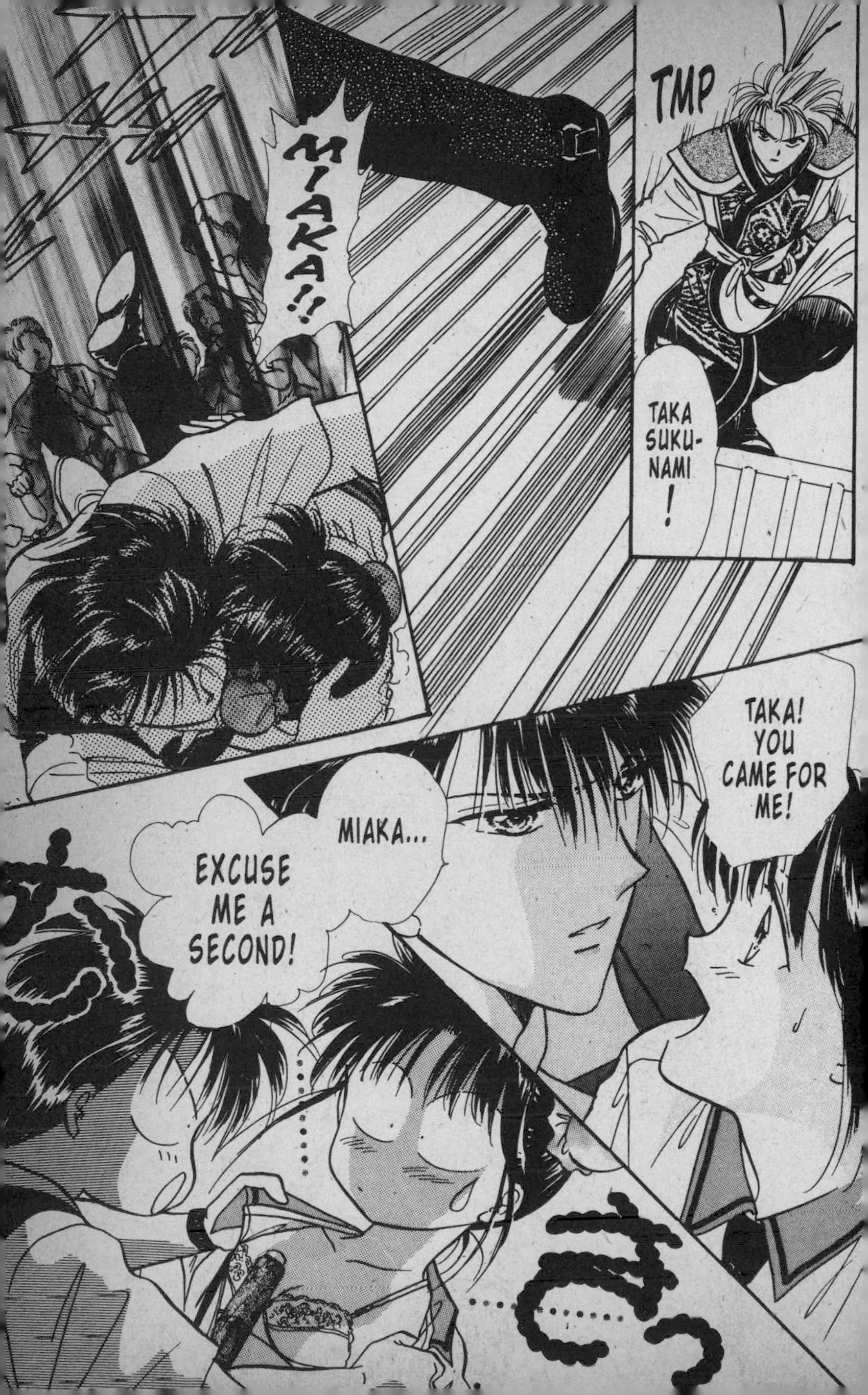
TMP
TAKA SUKU-NAMI!
MIAKA!!
TAKA! YOU CAME FOR ME!
MIAKA...
EXCUSE ME A SECOND!

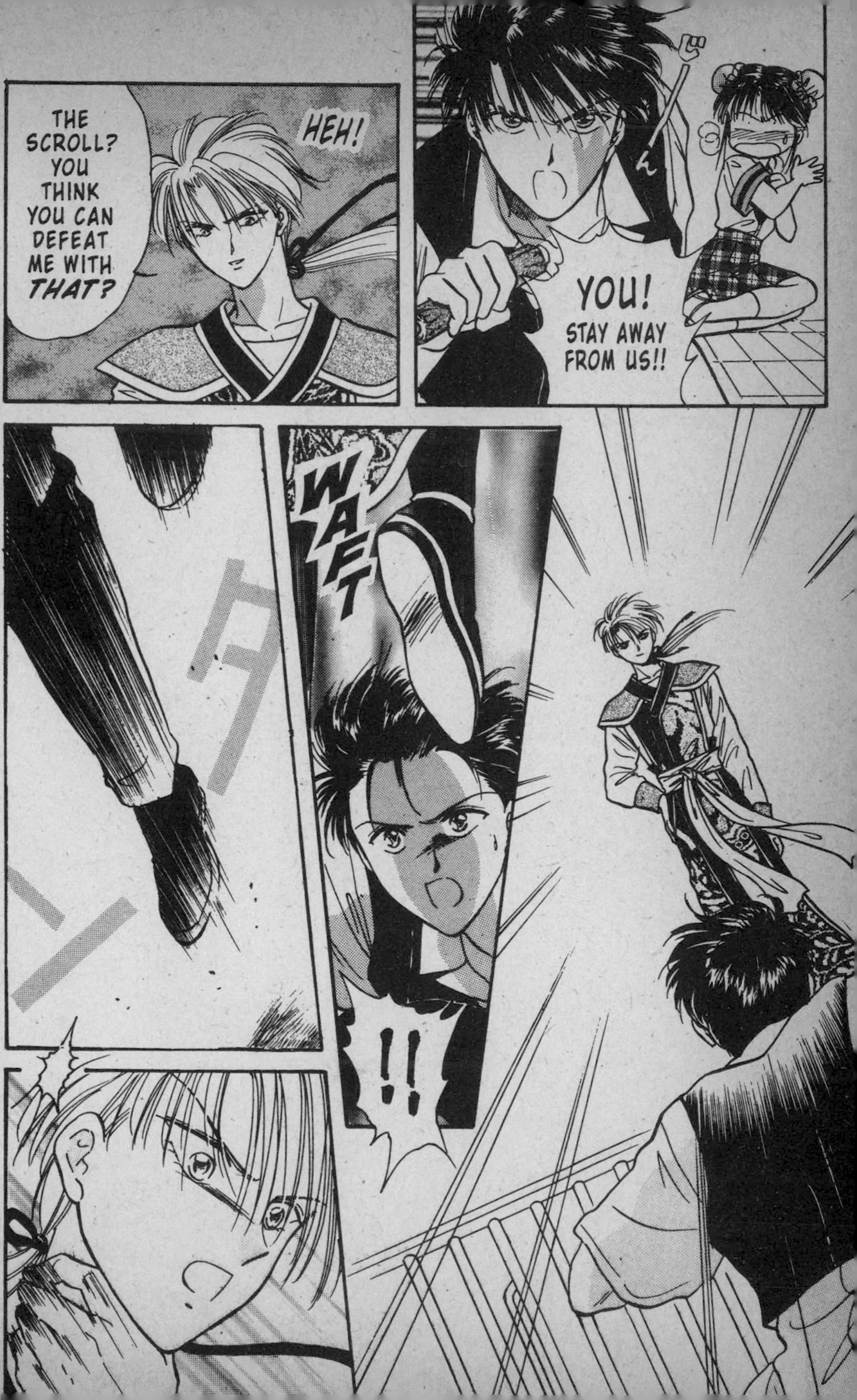
YOU!
STAY AWAY FROM US!!
HEH!
THE SCROLL? YOU THINK YOU CAN DEFEAT ME WITH *THAT?*
WAFT
!!

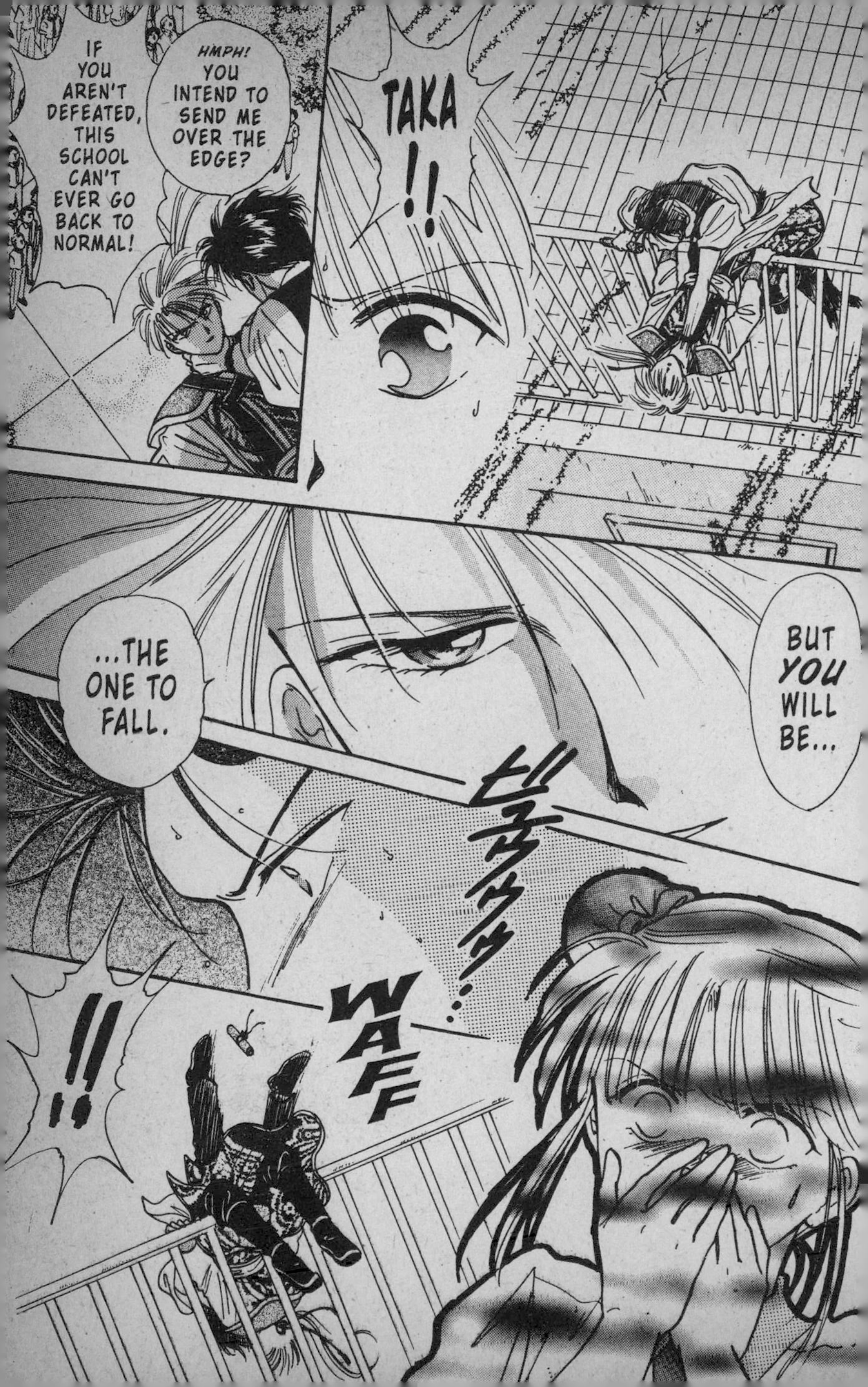
TAKA !!
HMPH! YOU INTEND TO SEND ME OVER THE EDGE?
IF YOU AREN'T DEFEATED, THIS SCHOOL CAN'T EVER GO BACK TO NORMAL!
BUT YOU WILL BE...
...THE ONE TO FALL.
WAFF
!!

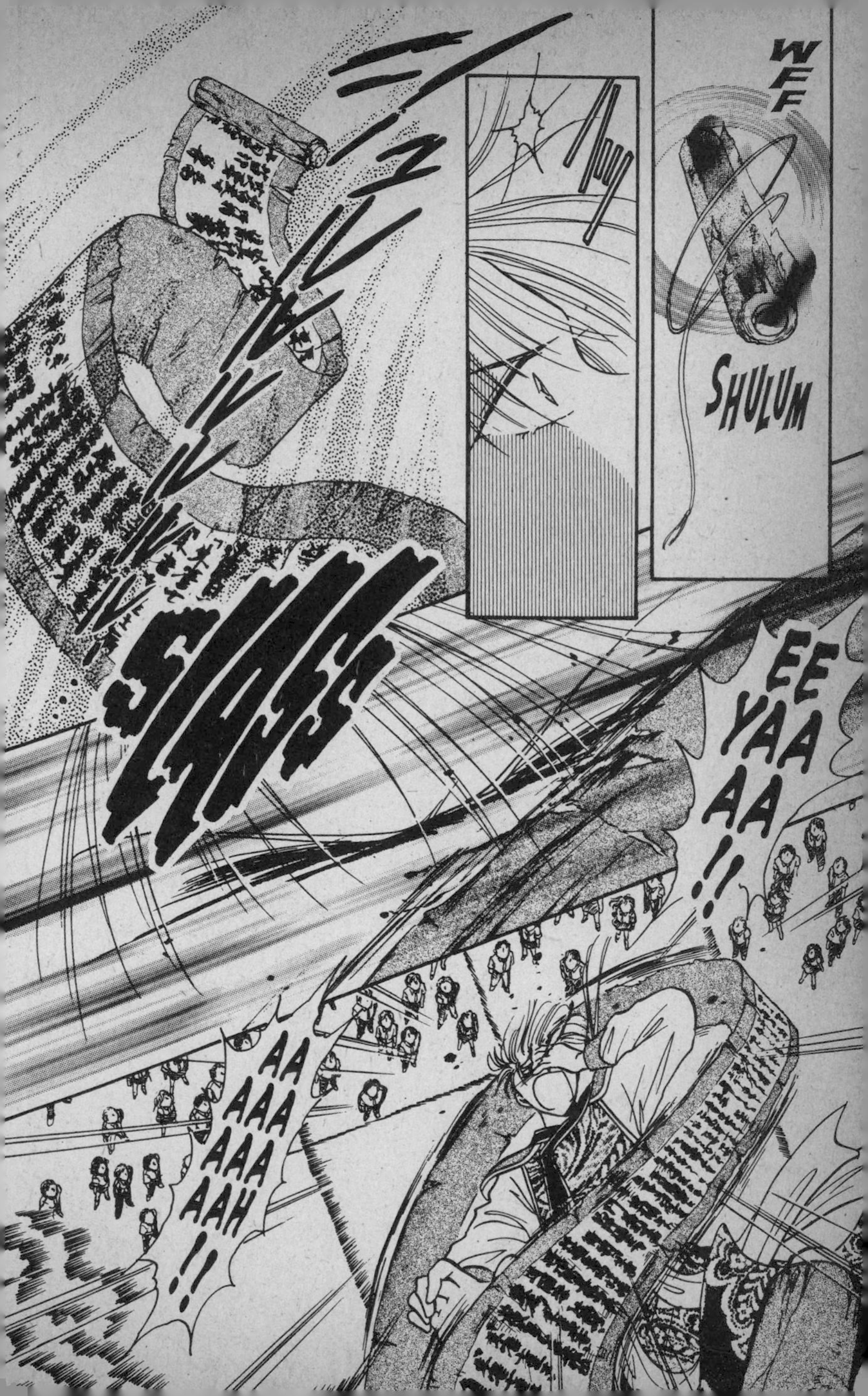
WFF
SHULUM
SHHS
EE YAAAAA!!
AAAAAAAAAAAAH!!

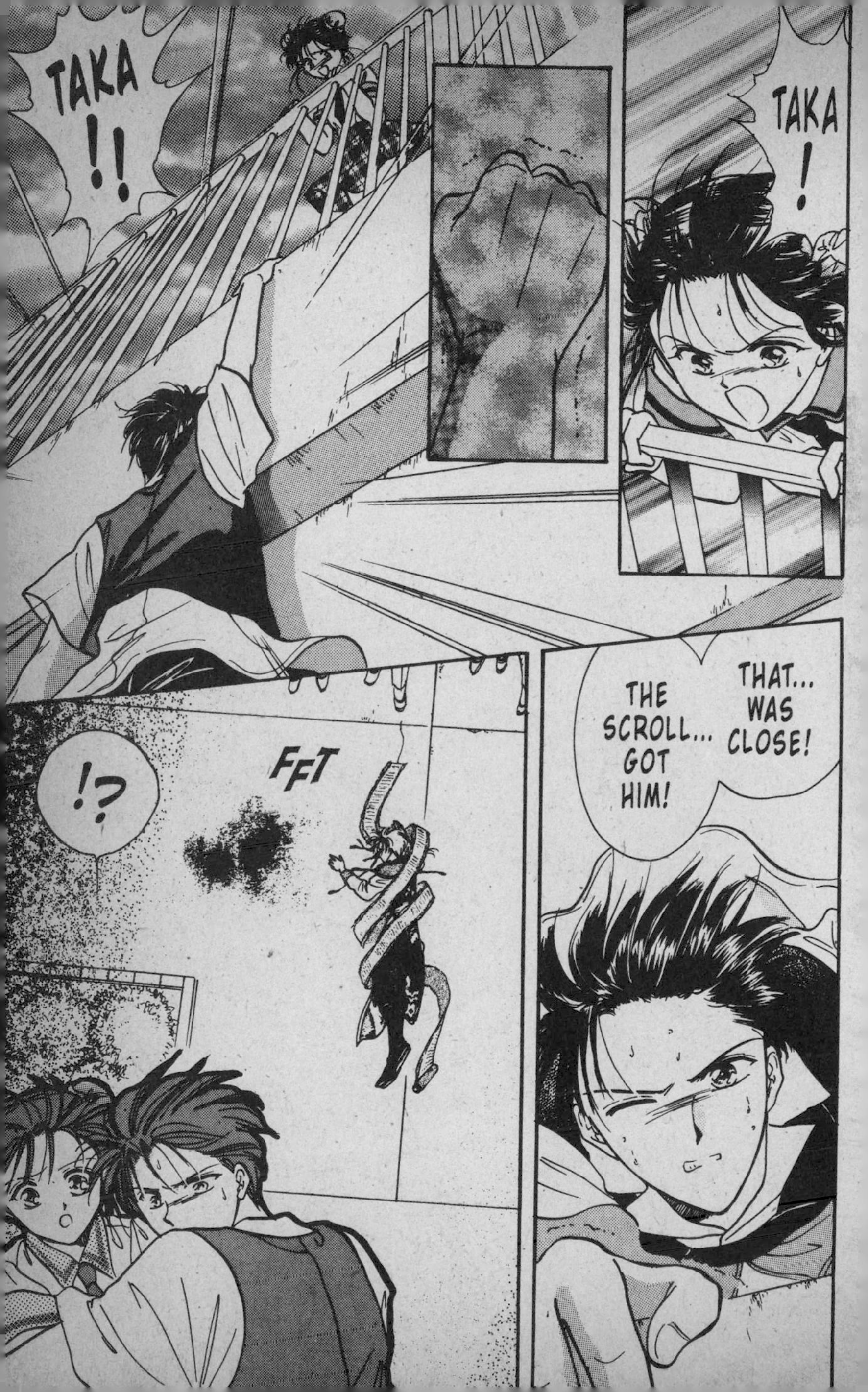
TAKA !
TAKA !!
THAT... WAS CLOSE!
THE SCROLL... GOT HIM!
FFT
!?

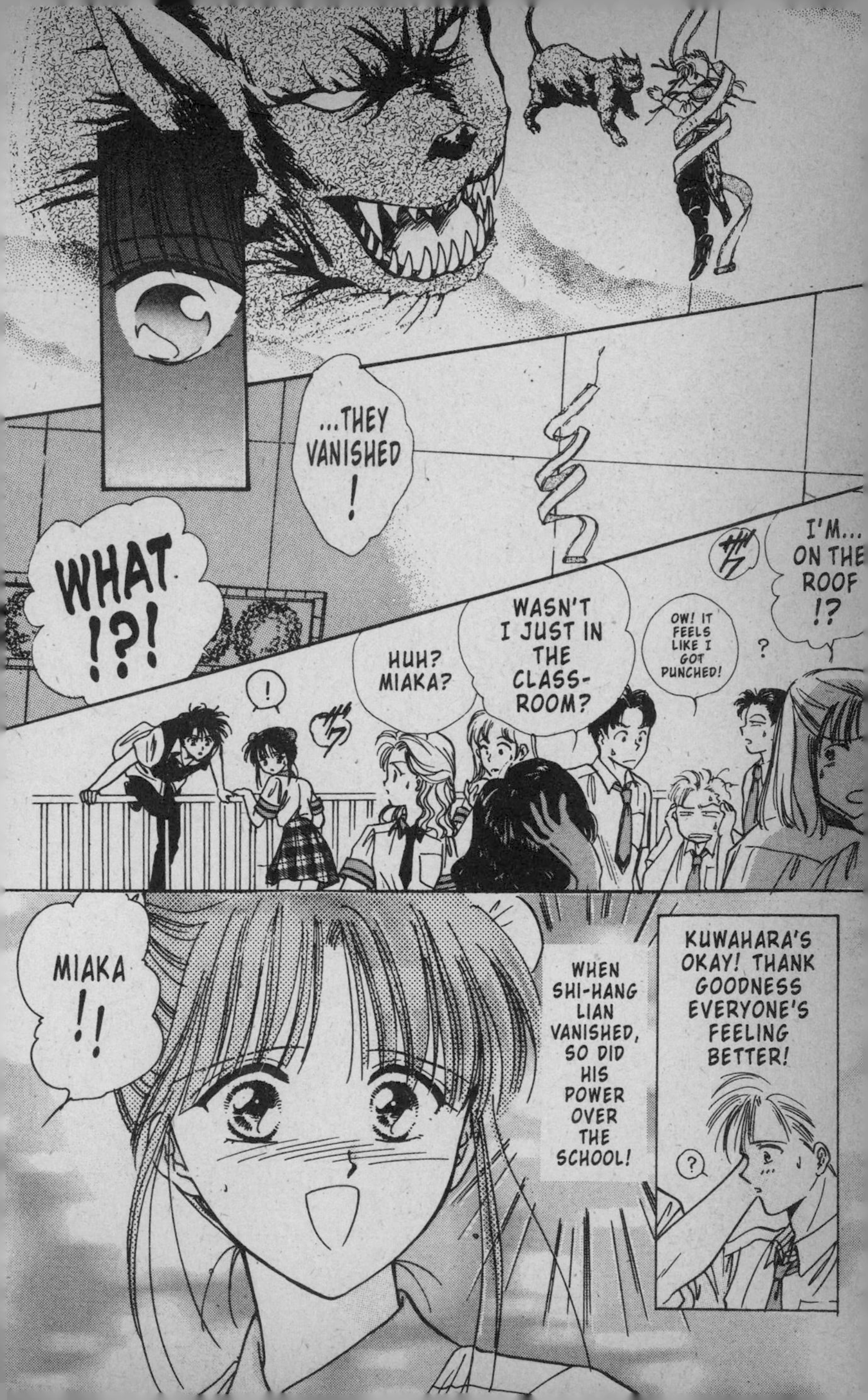
...THEY VANISHED!
I'M... ON THE ROOF!?
?
OW! IT FEELS LIKE I GOT PUNCHED!
WASN'T I JUST IN THE CLASS-ROOM?
HUH? MIAKA?
!
WHAT!?!
KUWAHARA'S OKAY! THANK GOODNESS EVERYONE'S FEELING BETTER!
?
WHEN SHI-HANG LIAN VANISHED, SO DID HIS POWER OVER THE SCHOOL!
MIAKA!!

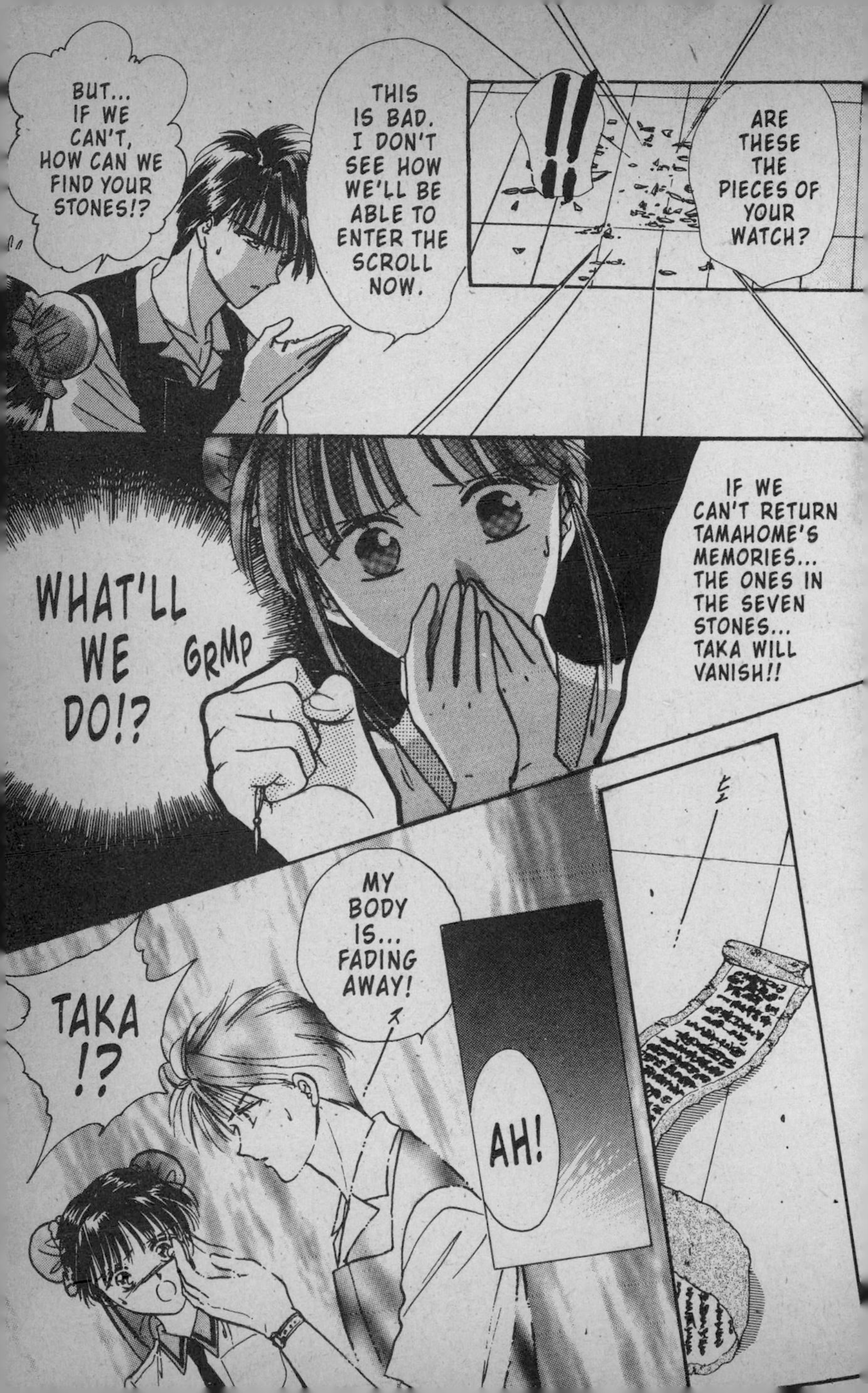
!!
ARE THESE THE PIECES OF YOUR WATCH?
THIS IS BAD. I DON'T SEE HOW WE'LL BE ABLE TO ENTER THE SCROLL NOW.
BUT... IF WE CAN'T, HOW CAN WE FIND YOUR STONES!?
IF WE CAN'T RETURN TAMAHOME'S MEMORIES... THE ONES IN THE SEVEN STONES... TAKA WILL VANISH!!
GRMP
WHAT'LL WE DO!?
AH!
MY BODY IS... FADING AWAY!
TAKA !?

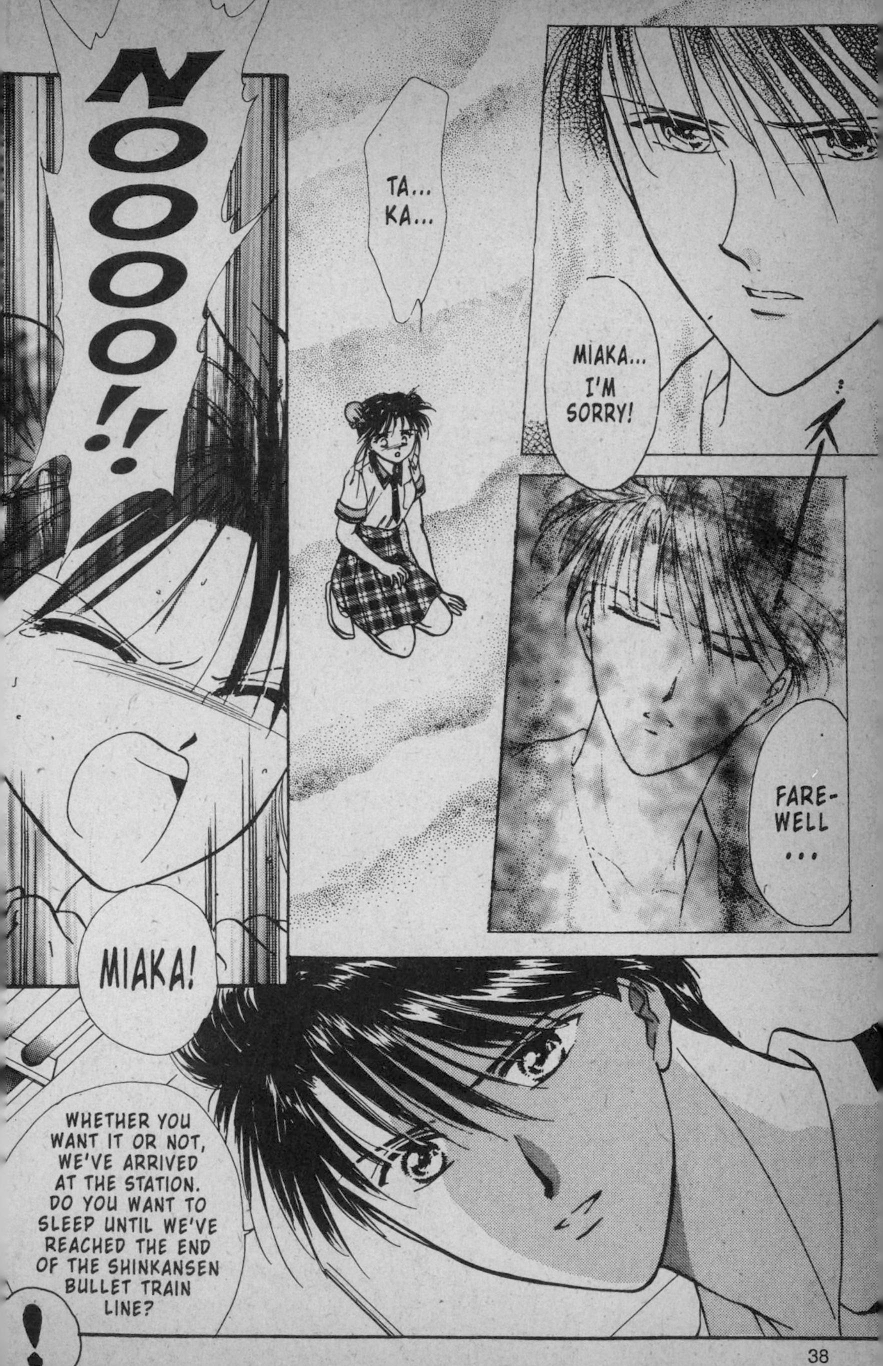
MIAKA... I'M SORRY!
FARE-WELL...
TA... KA...
NOOOO!!
MIAKA!
WHETHER YOU WANT IT OR NOT, WE'VE ARRIVED AT THE STATION. DO YOU WANT TO SLEEP UNTIL WE'VE REACHED THE END OF THE SHINKANSEN BULLET TRAIN LINE?
!

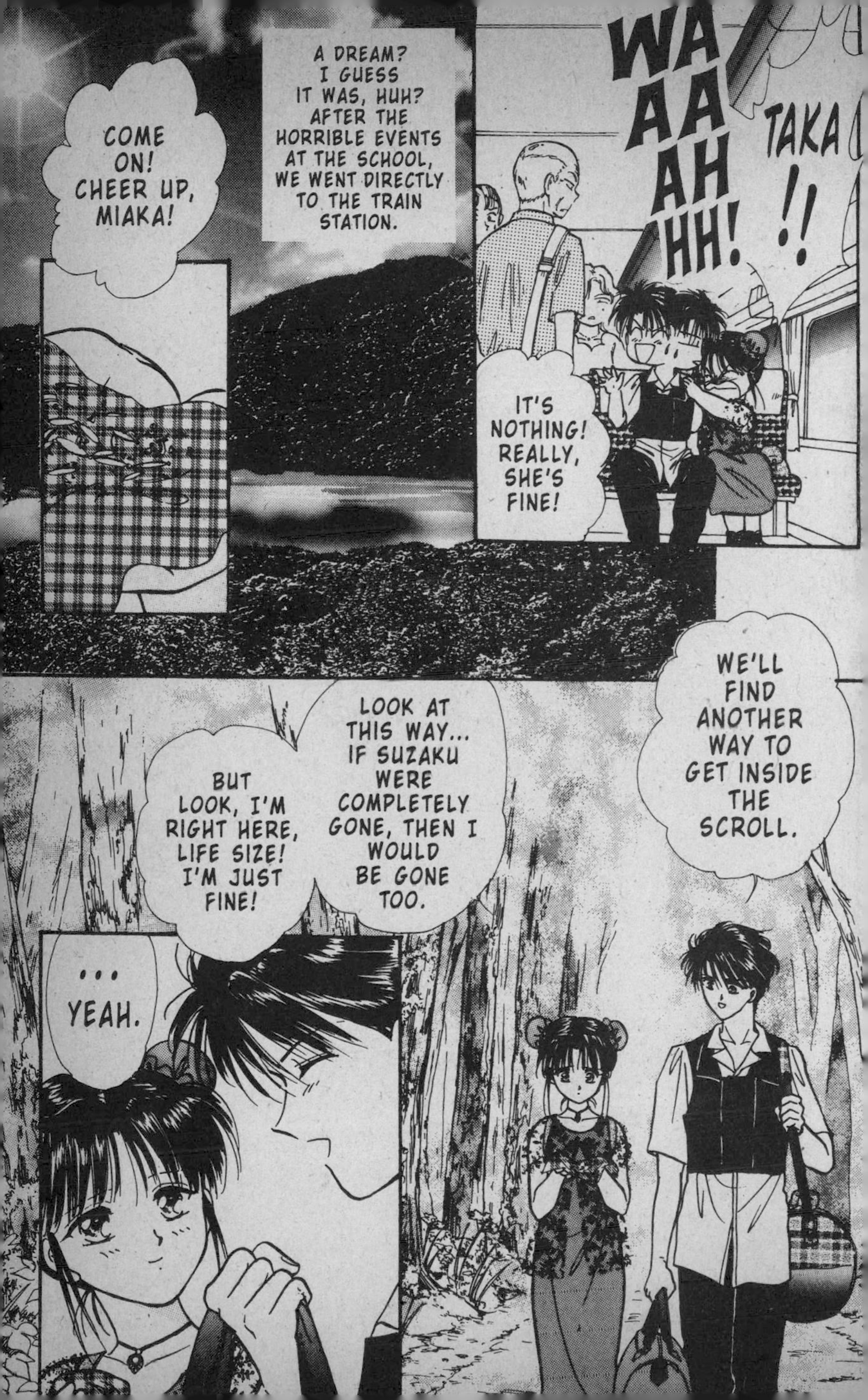
WAAAAHHH!
TAKA!!
IT'S NOTHING! REALLY, SHE'S FINE!
A DREAM? I GUESS IT WAS, HUH? AFTER THE HORRIBLE EVENTS AT THE SCHOOL, WE WENT DIRECTLY TO THE TRAIN STATION.
COME ON! CHEER UP, MIAKA!
WE'LL FIND ANOTHER WAY TO GET INSIDE THE SCROLL.
LOOK AT THIS WAY... IF SUZAKU WERE COMPLETELY GONE, THEN I WOULD BE GONE TOO.
BUT LOOK, I'M RIGHT HERE, LIFE SIZE! I'M JUST FINE!
... YEAH.

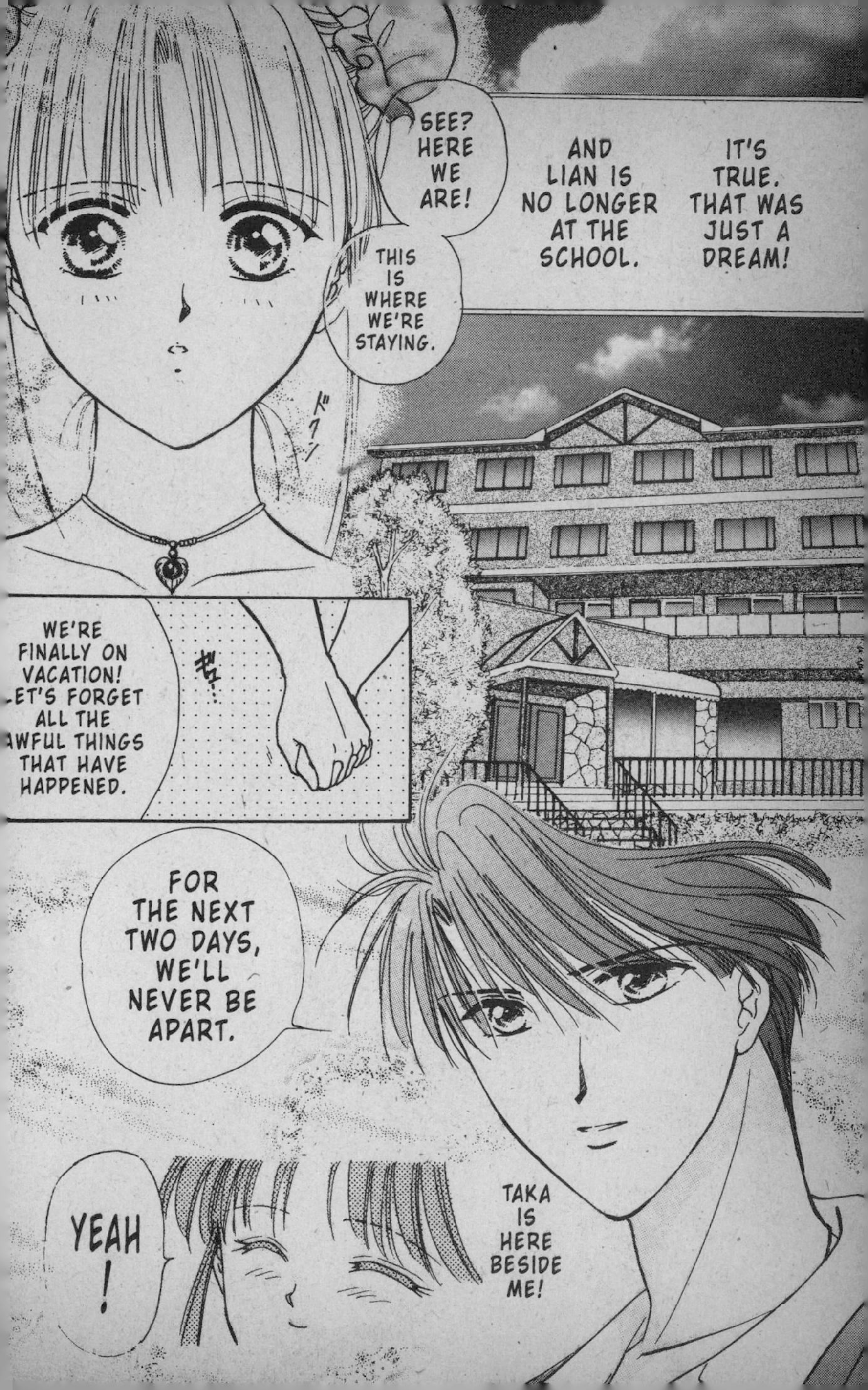
IT'S TRUE. THAT WAS JUST A DREAM!
AND LIAN IS NO LONGER AT THE SCHOOL.
SEE? HERE WE ARE!
THIS IS WHERE WE'RE STAYING.
WE'RE FINALLY ON VACATION! LET'S FORGET ALL THE AWFUL THINGS THAT HAVE HAPPENED.
FOR THE NEXT TWO DAYS, WE'LL NEVER BE APART.
TAKA IS HERE BESIDE ME!
YEAH!

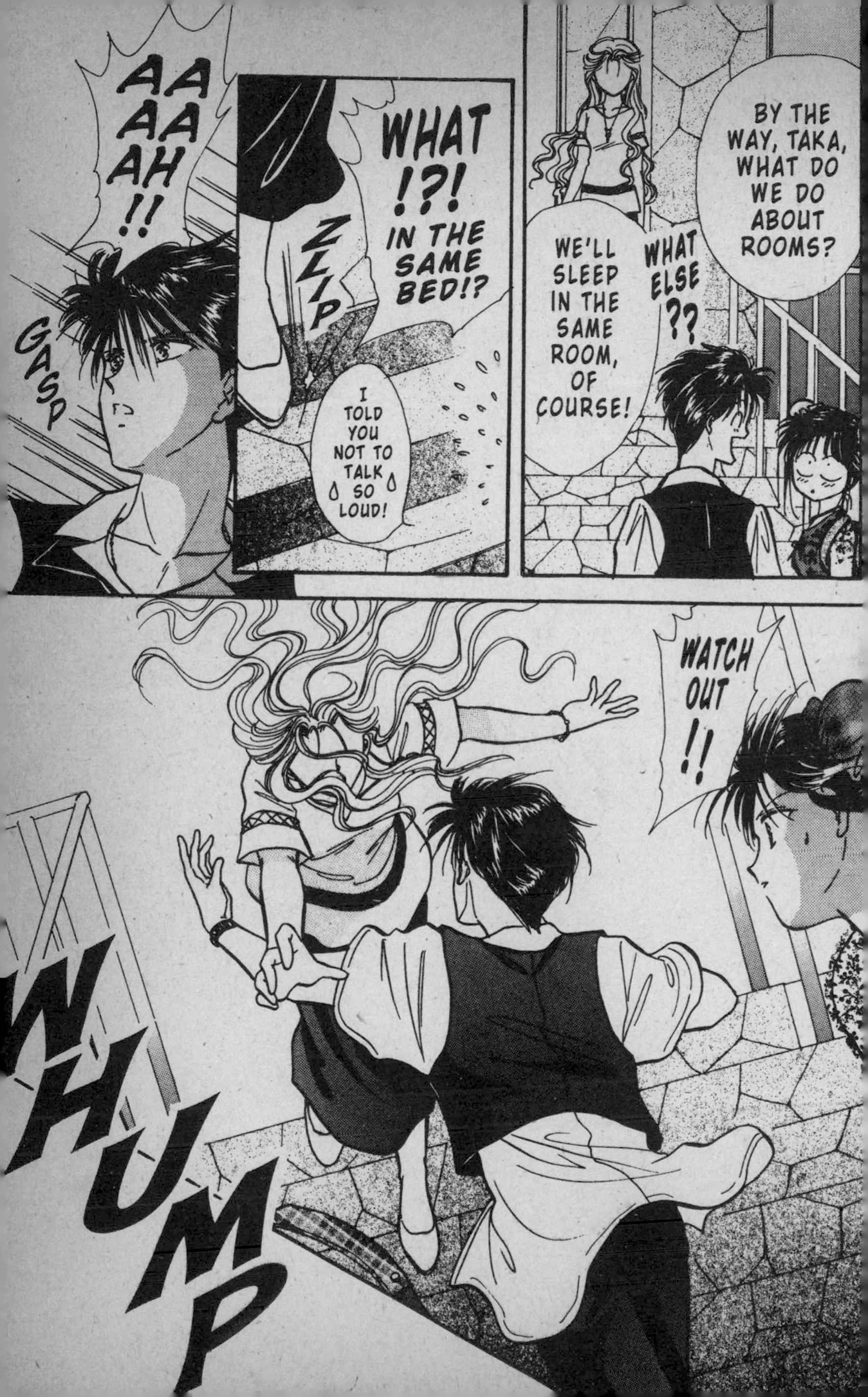
BY THE WAY, TAKA, WHAT DO WE DO ABOUT ROOMS?
WHAT ELSE ??
WE'LL SLEEP IN THE SAME ROOM, OF COURSE!
WHAT !?! IN THE SAME BED!?
ZLIP
I TOLD YOU NOT TO TALK SO LOUD!
AAAAH!!
GASP
WATCH OUT !!
WHUMP

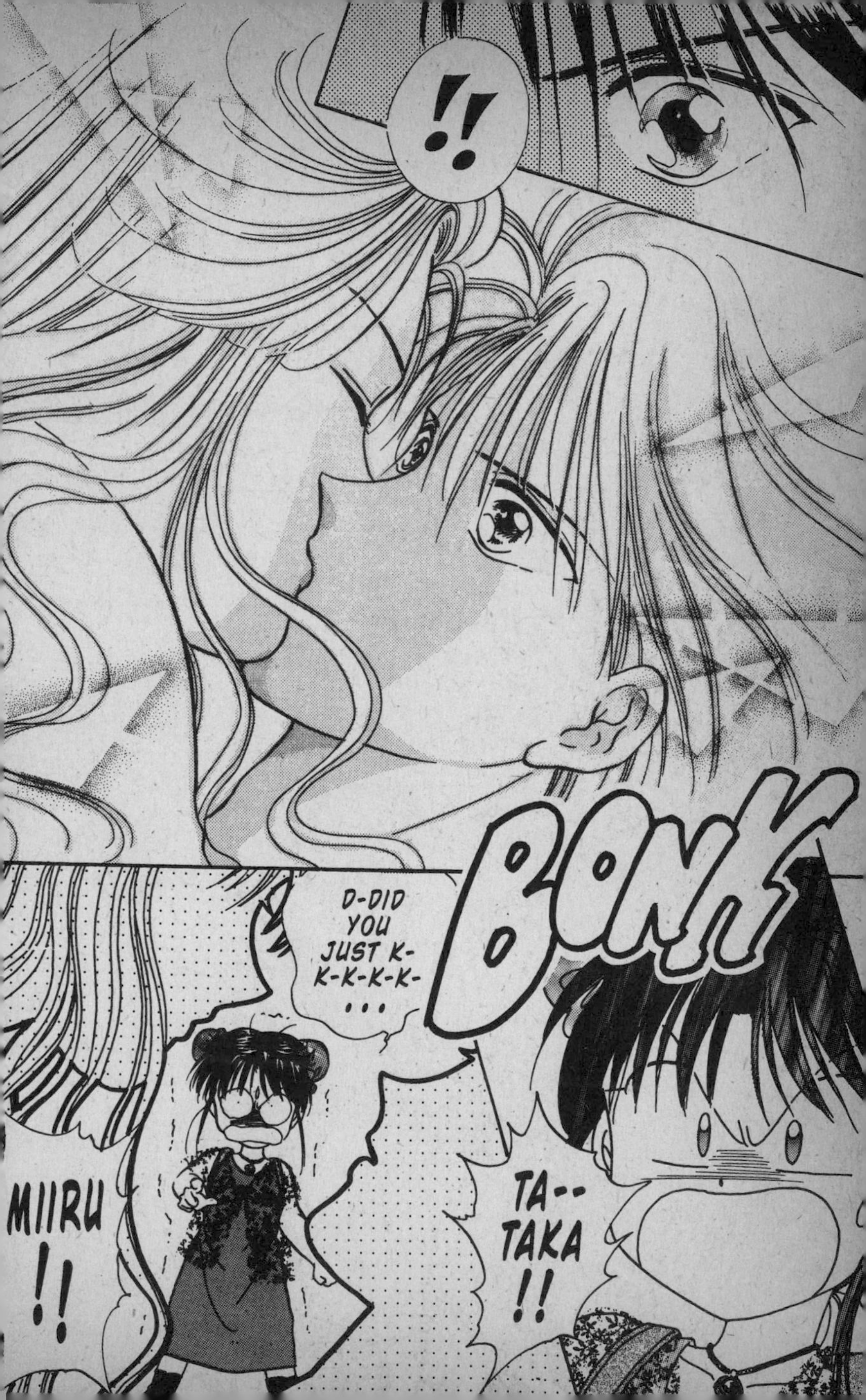
!!
BONK
D-DID YOU JUST K-K-K-K-K-...
TA--TAKA!!
MIIRU!!

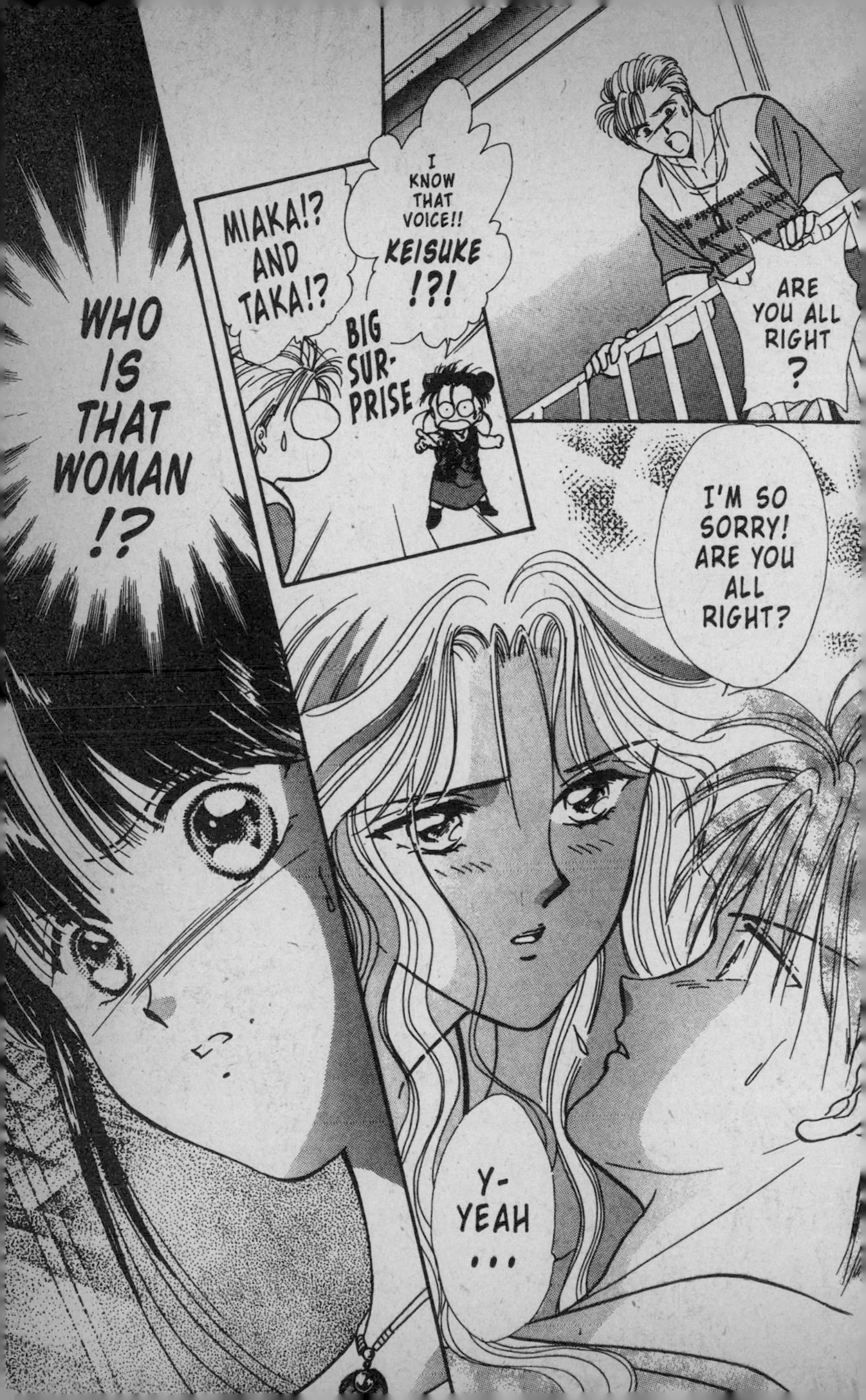
ARE YOU ALL RIGHT?
I KNOW THAT VOICE!! KEISUKE!?!
MIAKA!? AND TAKA!?
BIG SURPRISE
I'M SO SORRY! ARE YOU ALL RIGHT?
Y-YEAH...
WHO IS THAT WOMAN!?

I don't know what I'm talking about, but I'll talk anyway! If you don't like it, just skip to the next page!

There's a book out that has info on both the anime and manga of FUSHIGI YŪGI! They probably shouldn't have done it. I drew new illustrations of Miaka and each of the Seven Celestial Warriors for it! ☺ It also gives you a look at a voicing session and includes interviews with the voice actors and has a whole lot of other stuff, so be sure to check it out! Speaking of the voice actors, I recently attended a recording session and had the privilege of meeting them all face-to-face! Nakago (Mr. Furusawa) and Miaka (Ms. Araki) were at the same meeting I was in, and hearing their voices, I'd say, "Whoa! Huh?" ☺ While we were at dinner (Chinese food), my editor leaned over to me and said that behind us, Nuriko (Ms. Sakamoto) was talking! What was really interesting was when we were playing Bingo... Hotohori (Mr. Koyasu) was the master of ceremonies, but he turned to Mr. Midorikawa who had been eating the whole time and said, "Tamahome! Curb your gluttony," warning him in a very imperial voice. Mr. Seki would call out in Chichiri's voice (you know, like when he says "daaa!"), "I'm rich! No da!" or, "Bingo! No da!" Maybe it was because, from where I was seated, I couldn't see the voice actors, but listening to them all chatting in character during their meal made me feel... kind of weird. (?) ☺ At the end, mad-fan Watase had some signboards prepared (but not enough for everybody)! I couldn't get everyone's signatures, but most were kind enough to sign them for me. A large number of them also added personal comments, which made me very happy! I laughed when Mr. Ueda, who plays the twins, signed it "Big Brother!!" Mr. Koyasu and Mr. Midorikawa both signed for me in hiragana script even though they usually don't sign it this way, so it's especially valuable! Woo-hoo!

THAT'S A WRAP!
This day was the last day of work for Episode 27. I cried during episode 27. I thought Mr. Midorikawa's acting (the way he conveyed those emotions so realistically) was terrific! Really, he made me think, "If there is a single person who complains about Mr. Midorikawa's portrayal of Tamahome, I'm going to punch them out!" I really thought that! ☺ And when Nuriko died (episode 33), I just kept crying and crying... Ms. Sakamoto and Ms. Araki were so great! For anybody who hasn't seen the TV show, rent it if that's the only way, but please see it!! I was so emotional! There was a scene in it where Nuriko and Miaka go on a date in the real world. One of the staff told me, "It's a present for Nuriko." I think Nuriko would like that. There are so many episodes that I'd like to recommend that I wish I could do a commentary on the whole series! ☺ Everybody, please watch the videos!

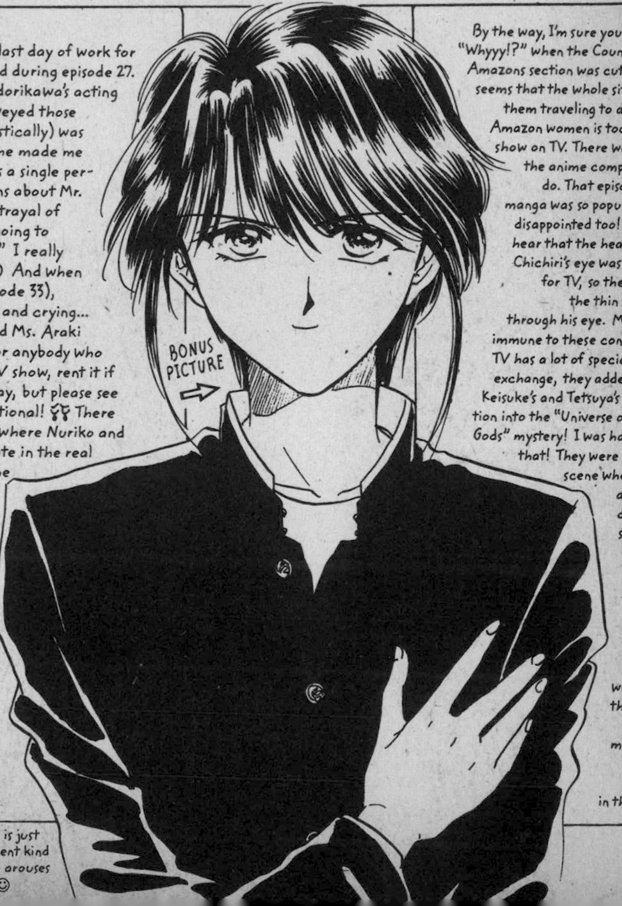
BONUS PICTURE

By the way, I'm sure you all yelled, "Whyyy!?" when the Country of the Amazons section was cut out! ☺ It seems that the whole situation of them traveling to a nation of Amazon women is too risqué to show on TV. There was nothing the anime company could do. That episode of the manga was so popular... I was disappointed too! Also, I hear that the heavy scar on Chichiri's eye was too much for TV, so they just had the thin scar going through his eye. Manga isn't immune to these concerns, but TV has a lot of special rules. In exchange, they added more to Keisuke's and Tetsuya's investigation into the "Universe of the Four Gods" mystery! I was happy about that! They were planning a scene where Tatara and Suzuno died at the same time, but events conspired against it, and they couldn't do it. But there were scenes that I didn't do in the manga that they were able to do in the anime!!

Miaka in episode 34 is just wonderful, in a different kind of way! ☺ Ms. Araki arouses my curiosity! ☺

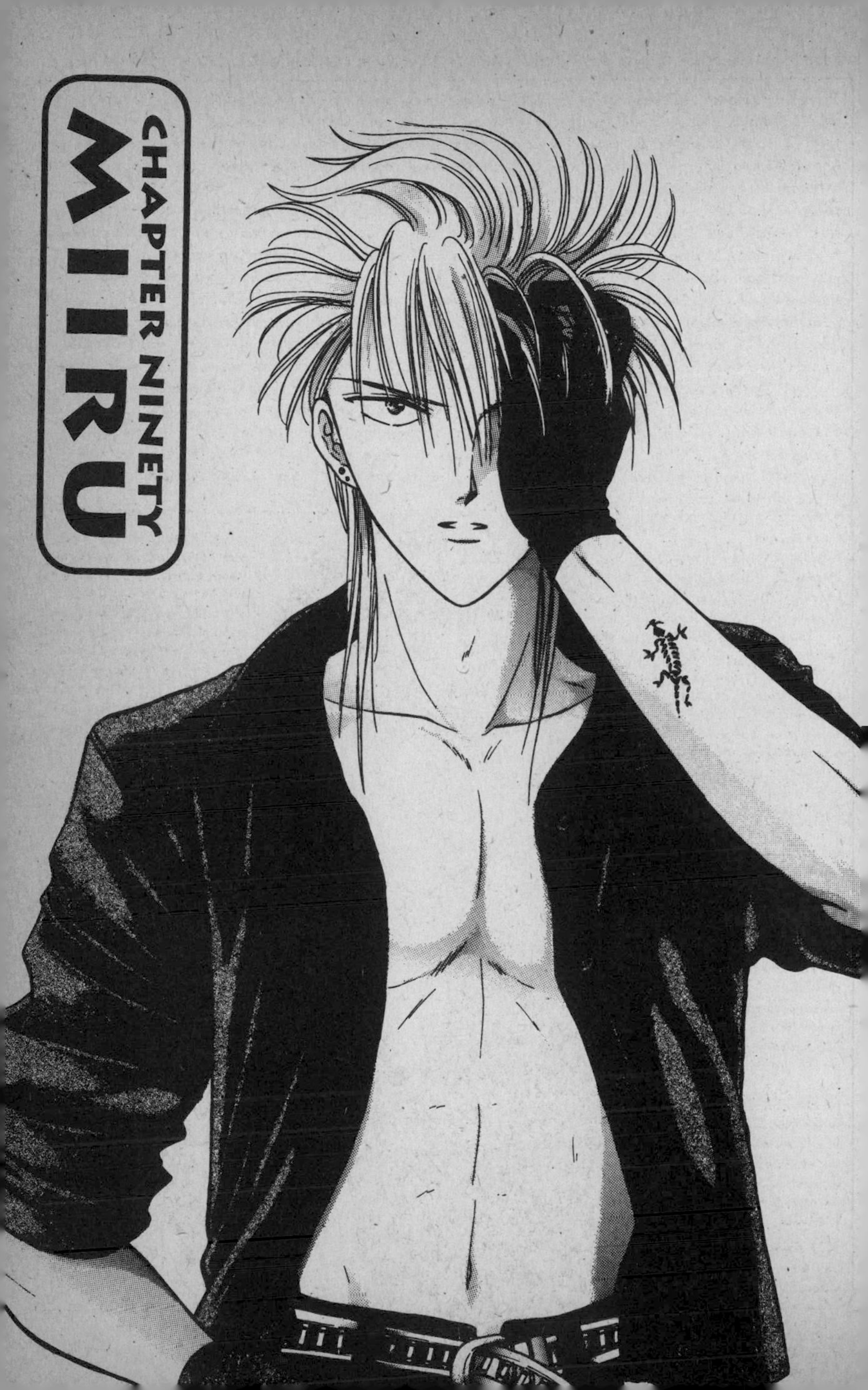
CHAPTER NINETY
MIIRU

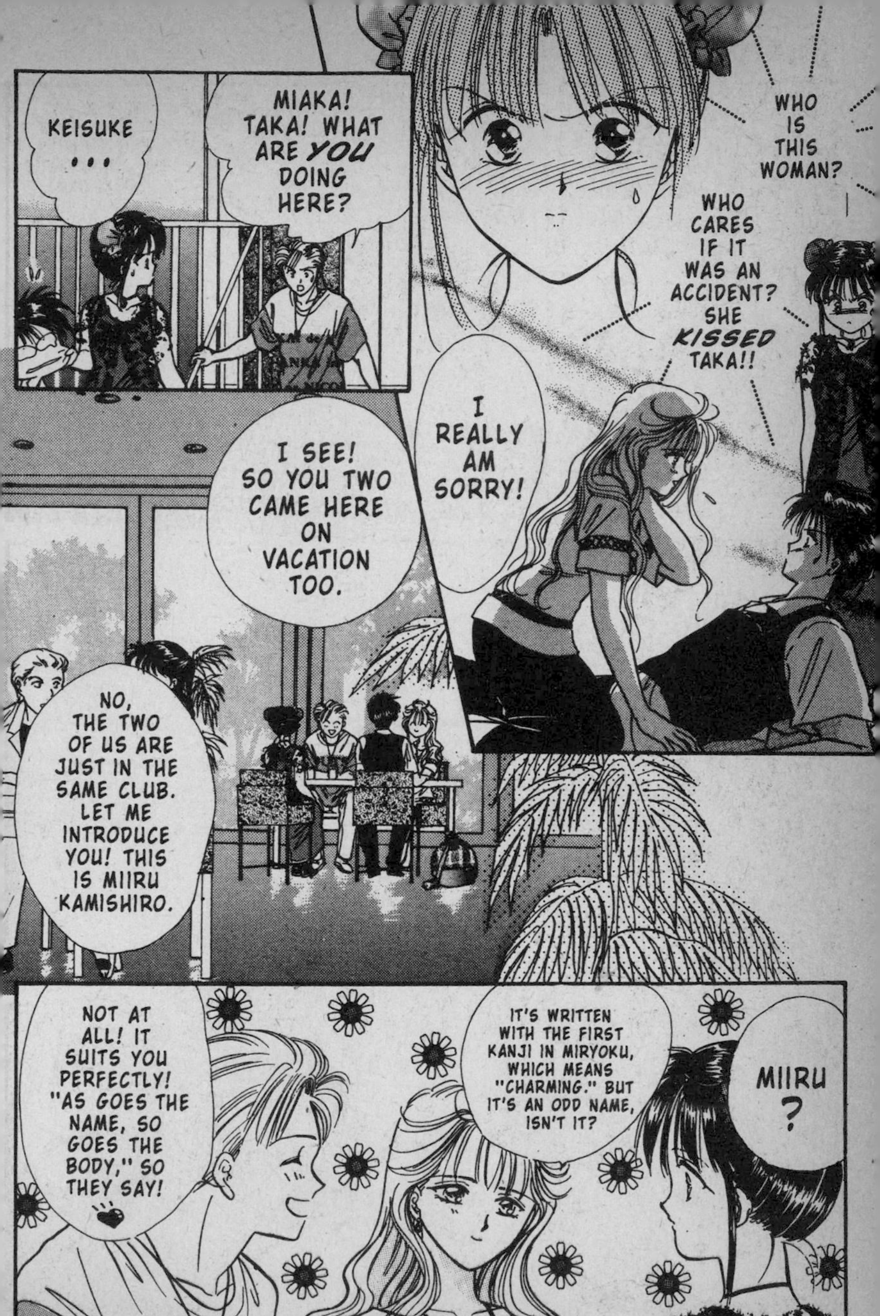
WHO IS THIS WOMAN?
WHO CARES IF IT WAS AN ACCIDENT? SHE *KISSED* TAKA!!
I REALLY AM SORRY!
MIAKA! TAKA! WHAT ARE *YOU* DOING HERE?
KEISUKE...
I SEE! SO YOU TWO CAME HERE ON VACATION TOO.
NO, THE TWO OF US ARE JUST IN THE SAME CLUB. LET ME INTRODUCE YOU! THIS IS MIIRU KAMISHIRO.
MIIRU?
IT'S WRITTEN WITH THE FIRST KANJI IN MIRYOKU, WHICH MEANS "CHARMING." BUT IT'S AN ODD NAME, ISN'T IT?
NOT AT ALL! IT SUITS YOU PERFECTLY! "AS GOES THE NAME, SO GOES THE BODY," SO THEY SAY!

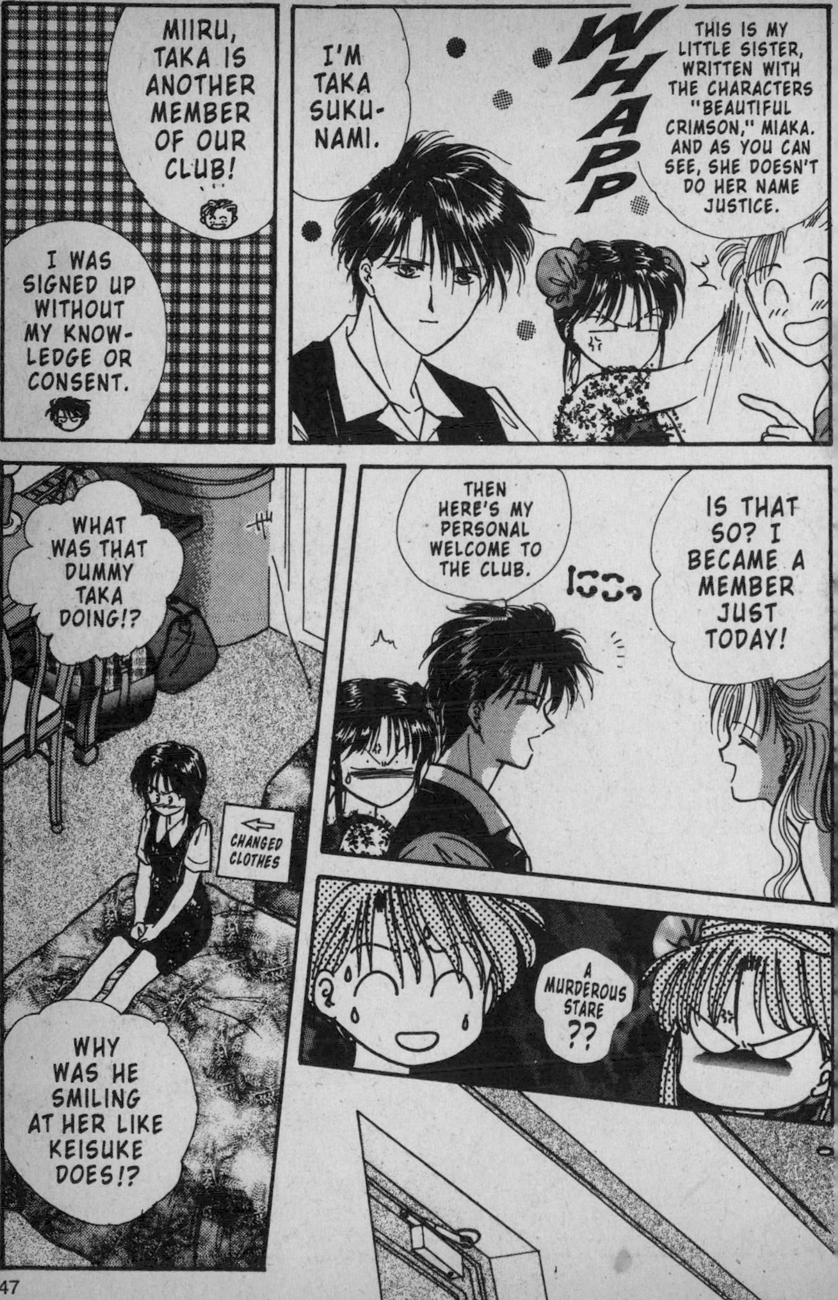
THIS IS MY LITTLE SISTER, WRITTEN WITH THE CHARACTERS "BEAUTIFUL CRIMSON," MIAKA. AND AS YOU CAN SEE, SHE DOESN'T DO HER NAME JUSTICE.
WHAPP
I'M TAKA SUKU-NAMI.
MIIRU, TAKA IS ANOTHER MEMBER OF OUR CLUB!
I WAS SIGNED UP WITHOUT MY KNOW-LEDGE OR CONSENT.
IS THAT SO? I BECAME A MEMBER JUST TODAY!
THEN HERE'S MY PERSONAL WELCOME TO THE CLUB.
A MURDEROUS STARE ??
WHAT WAS THAT DUMMY TAKA DOING!?
CHANGED CLOTHES
WHY WAS HE SMILING AT HER LIKE KEISUKE DOES!?

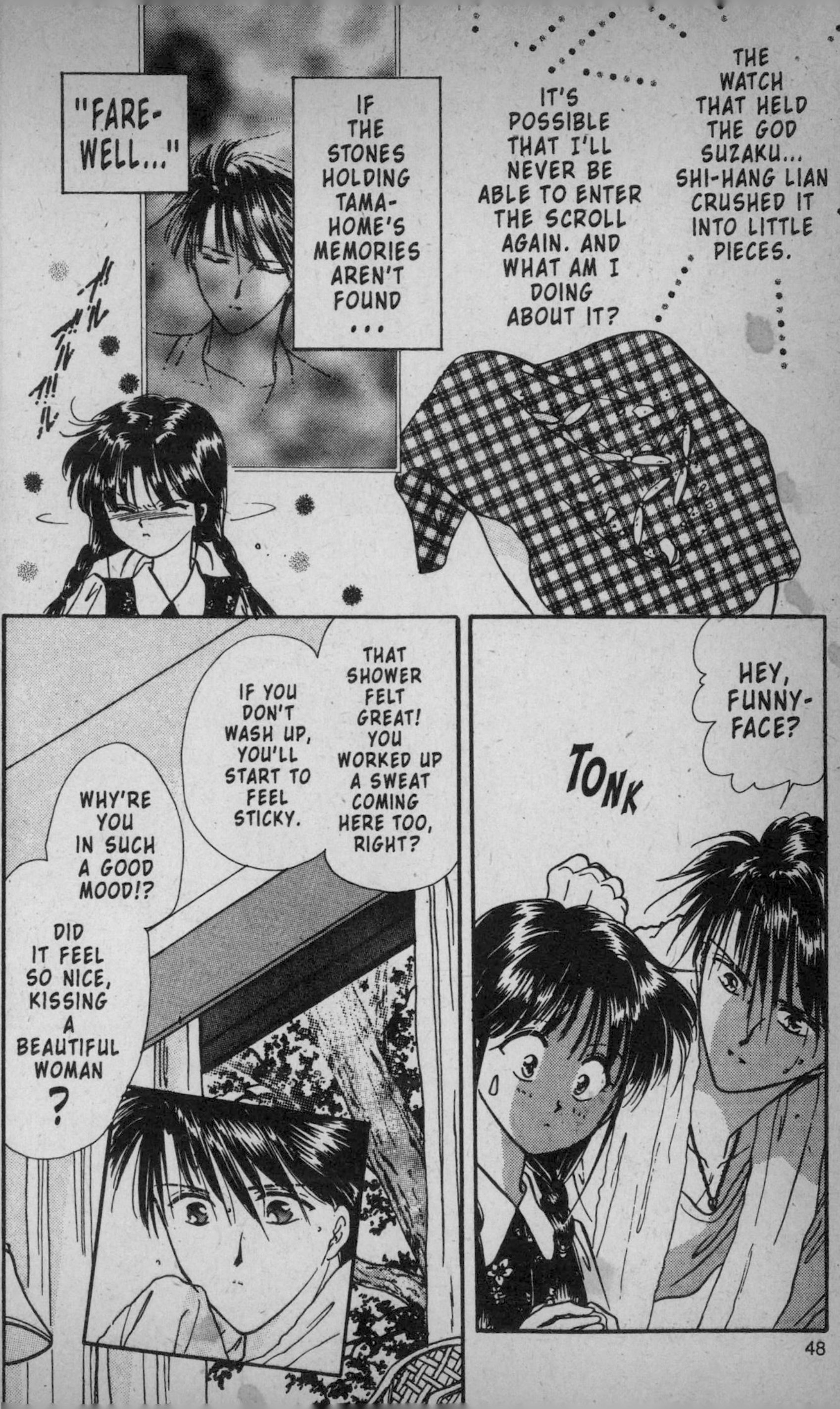
THE WATCH THAT HELD THE GOD SUZAKU... SHI-HANG LIAN CRUSHED IT INTO LITTLE PIECES.
IT'S POSSIBLE THAT I'LL NEVER BE ABLE TO ENTER THE SCROLL AGAIN. AND WHAT AM I DOING ABOUT IT?
IF THE STONES HOLDING TAMAHOME'S MEMORIES AREN'T FOUND...
"FAREWELL..."
HEY, FUNNY-FACE?
TONK
THAT SHOWER FELT GREAT! YOU WORKED UP A SWEAT COMING HERE TOO, RIGHT?
IF YOU DON'T WASH UP, YOU'LL START TO FEEL STICKY.
WHY'RE YOU IN SUCH A GOOD MOOD!?
DID IT FEEL SO NICE, KISSING A BEAUTIFUL WOMAN?

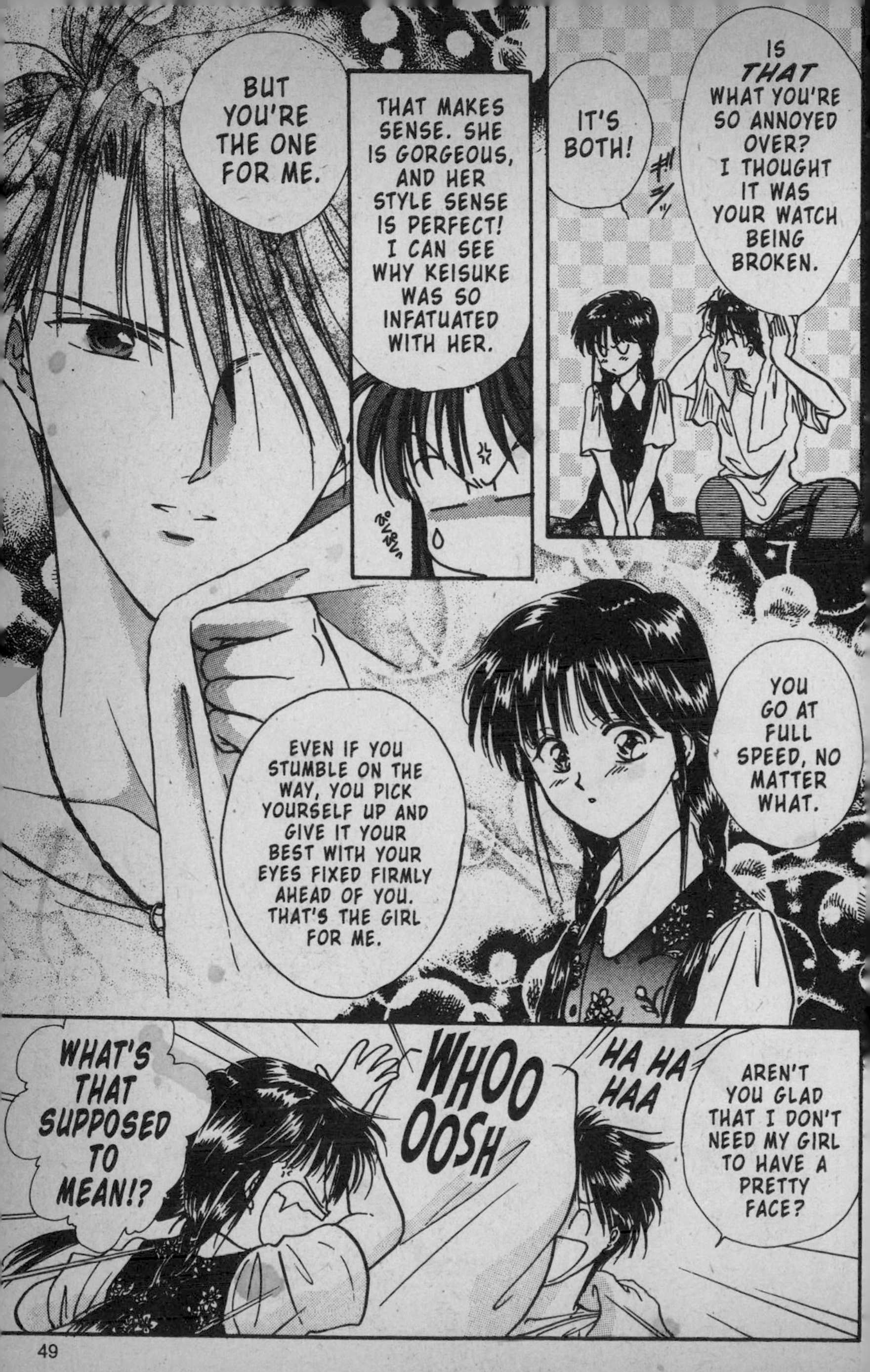
IS *THAT* WHAT YOU'RE SO ANNOYED OVER? I THOUGHT IT WAS YOUR WATCH BEING BROKEN.
IT'S BOTH!
THAT MAKES SENSE. SHE IS GORGEOUS, AND HER STYLE SENSE IS PERFECT! I CAN SEE WHY KEISUKE WAS SO INFATUATED WITH HER.
BUT YOU'RE THE ONE FOR ME.
YOU GO AT FULL SPEED, NO MATTER WHAT.
EVEN IF YOU STUMBLE ON THE WAY, YOU PICK YOURSELF UP AND GIVE IT YOUR BEST WITH YOUR EYES FIXED FIRMLY AHEAD OF YOU. THAT'S THE GIRL FOR ME.
AREN'T YOU GLAD THAT I DON'T NEED MY GIRL TO HAVE A PRETTY FACE?
HA HA HAA
WHOO OOSH
WHAT'S THAT SUPPOSED TO MEAN!?

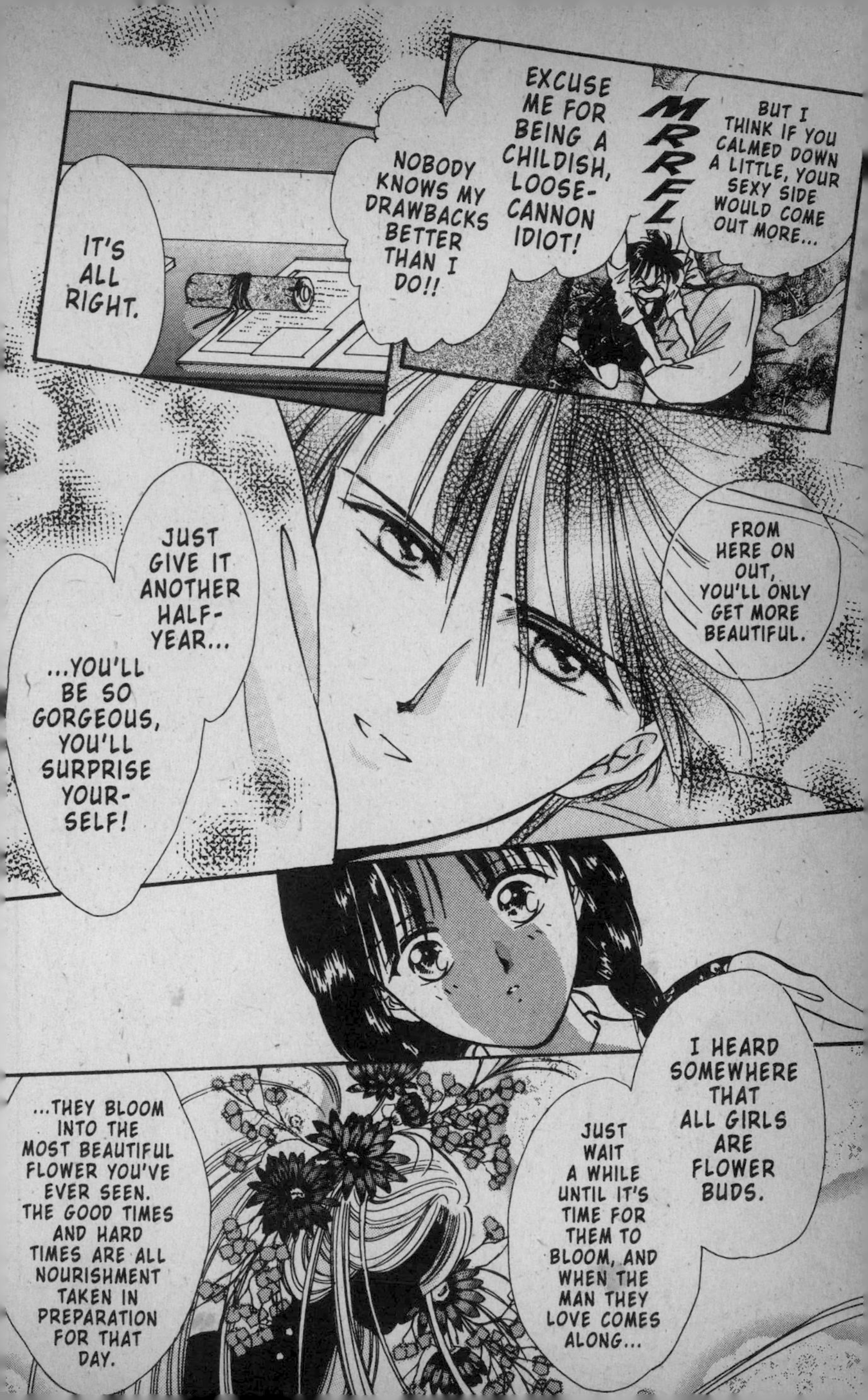
BUT I THINK IF YOU CALMED DOWN A LITTLE, YOUR SEXY SIDE WOULD COME OUT MORE...
MRRFL
EXCUSE ME FOR BEING A CHILDISH, LOOSE-CANNON IDIOT!
NOBODY KNOWS MY DRAWBACKS BETTER THAN I DO!!
IT'S ALL RIGHT.
FROM HERE ON OUT, YOU'LL ONLY GET MORE BEAUTIFUL.
JUST GIVE IT ANOTHER HALF-YEAR...
...YOU'LL BE SO GORGEOUS, YOU'LL SURPRISE YOUR-SELF!
I HEARD SOMEWHERE THAT ALL GIRLS ARE FLOWER BUDS.
JUST WAIT A WHILE UNTIL IT'S TIME FOR THEM TO BLOOM, AND WHEN THE MAN THEY LOVE COMES ALONG...
...THEY BLOOM INTO THE MOST BEAUTIFUL FLOWER YOU'VE EVER SEEN. THE GOOD TIMES AND HARD TIMES ARE ALL NOURISHMENT TAKEN IN PREPARATION FOR THAT DAY.

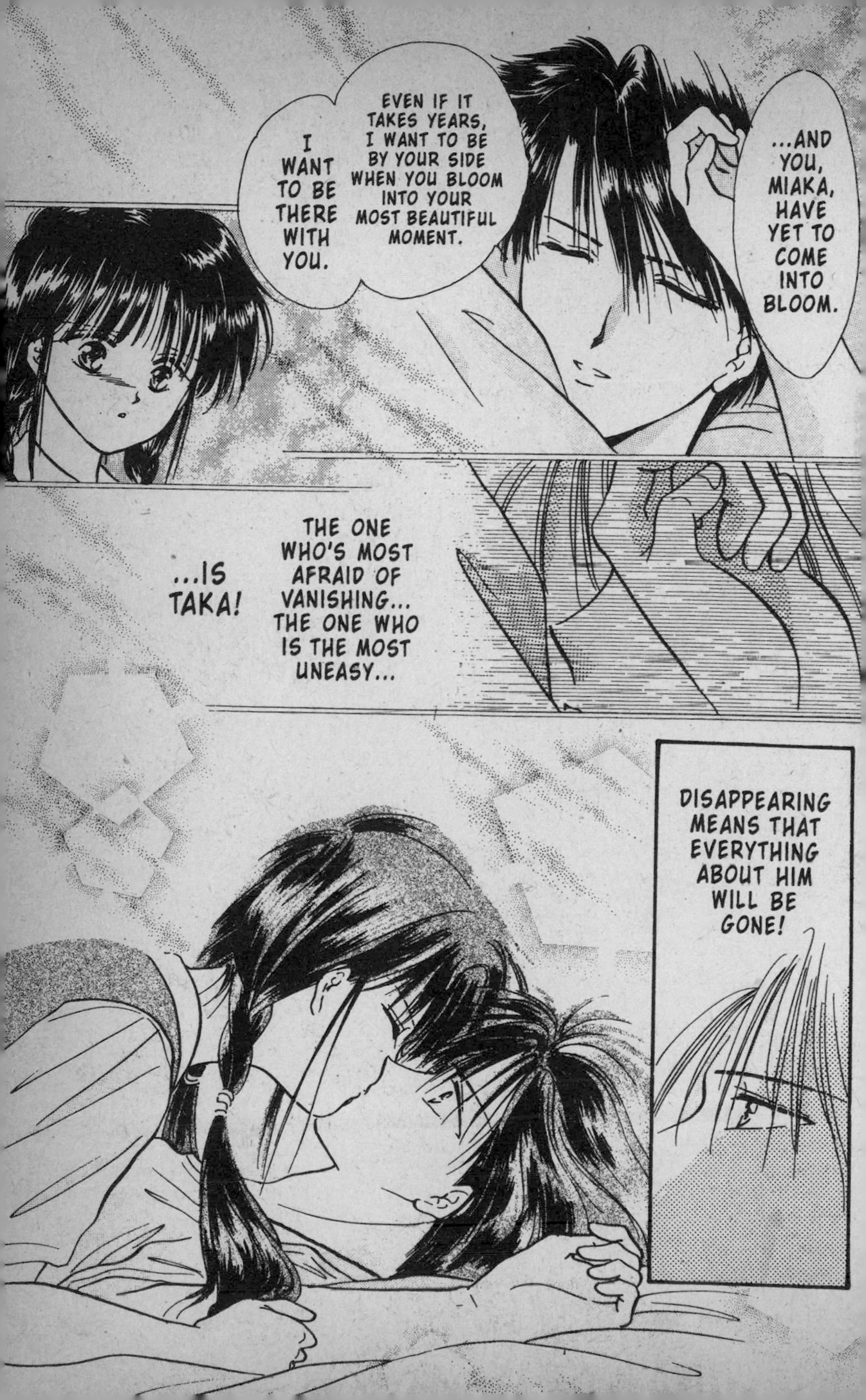
...AND YOU, MIAKA, HAVE YET TO COME INTO BLOOM.
EVEN IF IT TAKES YEARS, I WANT TO BE BY YOUR SIDE WHEN YOU BLOOM INTO YOUR MOST BEAUTIFUL MOMENT.
I WANT TO BE THERE WITH YOU.
THE ONE WHO'S MOST AFRAID OF VANISHING... THE ONE WHO IS THE MOST UNEASY...
...IS TAKA!
DISAPPEARING MEANS THAT EVERYTHING ABOUT HIM WILL BE GONE!

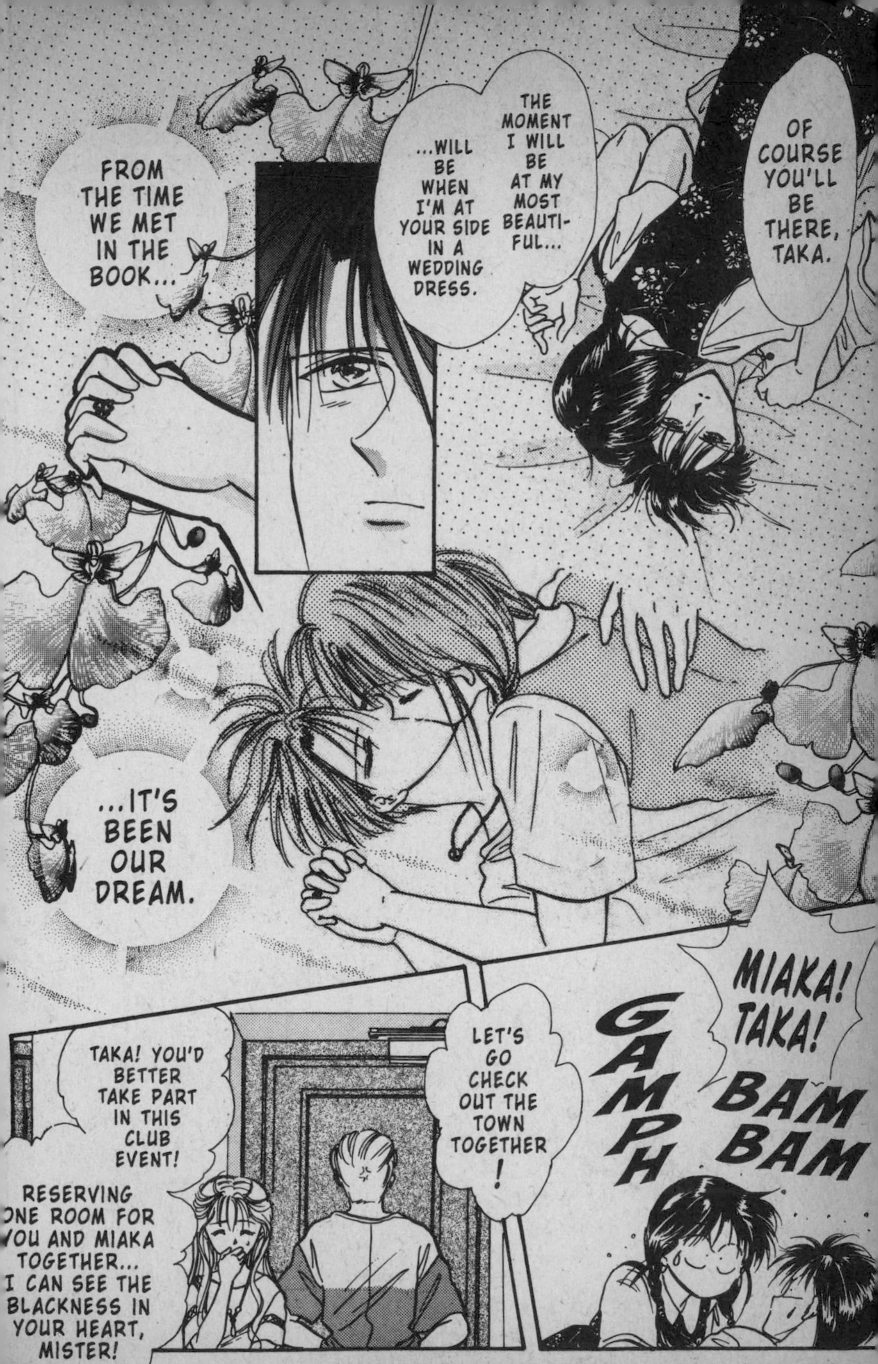
OF COURSE YOU'LL BE THERE, TAKA.
THE MOMENT I WILL BE AT MY MOST BEAUTIFUL...
...WILL BE WHEN I'M AT YOUR SIDE IN A WEDDING DRESS.
FROM THE TIME WE MET IN THE BOOK...
...IT'S BEEN OUR DREAM.
MIAKA! TAKA!
BAM BAM
GAMPH
LET'S GO CHECK OUT THE TOWN TOGETHER!
TAKA! YOU'D BETTER TAKE PART IN THIS CLUB EVENT!
RESERVING ONE ROOM FOR YOU AND MIAKA TOGETHER... I CAN SEE THE BLACKNESS IN YOUR HEART, MISTER!

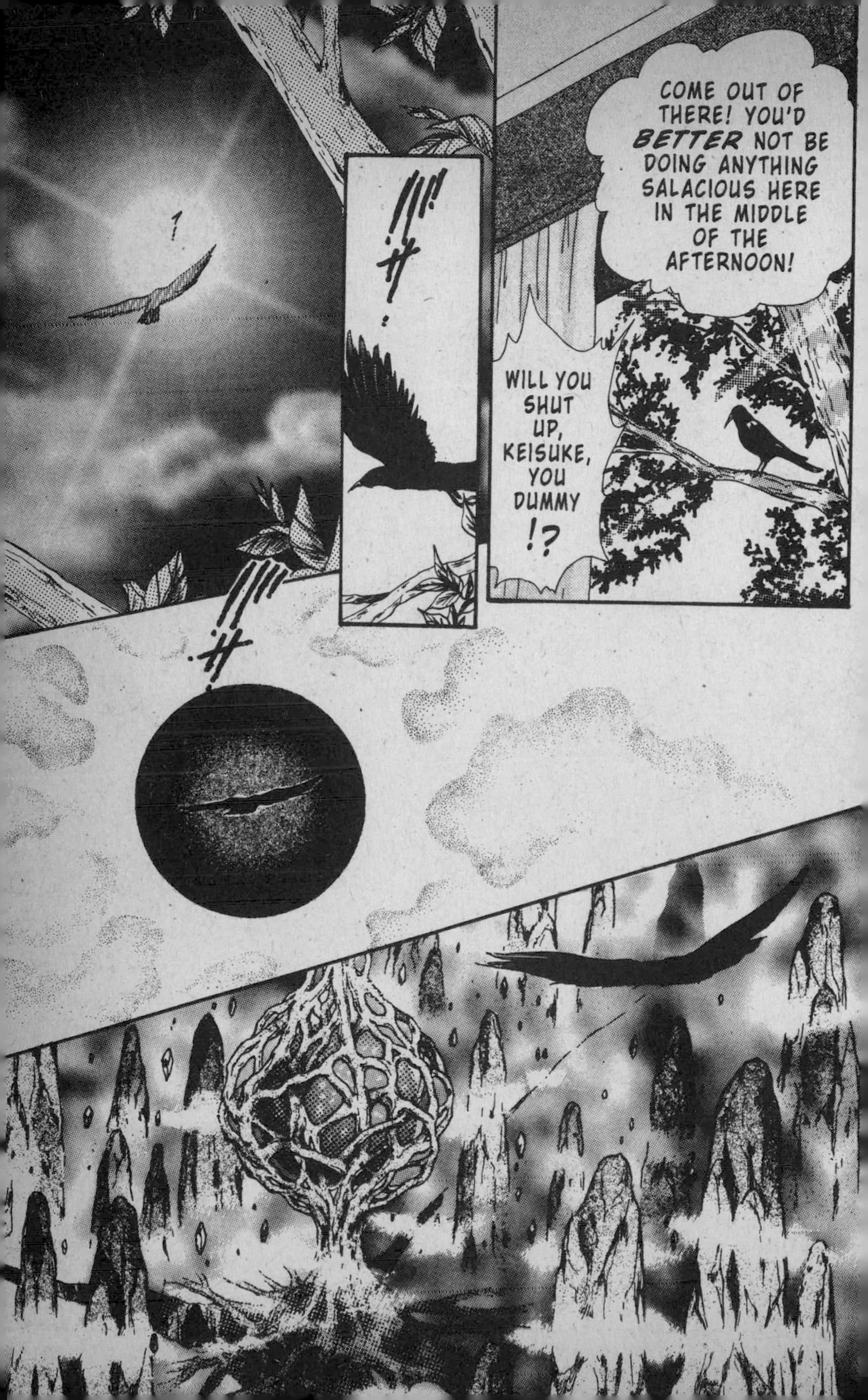
COME OUT OF THERE! YOU'D BETTER NOT BE DOING ANYTHING SALACIOUS HERE IN THE MIDDLE OF THE AFTERNOON!
WILL YOU SHUT UP, KEISUKE, YOU DUMMY !?

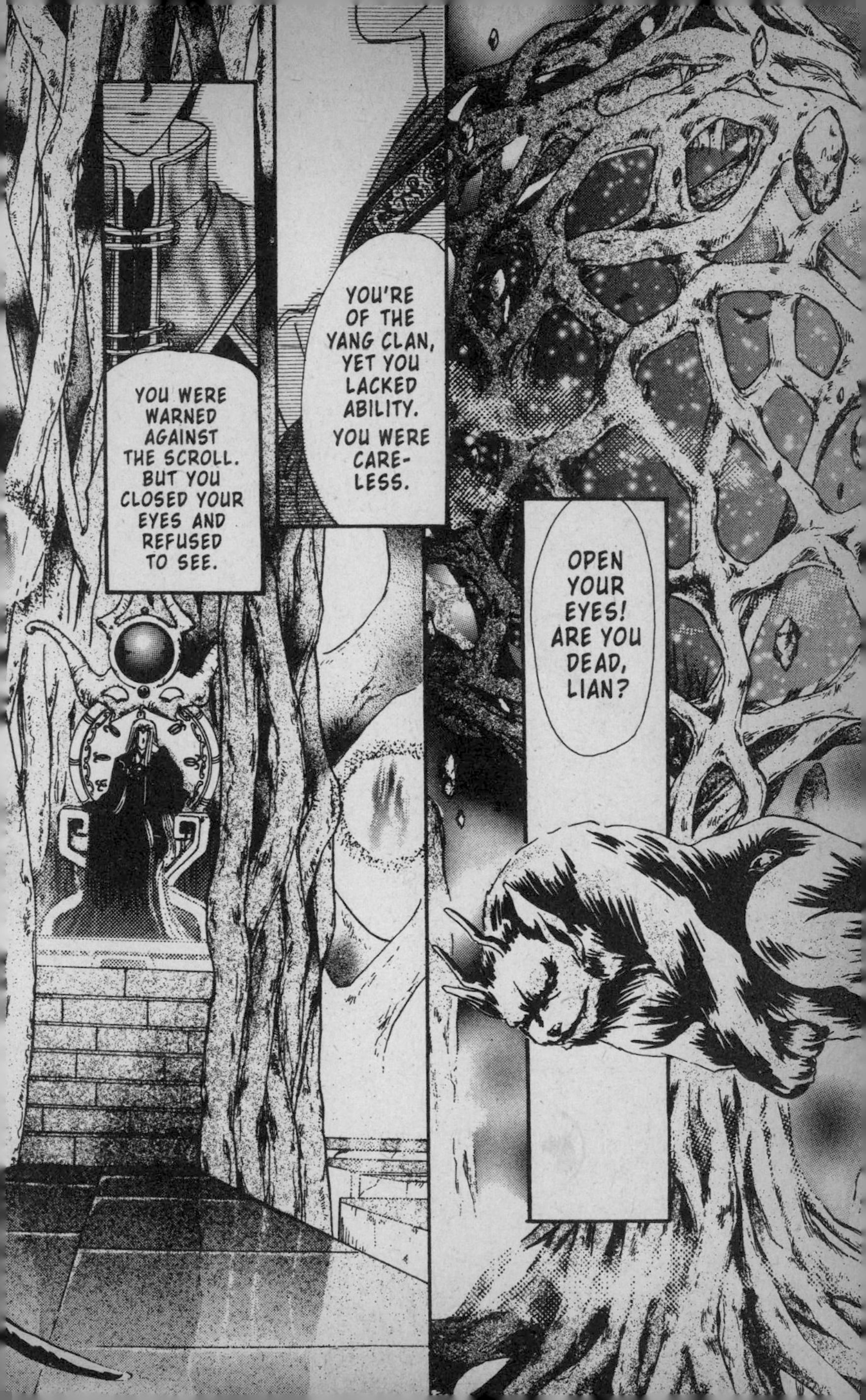
OPEN YOUR EYES! ARE YOU DEAD, LIAN?
YOU'RE OF THE YANG CLAN, YET YOU LACKED ABILITY.
YOU WERE CARE-LESS.
YOU WERE WARNED AGAINST THE SCROLL. BUT YOU CLOSED YOUR EYES AND REFUSED TO SEE.

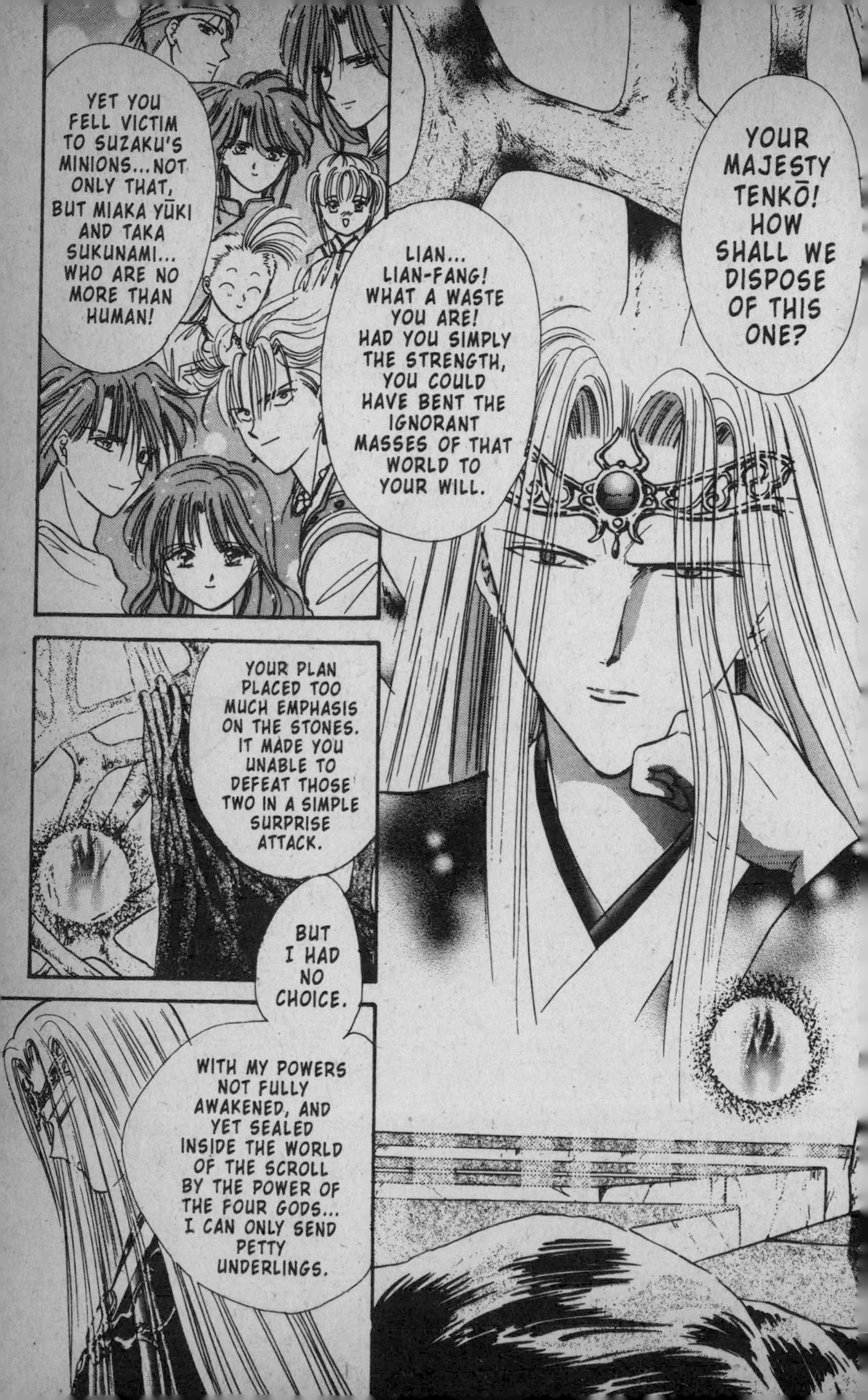

YOUR MAJESTY TENKŌ! HOW SHALL WE DISPOSE OF THIS ONE?
LIAN... LIAN-FANG! WHAT A WASTE YOU ARE! HAD YOU SIMPLY THE STRENGTH, YOU COULD HAVE BENT THE IGNORANT MASSES OF THAT WORLD TO YOUR WILL.
YET YOU FELL VICTIM TO SUZAKU'S MINIONS...NOT ONLY THAT, BUT MIAKA YŪKI AND TAKA SUKUNAMI... WHO ARE NO MORE THAN HUMAN!
YOUR PLAN PLACED TOO MUCH EMPHASIS ON THE STONES. IT MADE YOU UNABLE TO DEFEAT THOSE TWO IN A SIMPLE SURPRISE ATTACK.
BUT I HAD NO CHOICE.
WITH MY POWERS NOT FULLY AWAKENED, AND YET SEALED INSIDE THE WORLD OF THE SCROLL BY THE POWER OF THE FOUR GODS... I CAN ONLY SEND PETTY UNDERLINGS.

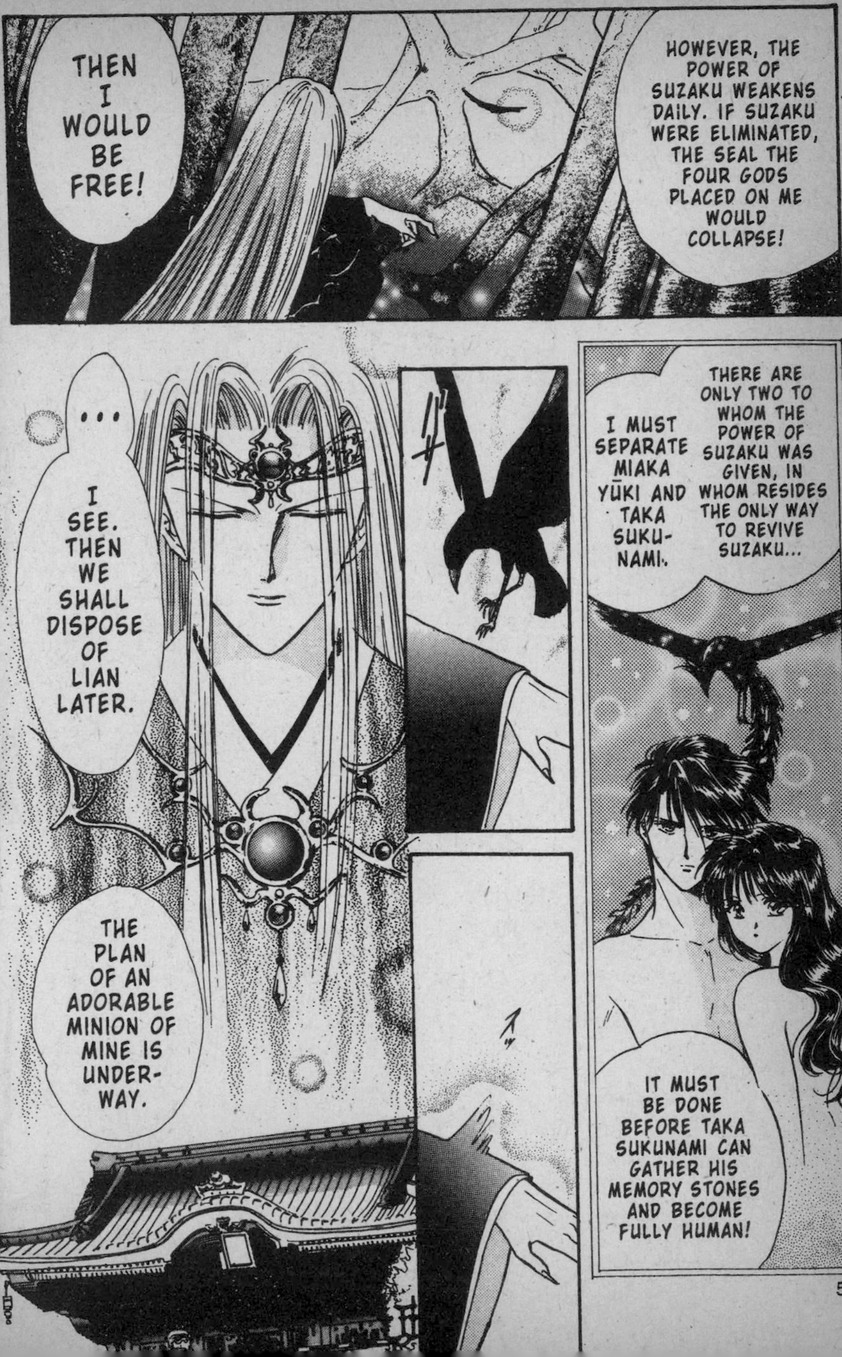
HOWEVER, THE POWER OF SUZAKU WEAKENS DAILY. IF SUZAKU WERE ELIMINATED, THE SEAL THE FOUR GODS PLACED ON ME WOULD COLLAPSE!
THEN I WOULD BE FREE!
THERE ARE ONLY TWO TO WHOM THE POWER OF SUZAKU WAS GIVEN, IN WHOM RESIDES THE ONLY WAY TO REVIVE SUZAKU...
I MUST SEPARATE MIAKA YŪKI AND TAKA SUKUNAMI.
IT MUST BE DONE BEFORE TAKA SUKUNAMI CAN GATHER HIS MEMORY STONES AND BECOME FULLY HUMAN!
...
I SEE. THEN WE SHALL DISPOSE OF LIAN LATER.
THE PLAN OF AN ADORABLE MINION OF MINE IS UNDERWAY.

So... I received a present through the president of Daran Publishing, and it was a Ming Dynasty (Did I say Ch'ing before? I know nothing!!) woman's jeweled seal that's a real treasure! (By the way, the president is a collector of rare treasures.) And he's got two jeweled necklaces!

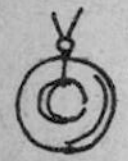

This is one type. The other is in the shape of a dragon.

▷ This one is definitely Ch'ing Dynasty. The jewel that's attached is a stone from the Pamirs region of India.
The dragon is from the Sung Dynasty. (Hong-Nan is based on this time.) The one above is Ming Dynasty. *I hope I got the period right!*
The most amazing thing I received was a loose jewel (not set into a necklace) from between two and three thousand years ago! Two to three thousand years old! Isn't it... just... *incredible?* I received other things, but this one was the most amazing. By the way, in China (...this is Taiwan...it's complicated) people keep their heirlooms close. When I was eating, I saw a waitress was wearing a seal on her bracelet. (Seals are very valuable items.) And to give me quite a number of such precious items... I'm really honored by their consideration!
One other thing: I was treated to the best tea in Taiwan by Daran Publishing's president! I even got some of the tea to take home! ☺ I wonder if it is proper to accept so many gifts! ☺
I want to thank all the people who were with me the whole time, Mr. Wong (he speaks Japanese perfectly!) and Mr. Zou...and Ms. Tomoko Takagishi from MSC, etc., etc. Thank you for everything you've done for me!
(And sorry I was so out of it!)

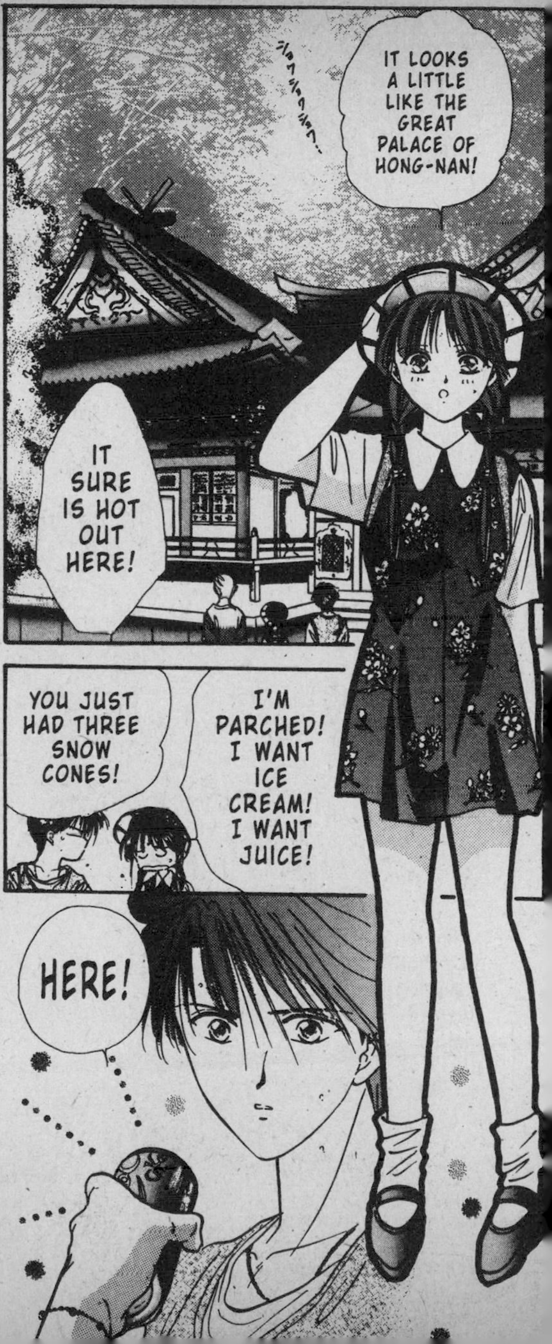
IT LOOKS A LITTLE LIKE THE GREAT PALACE OF HONG-NAN!
IT SURE IS HOT OUT HERE!
I'M PARCHED! I WANT ICE CREAM! I WANT JUICE!
YOU JUST HAD THREE SNOW CONES!
HERE!

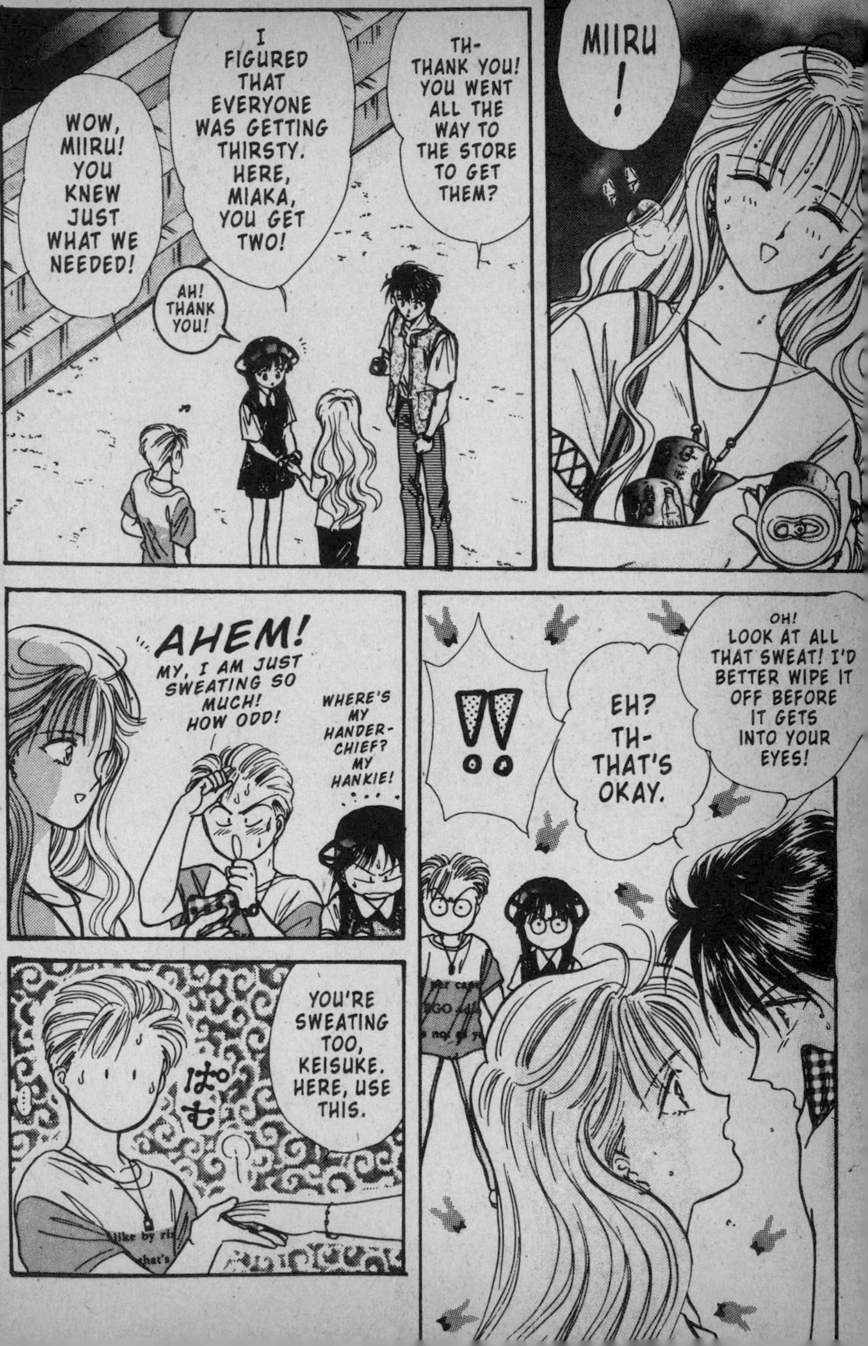
MIIRU!
TH- THANK YOU! YOU WENT ALL THE WAY TO THE STORE TO GET THEM?
I FIGURED THAT EVERYONE WAS GETTING THIRSTY. HERE, MIAKA, YOU GET TWO!
WOW, MIIRU! YOU KNEW JUST WHAT WE NEEDED!
AH! THANK YOU!
OH! LOOK AT ALL THAT SWEAT! I'D BETTER WIPE IT OFF BEFORE IT GETS INTO YOUR EYES!
EH? TH- THAT'S OKAY.
!!
AHEM!
MY, I AM JUST SWEATING SO MUCH! HOW ODD!
WHERE'S MY HANDER-CHIEF? MY HANKIE!
YOU'RE SWEATING TOO, KEISUKE. HERE, USE THIS.
ぱむ
...

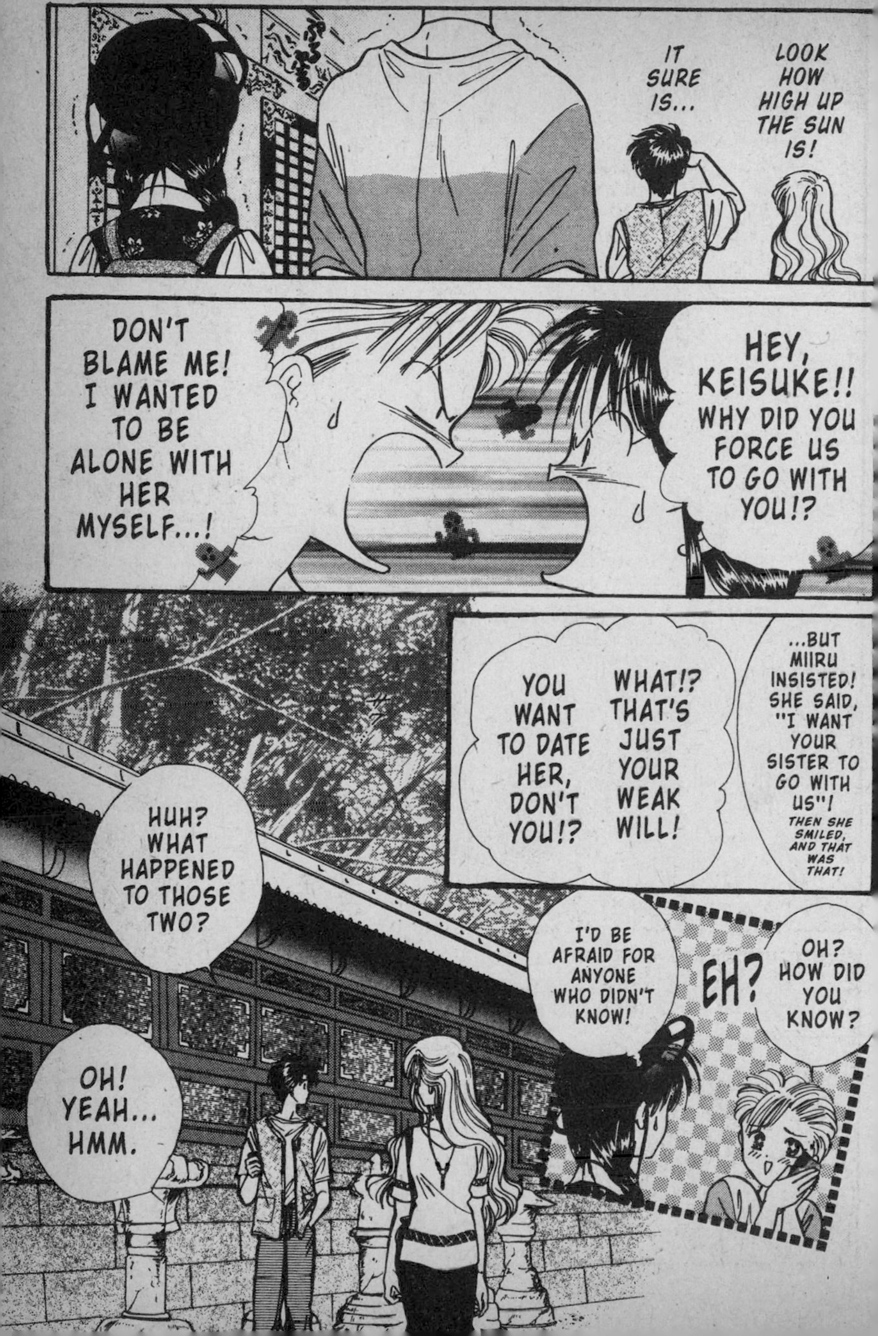
LOOK HOW HIGH UP THE SUN IS!
IT SURE IS...
HEY, KEISUKE!! WHY DID YOU FORCE US TO GO WITH YOU!?
DON'T BLAME ME! I WANTED TO BE ALONE WITH HER MYSELF...!
...BUT MIIRU INSISTED! SHE SAID, "I WANT YOUR SISTER TO GO WITH US"! THEN SHE SMILED, AND THAT WAS THAT!
WHAT!? THAT'S JUST YOUR WEAK WILL!
YOU WANT TO DATE HER, DON'T YOU!?
OH? HOW DID YOU KNOW?
EH?
I'D BE AFRAID FOR ANYONE WHO DIDN'T KNOW!
HUH? WHAT HAPPENED TO THOSE TWO?
OH! YEAH... HMM.

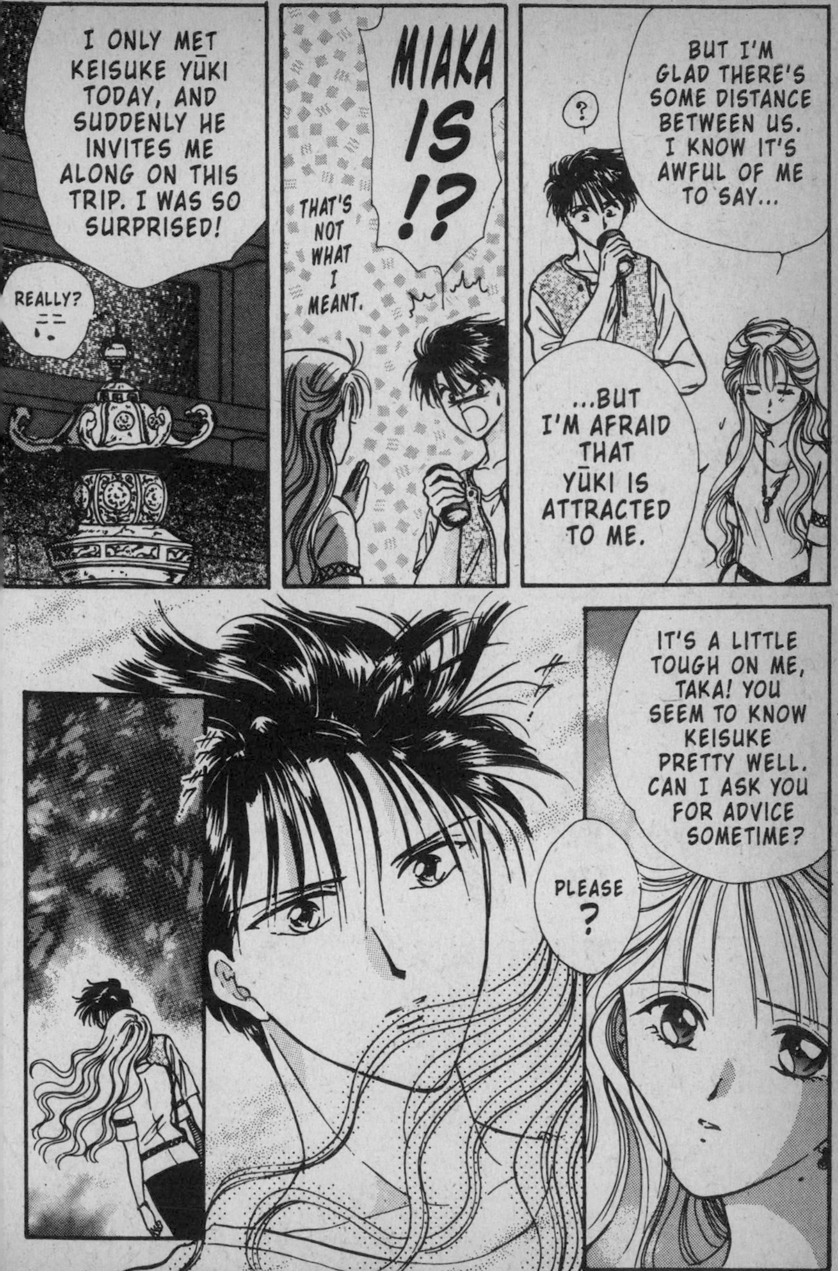
BUT I'M GLAD THERE'S SOME DISTANCE BETWEEN US. I KNOW IT'S AWFUL OF ME TO SAY...
?
...BUT I'M AFRAID THAT YŪKI IS ATTRACTED TO ME.
MIAKA IS !?
THAT'S NOT WHAT I MEANT.
I ONLY MET KEISUKE YŪKI TODAY, AND SUDDENLY HE INVITES ME ALONG ON THIS TRIP. I WAS SO SURPRISED!
REALLY?
IT'S A LITTLE TOUGH ON ME, TAKA! YOU SEEM TO KNOW KEISUKE PRETTY WELL. CAN I ASK YOU FOR ADVICE SOMETIME?
PLEASE ?

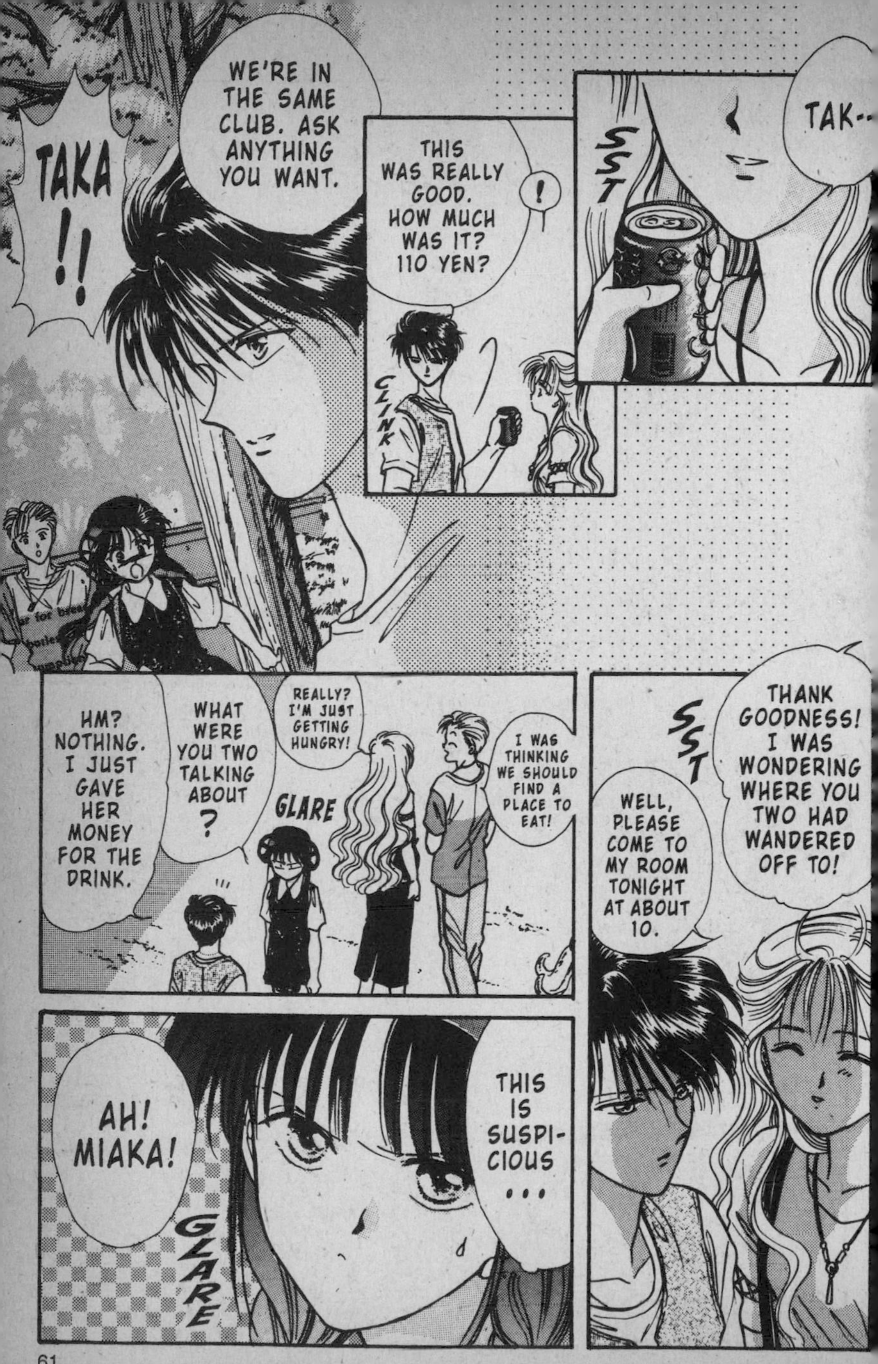
TAK--
SST
THIS WAS REALLY GOOD. HOW MUCH WAS IT? 110 YEN?
!
CLINK
WE'RE IN THE SAME CLUB. ASK ANYTHING YOU WANT.
TAKA!!
THANK GOODNESS! I WAS WONDERING WHERE YOU TWO HAD WANDERED OFF TO!
SST
WELL, PLEASE COME TO MY ROOM TONIGHT AT ABOUT 10.
I WAS THINKING WE SHOULD FIND A PLACE TO EAT!
REALLY? I'M JUST GETTING HUNGRY!
GLARE
WHAT WERE YOU TWO TALKING ABOUT?
HM? NOTHING. I JUST GAVE HER MONEY FOR THE DRINK.
THIS IS SUSPICIOUS...
GLARE
AH! MIAKA!

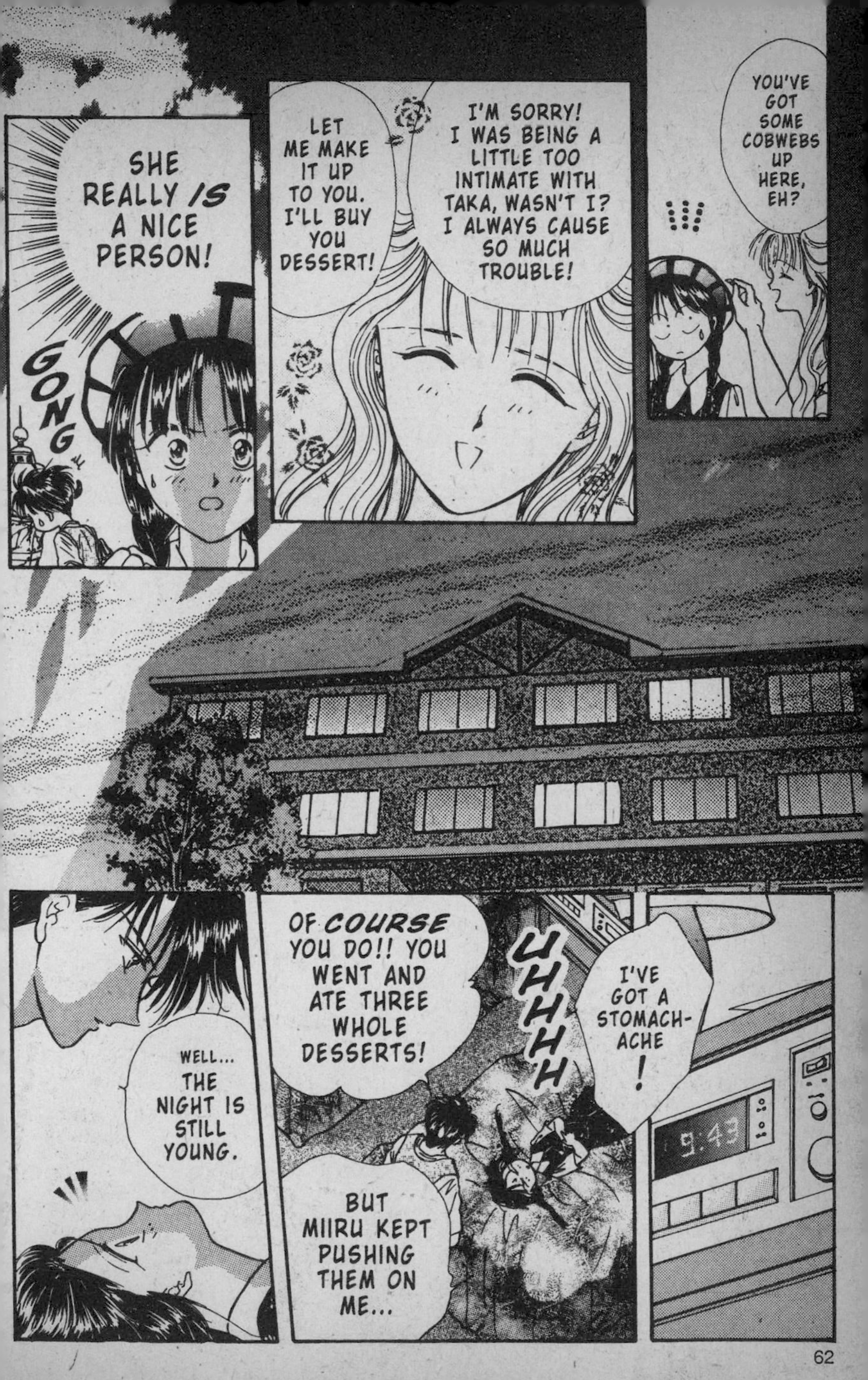
YOU'VE GOT SOME COBWEBS UP HERE, EH?
I'M SORRY! I WAS BEING A LITTLE TOO INTIMATE WITH TAKA, WASN'T I? I ALWAYS CAUSE SO MUCH TROUBLE!
LET ME MAKE IT UP TO YOU. I'LL BUY YOU DESSERT!
SHE REALLY *IS* A NICE PERSON!
GONG
I'VE GOT A STOMACH-ACHE!
UHHHH
OF *COURSE* YOU DO!! YOU WENT AND ATE THREE WHOLE DESSERTS!
BUT MIIRU KEPT PUSHING THEM ON ME...
WELL... THE NIGHT IS STILL YOUNG.

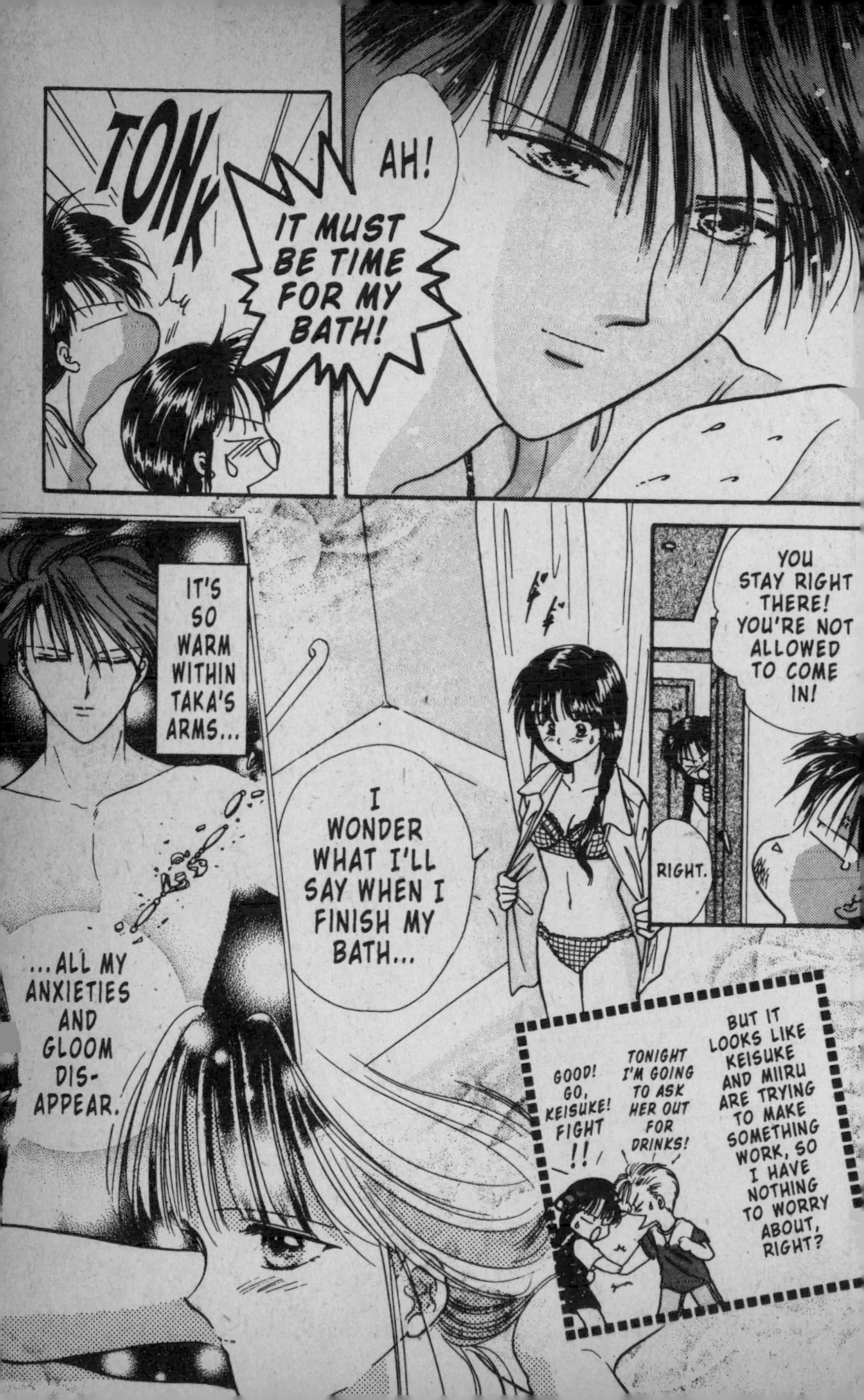
AH!
TONK
IT MUST BE TIME FOR MY BATH!
YOU STAY RIGHT THERE! YOU'RE NOT ALLOWED TO COME IN!
RIGHT.
I WONDER WHAT I'LL SAY WHEN I FINISH MY BATH...
BUT IT LOOKS LIKE KEISUKE AND MIIRU ARE TRYING TO MAKE SOMETHING WORK, SO I HAVE NOTHING TO WORRY ABOUT, RIGHT?
TONIGHT I'M GOING TO ASK HER OUT FOR DRINKS!
GOOD! GO, KEISUKE! FIGHT!!
IT'S SO WARM WITHIN TAKA'S ARMS...
...ALL MY ANXIETIES AND GLOOM DIS-APPEAR.

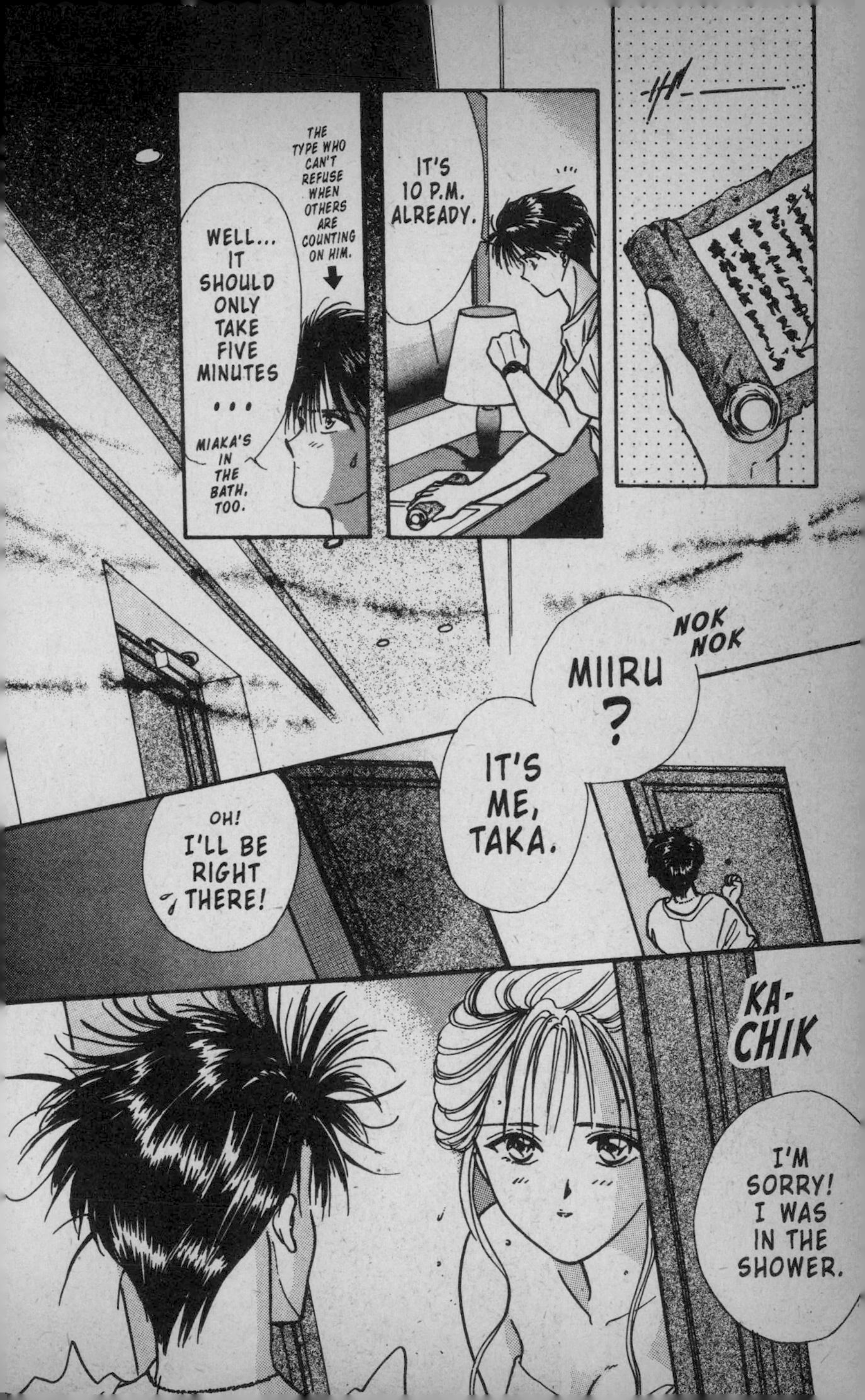
IT'S 10 P.M. ALREADY.
THE TYPE WHO CAN'T REFUSE WHEN OTHERS ARE COUNTING ON HIM.
WELL... IT SHOULD ONLY TAKE FIVE MINUTES ...
MIAKA'S IN THE BATH, TOO.
NOK NOK
MIIRU ?
IT'S ME, TAKA.
OH! I'LL BE RIGHT THERE!
KA-CHIK
I'M SORRY! I WAS IN THE SHOWER.

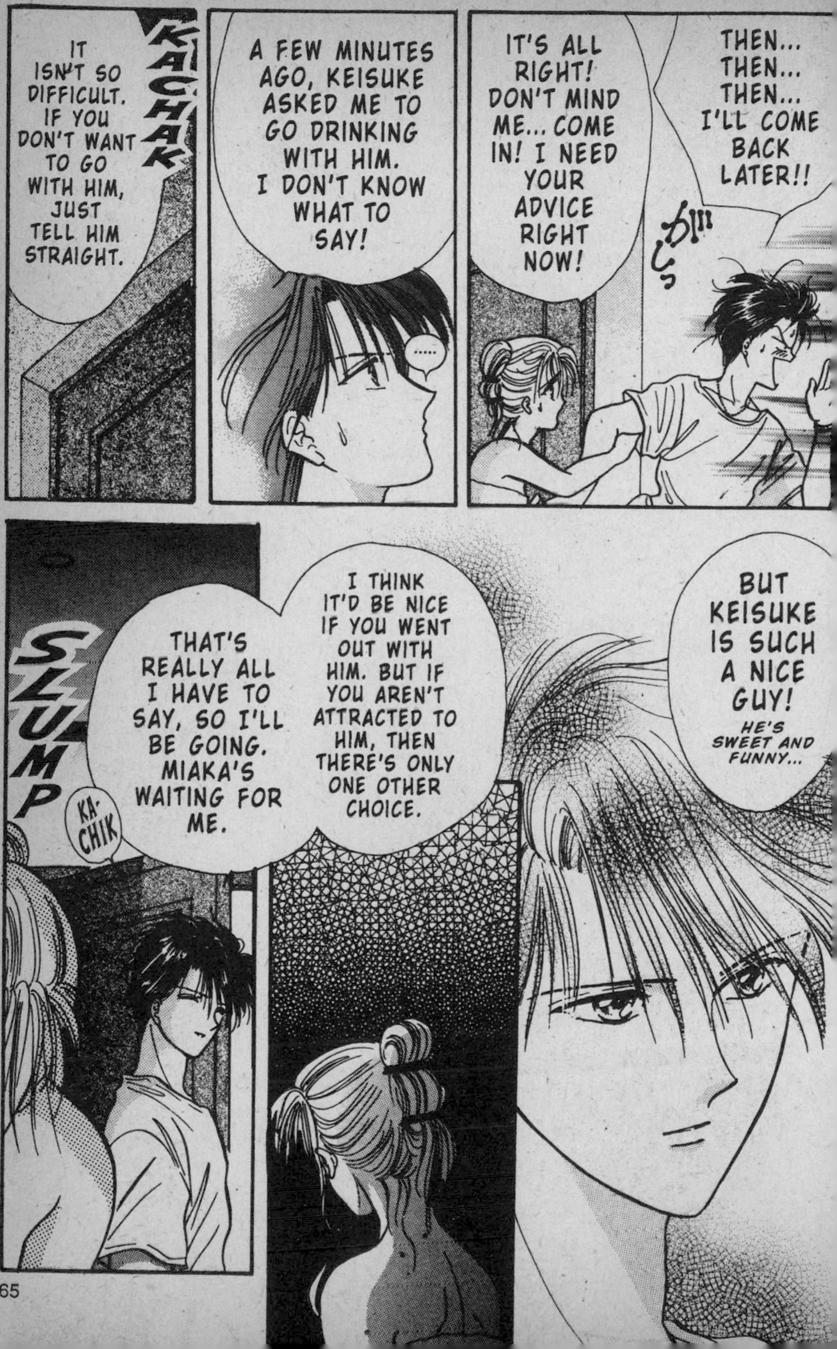
THEN... THEN... THEN... I'LL COME BACK LATER!!
IT'S ALL RIGHT! DON'T MIND ME... COME IN! I NEED YOUR ADVICE RIGHT NOW!
A FEW MINUTES AGO, KEISUKE ASKED ME TO GO DRINKING WITH HIM. I DON'T KNOW WHAT TO SAY!
.....
KACHAK
IT ISN'T SO DIFFICULT. IF YOU DON'T WANT TO GO WITH HIM, JUST TELL HIM STRAIGHT.
BUT KEISUKE IS SUCH A NICE GUY!
HE'S SWEET AND FUNNY...
I THINK IT'D BE NICE IF YOU WENT OUT WITH HIM. BUT IF YOU AREN'T ATTRACTED TO HIM, THEN THERE'S ONLY ONE OTHER CHOICE.
THAT'S REALLY ALL I HAVE TO SAY, SO I'LL BE GOING. MIAKA'S WAITING FOR ME.
SLUMP
KA-CHIK

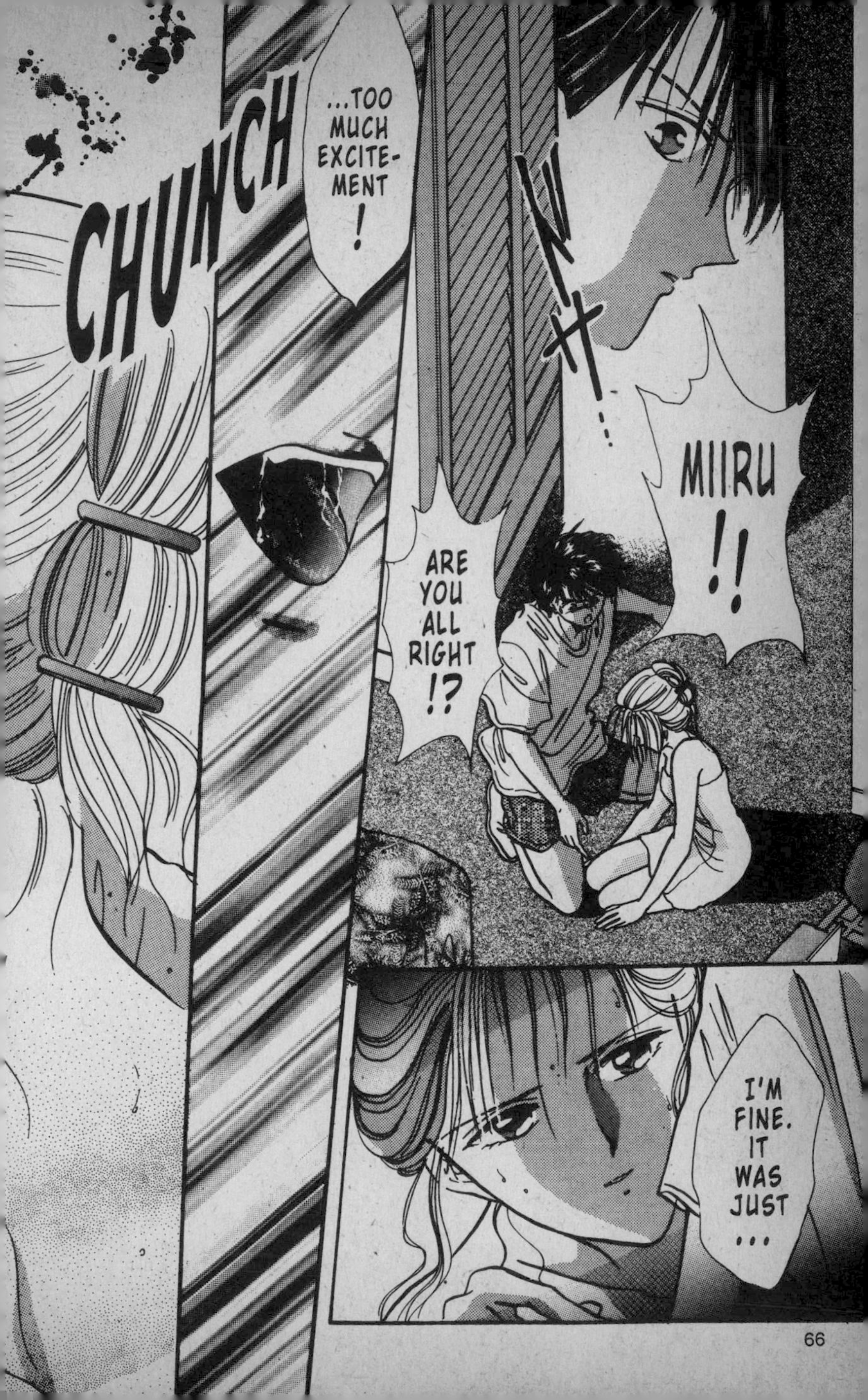
MIIRU!!
ARE YOU ALL RIGHT!?
I'M FINE. IT WAS JUST...
...TOO MUCH EXCITEMENT!
CHUNCH

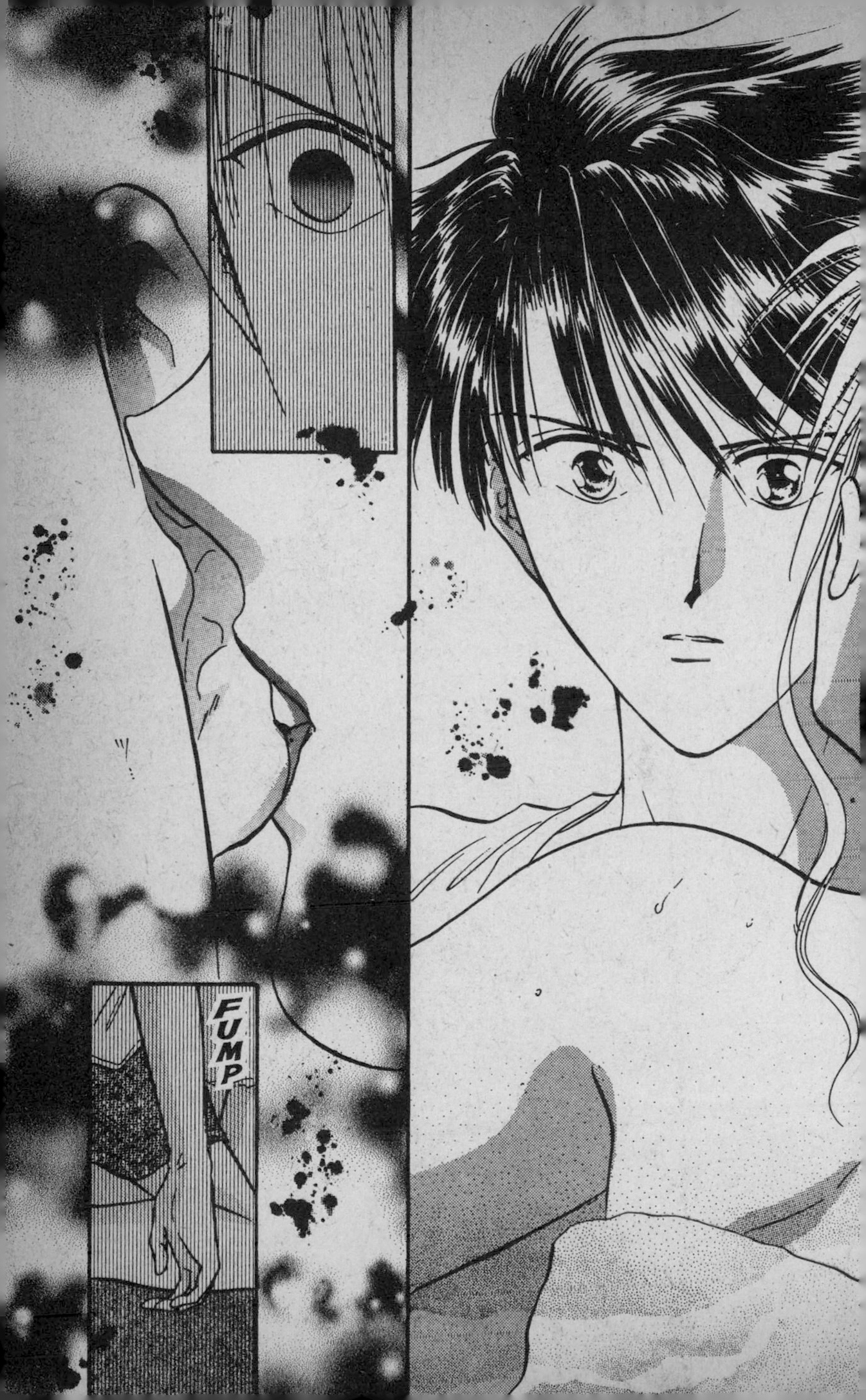
FUMP

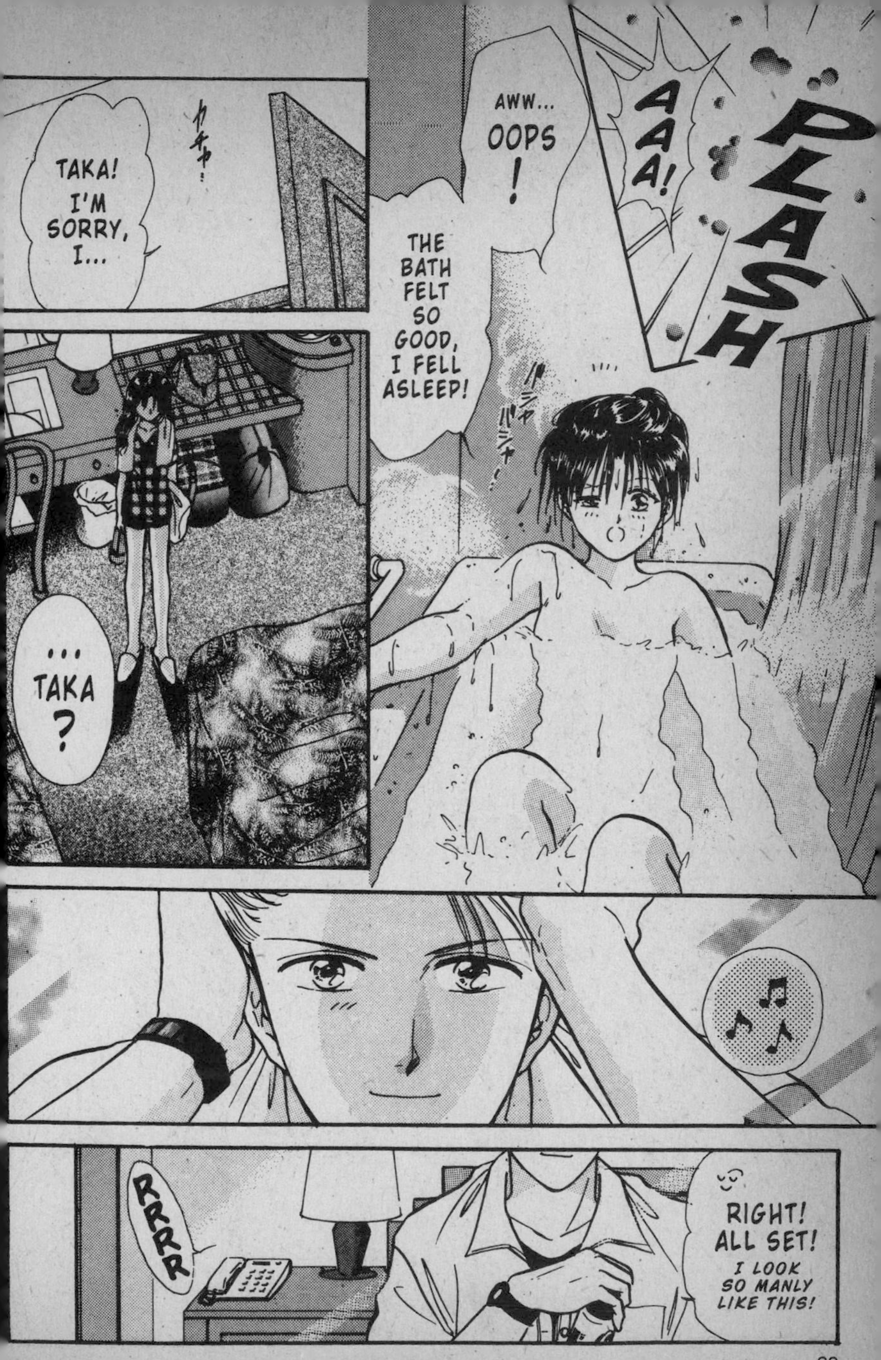
PLASH
AAA!
AWW... OOPS!
THE BATH FELT SO GOOD, I FELL ASLEEP!
バシャ バシャ
カチャ…
TAKA! I'M SORRY, I...
... TAKA?
RIGHT! ALL SET!
I LOOK SO MANLY LIKE THIS!
RRRR

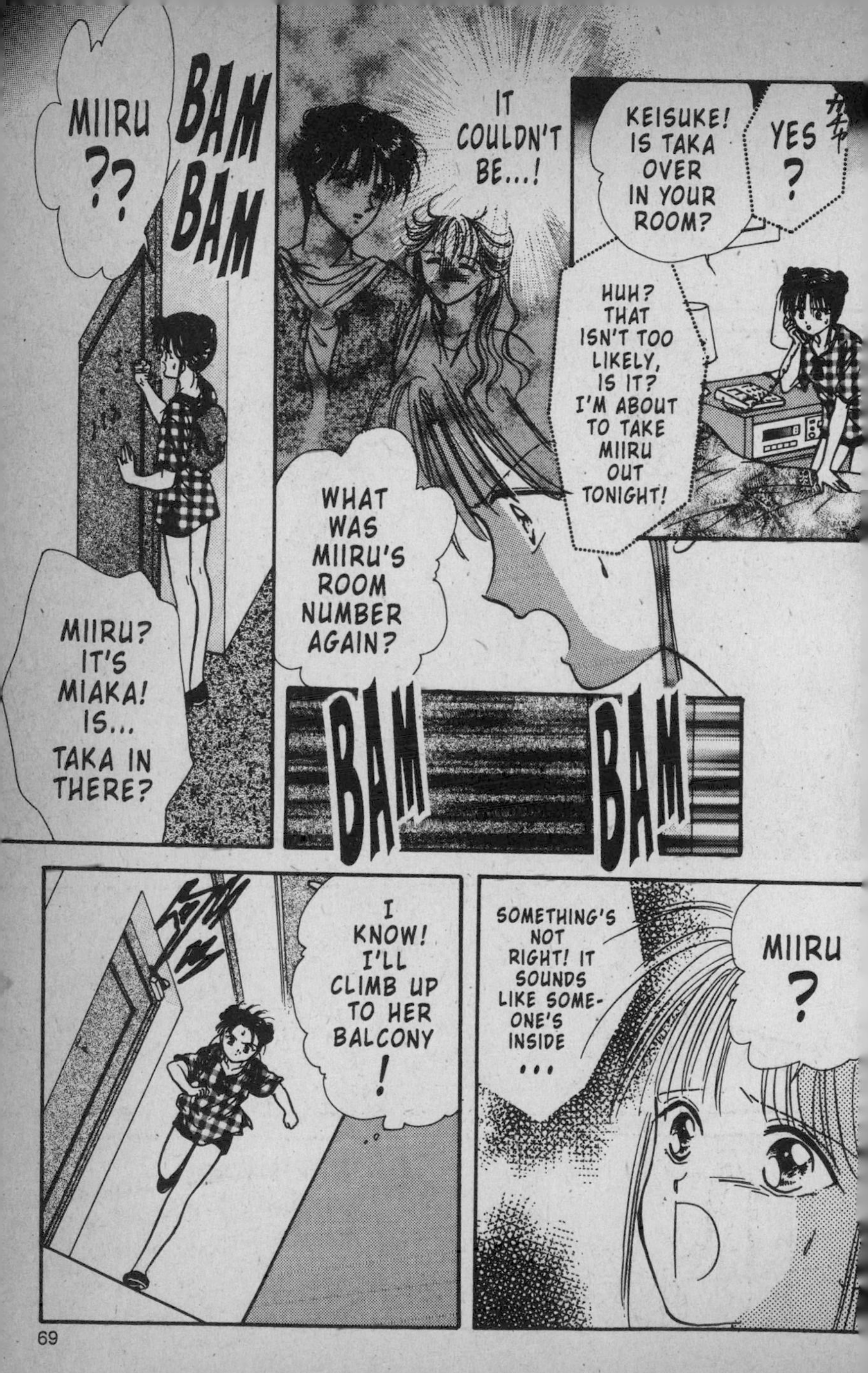
YES?
KEISUKE! IS TAKA OVER IN YOUR ROOM?
HUH? THAT ISN'T TOO LIKELY, IS IT? I'M ABOUT TO TAKE MIIRU OUT TONIGHT!
IT COULDN'T BE...!
WHAT WAS MIIRU'S ROOM NUMBER AGAIN?
BAM BAM
BAM BAM
MIIRU??
MIIRU? IT'S MIAKA! IS... TAKA IN THERE?
MIIRU?
SOMETHING'S NOT RIGHT! IT SOUNDS LIKE SOME-ONE'S INSIDE ...
I KNOW! I'LL CLIMB UP TO HER BALCONY!

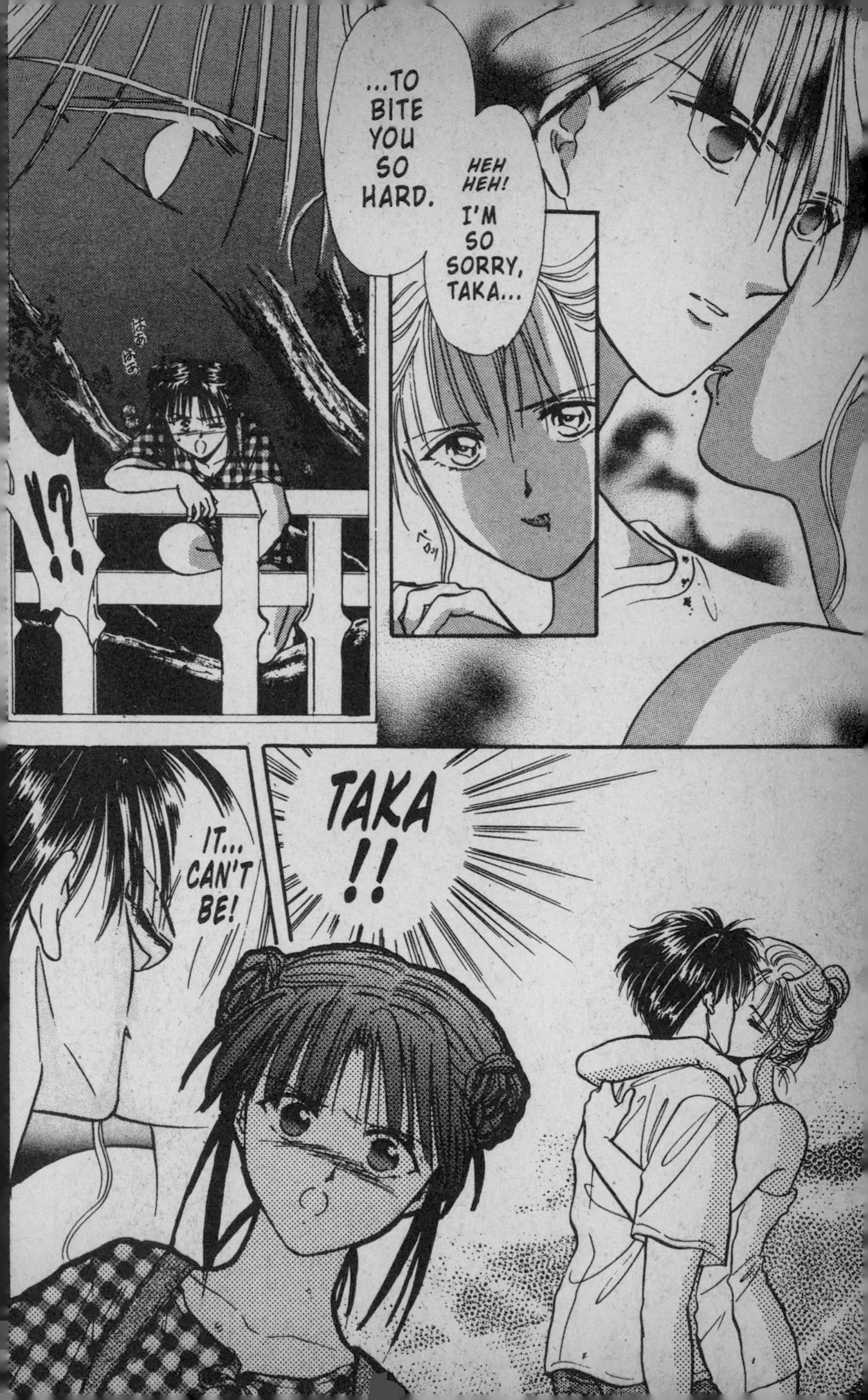

HEH HEH! I'M SO SORRY, TAKA...
...TO BITE YOU SO HARD.
!?!!
TAKA!!
IT... CAN'T BE!

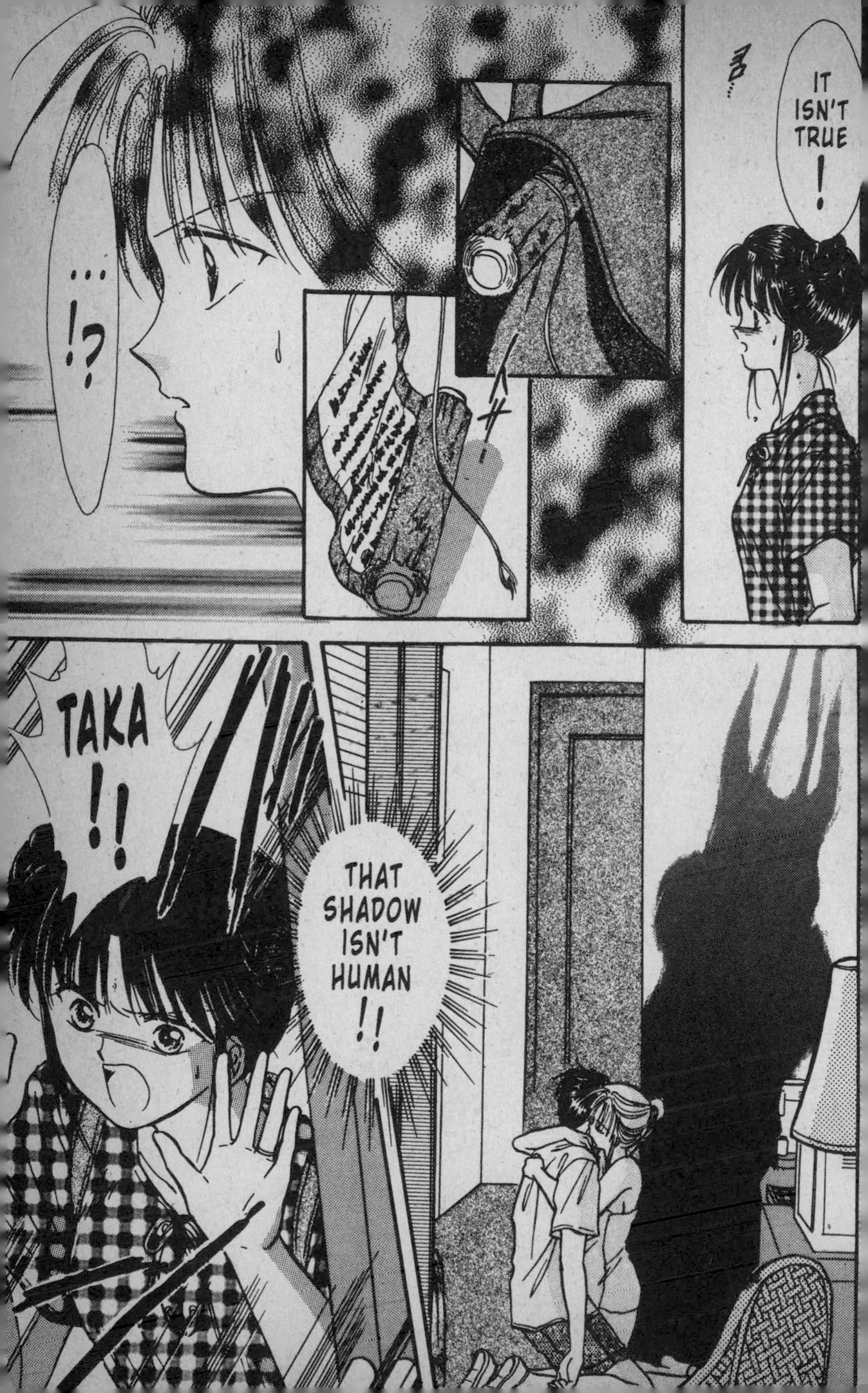
IT ISN'T TRUE!
...!?
TAKA!!
THAT SHADOW ISN'T HUMAN!!

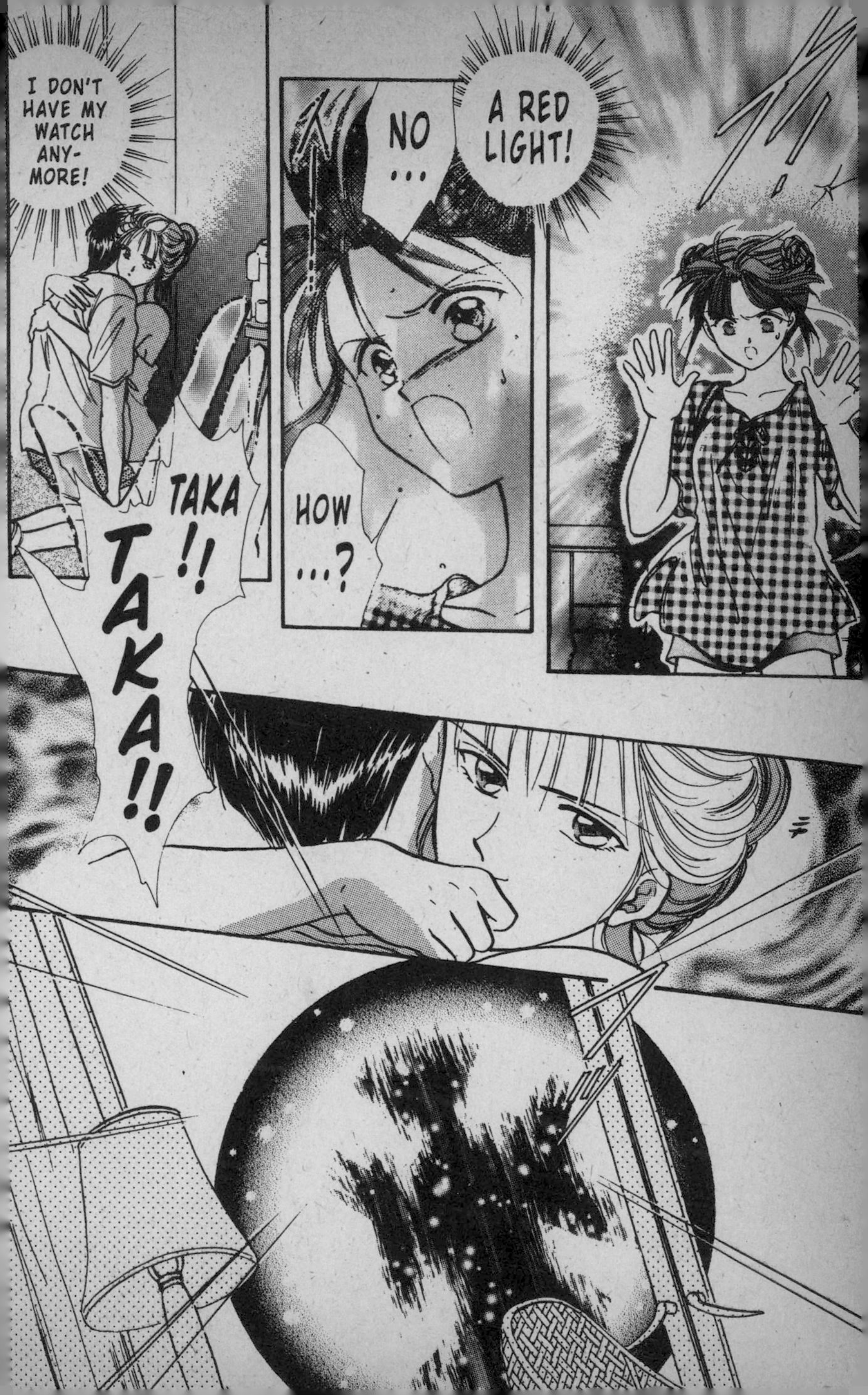
A RED LIGHT!
NO ...
HOW ...?
I DON'T HAVE MY WATCH ANY-MORE!
TAKA!!
TAKA!!

CHAPTER NINETY-ONE

THE MYSTIC FANG

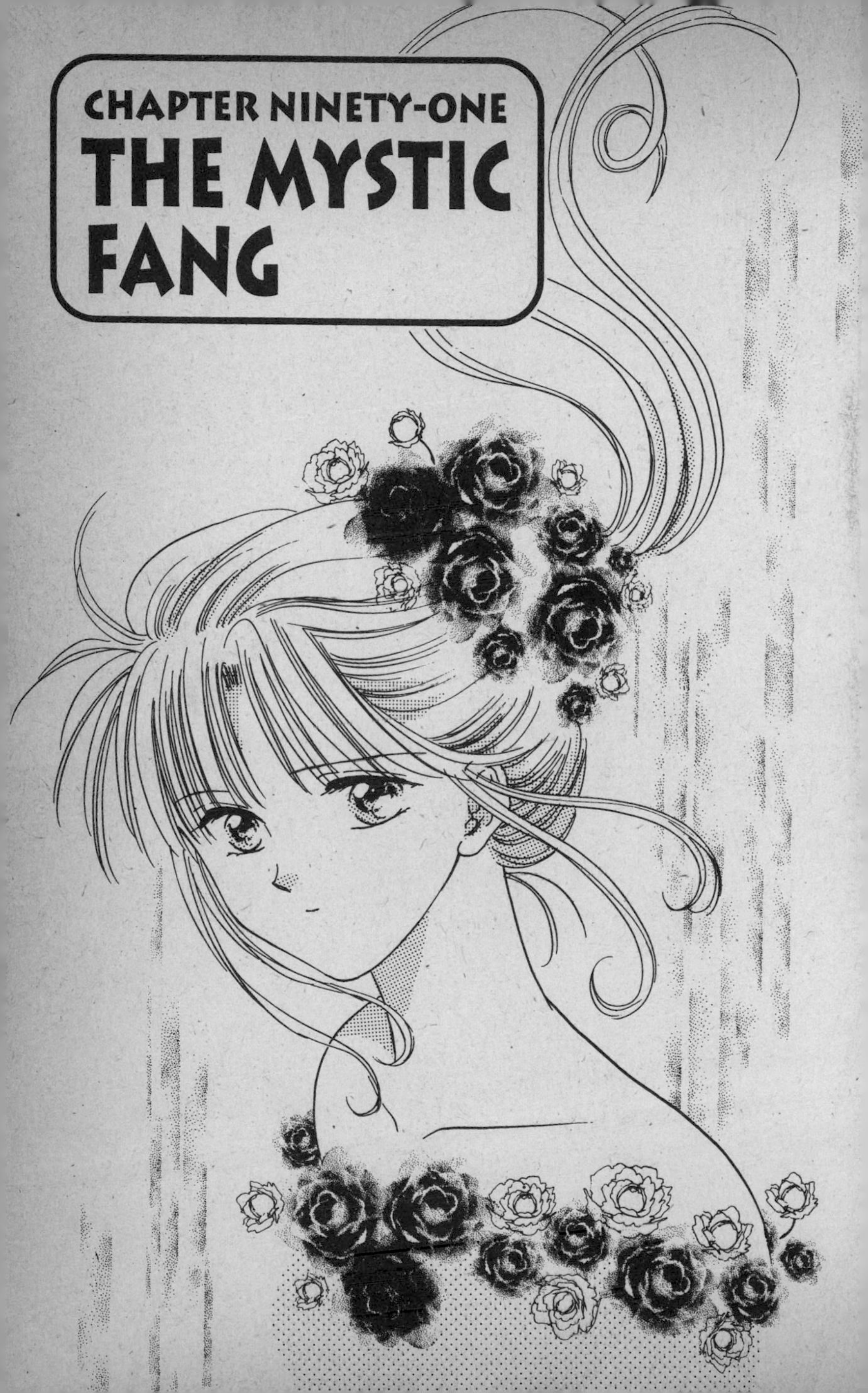

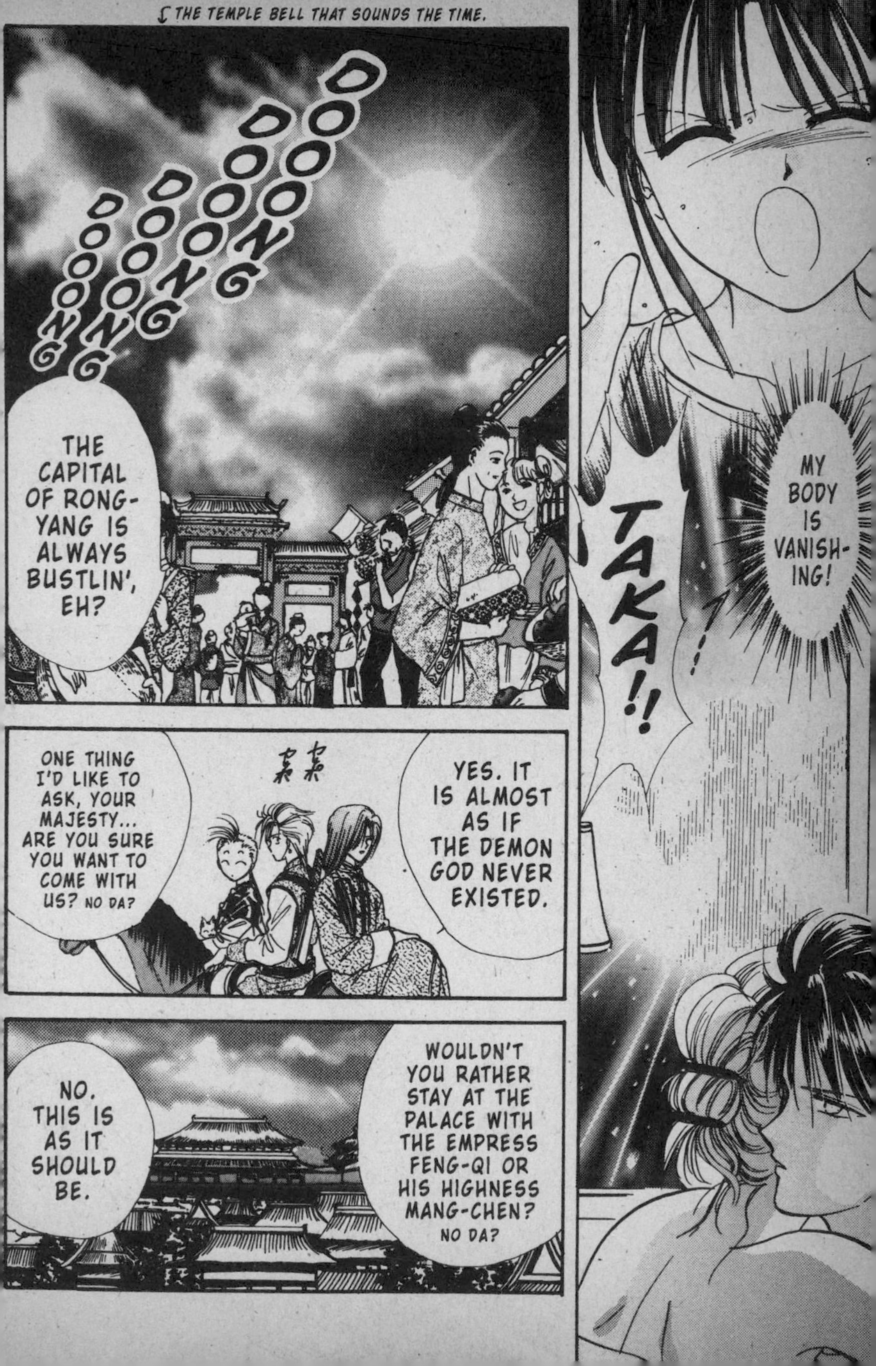
MY BODY IS VANISHING!
TAKA!!
THE TEMPLE BELL THAT SOUNDS THE TIME.
DOOONG
DOOONG
DOOONG
DOOOONG
THE CAPITAL OF RONG-YANG IS ALWAYS BUSTLIN', EH?
YES. IT IS ALMOST AS IF THE DEMON GOD NEVER EXISTED.
ONE THING I'D LIKE TO ASK, YOUR MAJESTY... ARE YOU SURE YOU WANT TO COME WITH US? NO DA?
WOULDN'T YOU RATHER STAY AT THE PALACE WITH THE EMPRESS FENG-QI OR HIS HIGHNESS MANG-CHEN? NO DA?
NO. THIS IS AS IT SHOULD BE.

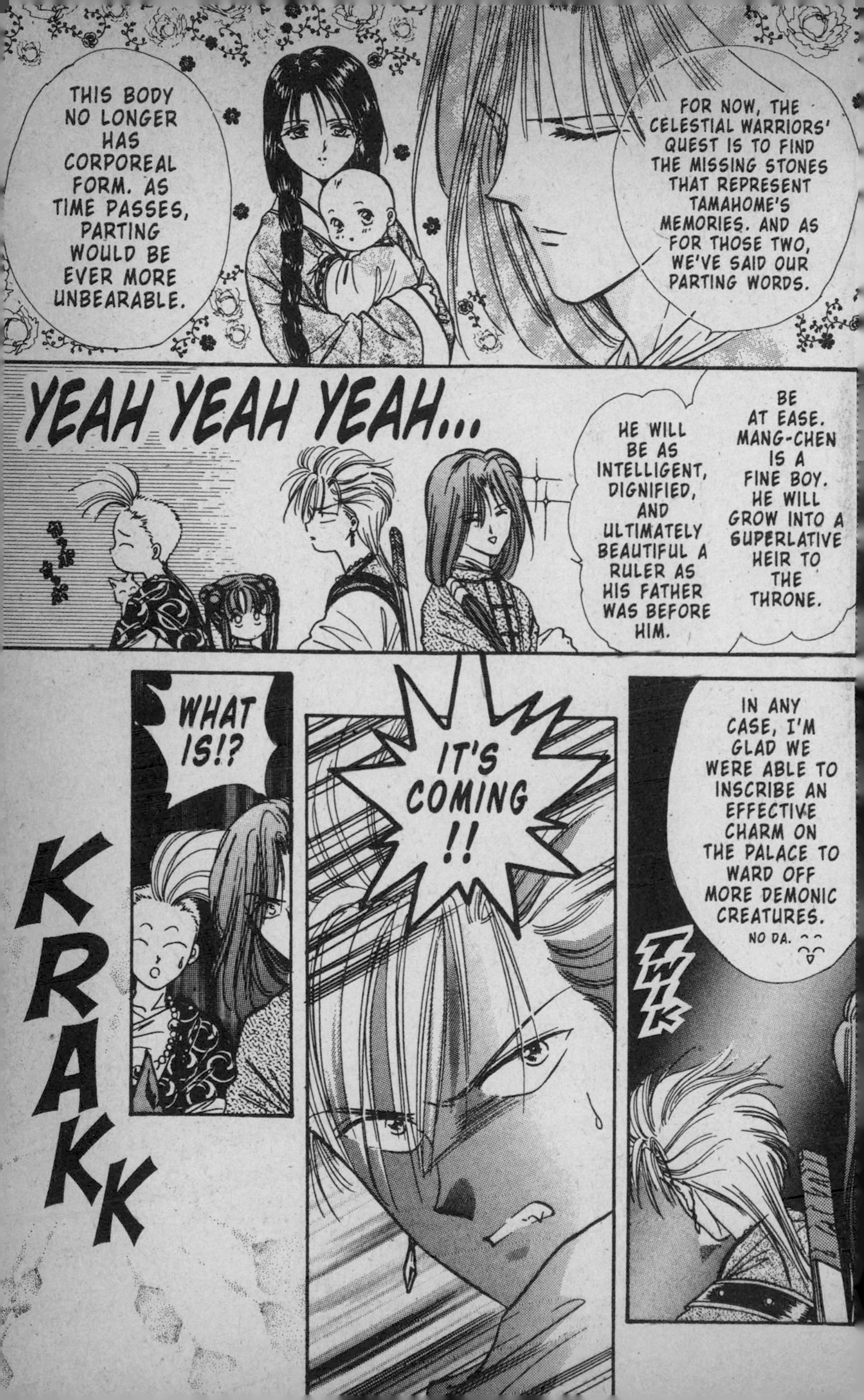
FOR NOW, THE CELESTIAL WARRIORS' QUEST IS TO FIND THE MISSING STONES THAT REPRESENT TAMAHOME'S MEMORIES. AND AS FOR THOSE TWO, WE'VE SAID OUR PARTING WORDS.
THIS BODY NO LONGER HAS CORPOREAL FORM. AS TIME PASSES, PARTING WOULD BE EVER MORE UNBEARABLE.
BE AT EASE. MANG-CHEN IS A FINE BOY. HE WILL GROW INTO A SUPERLATIVE HEIR TO THE THRONE.
HE WILL BE AS INTELLIGENT, DIGNIFIED, AND ULTIMATELY BEAUTIFUL A RULER AS HIS FATHER WAS BEFORE HIM.
YEAH YEAH YEAH...
IN ANY CASE, I'M GLAD WE WERE ABLE TO INSCRIBE AN EFFECTIVE CHARM ON THE PALACE TO WARD OFF MORE DEMONIC CREATURES.
NO DA.
TWIK
IT'S COMING!!
WHAT IS!?
KRAKK

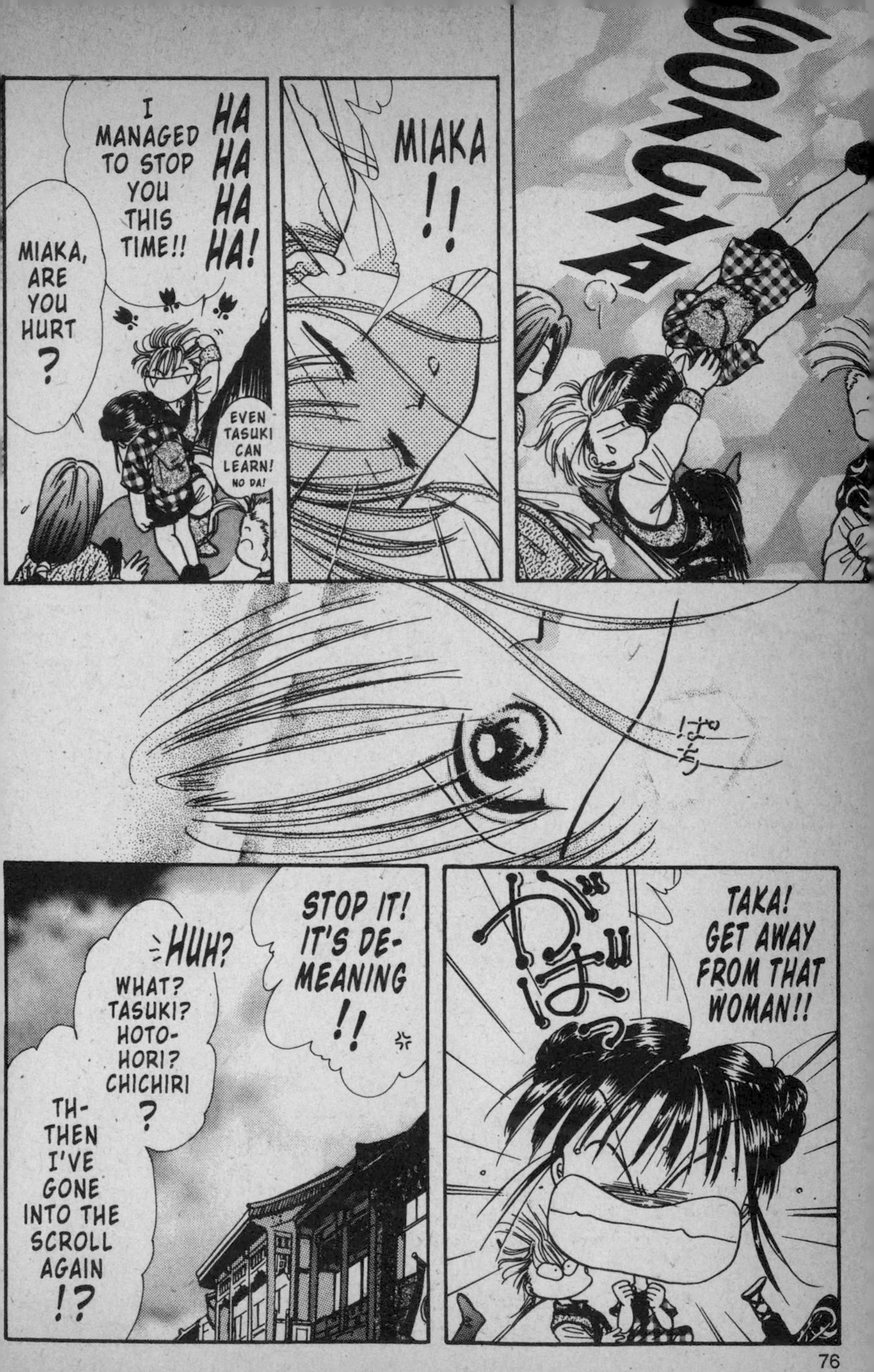
GOTCHA
MIAKA!!
HA HA HA HA!
I MANAGED TO STOP YOU THIS TIME!!
EVEN TASUKI CAN LEARN! NO DA!
MIAKA, ARE YOU HURT?
TAKA! GET AWAY FROM THAT WOMAN!!
STOP IT! IT'S DE-MEANING!!
HUH?
WHAT? TASUKI? HOTO-HORI? CHICHIRI?
TH-THEN I'VE GONE INTO THE SCROLL AGAIN!?

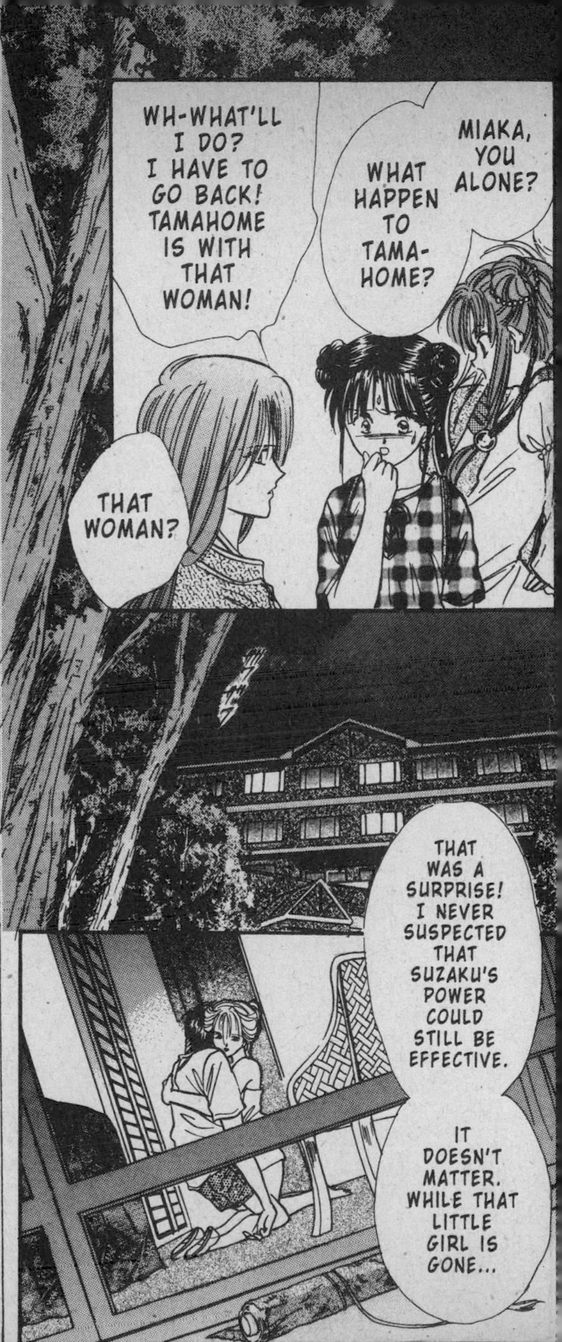
MIAKA, YOU ALONE?
WHAT HAPPEN TO TAMA-HOME?
WH-WHAT'LL I DO? I HAVE TO GO BACK! TAMAHOME IS WITH THAT WOMAN!
THAT WOMAN?
THAT WAS A SURPRISE! I NEVER SUSPECTED THAT SUZAKU'S POWER COULD STILL BE EFFECTIVE.
IT DOESN'T MATTER. WHILE THAT LITTLE GIRL IS GONE...

While I was in Taiwan, I was taken to a whole bunch of places! One was the Old Capital Museum (Was that the name?)... *I forget.* Because everything there was the real thing! ☺ I learned a lot! Also there was a village that looked like it was out of a movie! (It was incredible! An ancient Chinese village brought intact into modern times! I thought I was caught in a time warp!)
Oh, yeah! The president of the publishing company took me to a massage center! Some of it hurt so much, I cried out! ☺ And it went constantly for three hours! I could hear the cracking of bones, but by the end, it was like I had grown wings! (I felt so light!)
The market at night was a real Taiwan hot spot... or I should say it was crowded, crowded, crowded!! Even though it was 10 p.m., children were all over. It was like a night fair! And it happens every night! *I'm so jealous!* The feeling was like Sennichi-mae in Namba, Osaka (a big shopping promenade), but more impressive! (It really is amazing!) And the restaurants were so delicious! (My constitution was in better condition than it is in Japan.) I received some manga from some Taiwanese artists, but I had nothing to give back to them, so I handed them telephone cards.
I signed all sorts of things everywhere! ☺ But I still wonder why they were so enthusiastic after receiving only that. I had heard once that the Taiwanese manga scene grew out of the Japanese manga scene, so Japanese manga artists are treated like gods. Maybe it was true once, but now the Taiwanese artists are so accomplished! And the artwork I got from the readers was beautiful, too! If Japan doesn't pay attention, it could fall behind in manga. ☺ I still find it astonishing that manga can cross national and cultural barriers. I don't just mean the language barriers, but that there is no border that can hold back manga! That's what this trip taught me! I'll fondly remember this trip for the rest of my life! And to the people of Taiwan, thank you for letting me know that manga is a worldwide culture! *I'll come back soon!*

☺

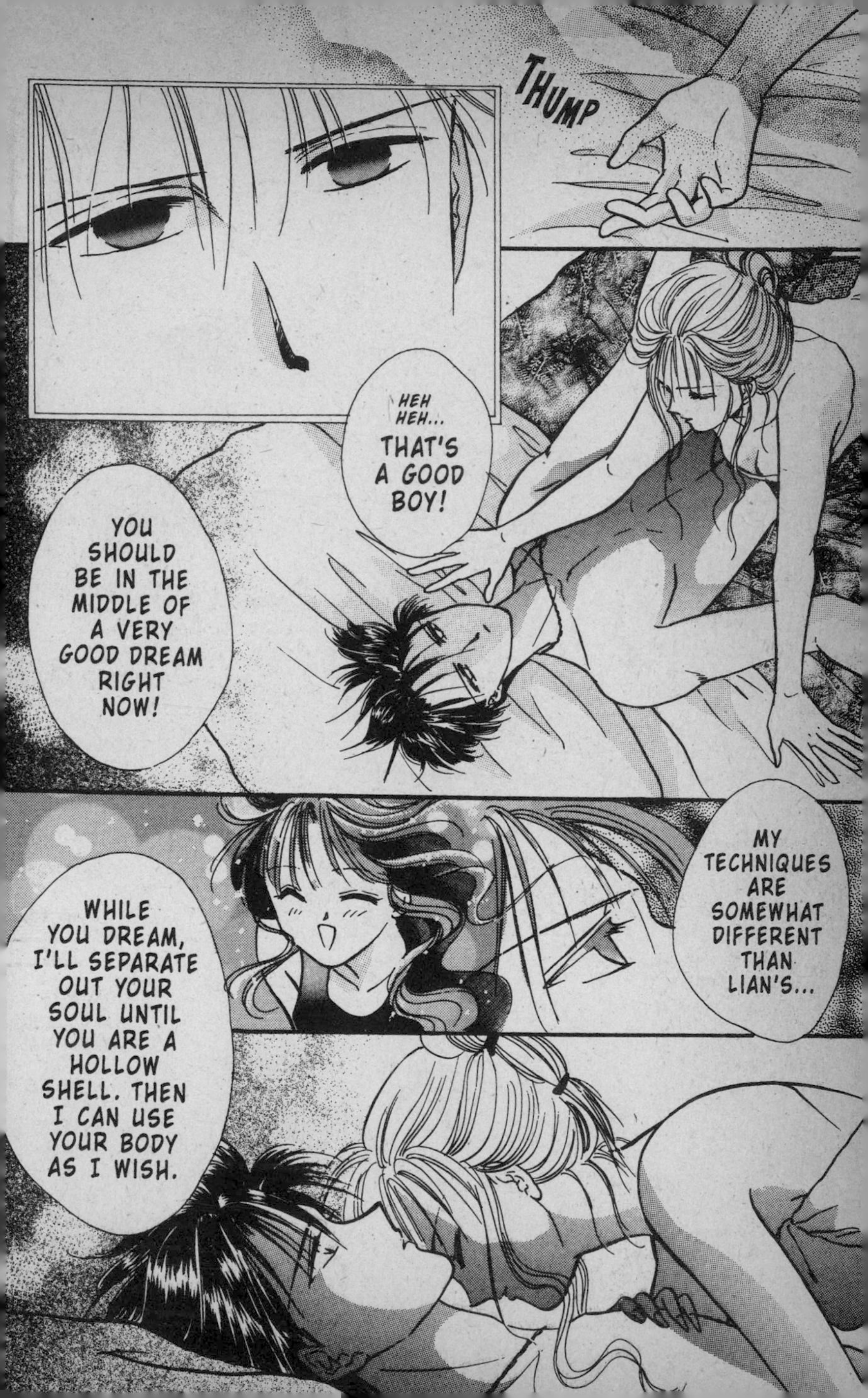
THUMP
HEH HEH... THAT'S A GOOD BOY!
YOU SHOULD BE IN THE MIDDLE OF A VERY GOOD DREAM RIGHT NOW!
MY TECHNIQUES ARE SOMEWHAT DIFFERENT THAN LIAN'S...
WHILE YOU DREAM, I'LL SEPARATE OUT YOUR SOUL UNTIL YOU ARE A HOLLOW SHELL. THEN I CAN USE YOUR BODY AS I WISH.

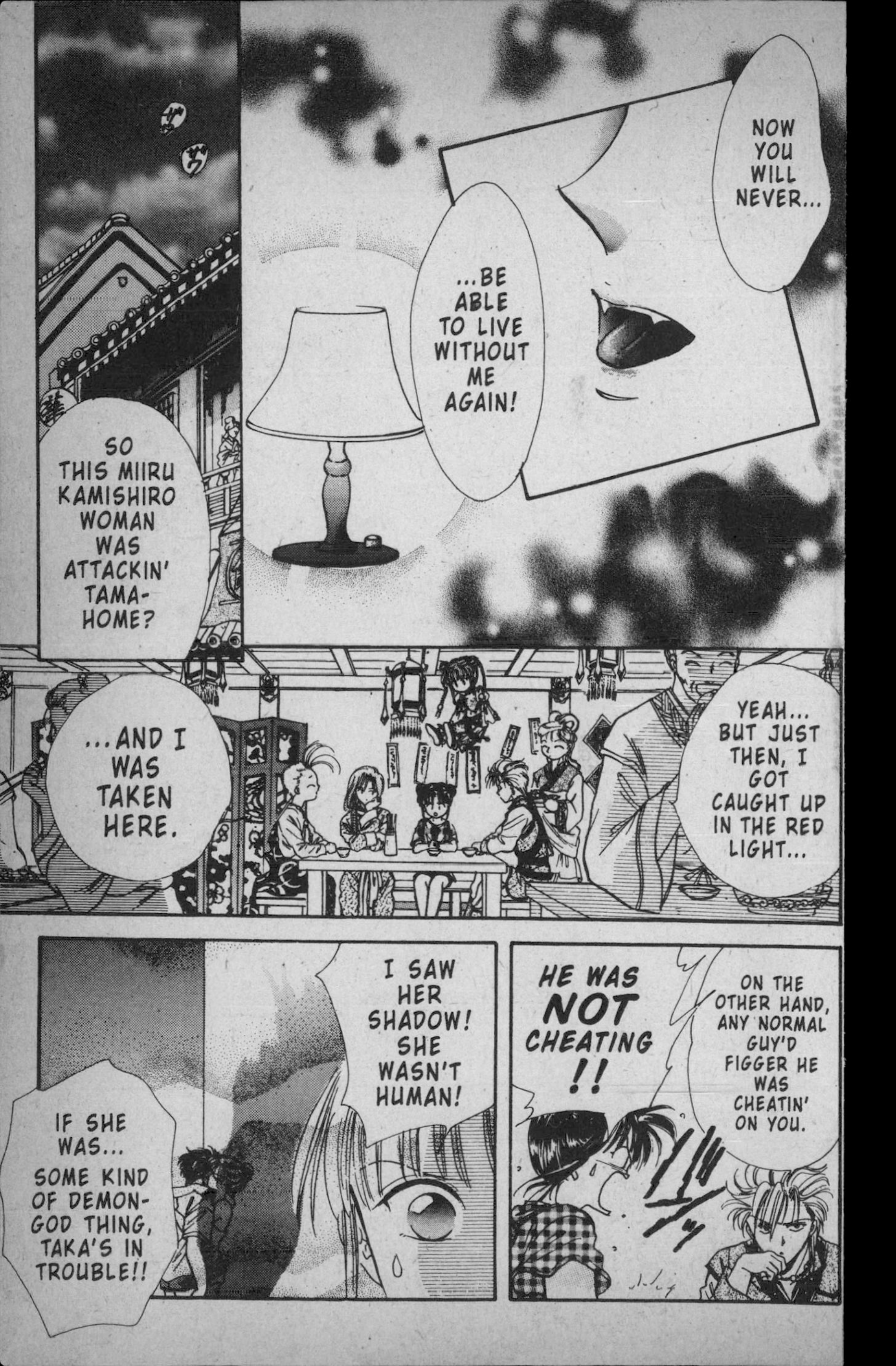
NOW YOU WILL NEVER...
...BE ABLE TO LIVE WITHOUT ME AGAIN!
SO THIS MIIRU KAMISHIRO WOMAN WAS ATTACKIN' TAMA-HOME?
YEAH... BUT JUST THEN, I GOT CAUGHT UP IN THE RED LIGHT...
...AND I WAS TAKEN HERE.
ON THE OTHER HAND, ANY NORMAL GUY'D FIGGER HE WAS CHEATIN' ON YOU.
HE WAS NOT CHEATING!!
I SAW HER SHADOW! SHE WASN'T HUMAN!
IF SHE WAS... SOME KIND OF DEMON-GOD THING, TAKA'S IN TROUBLE!!

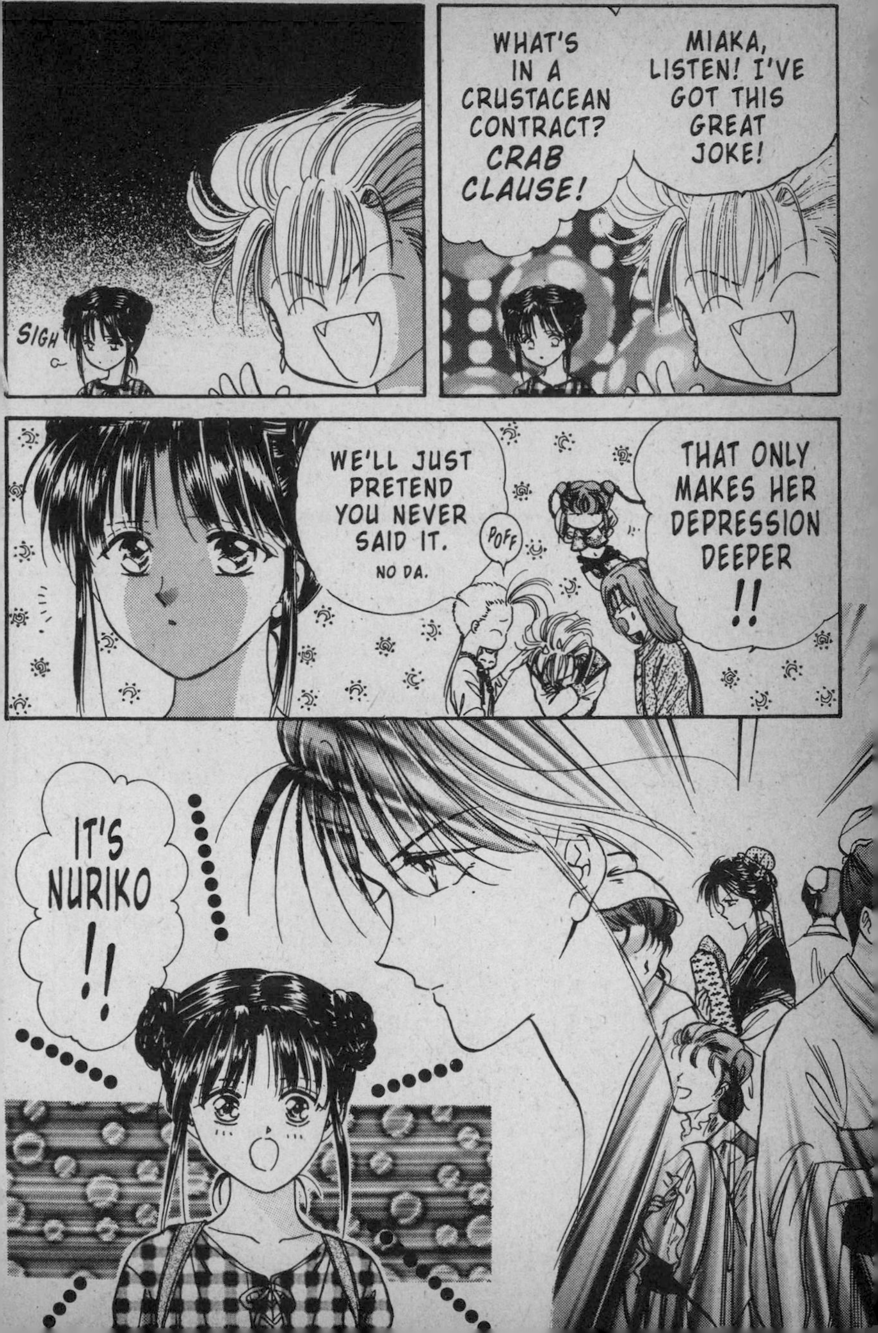
MIAKA, LISTEN! I'VE GOT THIS GREAT JOKE!
WHAT'S IN A CRUSTACEAN CONTRACT? CRAB CLAUSE!
SIGH
THAT ONLY MAKES HER DEPRESSION DEEPER !!
WE'LL JUST PRETEND YOU NEVER SAID IT. NO DA.
POFF
IT'S NURIKO !!

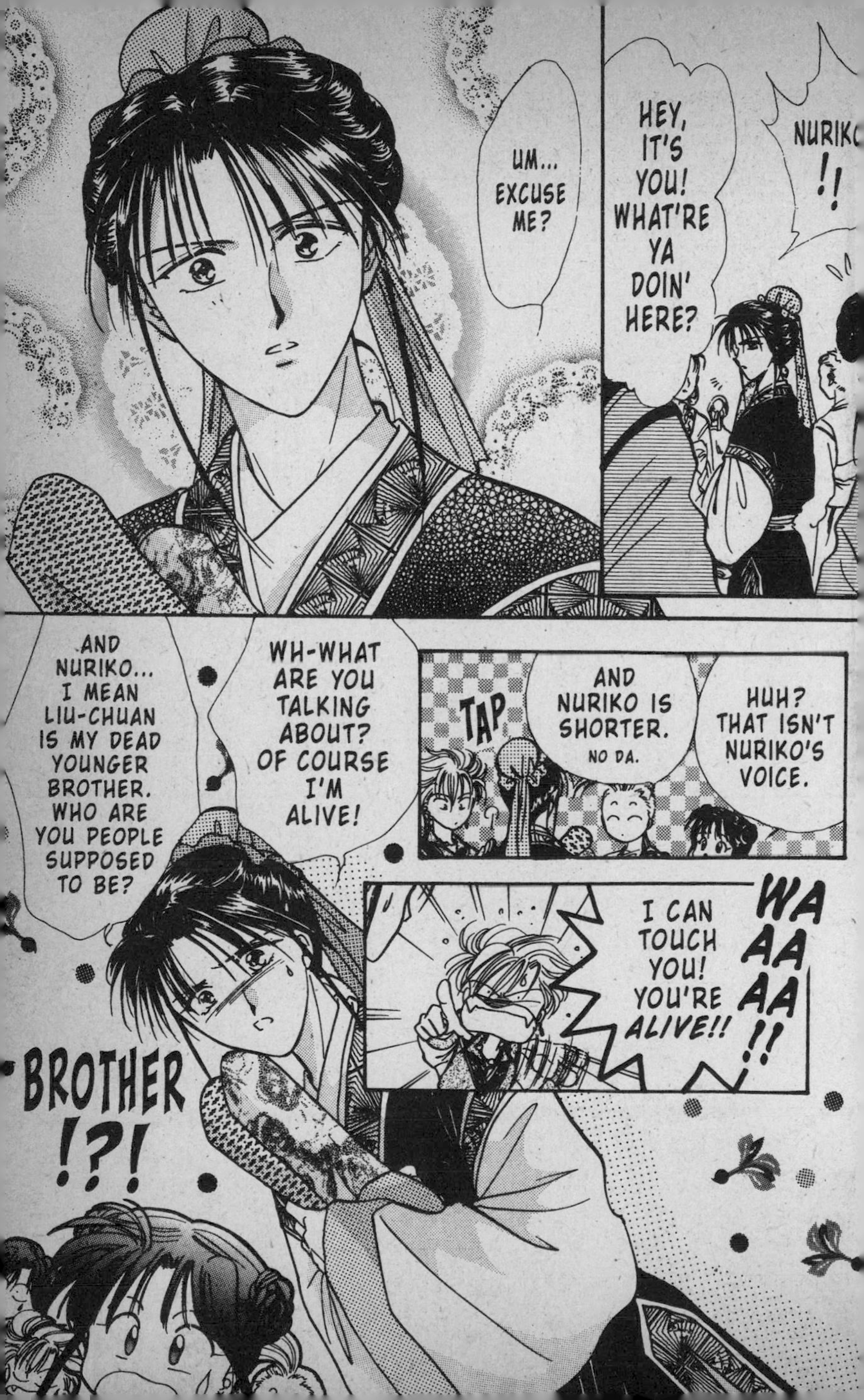
NURIKO !!
HEY, IT'S YOU! WHAT'RE YA DOIN' HERE?
UM... EXCUSE ME?
HUH? THAT ISN'T NURIKO'S VOICE.
AND NURIKO IS SHORTER. NO DA.
TAP
WAAAAA!!
I CAN TOUCH YOU! YOU'RE ALIVE!!
WH-WHAT ARE YOU TALKING ABOUT? OF COURSE I'M ALIVE!
AND NURIKO... I MEAN LIU-CHUAN IS MY DEAD YOUNGER BROTHER. WHO ARE YOU PEOPLE SUPPOSED TO BE?
BROTHER !?!

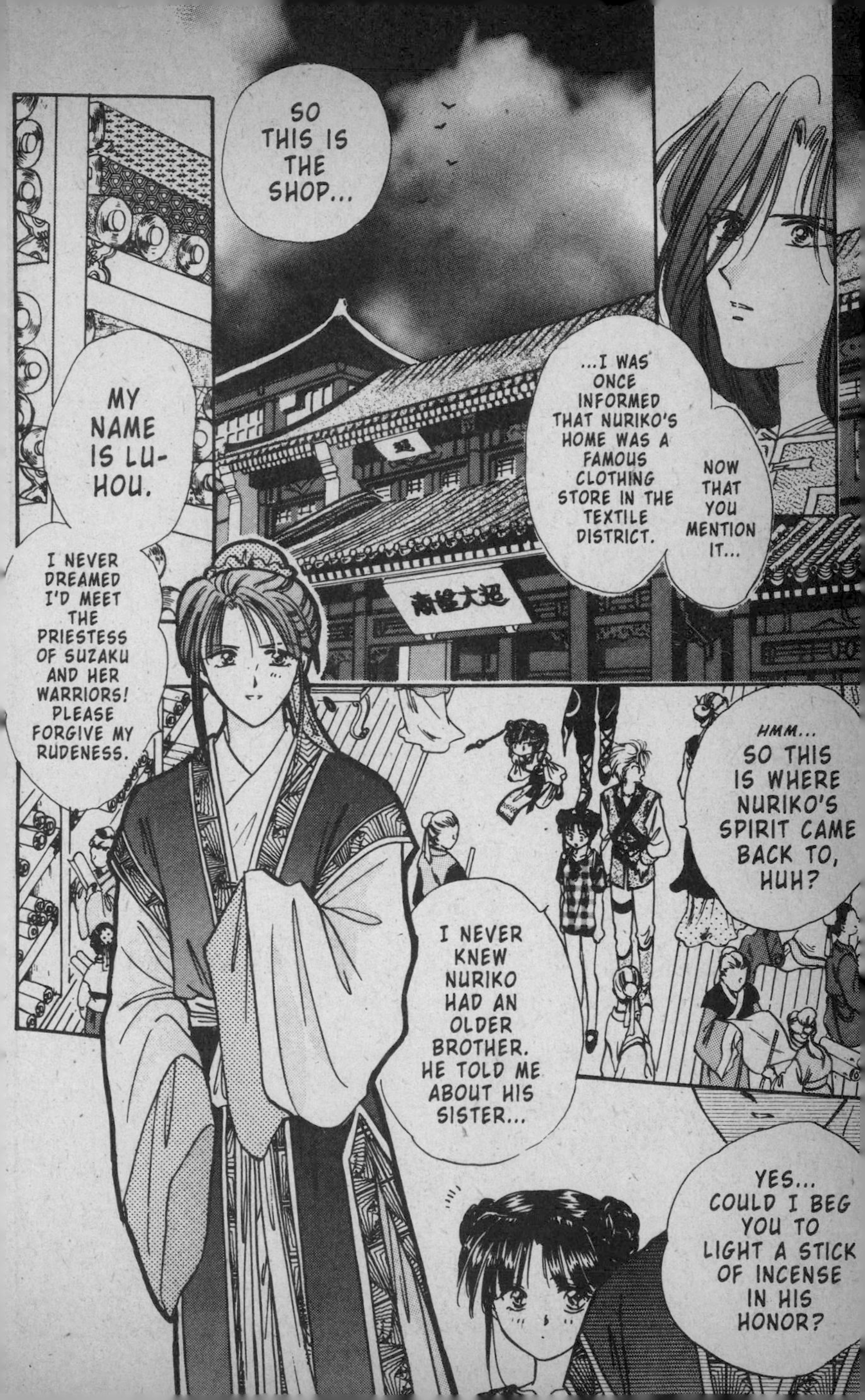
SO THIS IS THE SHOP...
NOW THAT YOU MENTION IT...
...I WAS ONCE INFORMED THAT NURIKO'S HOME WAS A FAMOUS CLOTHING STORE IN THE TEXTILE DISTRICT.
HMM... SO THIS IS WHERE NURIKO'S SPIRIT CAME BACK TO, HUH?
MY NAME IS LU-HOU.
I NEVER DREAMED I'D MEET THE PRIESTESS OF SUZAKU AND HER WARRIORS! PLEASE FORGIVE MY RUDENESS.
I NEVER KNEW NURIKO HAD AN OLDER BROTHER. HE TOLD ME ABOUT HIS SISTER...
YES... COULD I BEG YOU TO LIGHT A STICK OF INCENSE IN HIS HONOR?

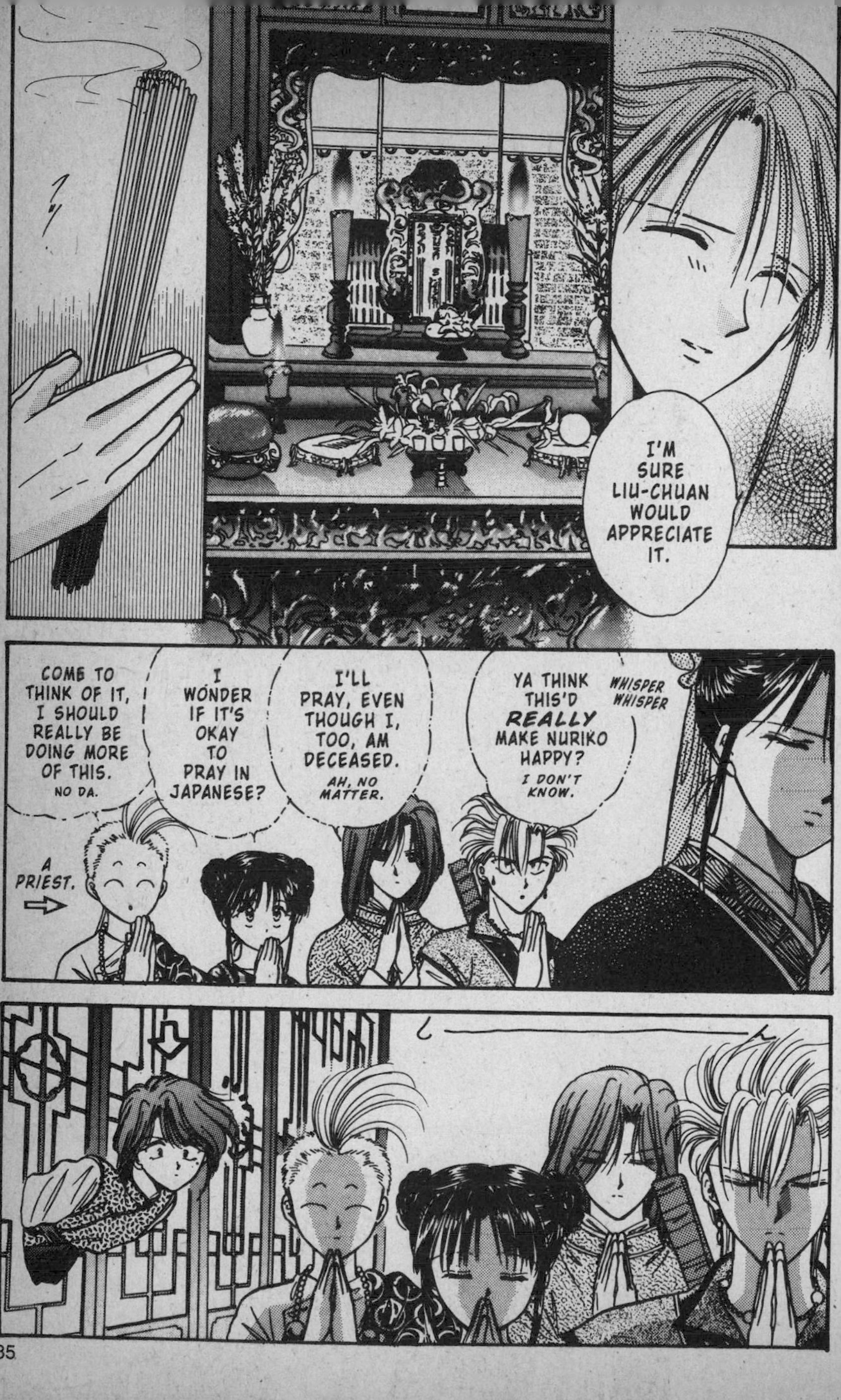
I'M SURE LIU-CHUAN WOULD APPRECIATE IT.
WHISPER WHISPER
YA THINK THIS'D REALLY MAKE NURIKO HAPPY?
I DON'T KNOW.
I'LL PRAY, EVEN THOUGH I, TOO, AM DECEASED.
AH, NO MATTER.
I WONDER IF IT'S OKAY TO PRAY IN JAPANESE?
COME TO THINK OF IT, I SHOULD REALLY BE DOING MORE OF THIS.
NO DA.
A PRIEST.

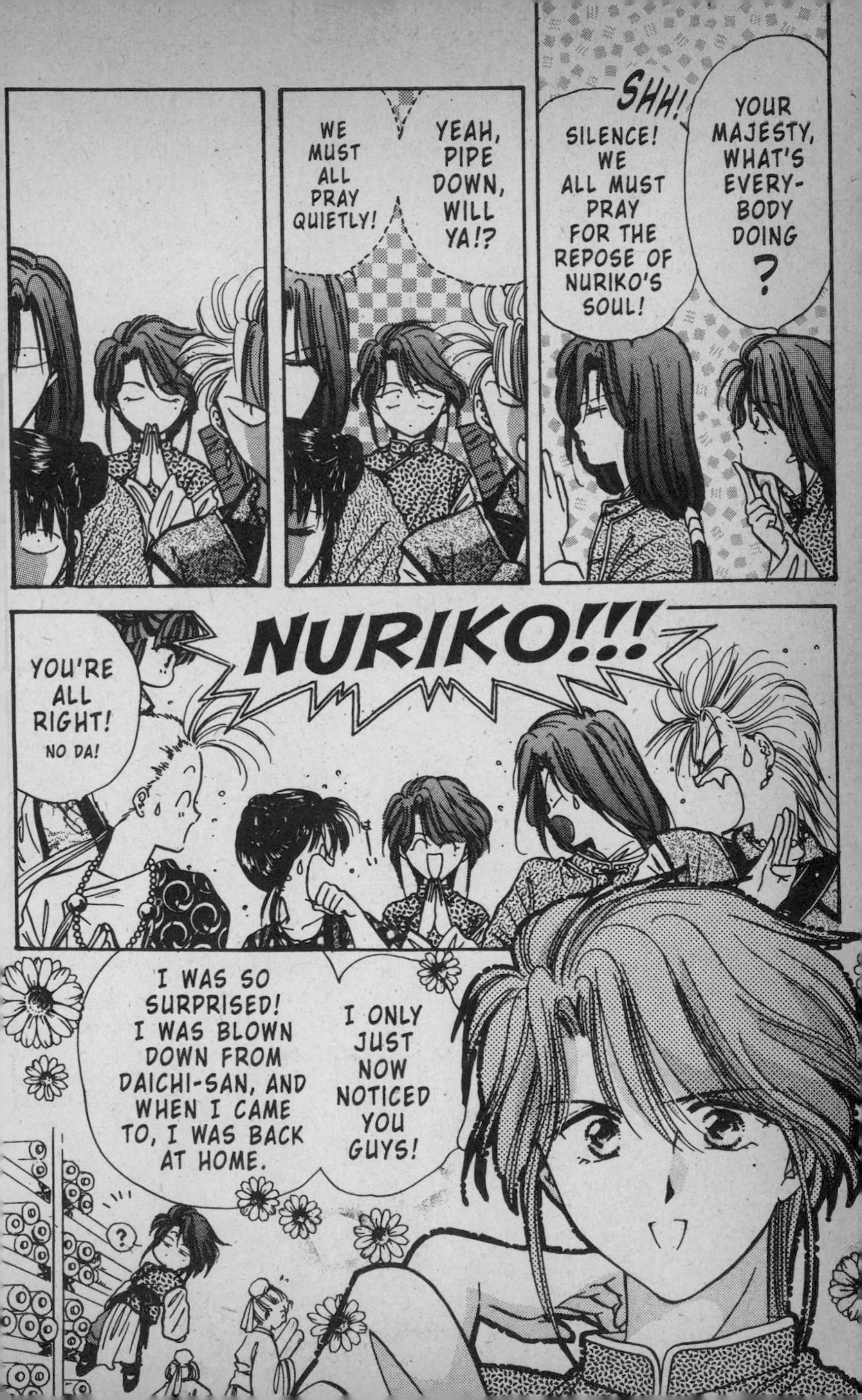
YOUR MAJESTY, WHAT'S EVERYBODY DOING?
SHH!
SILENCE! WE ALL MUST PRAY FOR THE REPOSE OF NURIKO'S SOUL!
YEAH, PIPE DOWN, WILL YA!?
WE MUST ALL PRAY QUIETLY!
NURIKO!!!
YOU'RE ALL RIGHT! NO DA!
I ONLY JUST NOW NOTICED YOU GUYS!
I WAS SO SURPRISED! I WAS BLOWN DOWN FROM DAICHI-SAN, AND WHEN I CAME TO, I WAS BACK AT HOME.

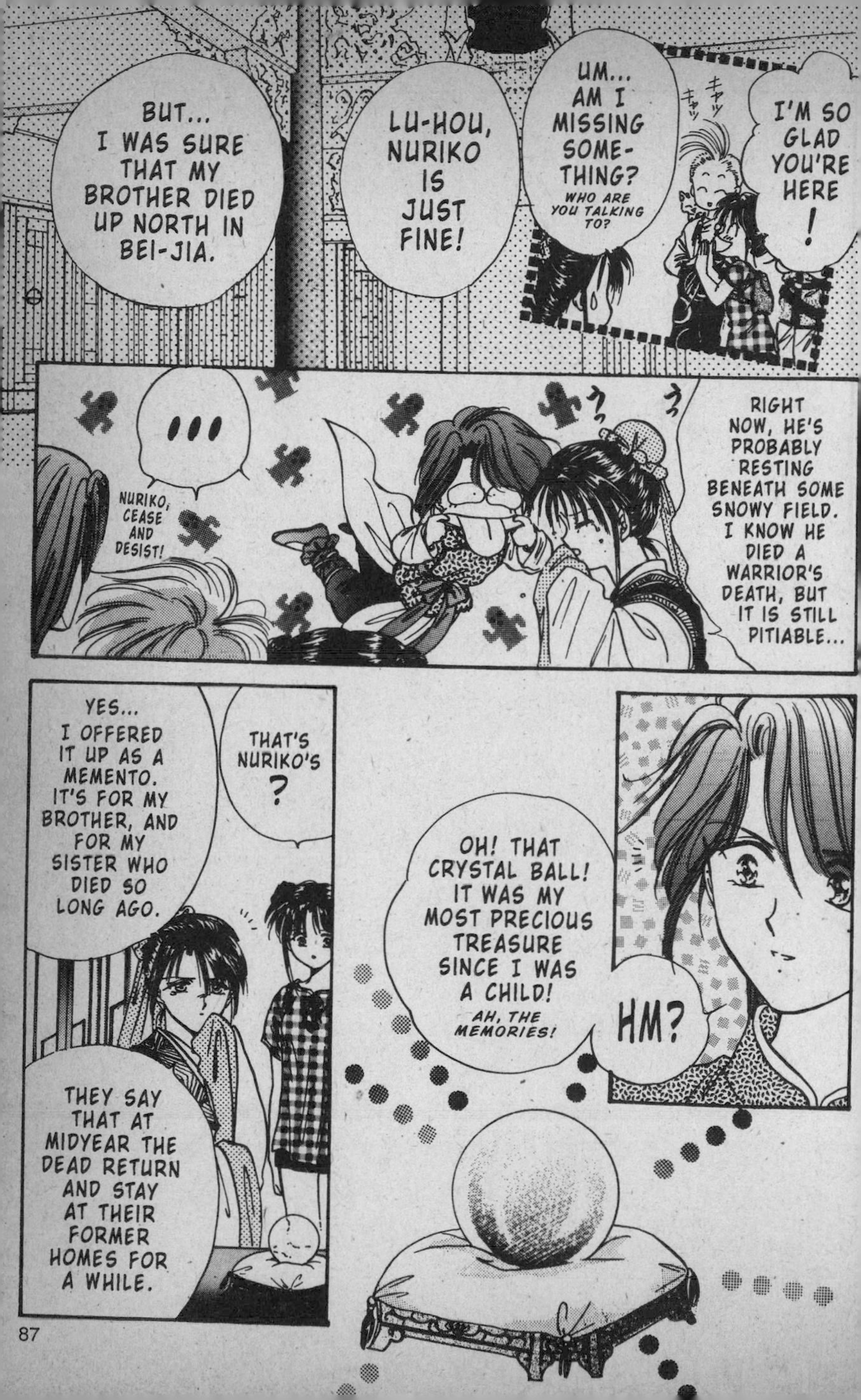
BUT... I WAS SURE THAT MY BROTHER DIED UP NORTH IN BEI-JIA.
LU-HOU, NURIKO IS JUST FINE!
UM... AM I MISSING SOME-THING?
WHO ARE YOU TALKING TO?
キャッキャッ
I'M SO GLAD YOU'RE HERE!
RIGHT NOW, HE'S PROBABLY RESTING BENEATH SOME SNOWY FIELD. I KNOW HE DIED A WARRIOR'S DEATH, BUT IT IS STILL PITIABLE...
...
NURIKO, CEASE AND DESIST!
THAT'S NURIKO'S?
YES... I OFFERED IT UP AS A MEMENTO. IT'S FOR MY BROTHER, AND FOR MY SISTER WHO DIED SO LONG AGO.
THEY SAY THAT AT MIDYEAR THE DEAD RETURN AND STAY AT THEIR FORMER HOMES FOR A WHILE.
HM?
OH! THAT CRYSTAL BALL! IT WAS MY MOST PRECIOUS TREASURE SINCE I WAS A CHILD!
AH, THE MEMORIES!

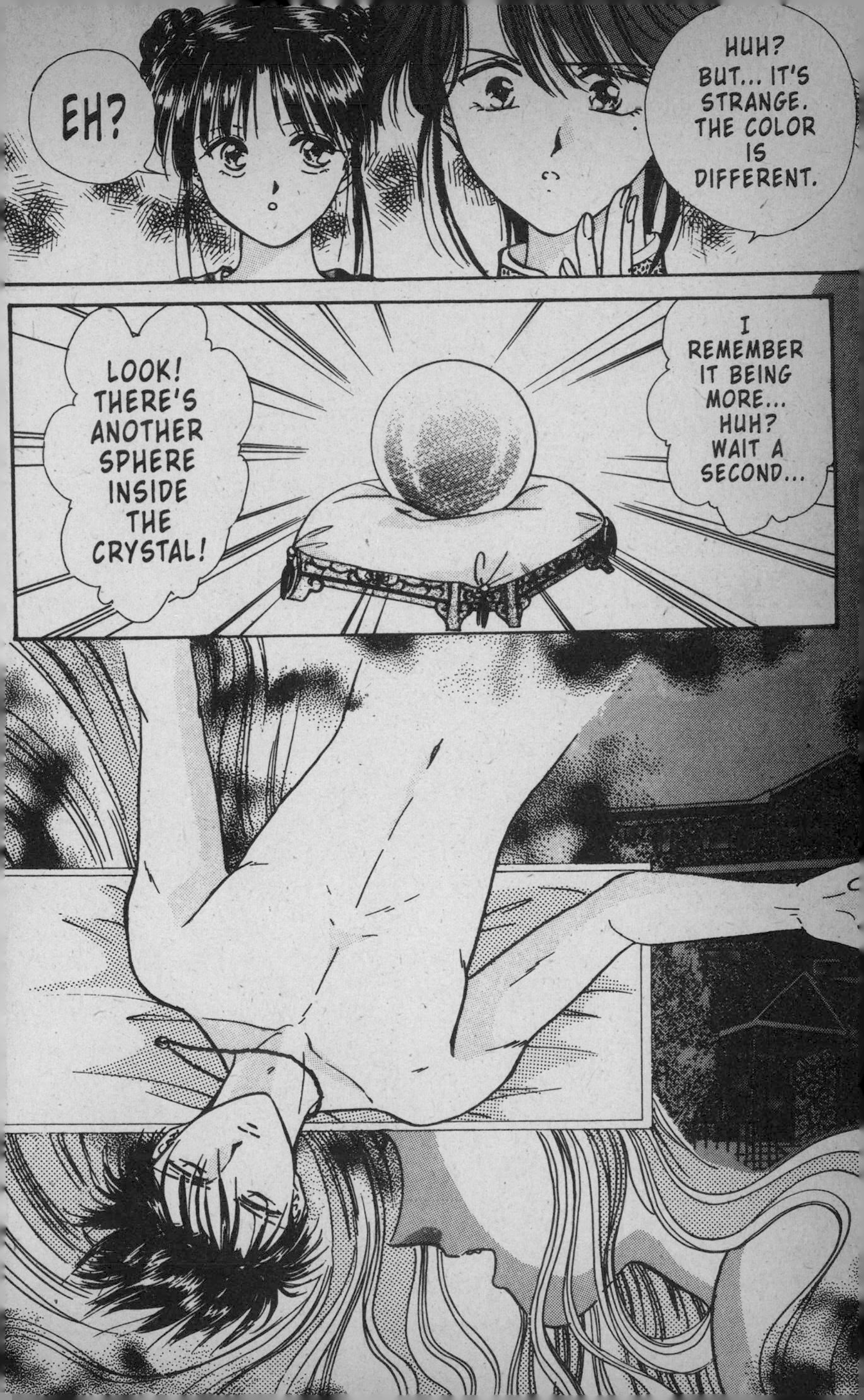
HUH? BUT... IT'S STRANGE. THE COLOR IS DIFFERENT.
EH?
I REMEMBER IT BEING MORE... HUH? WAIT A SECOND...
LOOK! THERE'S ANOTHER SPHERE INSIDE THE CRYSTAL!

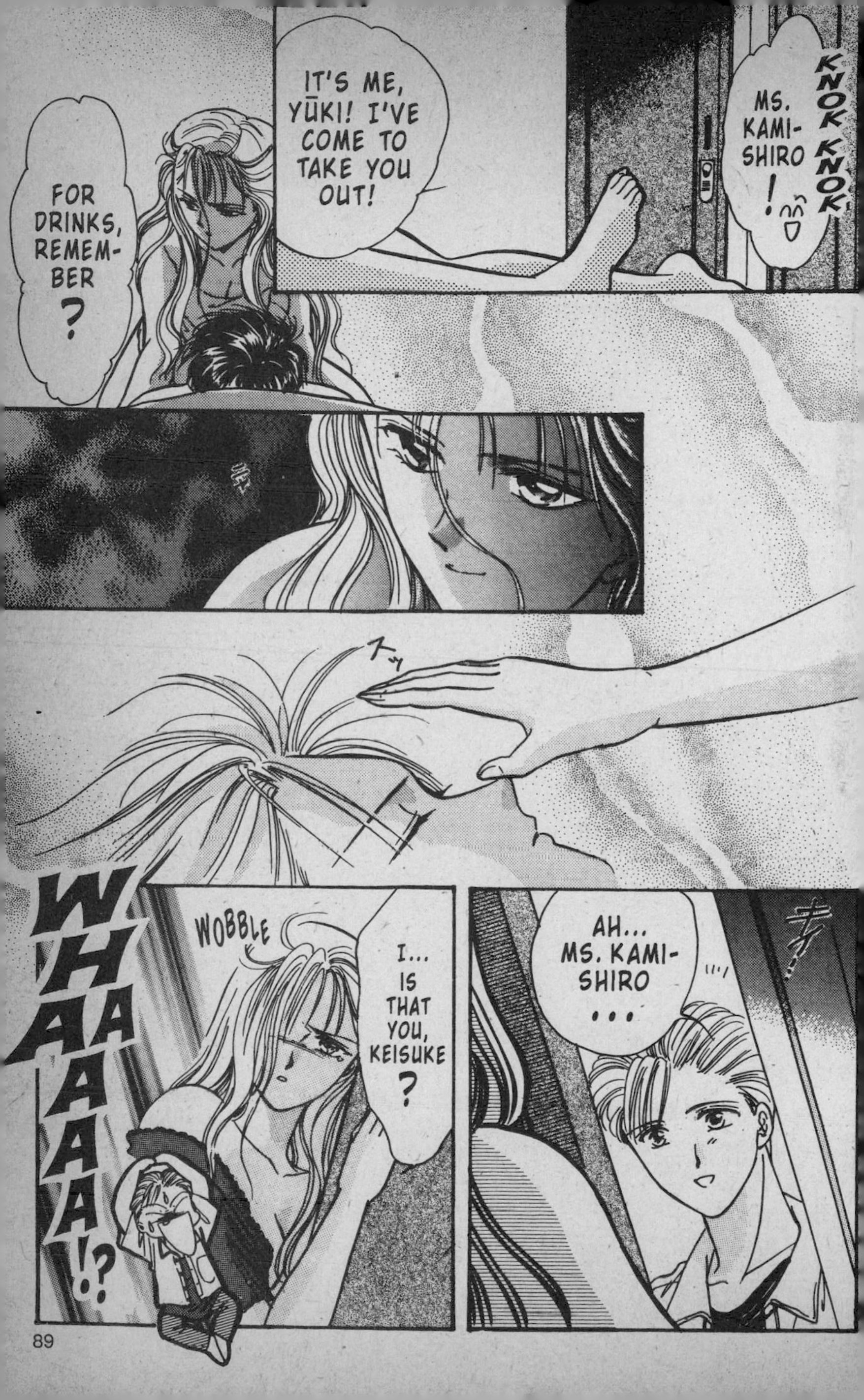
KNOK KNOK
MS. KAMI-SHIRO!
IT'S ME, YŪKI! I'VE COME TO TAKE YOU OUT!
FOR DRINKS, REMEMBER?
AH... MS. KAMI-SHIRO...
WOBBLE
I... IS THAT YOU, KEISUKE?
WHAAAAAA!?

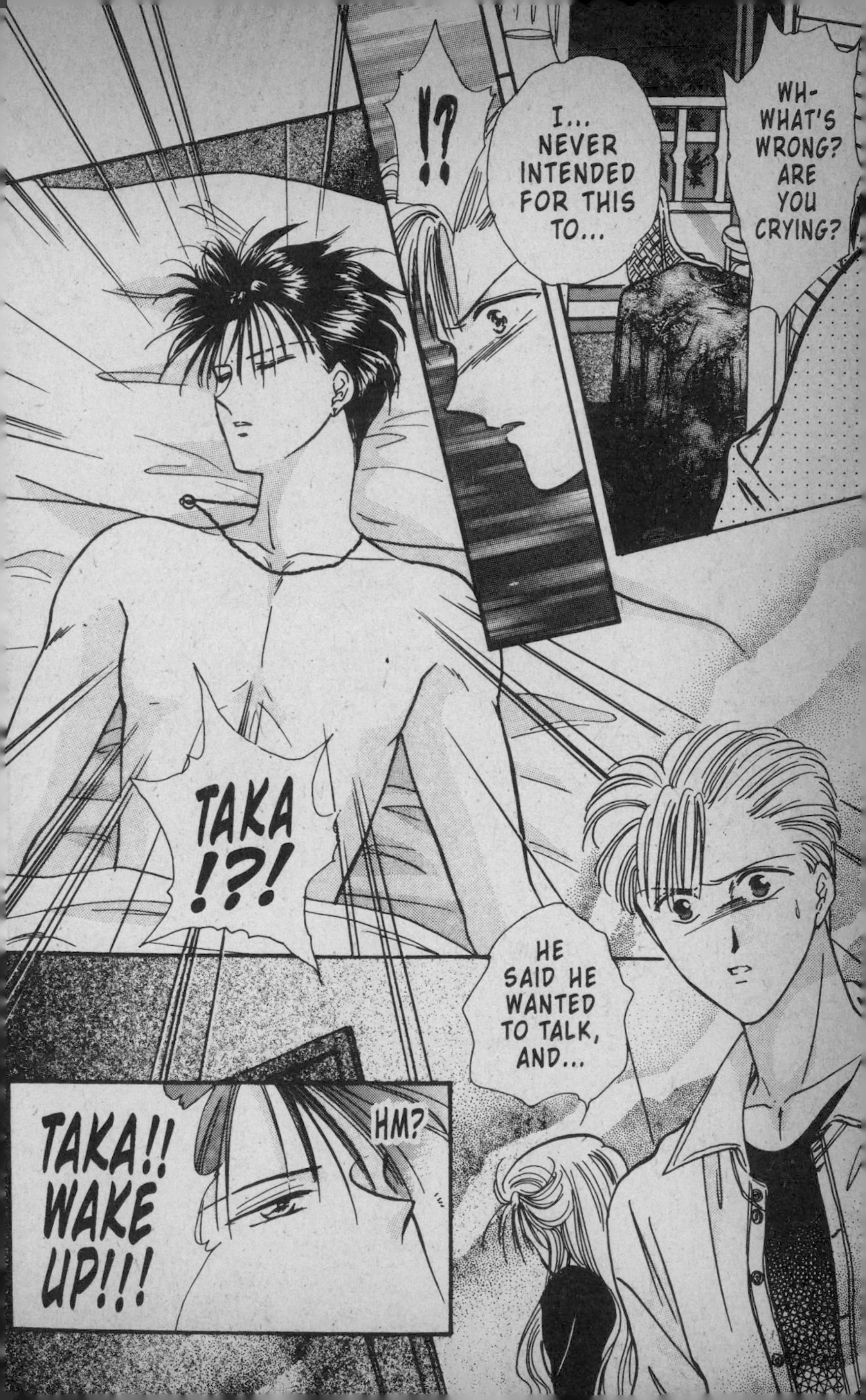
WH- WHAT'S WRONG? ARE YOU CRYING?
!?
I... NEVER INTENDED FOR THIS TO...
HE SAID HE WANTED TO TALK, AND...
TAKA !?!
TAKA!! WAKE UP!!!
HM?

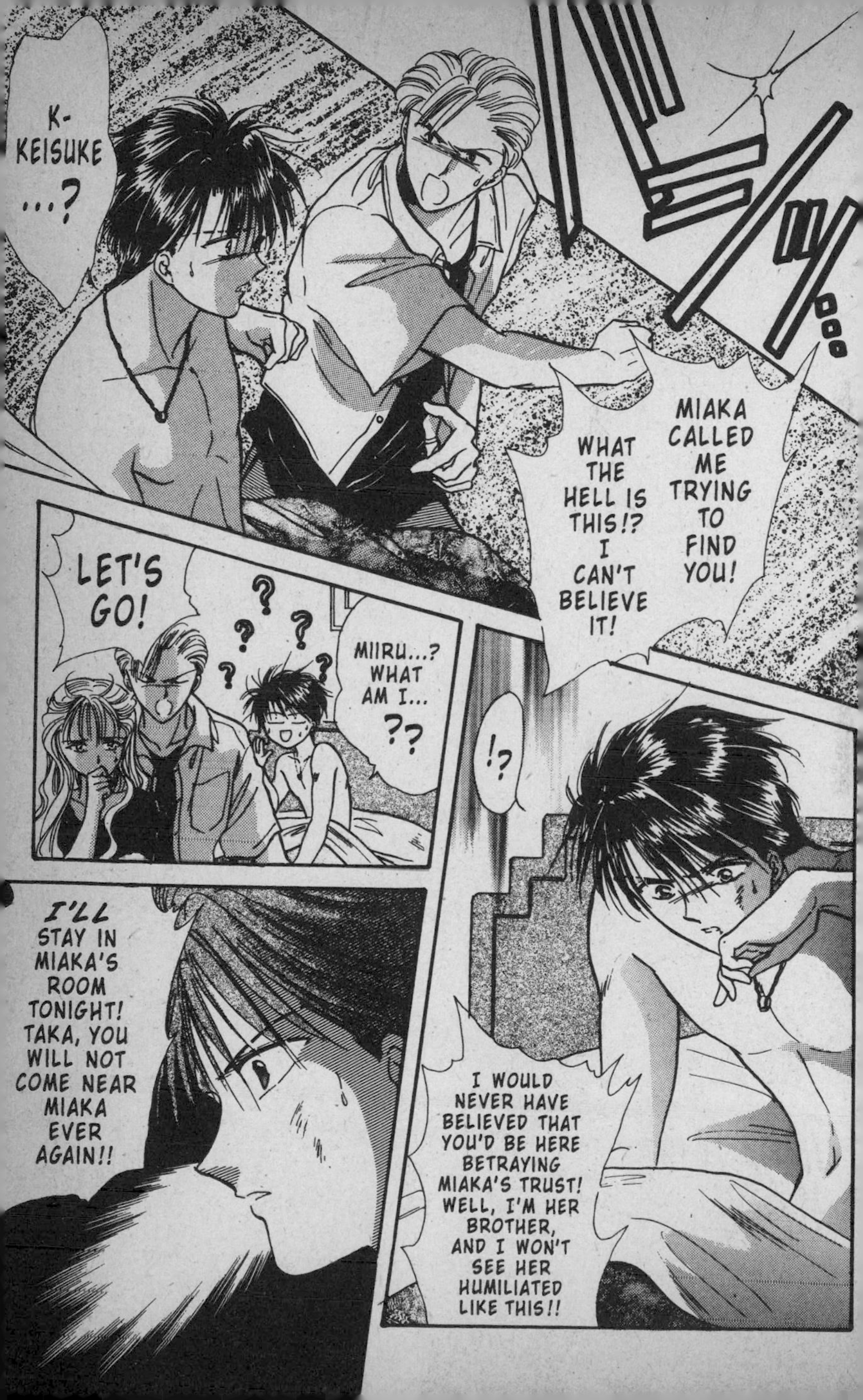
MIAKA CALLED ME TRYING TO FIND YOU!
WHAT THE HELL IS THIS!? I CAN'T BELIEVE IT!
K-KEISUKE ...?
!?
I WOULD NEVER HAVE BELIEVED THAT YOU'D BE HERE BETRAYING MIAKA'S TRUST! WELL, I'M HER BROTHER, AND I WON'T SEE HER HUMILIATED LIKE THIS!!
MIIRU...? WHAT AM I... ??
LET'S GO!
I'LL STAY IN MIAKA'S ROOM TONIGHT! TAKA, YOU WILL NOT COME NEAR MIAKA EVER AGAIN!!

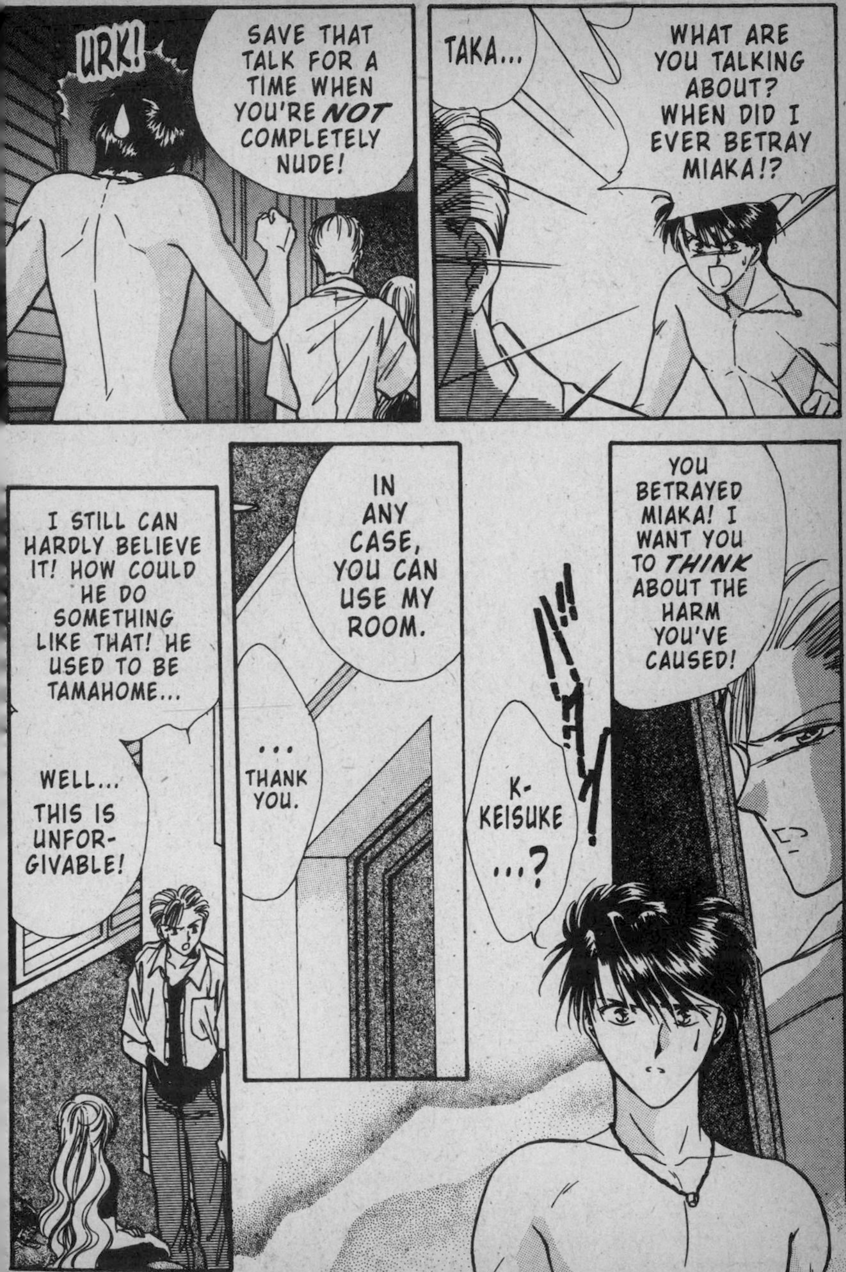
WHAT ARE YOU TALKING ABOUT? WHEN DID I EVER BETRAY MIAKA!?
TAKA...
SAVE THAT TALK FOR A TIME WHEN YOU'RE *NOT* COMPLETELY NUDE!
URK!
YOU BETRAYED MIAKA! I WANT YOU TO *THINK* ABOUT THE HARM YOU'VE CAUSED!
K-KEISUKE ...?
IN ANY CASE, YOU CAN USE MY ROOM.
... THANK YOU.
I STILL CAN HARDLY BELIEVE IT! HOW COULD HE DO SOMETHING LIKE THAT! HE USED TO BE TAMAHOME...
WELL... THIS IS UNFORGIVABLE!

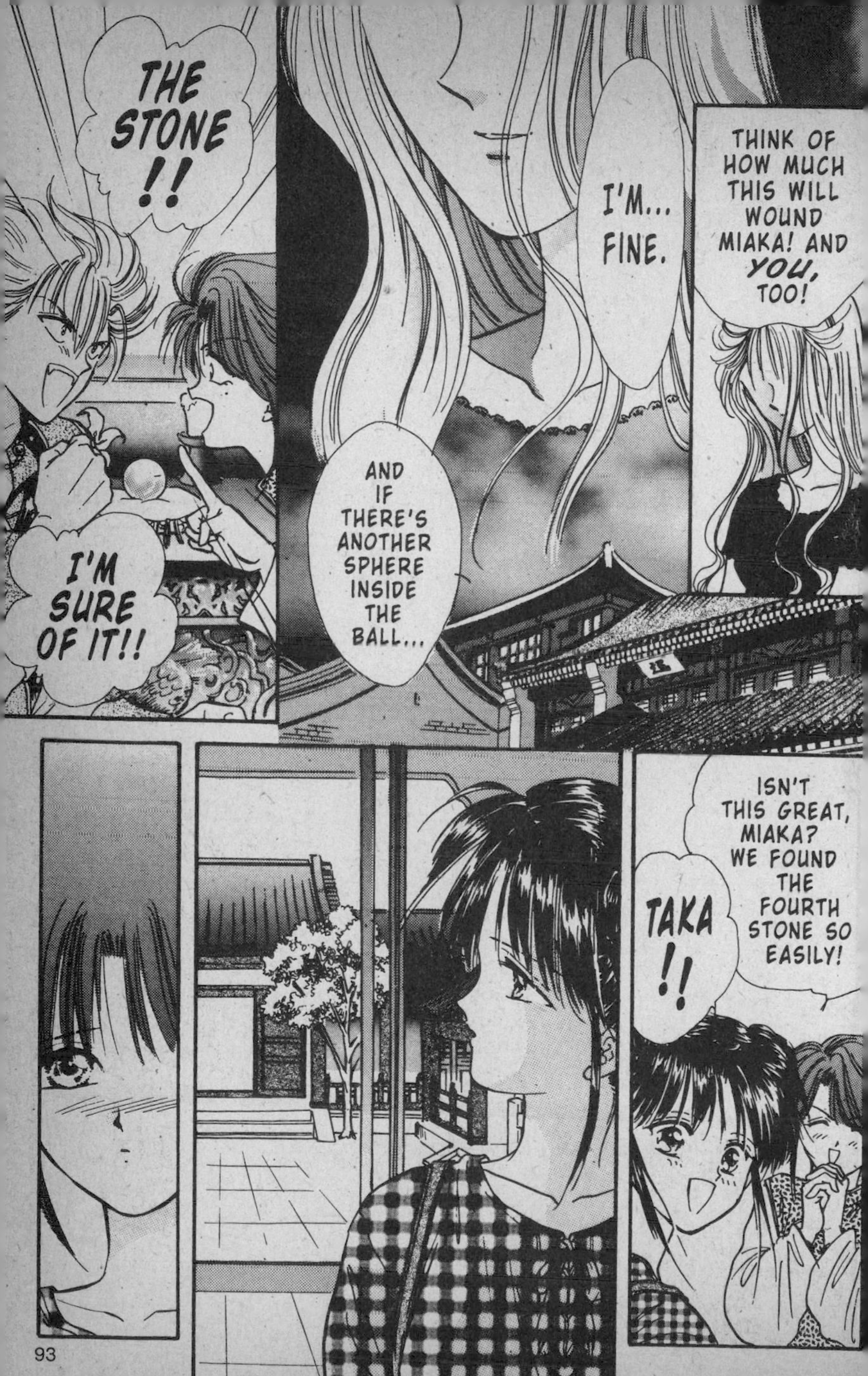
THINK OF HOW MUCH THIS WILL WOUND MIAKA! AND YOU, TOO!
I'M... FINE.
AND IF THERE'S ANOTHER SPHERE INSIDE THE BALL...
THE STONE!!
I'M SURE OF IT!!
ISN'T THIS GREAT, MIAKA? WE FOUND THE FOURTH STONE SO EASILY!
TAKA!!

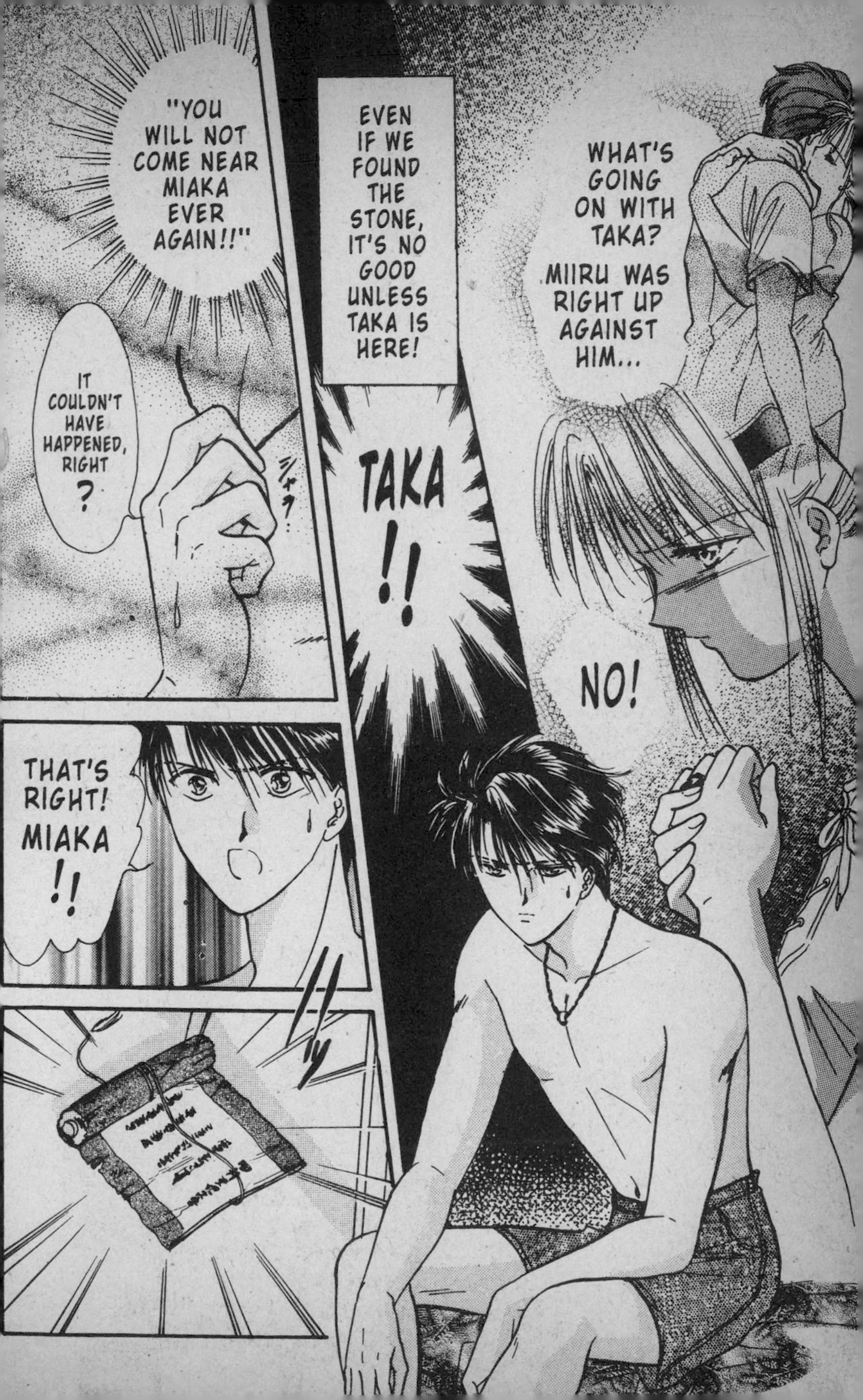
WHAT'S GOING ON WITH TAKA?
MIIRU WAS RIGHT UP AGAINST HIM...
NO!
EVEN IF WE FOUND THE STONE, IT'S NO GOOD UNLESS TAKA IS HERE!
TAKA!!
"YOU WILL NOT COME NEAR MIAKA EVER AGAIN!!"
IT COULDN'T HAVE HAPPENED, RIGHT?
THAT'S RIGHT! MIAKA!!

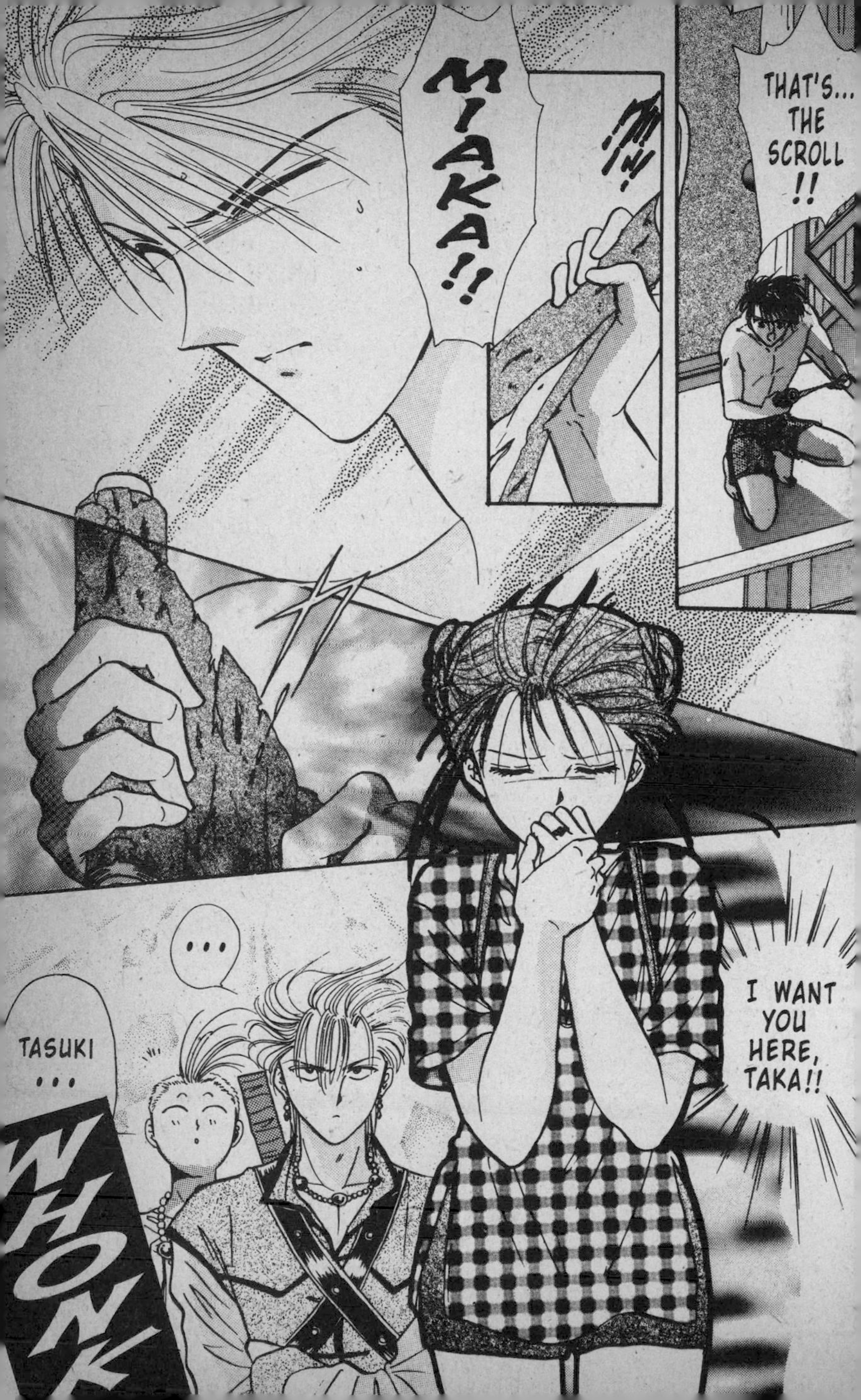
THAT'S... THE SCROLL!!
MIAKA!!
I WANT YOU HERE, TAKA!!
...
TASUKI...
THONK

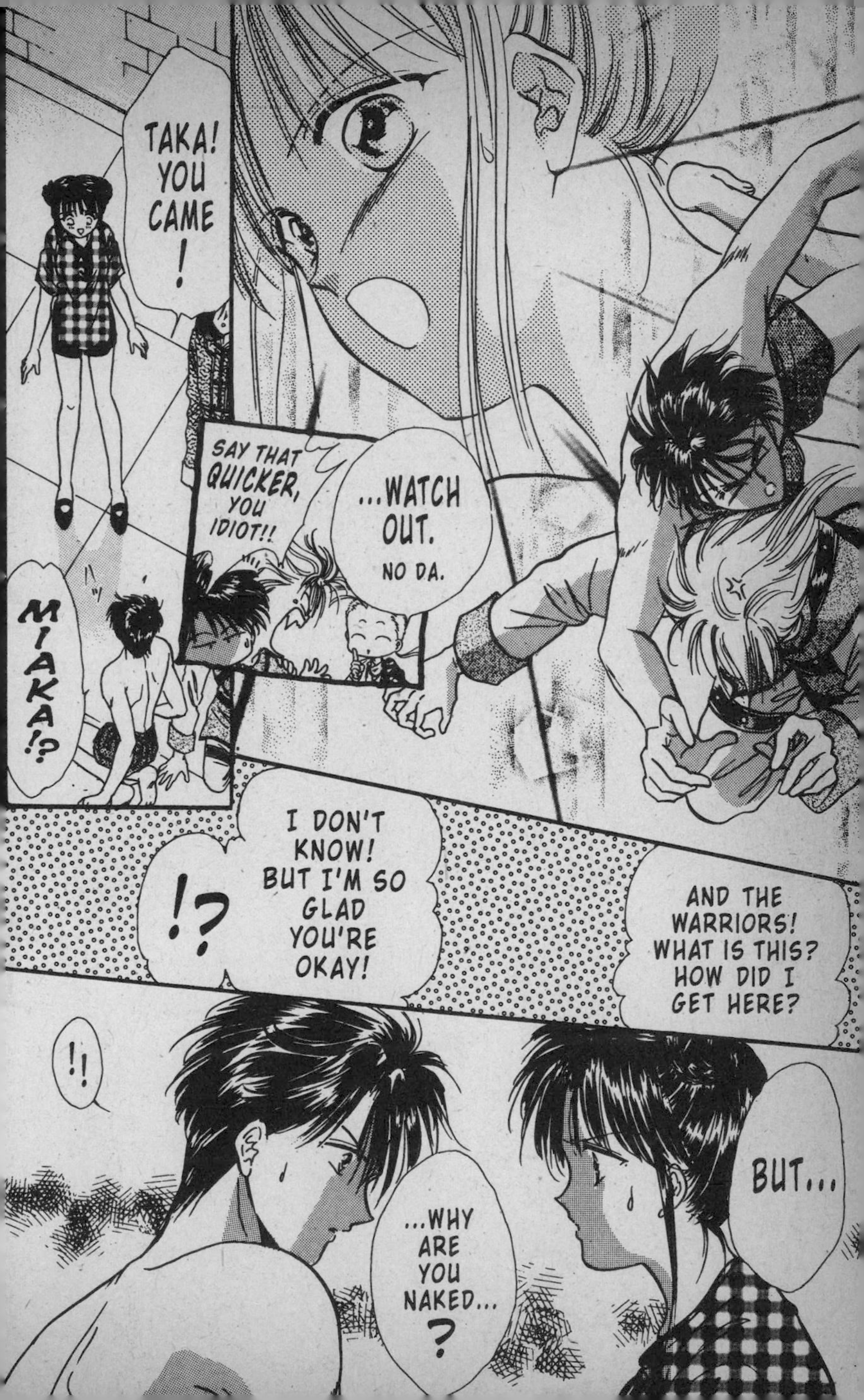
...WATCH OUT. NO DA.
SAY THAT QUICKER, YOU IDIOT!!
TAKA! YOU CAME!
MIAKA!?
AND THE WARRIORS! WHAT IS THIS? HOW DID I GET HERE?
I DON'T KNOW! BUT I'M SO GLAD YOU'RE OKAY!
!?
BUT...
...WHY ARE YOU NAKED...?
!!

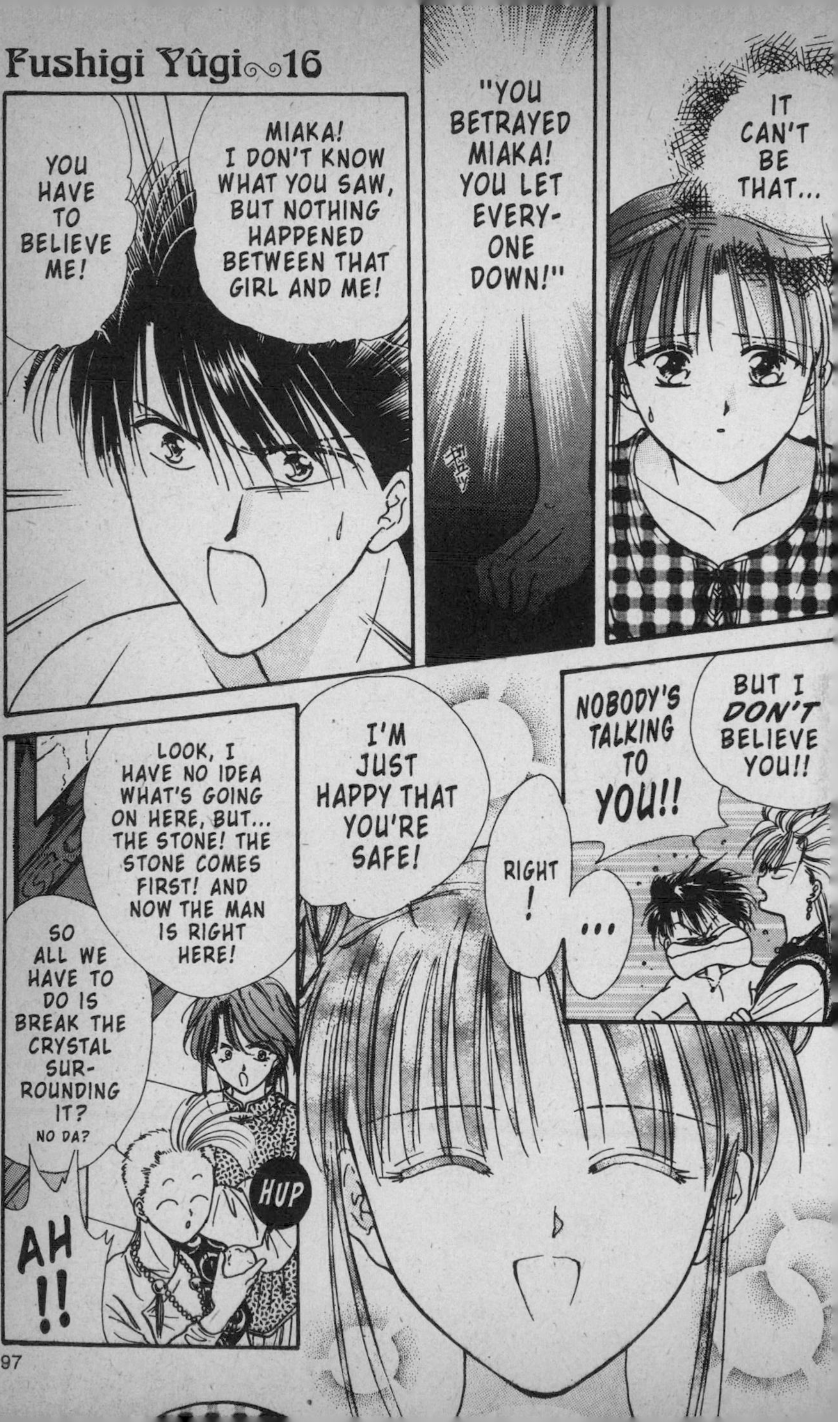
IT CAN'T BE THAT...
"YOU BETRAYED MIAKA! YOU LET EVERY-ONE DOWN!"
MIAKA! I DON'T KNOW WHAT YOU SAW, BUT NOTHING HAPPENED BETWEEN THAT GIRL AND ME!
YOU HAVE TO BELIEVE ME!
BUT I *DON'T* BELIEVE YOU!!
NOBODY'S TALKING TO YOU!!
...
I'M JUST HAPPY THAT YOU'RE SAFE!
RIGHT!
LOOK, I HAVE NO IDEA WHAT'S GOING ON HERE, BUT... THE STONE! THE STONE COMES FIRST! AND NOW THE MAN IS RIGHT HERE!
SO ALL WE HAVE TO DO IS BREAK THE CRYSTAL SUR-ROUNDING IT? NO DA?
HUP
AH!!

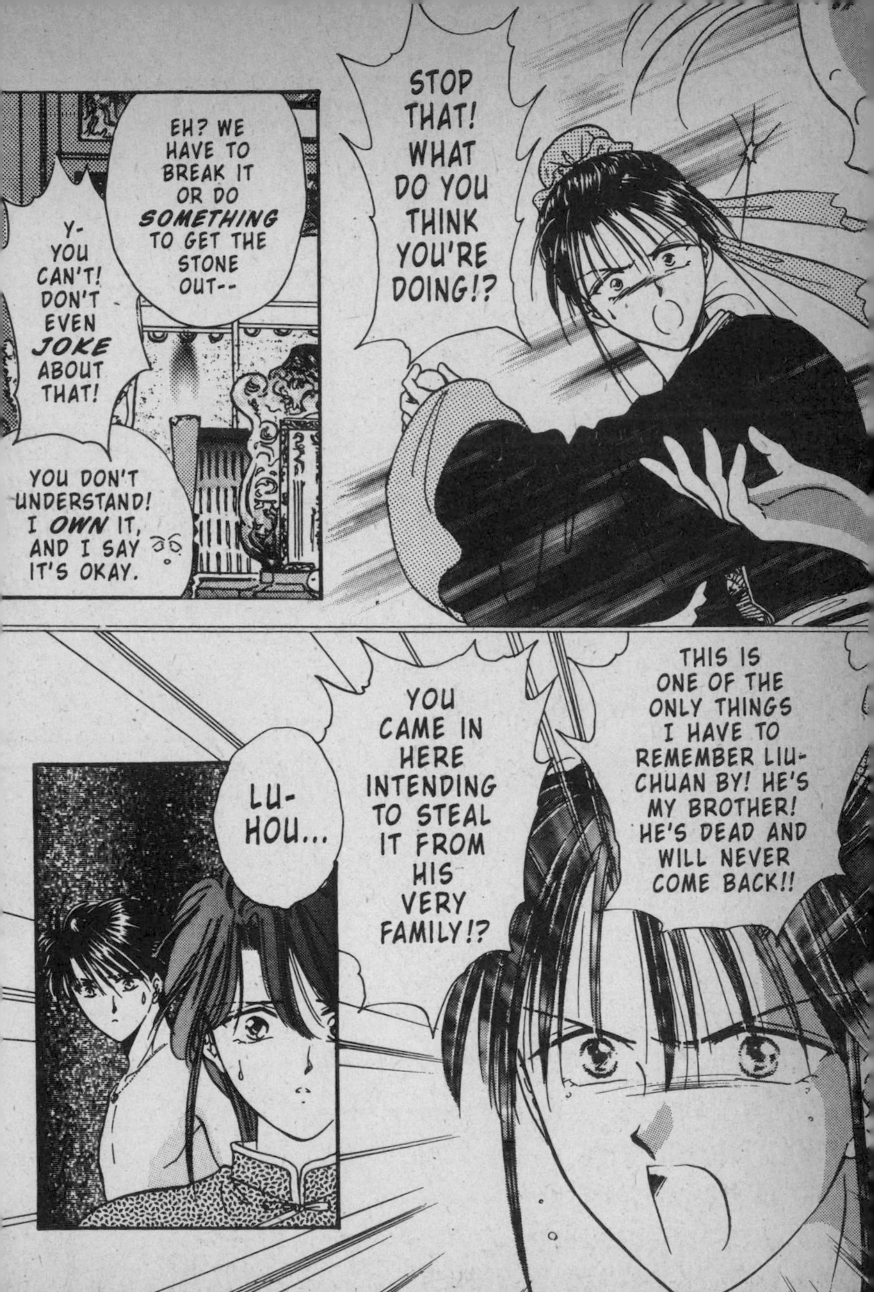
STOP THAT! WHAT DO YOU THINK YOU'RE DOING!?
EH? WE HAVE TO BREAK IT OR DO *SOMETHING* TO GET THE STONE OUT--
Y- YOU CAN'T! DON'T EVEN *JOKE* ABOUT THAT!
YOU DON'T UNDERSTAND! I *OWN* IT, AND I SAY IT'S OKAY.
THIS IS ONE OF THE ONLY THINGS I HAVE TO REMEMBER LIU-CHUAN BY! HE'S MY BROTHER! HE'S DEAD AND WILL NEVER COME BACK!!
YOU CAME IN HERE INTENDING TO STEAL IT FROM HIS VERY FAMILY!?
LU-HOU...

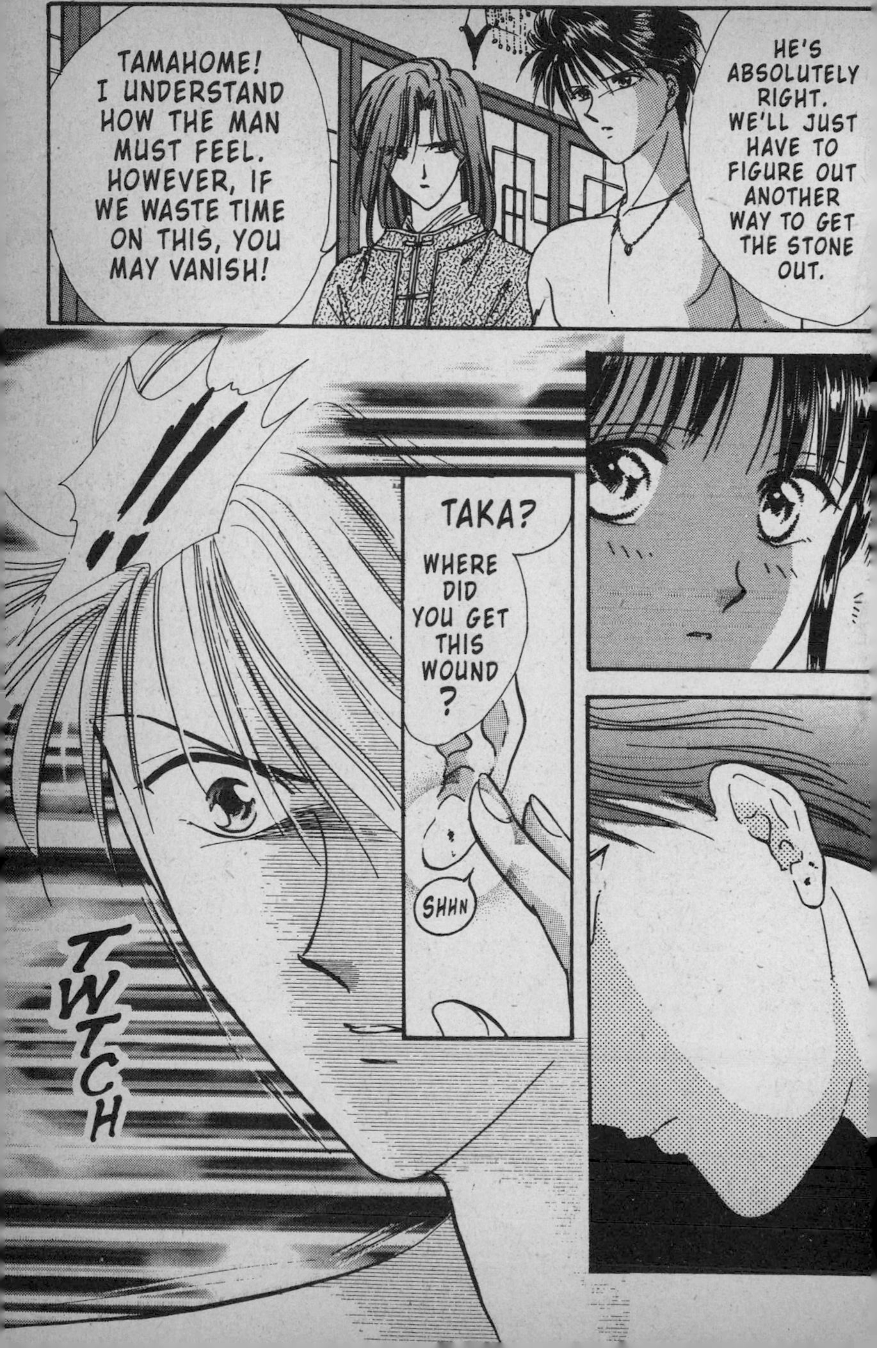
TAMAHOME! I UNDERSTAND HOW THE MAN MUST FEEL. HOWEVER, IF WE WASTE TIME ON THIS, YOU MAY VANISH!
HE'S ABSOLUTELY RIGHT. WE'LL JUST HAVE TO FIGURE OUT ANOTHER WAY TO GET THE STONE OUT.
TAKA?
WHERE DID YOU GET THIS WOUND?
SHHN
TWITCH

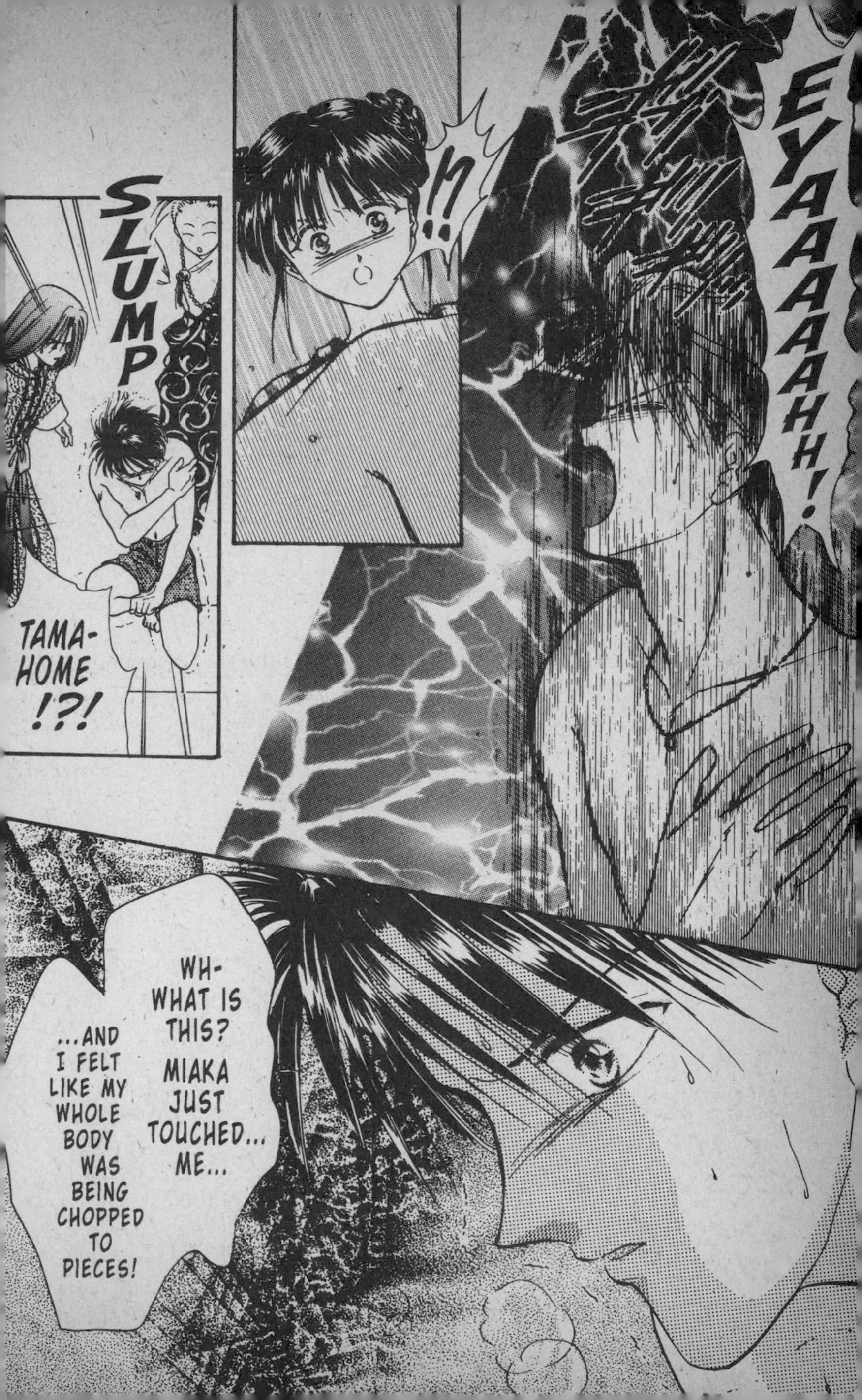
EYAAAAAAHH!
!!
SLUMP
TAMA-HOME !?!
WH- WHAT IS THIS? MIAKA JUST TOUCHED... ME...
...AND I FELT LIKE MY WHOLE BODY WAS BEING CHOPPED TO PIECES!

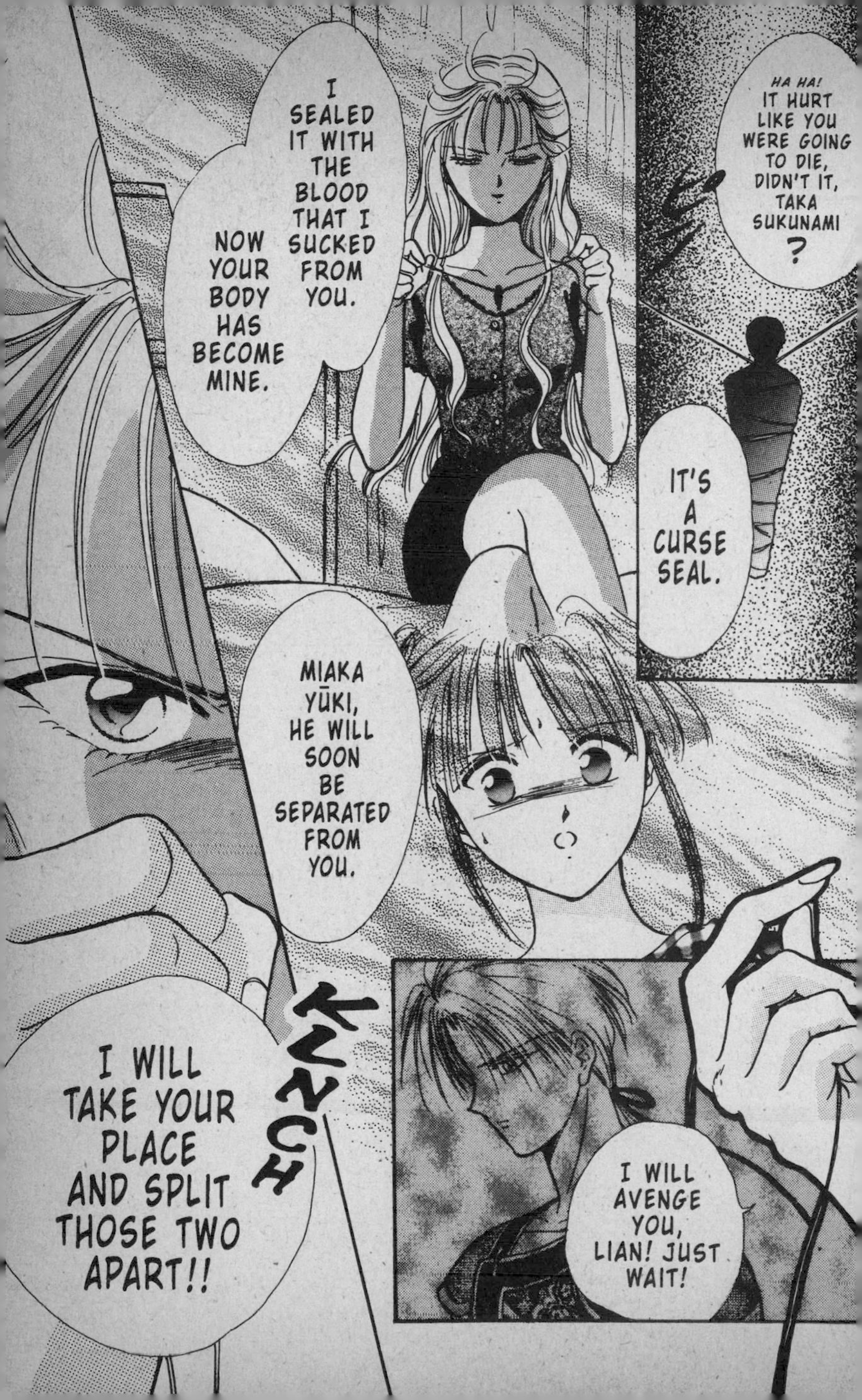
HA HA! IT HURT LIKE YOU WERE GOING TO DIE, DIDN'T IT, TAKA SUKUNAMI?
IT'S A CURSE SEAL.
I SEALED IT WITH THE BLOOD THAT I SUCKED FROM YOU.
NOW YOUR BODY HAS BECOME MINE.
MIAKA YŪKI, HE WILL SOON BE SEPARATED FROM YOU.
I WILL AVENGE YOU, LIAN! JUST WAIT!
KLNCH
I WILL TAKE YOUR PLACE AND SPLIT THOSE TWO APART!!

CHAPTER NINETY-TWO
THE BROKEN PLAN

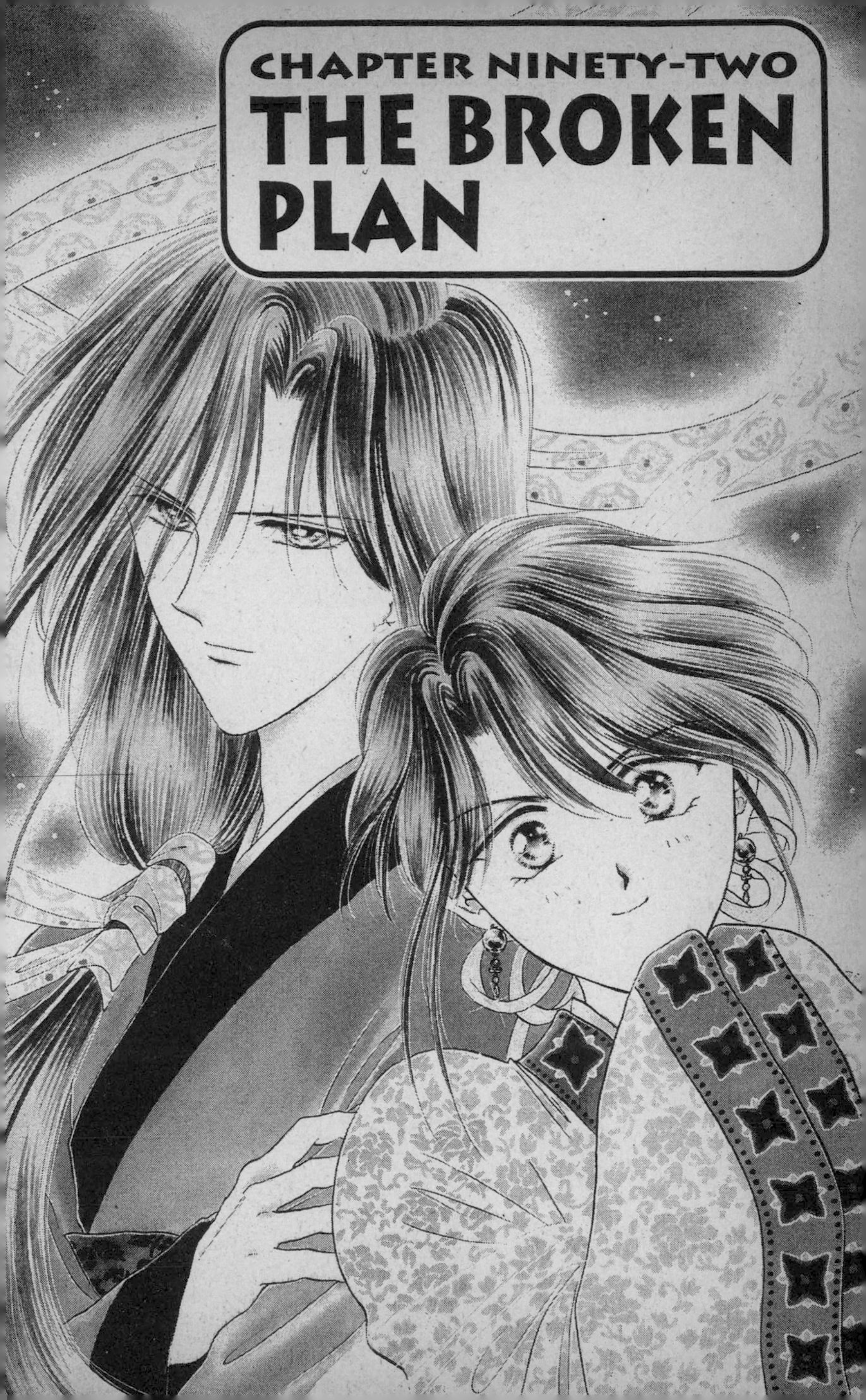

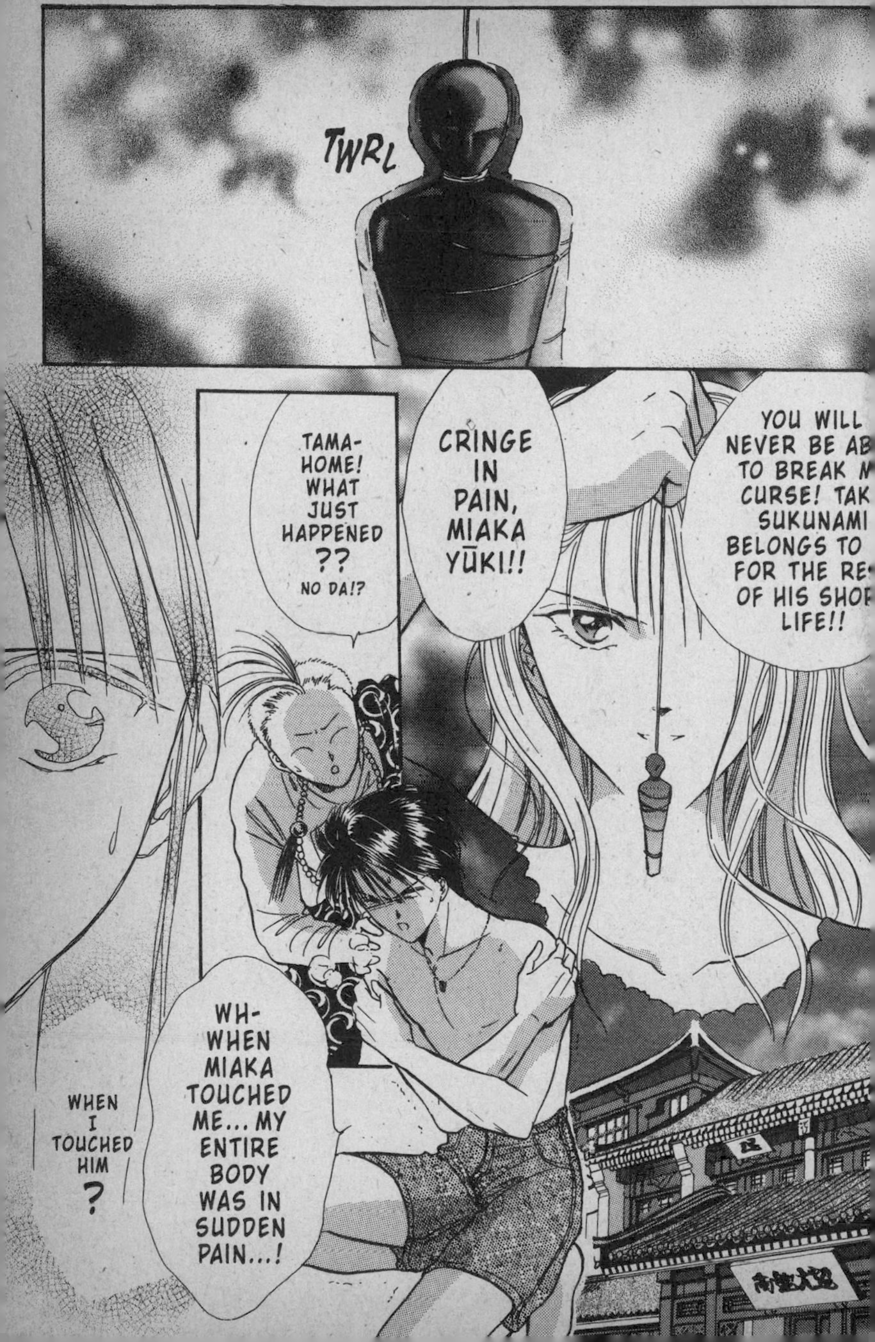
TWRL
YOU WILL NEVER BE AB TO BREAK M CURSE! TAK SUKUNAMI BELONGS TO FOR THE RE OF HIS SHOR LIFE!!
CRINGE IN PAIN, MIAKA YŪKI!!
TAMA-HOME! WHAT JUST HAPPENED?? NO DA!?
WH-WHEN MIAKA TOUCHED ME... MY ENTIRE BODY WAS IN SUDDEN PAIN...!
WHEN I TOUCHED HIM?

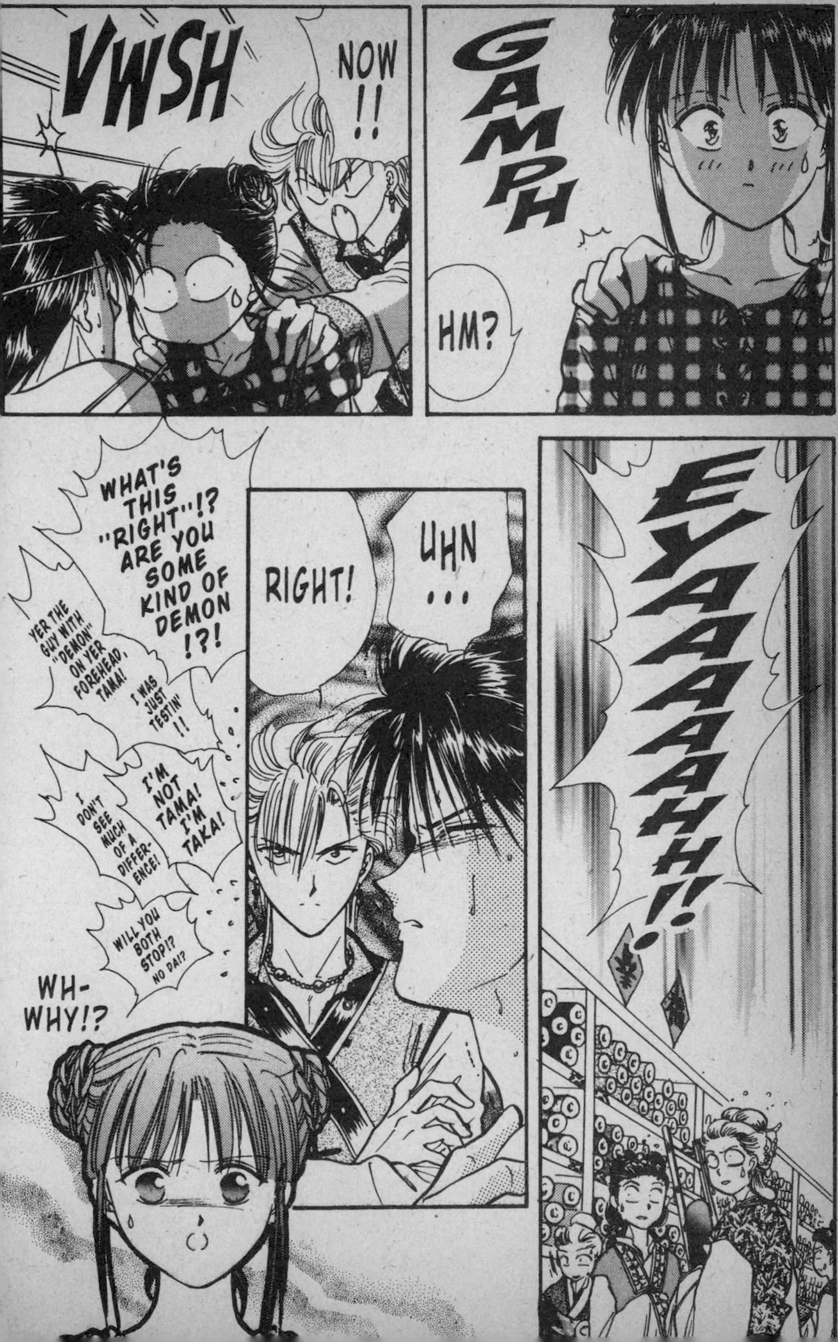
GAMPH
HM?
NOW!!
VWSH
EYAAAAAHH!!
UHN...
RIGHT!
WHAT'S THIS "RIGHT"!? ARE YOU SOME KIND OF DEMON!?!
YER THE GUY WITH "DEMON" ON YER FOREHEAD, TAMA!
I WAS JUST TESTIN'!!
I'M NOT TAMA! I'M TAKA!
I DON'T SEE MUCH OF A DIFFERENCE!
WILL YOU BOTH STOP!? NO DA!?
WH-WHY!?

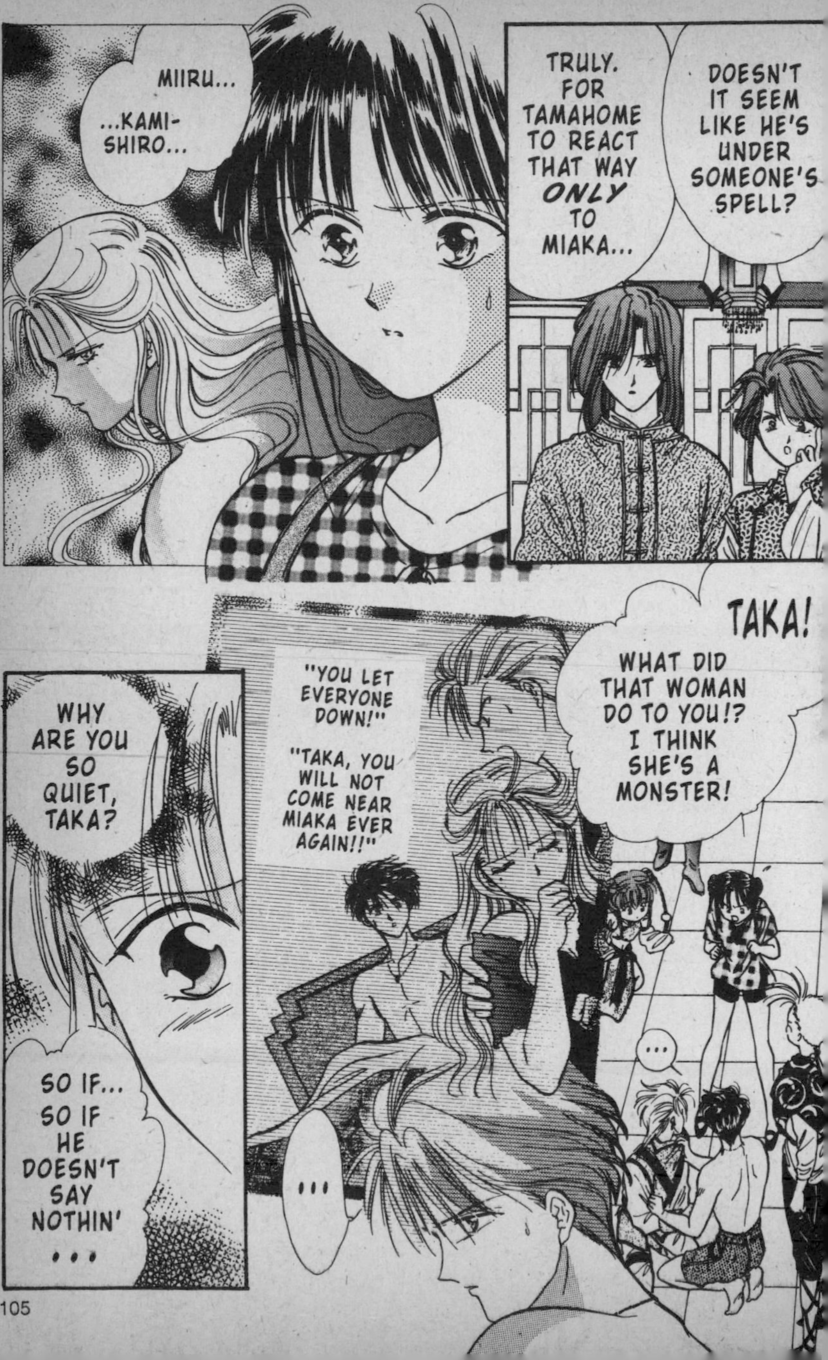
DOESN'T IT SEEM LIKE HE'S UNDER SOMEONE'S SPELL?
TRULY. FOR TAMAHOME TO REACT THAT WAY ONLY TO MIAKA...
MIIRU...
...KAMI-SHIRO...
TAKA!
WHAT DID THAT WOMAN DO TO YOU!? I THINK SHE'S A MONSTER!
...
"YOU LET EVERYONE DOWN!"
"TAKA, YOU WILL NOT COME NEAR MIAKA EVER AGAIN!!"
...
WHY ARE YOU SO QUIET, TAKA?
SO IF... SO IF HE DOESN'T SAY NOTHIN' ...

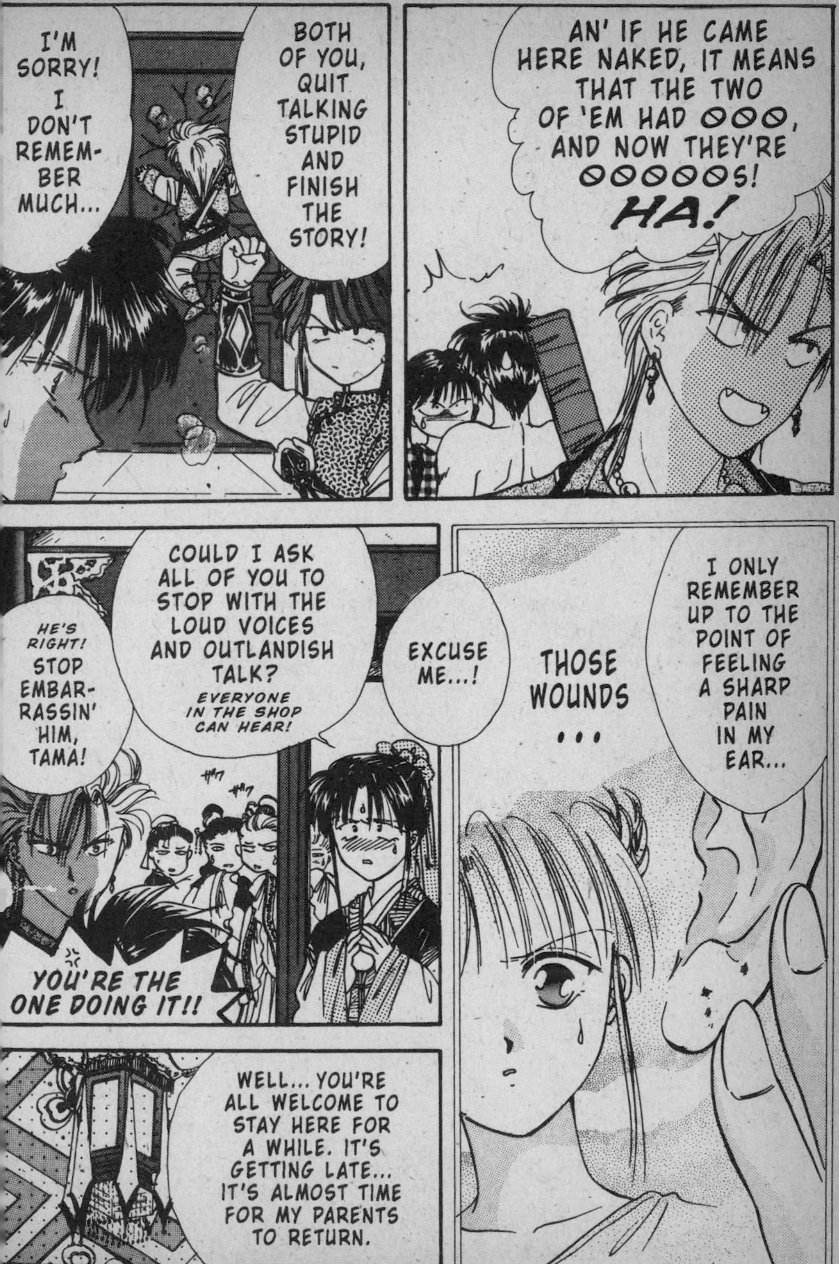
AN' IF HE CAME HERE NAKED, IT MEANS THAT THE TWO OF 'EM HAD OOO, AND NOW THEY'RE OOOOOS!
HA!
BOTH OF YOU, QUIT TALKING STUPID AND FINISH THE STORY!
I'M SORRY! I DON'T REMEMBER MUCH...
I ONLY REMEMBER UP TO THE POINT OF FEELING A SHARP PAIN IN MY EAR...
THOSE WOUNDS ...
EXCUSE ME...!
COULD I ASK ALL OF YOU TO STOP WITH THE LOUD VOICES AND OUTLANDISH TALK?
EVERYONE IN THE SHOP CAN HEAR!
HE'S RIGHT! STOP EMBARRASSIN' HIM, TAMA!
YOU'RE THE ONE DOING IT!!
WELL... YOU'RE ALL WELCOME TO STAY HERE FOR A WHILE. IT'S GETTING LATE... IT'S ALMOST TIME FOR MY PARENTS TO RETURN.

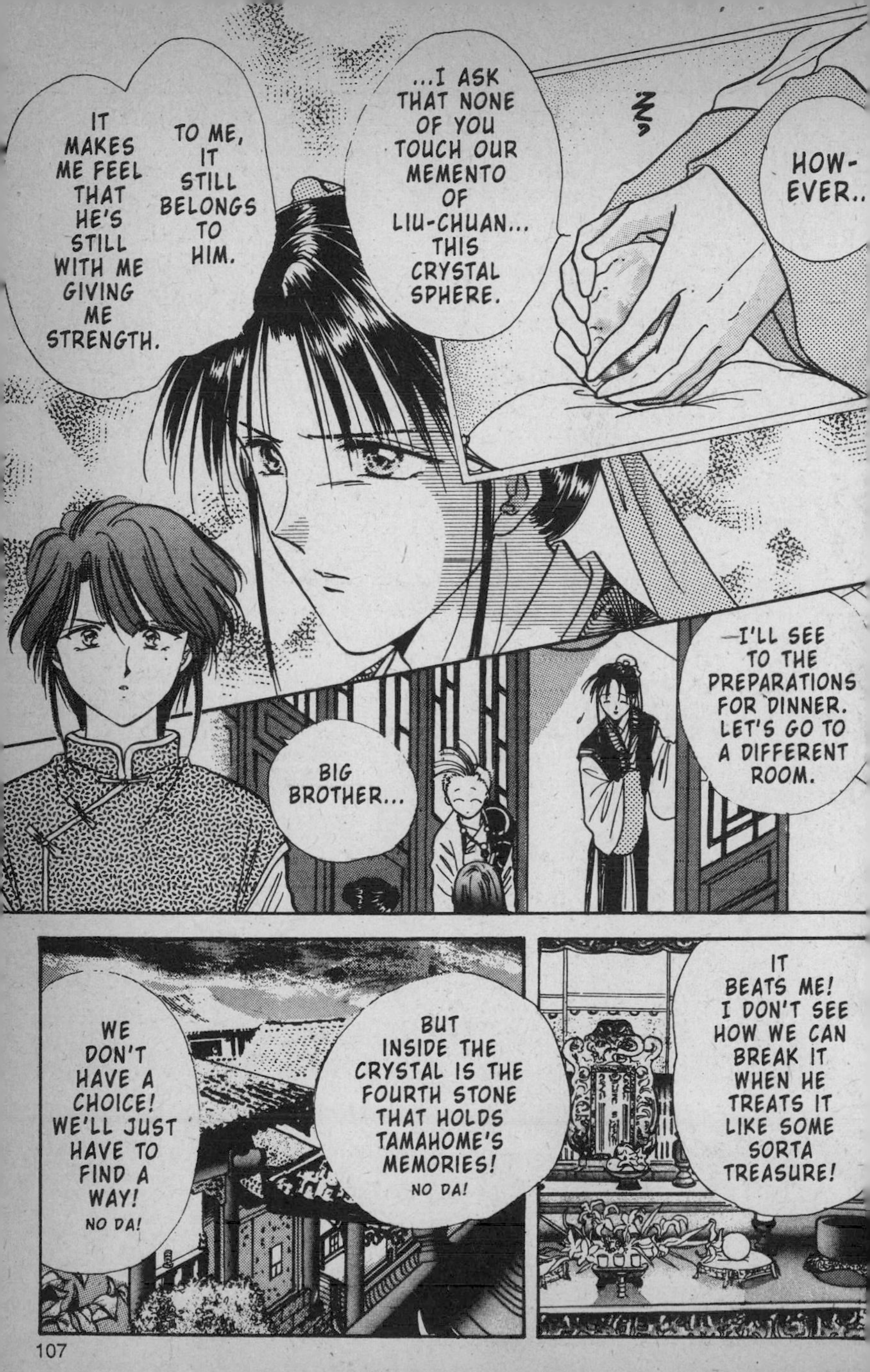
HOW-EVER...
...I ASK THAT NONE OF YOU TOUCH OUR MEMENTO OF LIU-CHUAN... THIS CRYSTAL SPHERE.
TO ME, IT STILL BELONGS TO HIM.
IT MAKES ME FEEL THAT HE'S STILL WITH ME GIVING ME STRENGTH.
—I'LL SEE TO THE PREPARATIONS FOR DINNER. LET'S GO TO A DIFFERENT ROOM.
BIG BROTHER...
IT BEATS ME! I DON'T SEE HOW WE CAN BREAK IT WHEN HE TREATS IT LIKE SOME SORTA TREASURE!
BUT INSIDE THE CRYSTAL IS THE FOURTH STONE THAT HOLDS TAMAHOME'S MEMORIES! NO DA!
WE DON'T HAVE A CHOICE! WE'LL JUST HAVE TO FIND A WAY! NO DA!

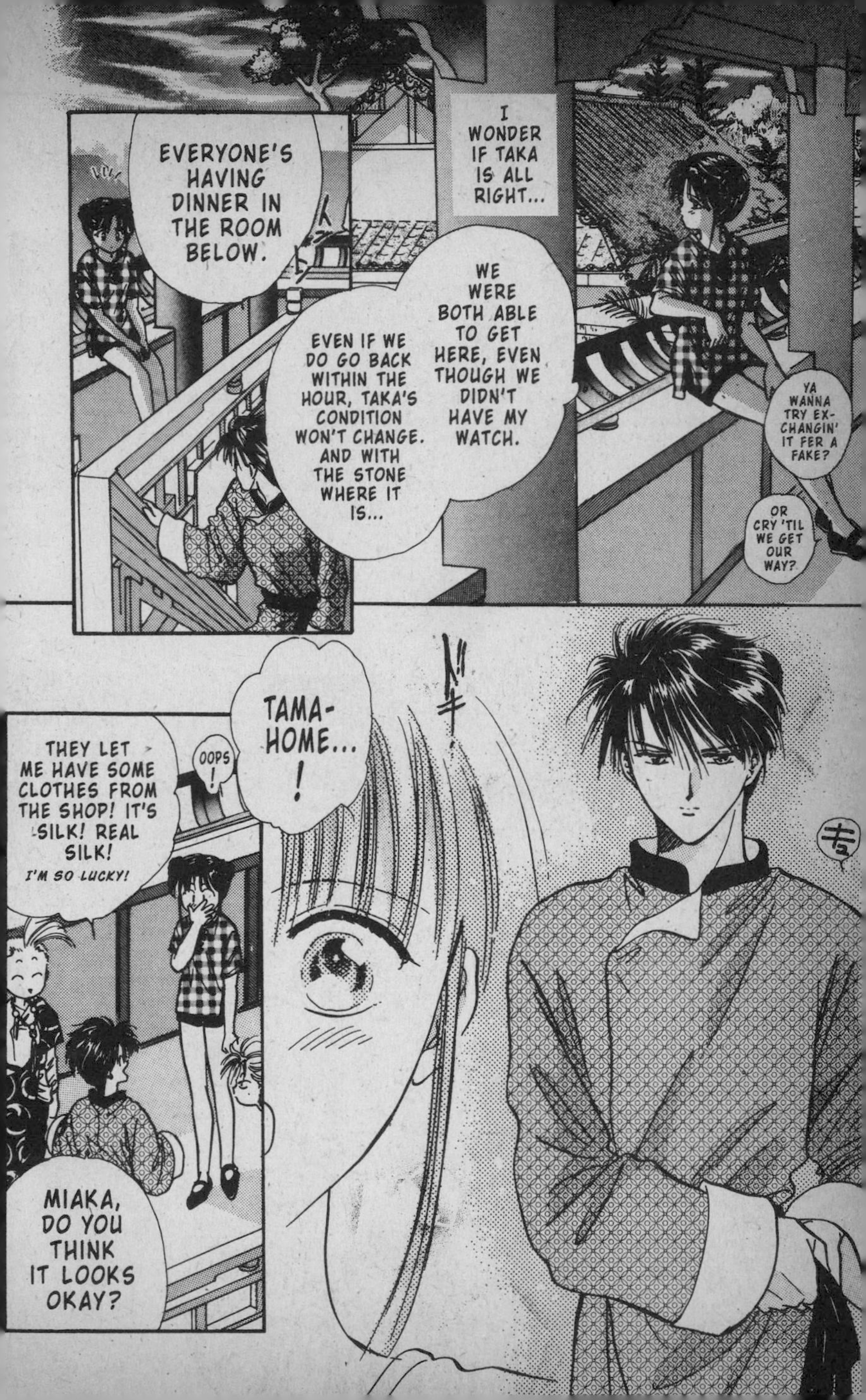
I WONDER IF TAKA IS ALL RIGHT...
WE WERE BOTH ABLE TO GET HERE, EVEN THOUGH WE DIDN'T HAVE MY WATCH.
EVEN IF WE DO GO BACK WITHIN THE HOUR, TAKA'S CONDITION WON'T CHANGE. AND WITH THE STONE WHERE IT IS...
YA WANNA TRY EX-CHANGIN' IT FER A FAKE?
OR CRY 'TIL WE GET OUR WAY?
EVERYONE'S HAVING DINNER IN THE ROOM BELOW.
TAMA-HOME...!
OOPS!
THEY LET ME HAVE SOME CLOTHES FROM THE SHOP! IT'S SILK! REAL SILK!
I'M SO LUCKY!
MIAKA, DO YOU THINK IT LOOKS OKAY?

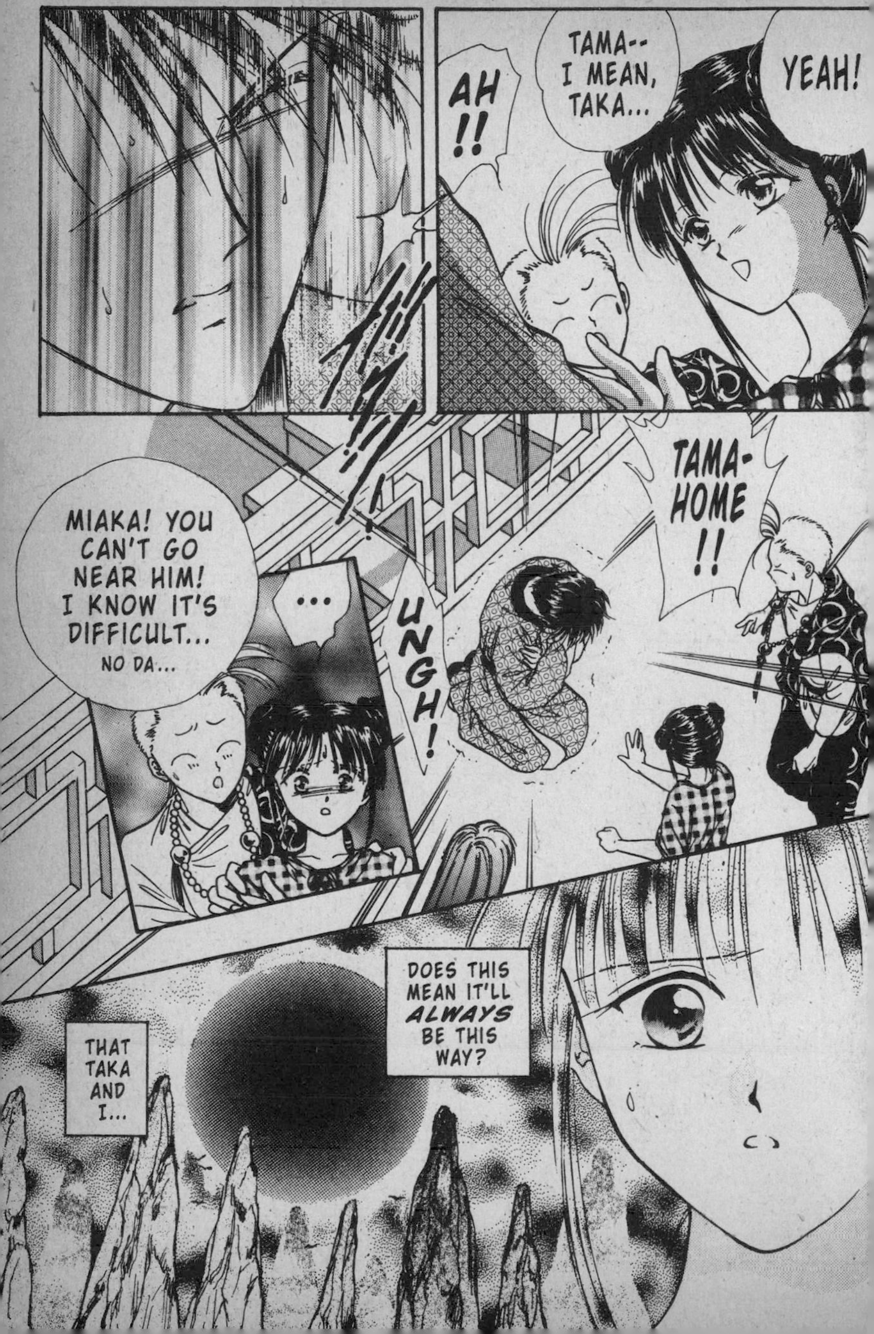
YEAH!
TAMA-- I MEAN, TAKA...
AH !!
TAMA-HOME !!
UNGH!
MIAKA! YOU CAN'T GO NEAR HIM! I KNOW IT'S DIFFICULT... NO DA...
...
DOES THIS MEAN IT'LL *ALWAYS* BE THIS WAY?
THAT TAKA AND I...

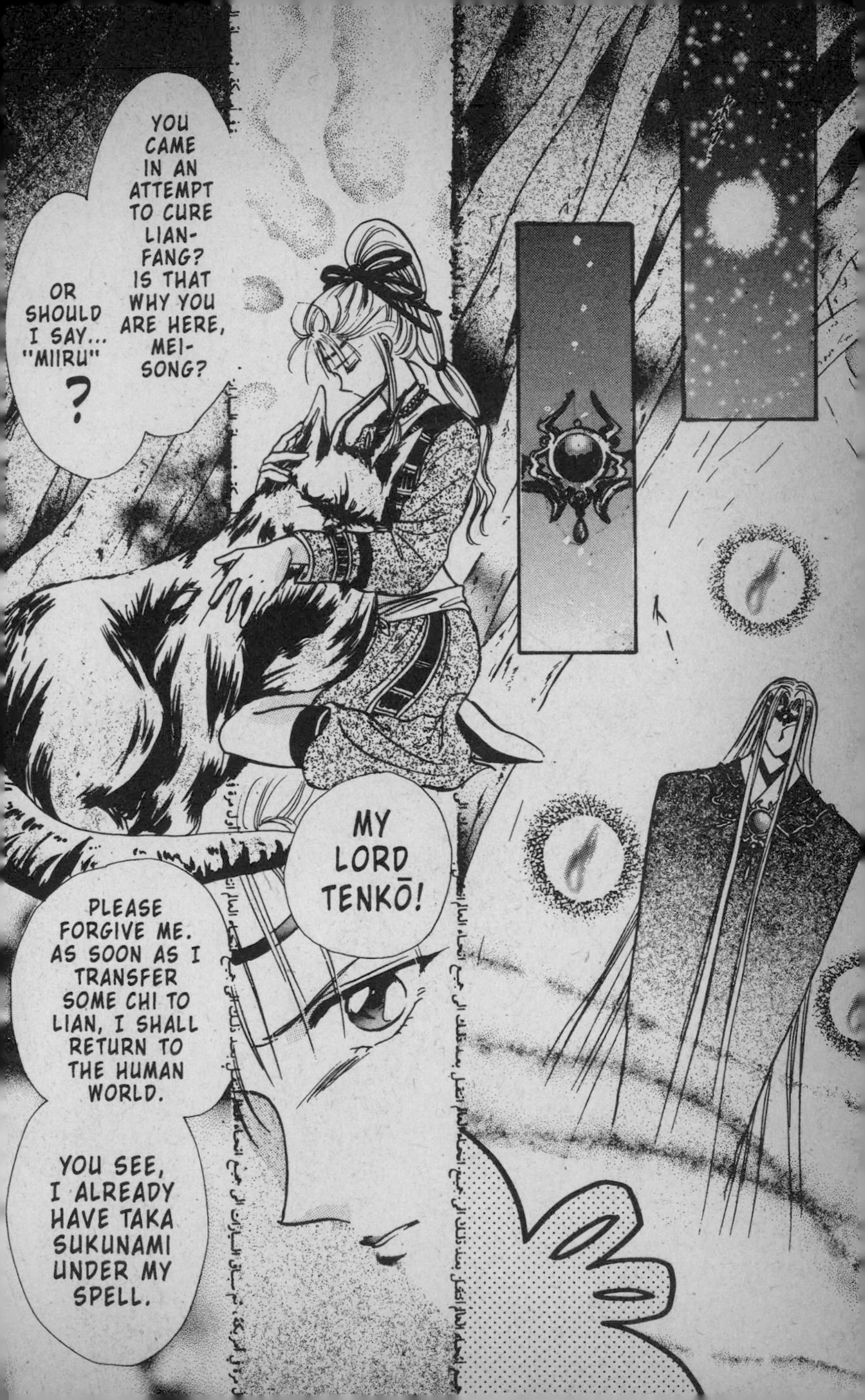
YOU CAME IN AN ATTEMPT TO CURE LIAN-FANG? IS THAT WHY YOU ARE HERE, MEI-SONG?
OR SHOULD I SAY... "MIIRU" ?
MY LORD TENKŌ!
PLEASE FORGIVE ME. AS SOON AS I TRANSFER SOME CHI TO LIAN, I SHALL RETURN TO THE HUMAN WORLD.
YOU SEE, I ALREADY HAVE TAKA SUKUNAMI UNDER MY SPELL.

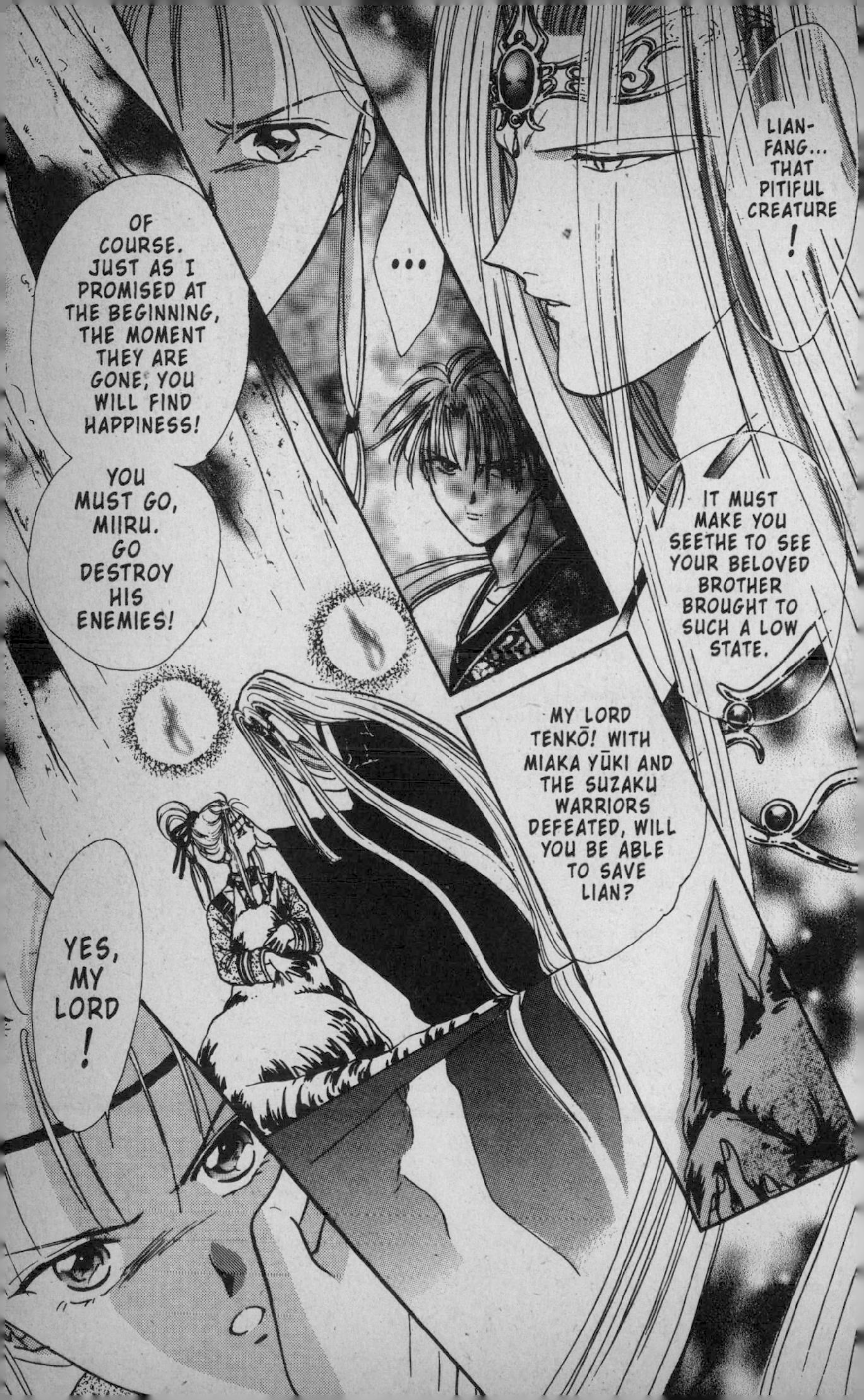
LIAN-FANG... THAT PITIFUL CREATURE!
...
IT MUST MAKE YOU SEETHE TO SEE YOUR BELOVED BROTHER BROUGHT TO SUCH A LOW STATE.
MY LORD TENKŌ! WITH MIAKA YŪKI AND THE SUZAKU WARRIORS DEFEATED, WILL YOU BE ABLE TO SAVE LIAN?
OF COURSE. JUST AS I PROMISED AT THE BEGINNING, THE MOMENT THEY ARE GONE, YOU WILL FIND HAPPINESS!
YOU MUST GO, MIIRU. GO DESTROY HIS ENEMIES!
YES, MY LORD!

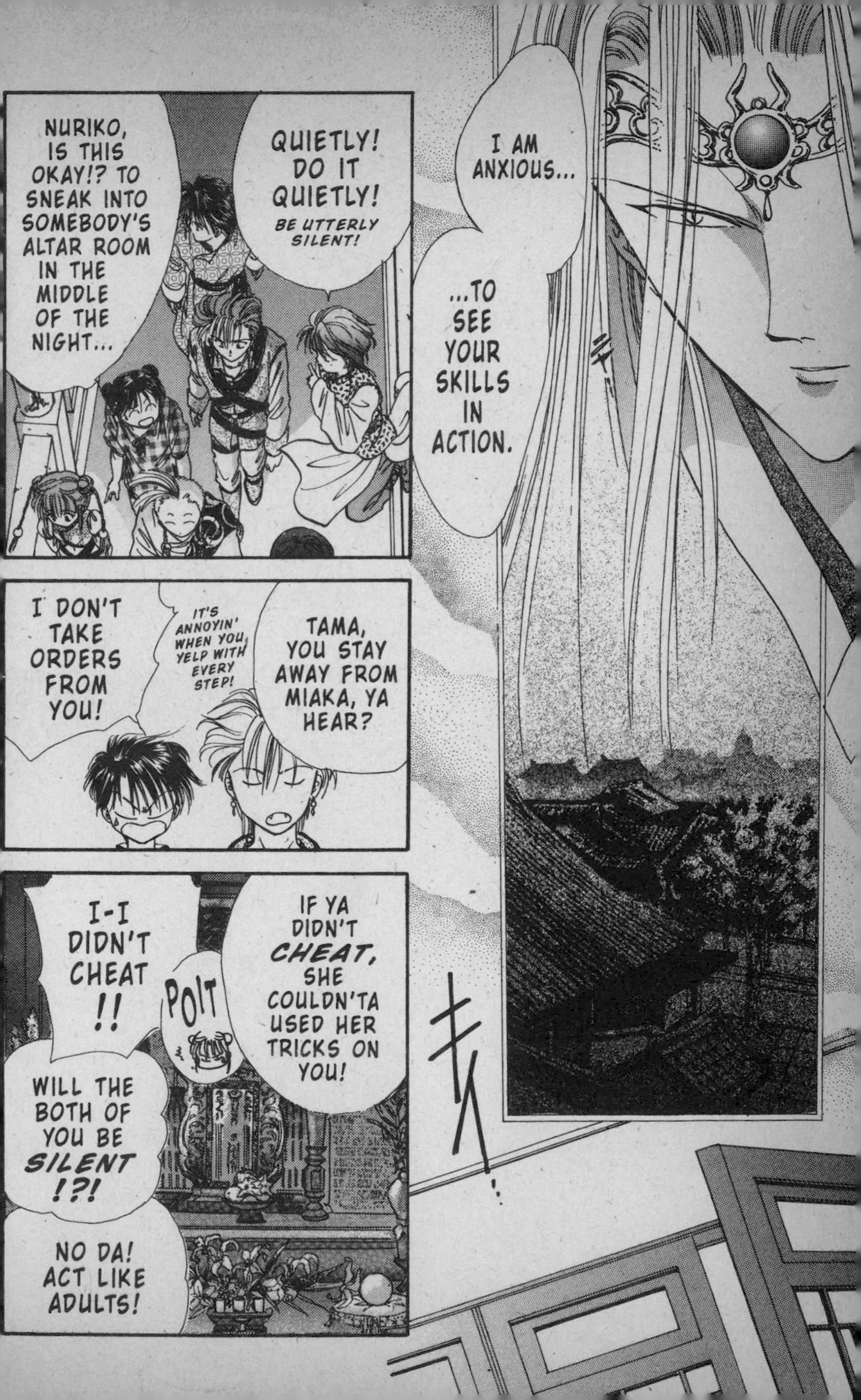
I AM ANXIOUS...
...TO SEE YOUR SKILLS IN ACTION.
QUIETLY! DO IT QUIETLY!
BE UTTERLY SILENT!
NURIKO, IS THIS OKAY!? TO SNEAK INTO SOMEBODY'S ALTAR ROOM IN THE MIDDLE OF THE NIGHT...
TAMA, YOU STAY AWAY FROM MIAKA, YA HEAR?
IT'S ANNOYIN' WHEN YOU YELP WITH EVERY STEP!
I DON'T TAKE ORDERS FROM YOU!
IF YA DIDN'T CHEAT, SHE COULDN'TA USED HER TRICKS ON YOU!
POIT
I-I DIDN'T CHEAT!!
WILL THE BOTH OF YOU BE SILENT!?!
NO DA! ACT LIKE ADULTS!

Assassin

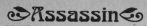

In an earlier section, I talked about readers who said that they wouldn't acknowledge fans who became fans just because of the anime. Before long, I got a lot of letters complaining about that opinion saying, "I could cry," or "no fair!" Many said things like this, "Hey, I saw an episode or two of the anime, and I went right out and bought all of the graphic novels! That could be considered becoming a fan through the original work, too!!" Ahh... yeah. ☺ The people writing in have a point. There are people who never had the chance to hear about *Fushigi Yûgi* until the anime came out, but once they did, their love for the series was just as strong as anyone else's. Those people fell in love with the story, and it makes me very happy that the number of fans increased after it became an anime. I can only say I'm moved that a whole lot of new people are emotionally affected by a story that came from the bottom of my heart. People can make a lot of friends through fan groups and have something to talk about. Even if they have different perspectives or have different favorite characters, they can have their worlds expanded by the points of view of others. At least, that's what I'd like to see happen. I'm so mature! If I were childish, I'd want to monopolize the work only for myself! ☺ So, everyone, be sure to go forward with an open heart! Remember there will be new readers too... so to you long-time readers, don't look disparagingly on any of the new fans!

While I was thinking all of those things, I got this letter that said, "I knew that shōjo manga = high school romance, ♥♥♥ so I never read your stuff." KA-WHUMP.

A lot of people think shōjo manga is boring, huh? No, I understand their point. ☺ When I was in 6th grade, there was someone I knew who said, "Shōjo manga are just boring romances," and threw the books out. But why bring it up now? Humph! Is all of this just revenge for ancient humiliations? ☺

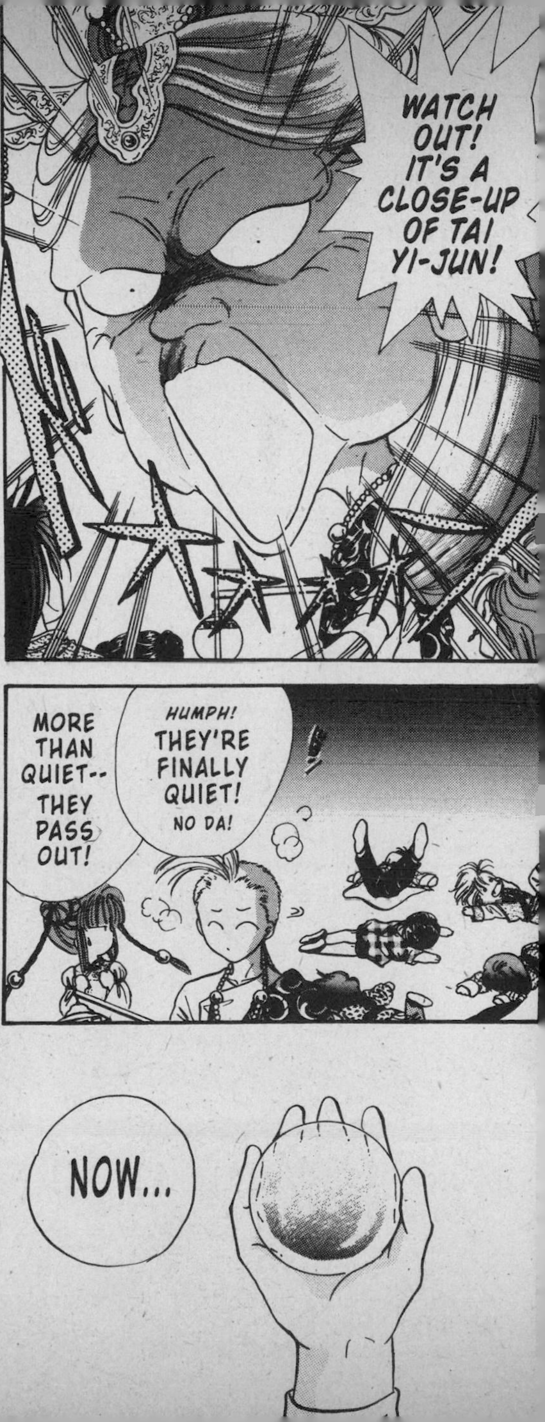
WATCH OUT! IT'S A CLOSE-UP OF TAI YI-JUN!
HUMPH! THEY'RE FINALLY QUIET! NO DA!
MORE THAN QUIET-- THEY PASS OUT!
NOW...

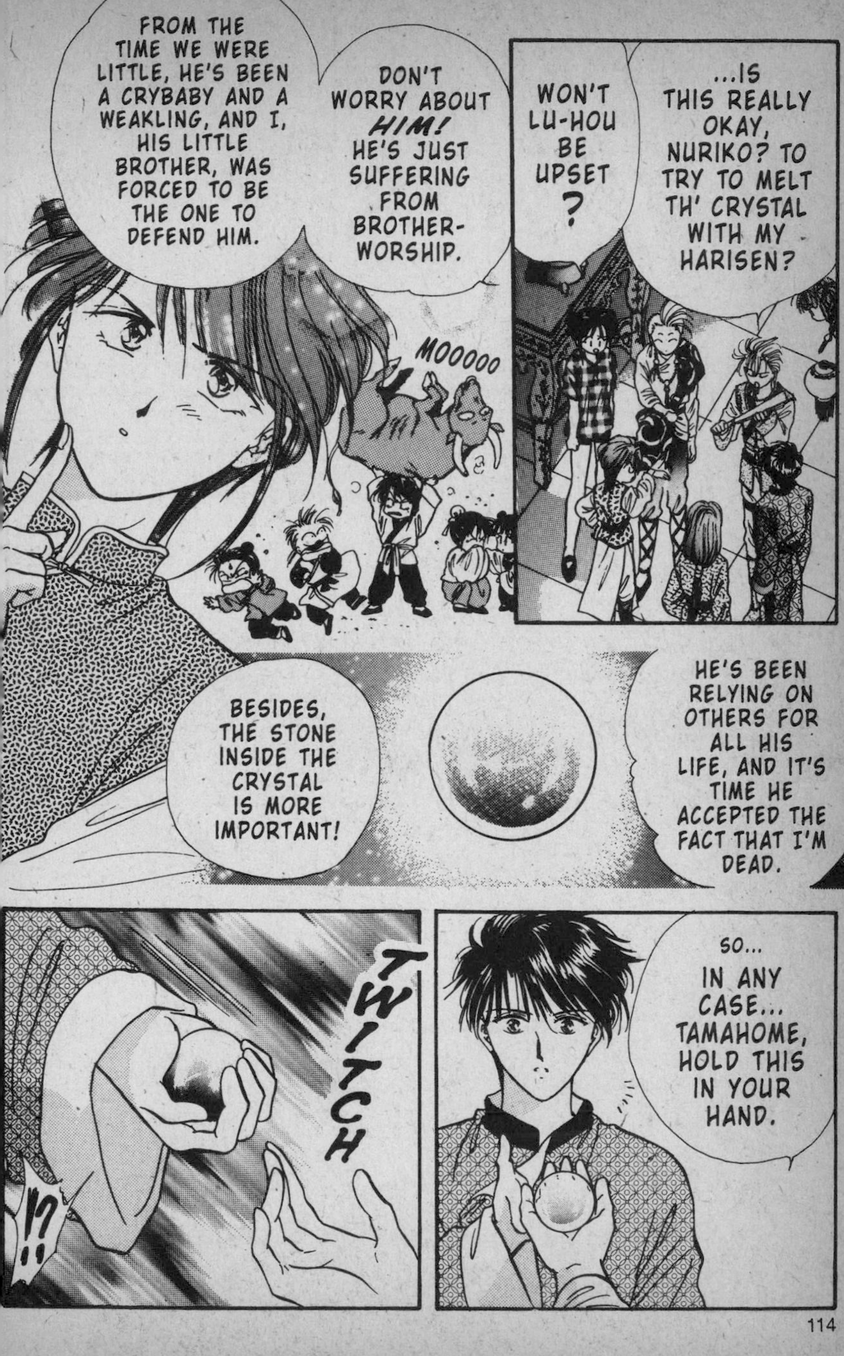
...IS THIS REALLY OKAY, NURIKO? TO TRY TO MELT TH' CRYSTAL WITH MY HARISEN?
WON'T LU-HOU BE UPSET?
DON'T WORRY ABOUT *HIM!* HE'S JUST SUFFERING FROM BROTHER-WORSHIP.
FROM THE TIME WE WERE LITTLE, HE'S BEEN A CRYBABY AND A WEAKLING, AND I, HIS LITTLE BROTHER, WAS FORCED TO BE THE ONE TO DEFEND HIM.
MOOOOO
HE'S BEEN RELYING ON OTHERS FOR ALL HIS LIFE, AND IT'S TIME HE ACCEPTED THE FACT THAT I'M DEAD.
BESIDES, THE STONE INSIDE THE CRYSTAL IS MORE IMPORTANT!
SO... IN ANY CASE... TAMAHOME, HOLD THIS IN YOUR HAND.
TWITCH
!?

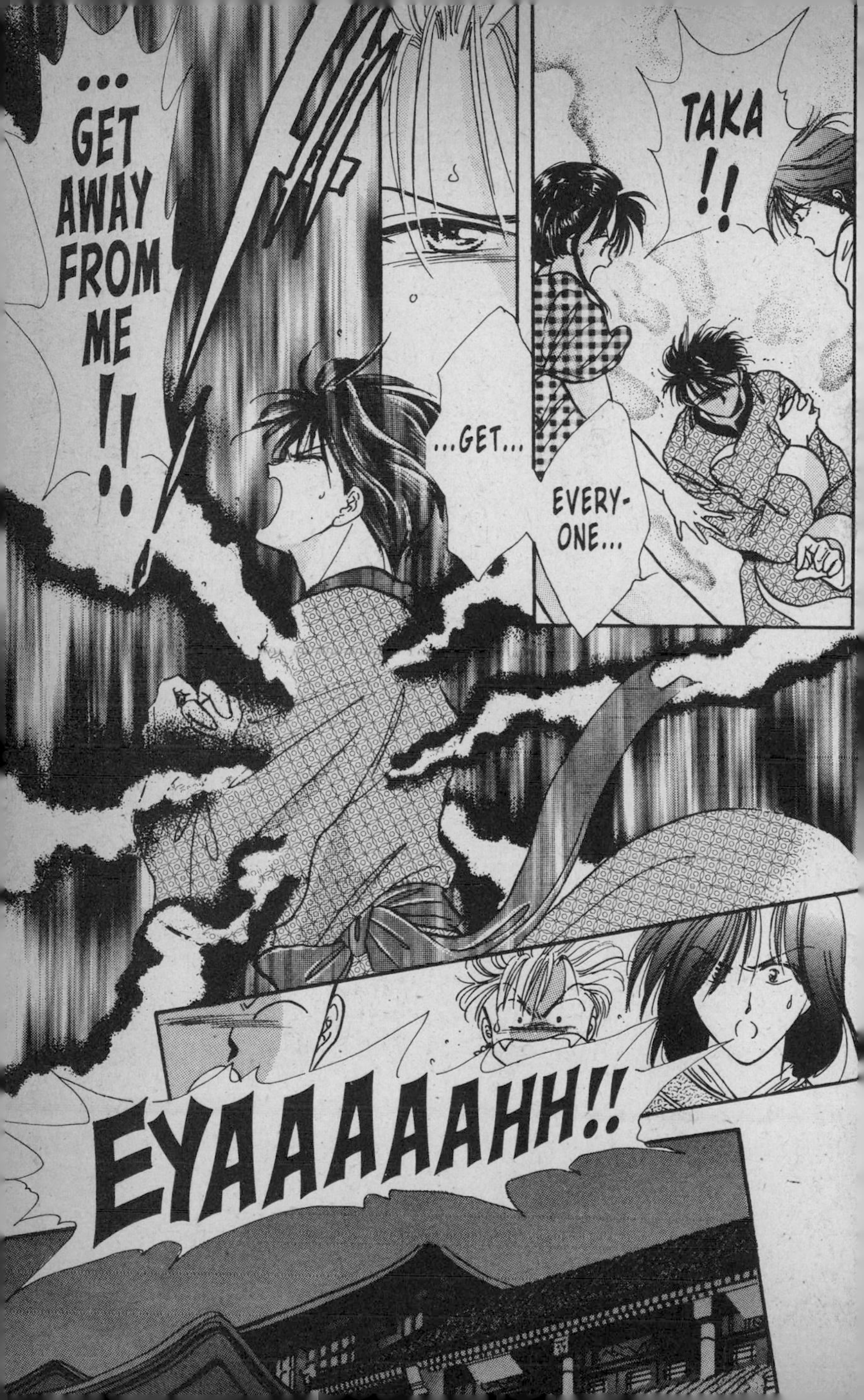
TAKA!!
...GET...
EVERY-ONE...
...GET AWAY FROM ME!!
EYAAAAAHH!!

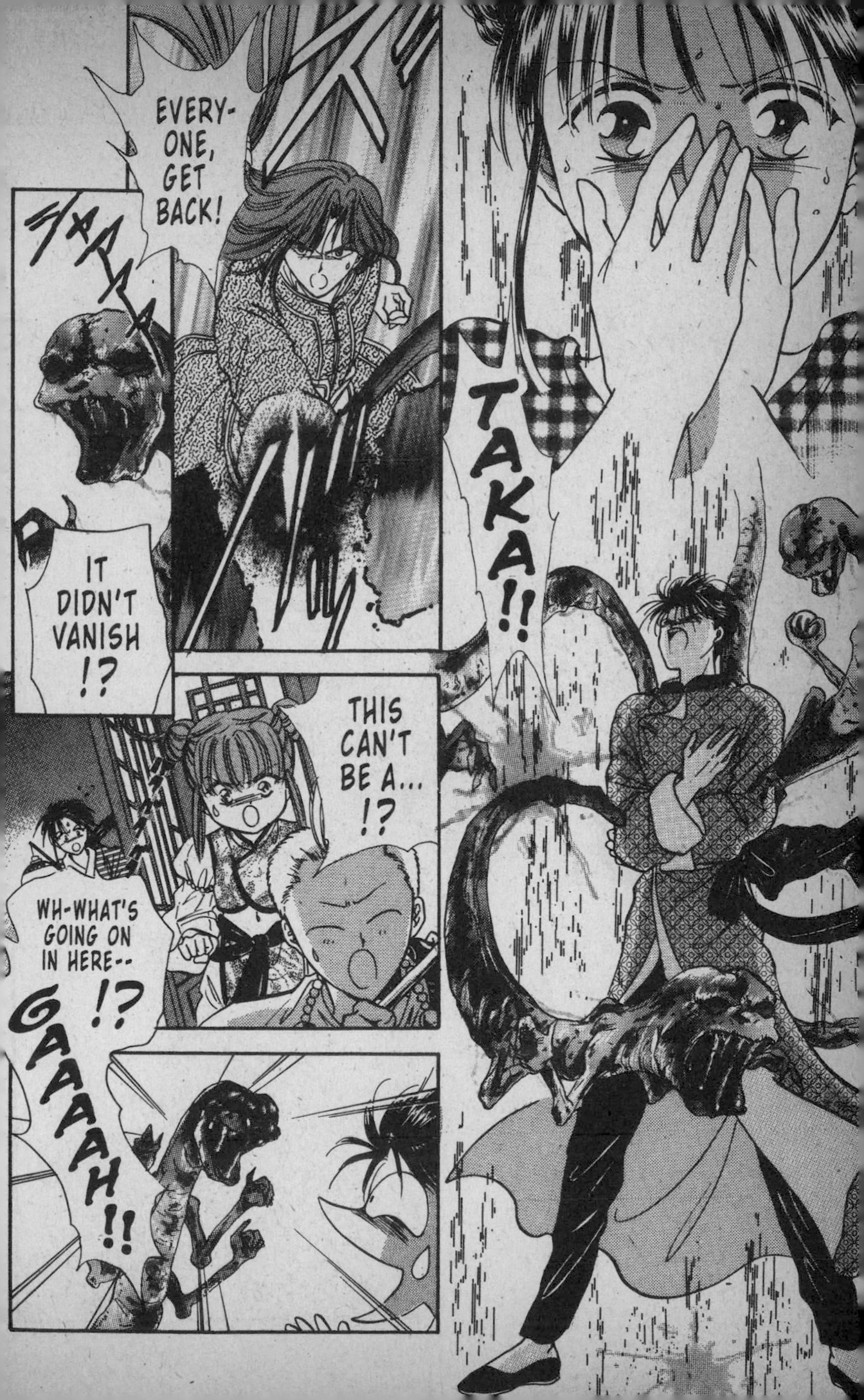
TAKA!!
EVERY-ONE, GET BACK!
IT DIDN'T VANISH!?
THIS CAN'T BE A...!?
WH-WHAT'S GOING ON IN HERE--!?
GAAAAH!!

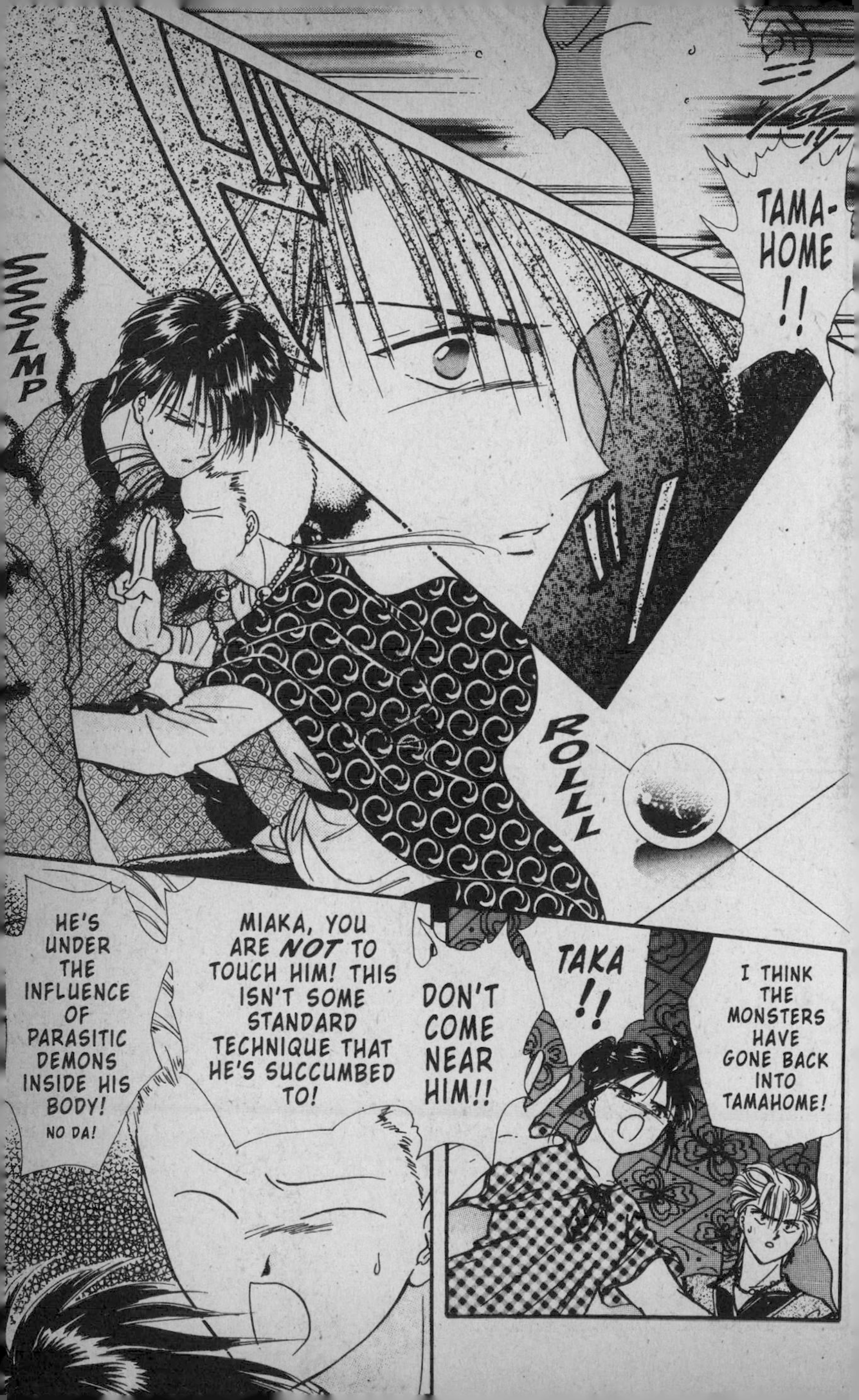
TAMA-HOME!!
SSSLMP
ROLLL
I THINK THE MONSTERS HAVE GONE BACK INTO TAMAHOME!
TAKA!!
DON'T COME NEAR HIM!!
MIAKA, YOU ARE NOT TO TOUCH HIM! THIS ISN'T SOME STANDARD TECHNIQUE THAT HE'S SUCCUMBED TO!
HE'S UNDER THE INFLUENCE OF PARASITIC DEMONS INSIDE HIS BODY!
NO DA!

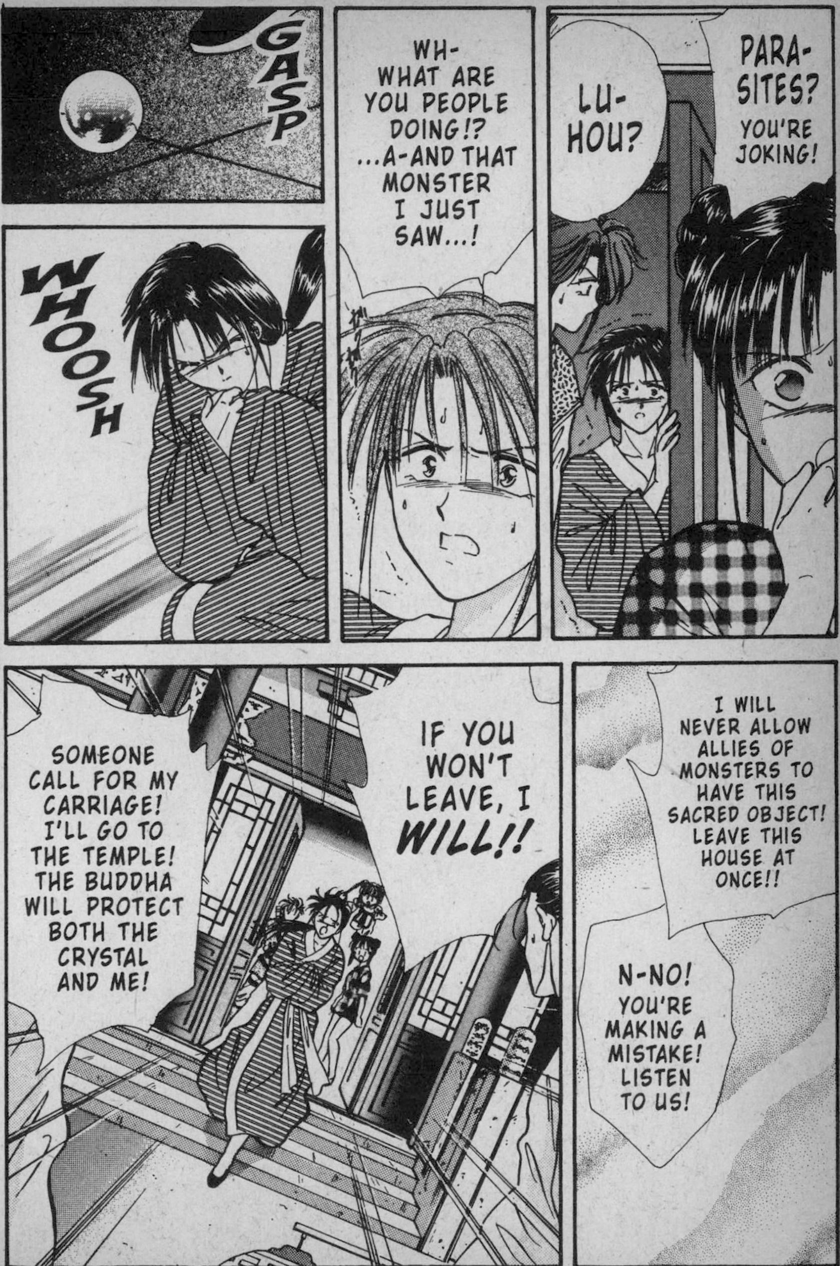
PARA-SITES? YOU'RE JOKING!
LU-HOU?
WH- WHAT ARE YOU PEOPLE DOING!? ...A-AND THAT MONSTER I JUST SAW...!
GASP
WHOOSH
I WILL NEVER ALLOW ALLIES OF MONSTERS TO HAVE THIS SACRED OBJECT! LEAVE THIS HOUSE AT ONCE!!
N-NO! YOU'RE MAKING A MISTAKE! LISTEN TO US!
IF YOU WON'T LEAVE, I *WILL!!*
SOMEONE CALL FOR MY CARRIAGE! I'LL GO TO THE TEMPLE! THE BUDDHA WILL PROTECT BOTH THE CRYSTAL AND ME!

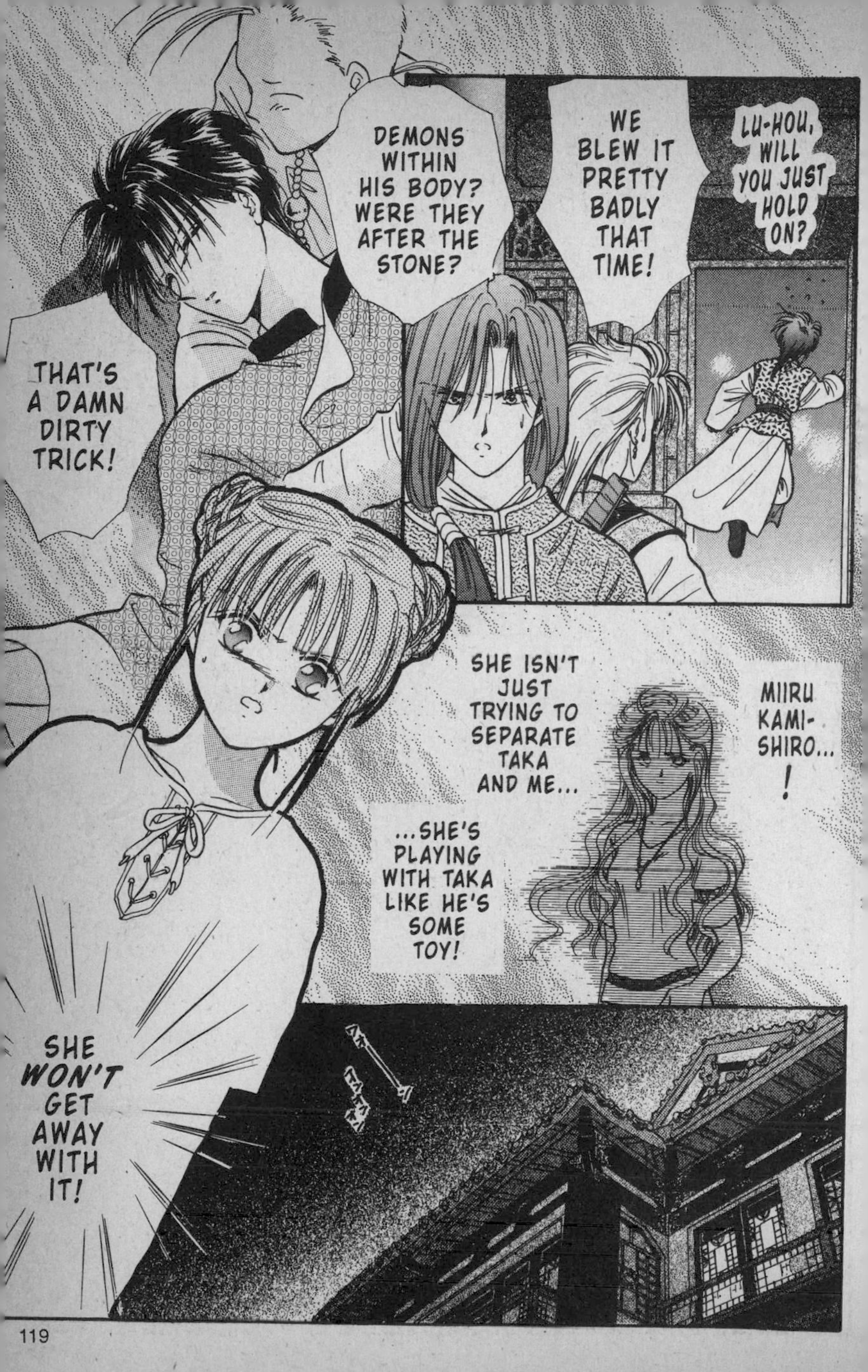
LU-HOU, WILL YOU JUST HOLD ON?
WE BLEW IT PRETTY BADLY THAT TIME!
DEMONS WITHIN HIS BODY? WERE THEY AFTER THE STONE?
THAT'S A DAMN DIRTY TRICK!
MIIRU KAMI-SHIRO...!
SHE ISN'T JUST TRYING TO SEPARATE TAKA AND ME...
...SHE'S PLAYING WITH TAKA LIKE HE'S SOME TOY!
SHE *WON'T* GET AWAY WITH IT!

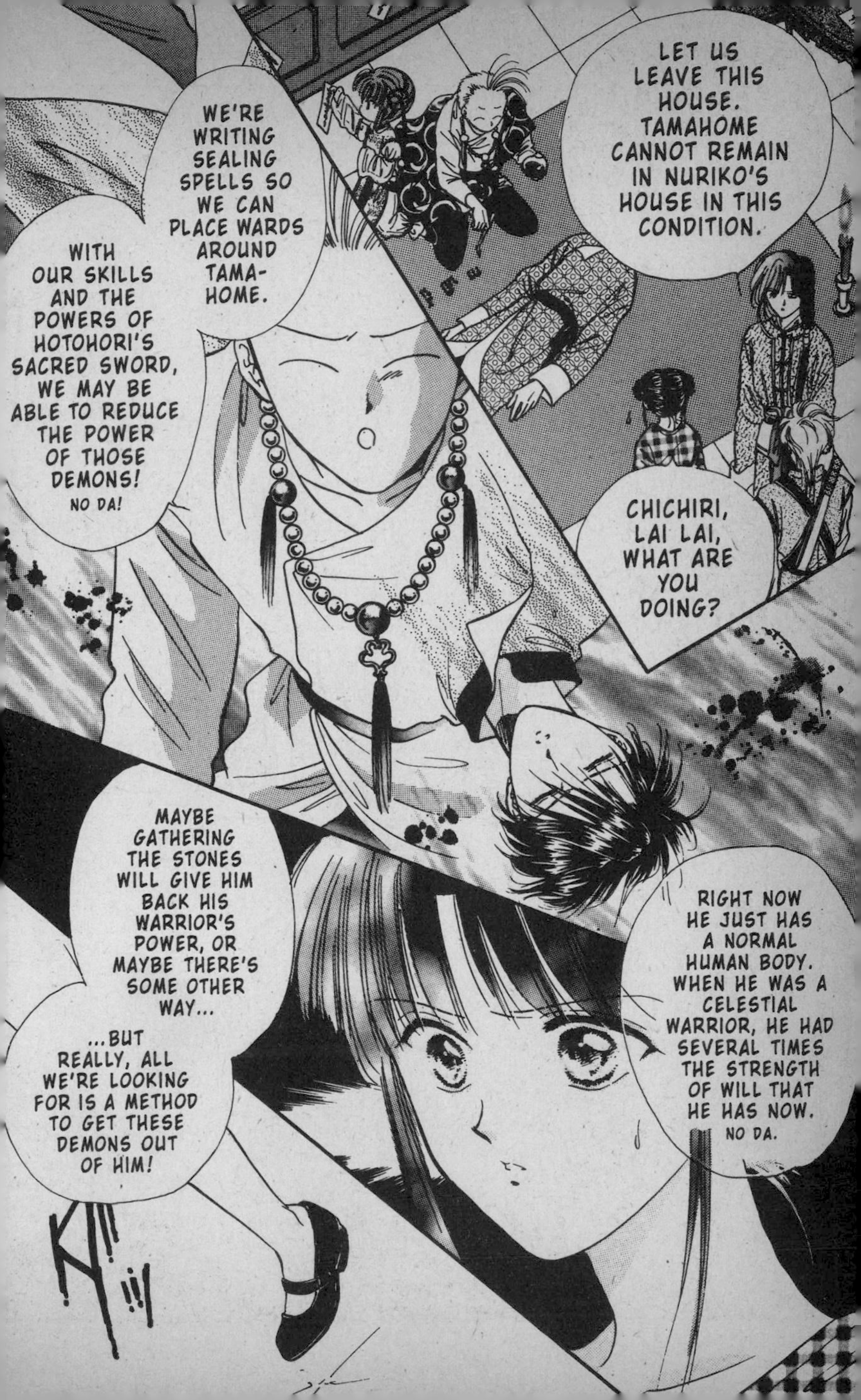
LET US LEAVE THIS HOUSE. TAMAHOME CANNOT REMAIN IN NURIKO'S HOUSE IN THIS CONDITION.
CHICHIRI, LAI LAI, WHAT ARE YOU DOING?
WE'RE WRITING SEALING SPELLS SO WE CAN PLACE WARDS AROUND TAMA-HOME.
WITH OUR SKILLS AND THE POWERS OF HOTOHORI'S SACRED SWORD, WE MAY BE ABLE TO REDUCE THE POWER OF THOSE DEMONS! NO DA!
RIGHT NOW HE JUST HAS A NORMAL HUMAN BODY. WHEN HE WAS A CELESTIAL WARRIOR, HE HAD SEVERAL TIMES THE STRENGTH OF WILL THAT HE HAS NOW. NO DA.
MAYBE GATHERING THE STONES WILL GIVE HIM BACK HIS WARRIOR'S POWER, OR MAYBE THERE'S SOME OTHER WAY...
...BUT REALLY, ALL WE'RE LOOKING FOR IS A METHOD TO GET THESE DEMONS OUT OF HIM!

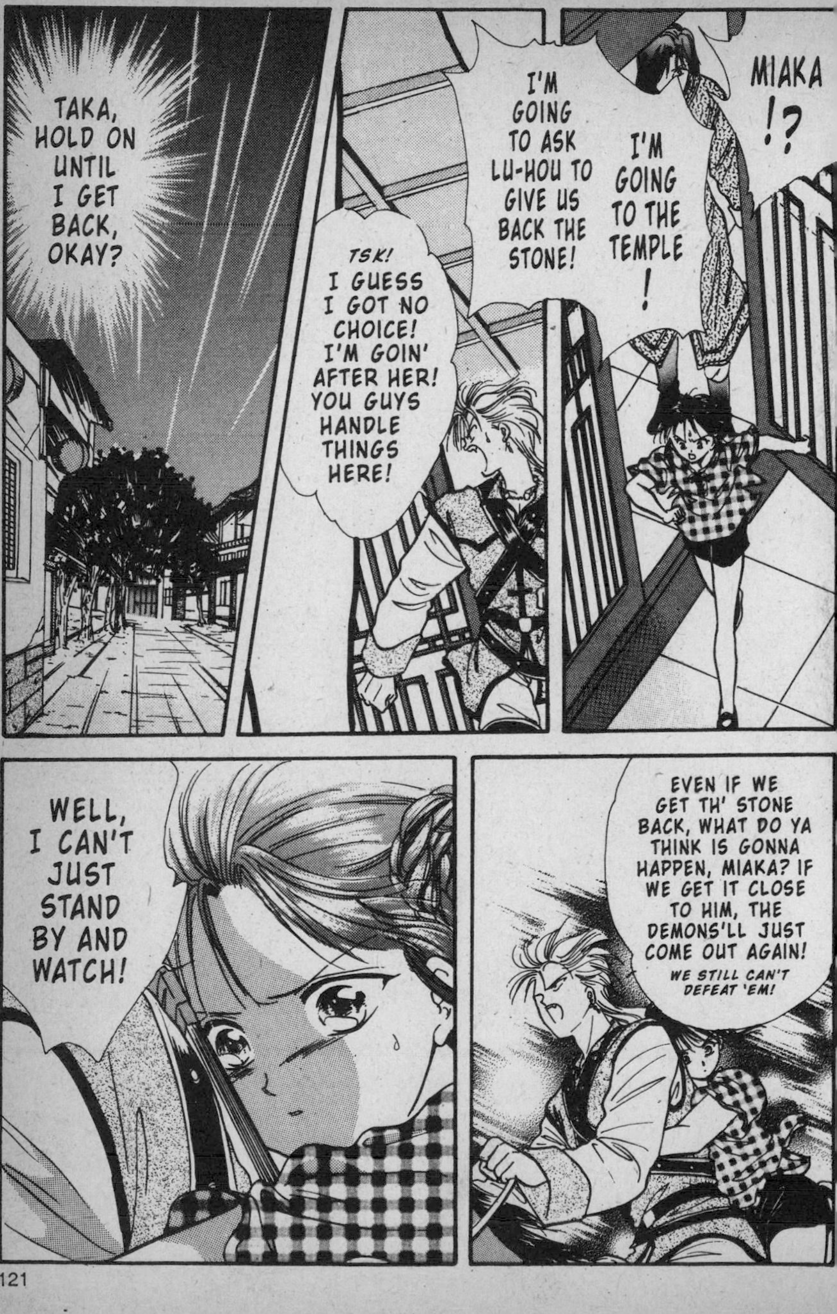
MIAKA !?
I'M GOING TO THE TEMPLE!
I'M GOING TO ASK LU-HOU TO GIVE US BACK THE STONE!
TSK! I GUESS I GOT NO CHOICE! I'M GOIN' AFTER HER! YOU GUYS HANDLE THINGS HERE!
TAKA, HOLD ON UNTIL I GET BACK, OKAY?
EVEN IF WE GET TH' STONE BACK, WHAT DO YA THINK IS GONNA HAPPEN, MIAKA? IF WE GET IT CLOSE TO HIM, THE DEMONS'LL JUST COME OUT AGAIN! WE STILL CAN'T DEFEAT 'EM!
WELL, I CAN'T JUST STAND BY AND WATCH!

LISTEN, I CAN'T BE NEAR HIM, SO THE LEAST I CAN DO IS TRY TO GET THE STONE BACK!
DON'T IT JUST PISS YOU OFF?
EH?
IF YA ASK ME, HIS GETTIN' CURSED LIKE THIS IS ALL HIS OWN FAULT!
TAMAHOME WENT T' THAT WOMAN ON HIS OWN, RIGHT? AND HIS EXCUSE THAT HE DON'T REMEMBER IS TOO EASY AN ANSWER!
WHOOSH
Y'KNOW WHAT I MEAN! THE WAY SOMETHIN' HAPPENED BETWEEN THIS MIIRU WOMAN AND TAMA-HOME!
!

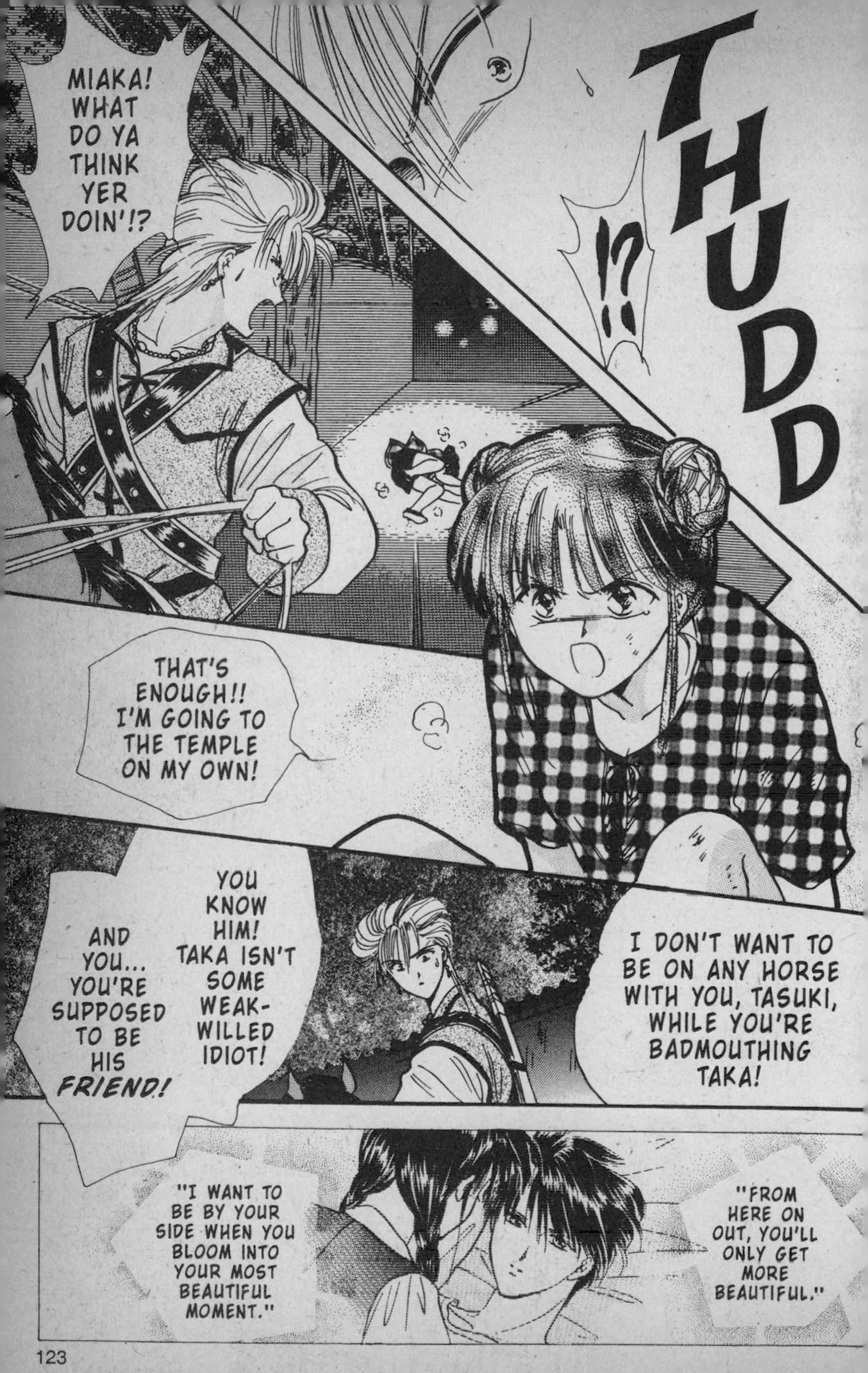
THUD
!?!!
MIAKA! WHAT DO YA THINK YER DOIN'!?
THAT'S ENOUGH!! I'M GOING TO THE TEMPLE ON MY OWN!
I DON'T WANT TO BE ON ANY HORSE WITH YOU, TASUKI, WHILE YOU'RE BADMOUTHING TAKA!
YOU KNOW HIM! TAKA ISN'T SOME WEAK-WILLED IDIOT!
AND YOU... YOU'RE SUPPOSED TO BE HIS *FRIEND!*
"FROM HERE ON OUT, YOU'LL ONLY GET MORE BEAUTIFUL."
"I WANT TO BE BY YOUR SIDE WHEN YOU BLOOM INTO YOUR MOST BEAUTIFUL MOMENT."

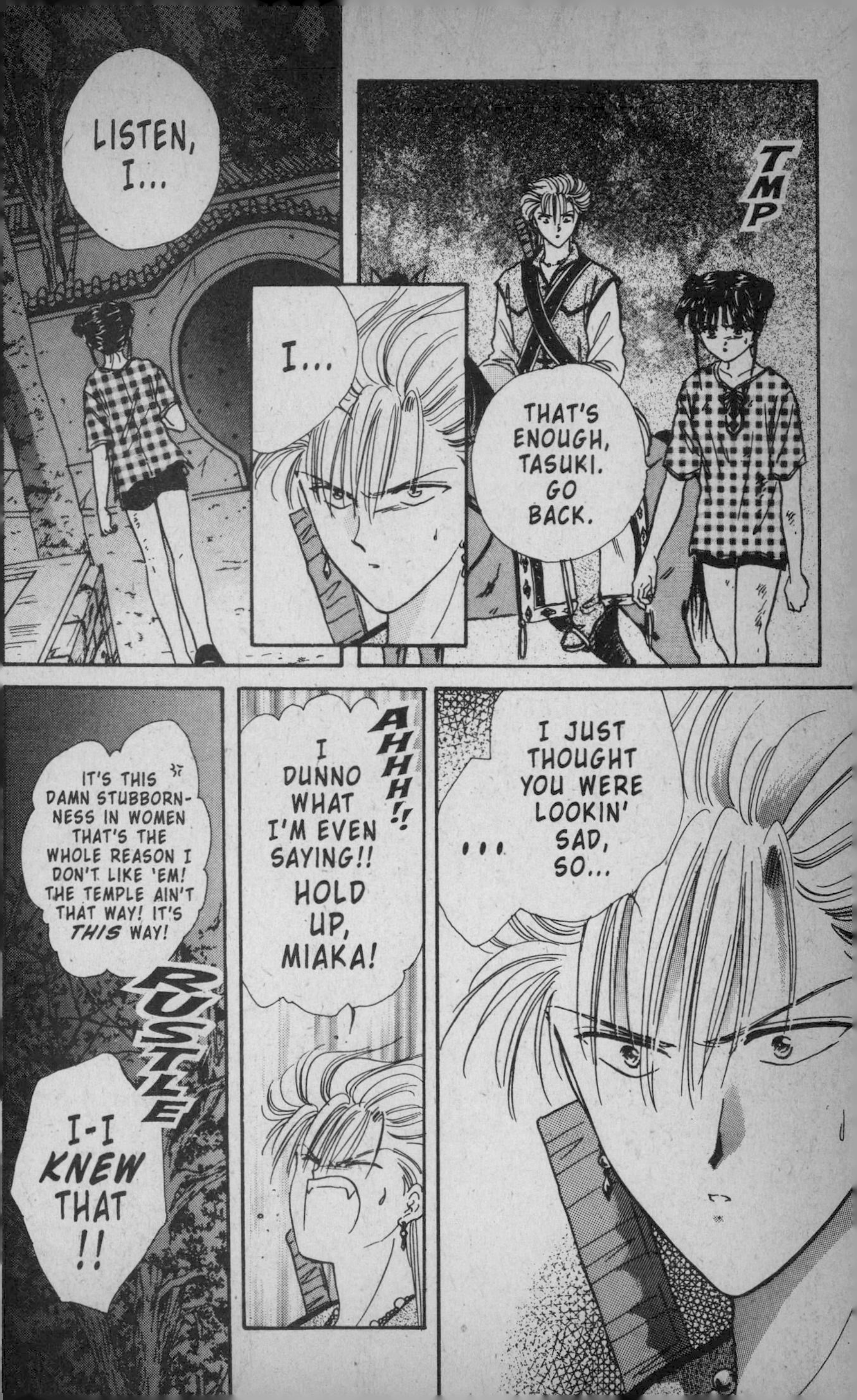
TMP
THAT'S ENOUGH, TASUKI. GO BACK.
I...
LISTEN, I...
I JUST THOUGHT YOU WERE LOOKIN' SAD, SO...
...
AHHHH!!
I DUNNO WHAT I'M EVEN SAYING!! HOLD UP, MIAKA!
IT'S THIS DAMN STUBBORN-NESS IN WOMEN THAT'S THE WHOLE REASON I DON'T LIKE 'EM! THE TEMPLE AIN'T THAT WAY! IT'S THIS WAY!
RUSTLE
I-I KNEW THAT !!

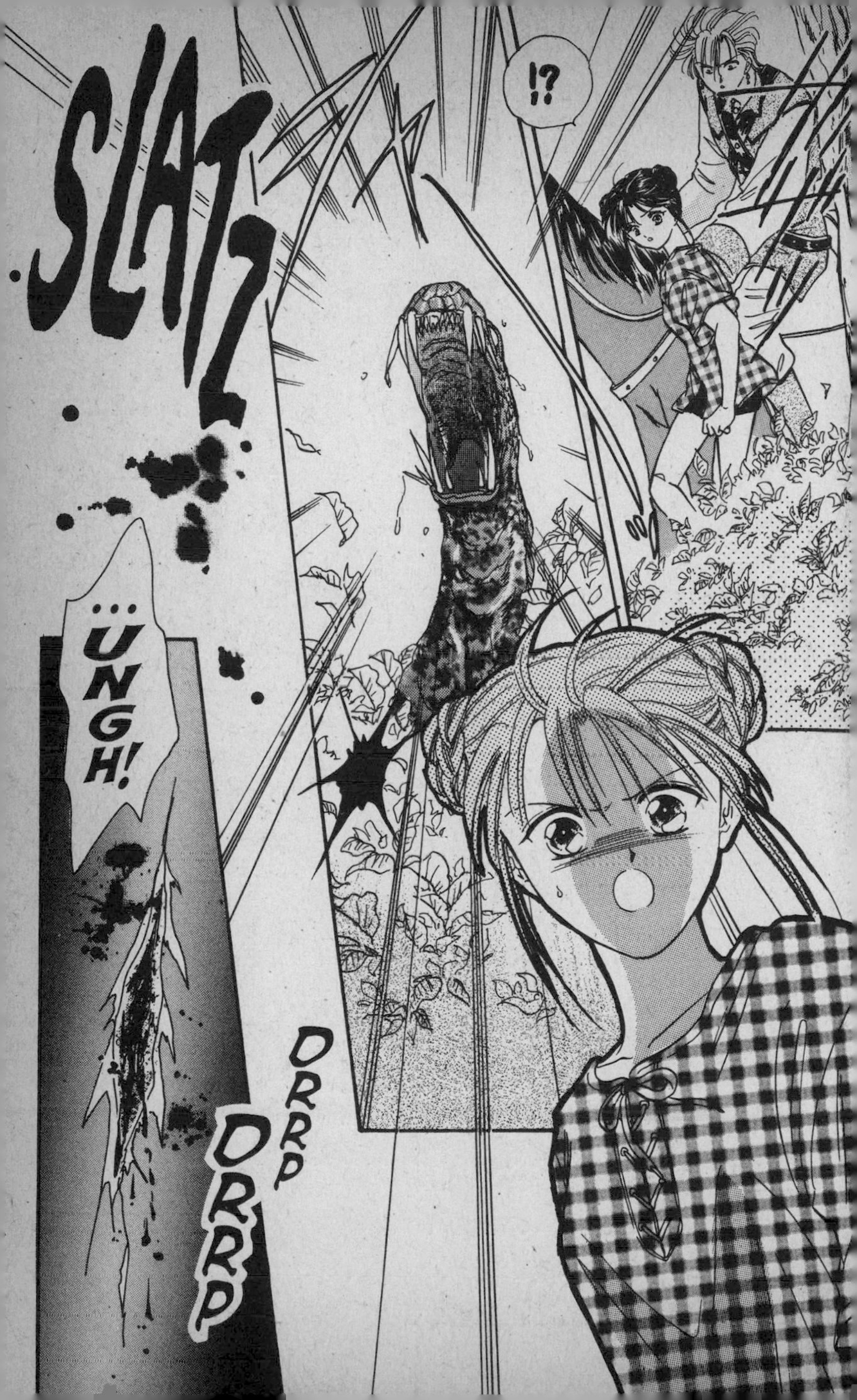
!?
SLAT
...ÜNGH!
DRRP
DRRP

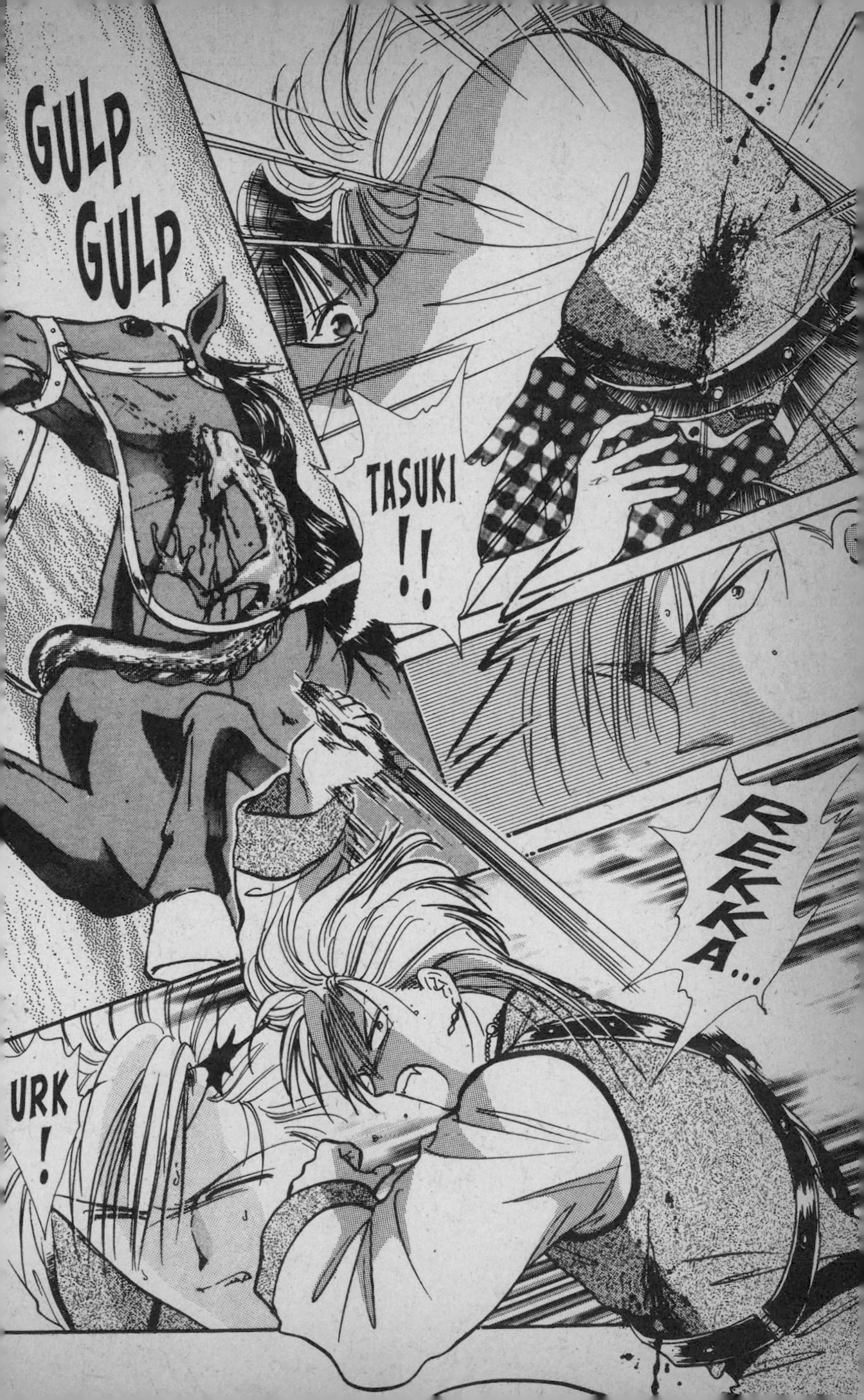
TASUKI !!
GULP GULP
REKKA...
URK !

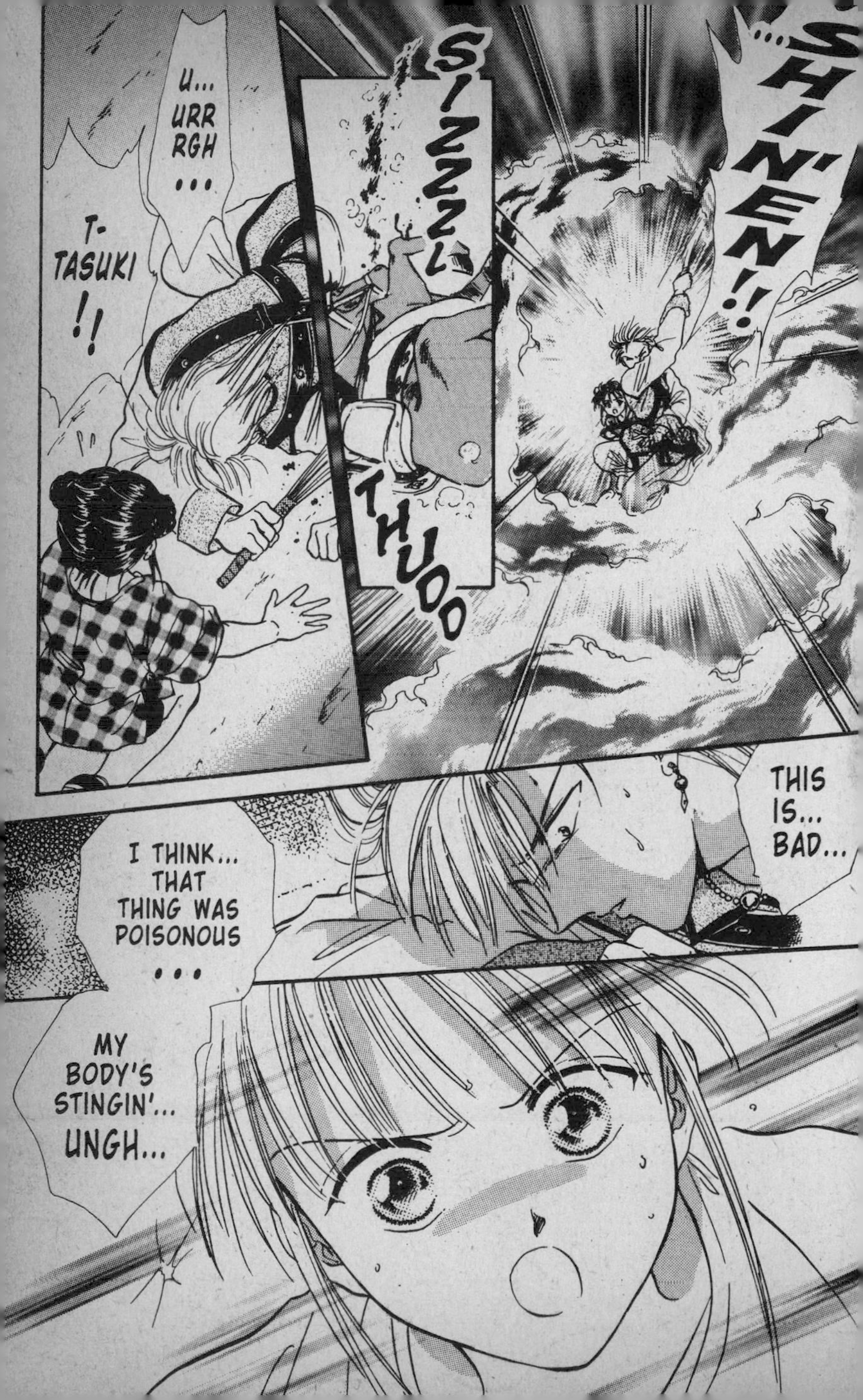
...SHIN'EN!!
SIZZZL
THUDD
U... URRRGH...
T-TASUKI!!
THIS IS... BAD...
I THINK... THAT THING WAS POISONOUS...
MY BODY'S STINGIN'... UNGH...

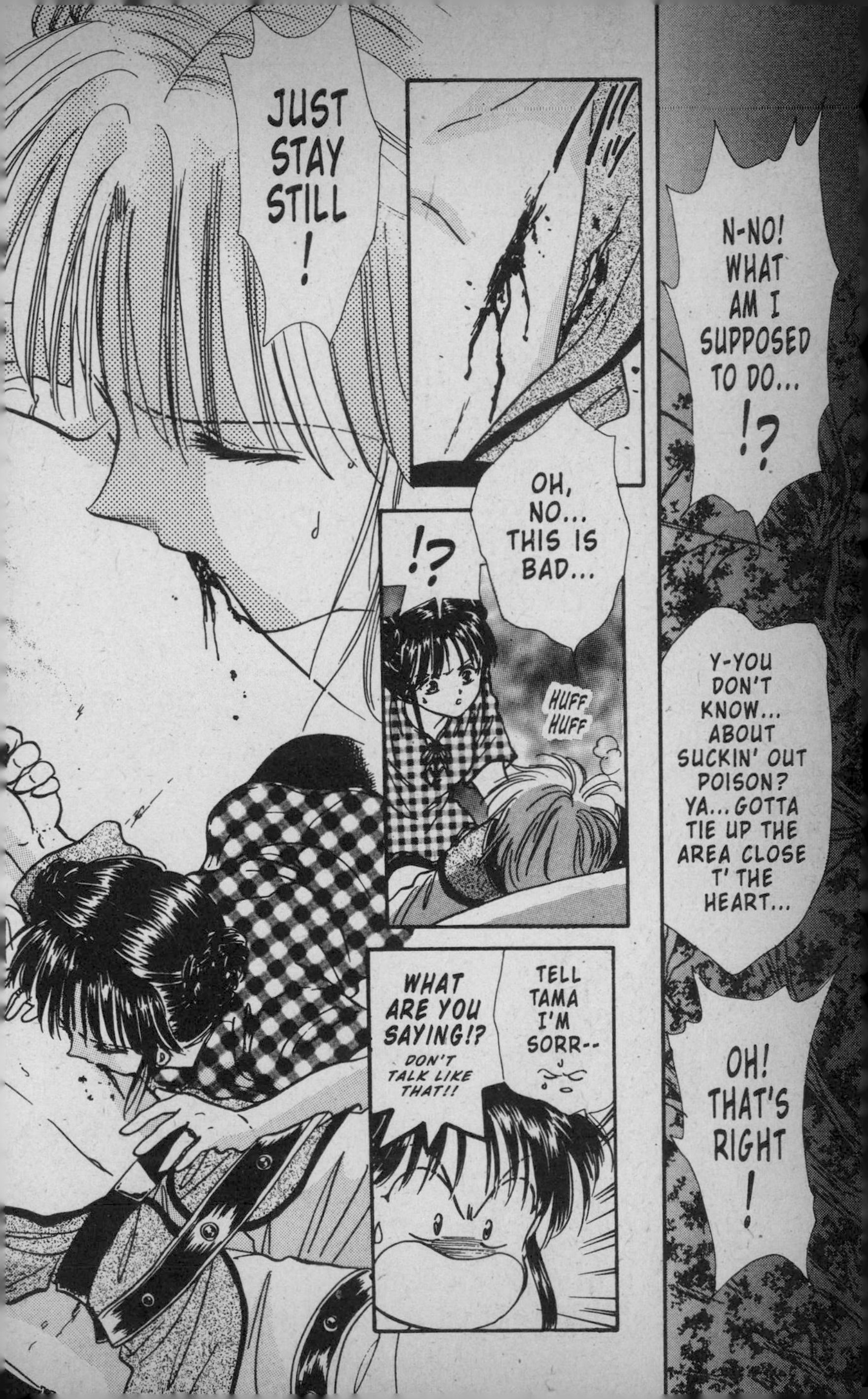
N-NO! WHAT AM I SUPPOSED TO DO...!?
Y-YOU DON'T KNOW... ABOUT SUCKIN' OUT POISON? YA...GOTTA TIE UP THE AREA CLOSE T' THE HEART...
OH! THAT'S RIGHT!
OH, NO... THIS IS BAD...
!?
HUFF HUFF
TELL TAMA I'M SORR--
WHAT ARE YOU SAYING!?
DON'T TALK LIKE THAT!!
JUST STAY STILL!

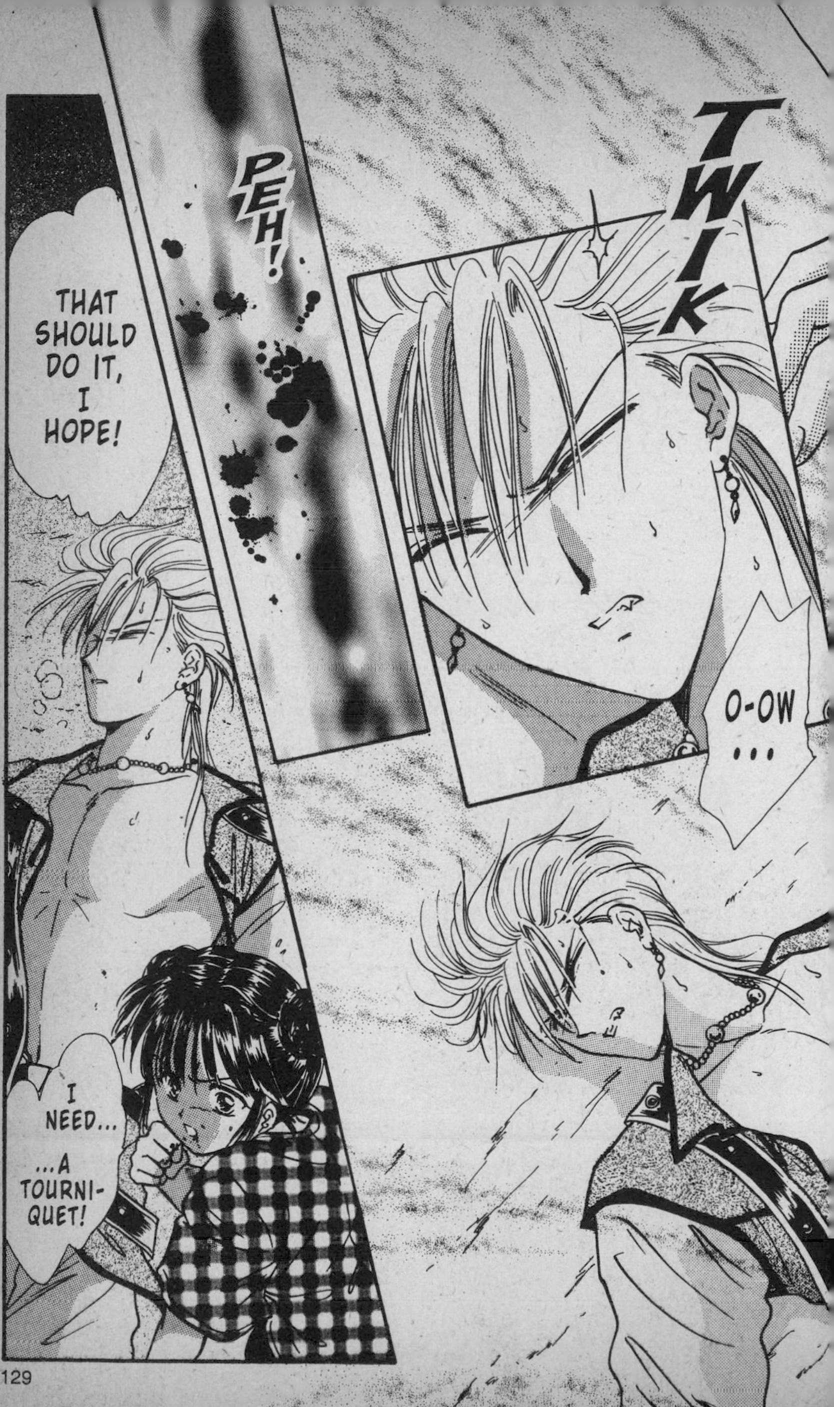
TWIK
O-OW ...
PEH!
THAT SHOULD DO IT, I HOPE!
I NEED...
...A TOURNIQUET!

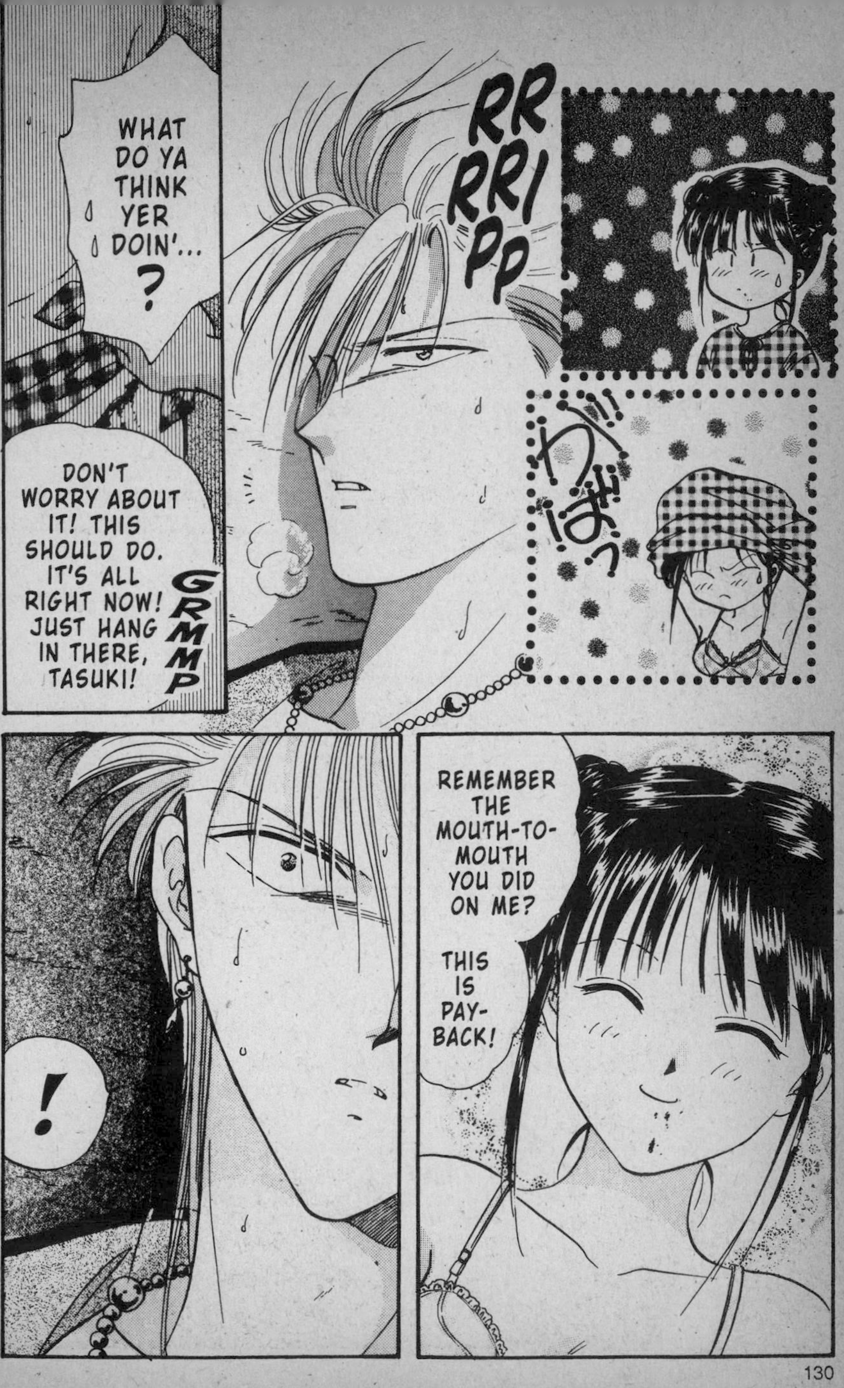

わばっ!!
RR RRIPP
WHAT DO YA THINK YER DOIN'...?
DON'T WORRY ABOUT IT! THIS SHOULD DO. IT'S ALL RIGHT NOW! JUST HANG IN THERE, TASUKI!
GRMMP
REMEMBER THE MOUTH-TO-MOUTH YOU DID ON ME?
THIS IS PAY-BACK!
!

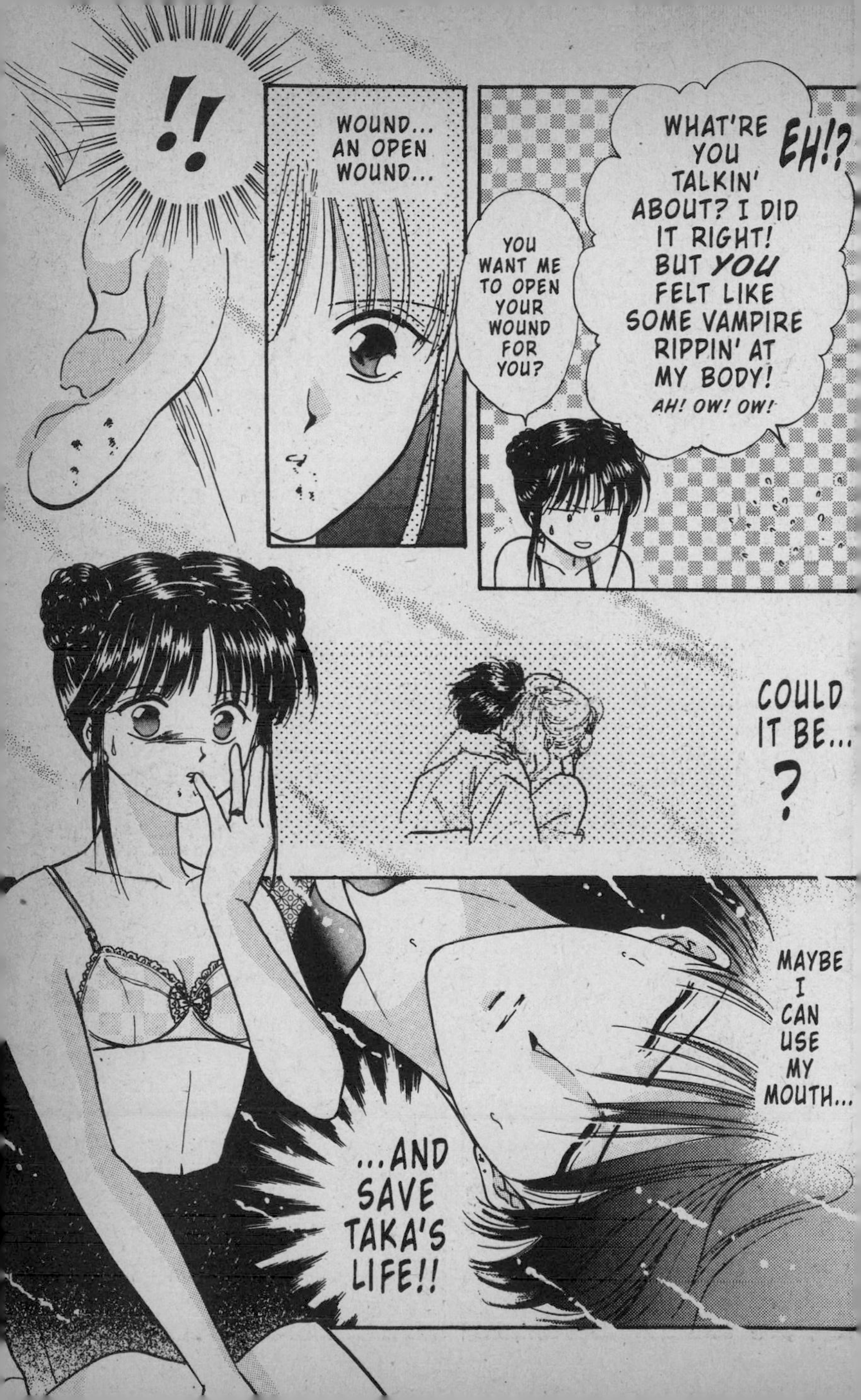
EH!?
WHAT'RE YOU TALKIN' ABOUT? I DID IT RIGHT! BUT YOU FELT LIKE SOME VAMPIRE RIPPIN' AT MY BODY!
AH! OW! OW!
YOU WANT ME TO OPEN YOUR WOUND FOR YOU?
WOUND... AN OPEN WOUND...
!!
COULD IT BE...?
MAYBE I CAN USE MY MOUTH...
...AND SAVE TAKA'S LIFE!!

It's now November '95.
Some of the character merchandise things I talked about before were unconfirmed when I talked about them, so don't get upset if you can't find them, okay?
Oh, yeah! There's a jigsaw puzzle from Seika Notebooks! They come in three sizes: small, medium, and large. And the pictures they chose were great! The Suzaku warriors look cool! And the shot with Miaka and Tama is so cute!
Another thing! Was everybody able to get their hands on a calendar this year? No, not mine... the two versions of the anime calendar! The pictures in them are beautiful! I love them both, but the one sold by Movic (I mean, the thing's just huge!!)... I'm still wondering about the May/June picture!☺ Those nudes get me every time! *Fantastic!*☆ Both the Suzaku and Seiryu are just cool! Nakago and Soi... Now that was just too good!!
Oh, also the phone cards (the ones you can pick up for 20 yen), those are dead-on! Chichiri is especially cool!
He's got a profile on the card!

I wonder if they're still on sale?

ふしぎ悪戯 FUSHIGI AKUGI THE MALICIOUS PLAY (13)

Idea by Ms. Rui Suzuki.

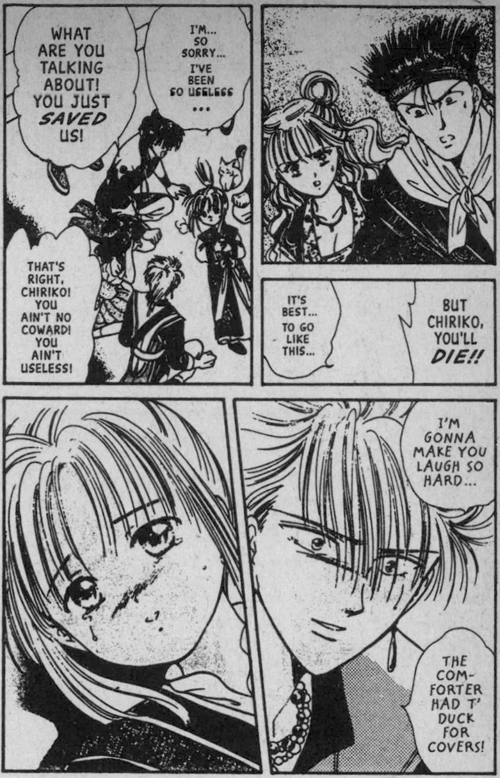
BUT CHIRIKO, YOU'LL *DIE!!*
IT'S BEST... TO GO LIKE THIS...
I'M... SO SORRY... I'VE BEEN SO USELESS...
WHAT ARE YOU TALKING ABOUT! YOU JUST *SAVED* US!
THAT'S RIGHT, CHIRIKO! YOU AIN'T NO COWARD! YOU AIN'T USELESS!
I'M GONNA MAKE YOU LAUGH SO HARD...
THE COMFORTER HAD T' DUCK FOR COVERS!

The title is "Hey, hey, Tasuki!" Whether you should laugh or cry is up to you. We all burst out laughing.

• CD Book (5) (All finished!)... Have you all had a chance to listen to it?
Well, Watase just got goosebumps listening to it! The background music by 135 was just terrific! (On book (4), I loved "19"!)
The scene where Seiryu consumes Yui! The scene where Miaka begins the chant to call Suzaku!! Nakago being so noble in the tale from long ago! The last scene! I just love the songs! And the brilliant acting by the voice actors! And the wonderful sound effects! I honestly feel that this is the best one yet among the five!
And Nakago's final "Mother!" had his voice overlaid with the voice from his youth! Tra-la! ★★★
Of course, at the scene where Suzaku is summoned, I got all shivery! It's really incredible when they put this to sound! The "Suzaku Theme" they used in the opening was so cool, I fell in love with it!
All the other songs were great too! Nakago's theme was just what the doctor ordered! ☺ And Miaka and Tamahome's theme left me spellbound. I swear, when I heard "Subete ni Wo Ai Ni" ("Everything is Wo Ai Ni") the tears started to flow! And "Sayonara Iranai" ("No Need for Goodbyes")!! I was a crying wreck just listening to the songs! ☺ I had this image of the universe and the heavens...
It seems that the songs had an effect on my assistants, too. They were a little too on-target. *Waaaah!*
There was some dialog between Nakago and Yui on this CD. It didn't happen in the original, but last time, I talked all about Nakago to the scriptwriters, and maybe that was the reason for it. This stuff was always a part of Nakago's feelings and motivations, but because of page counts and other considerations it was left out. It's like they put it back in just for me... so listen closely!!
Sincerely, to all of the production people, and all of the actors who have stuck with the CD book series for more than three years, and everyone, etc. etc., you guys did such a great job!!

If you readers can get your hands on all five, be sure to give them a listen! Everyone who worked on it is a genius! (No, really. It's true!) But people like Makoto Nagai and the voice actors... I doubt they'll ever gather in the same place again!

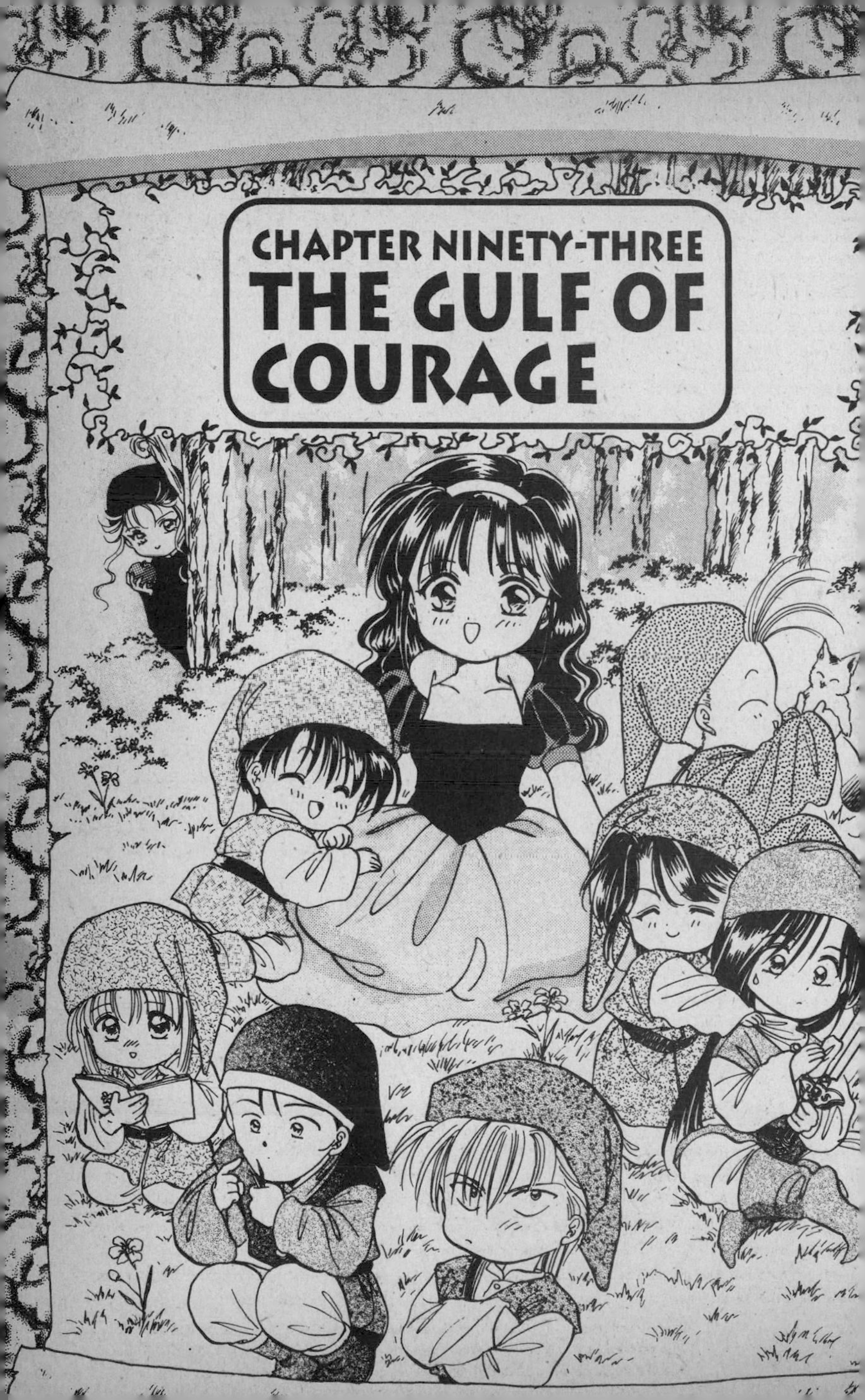
CHAPTER NINETY-THREE
THE GULF OF COURAGE

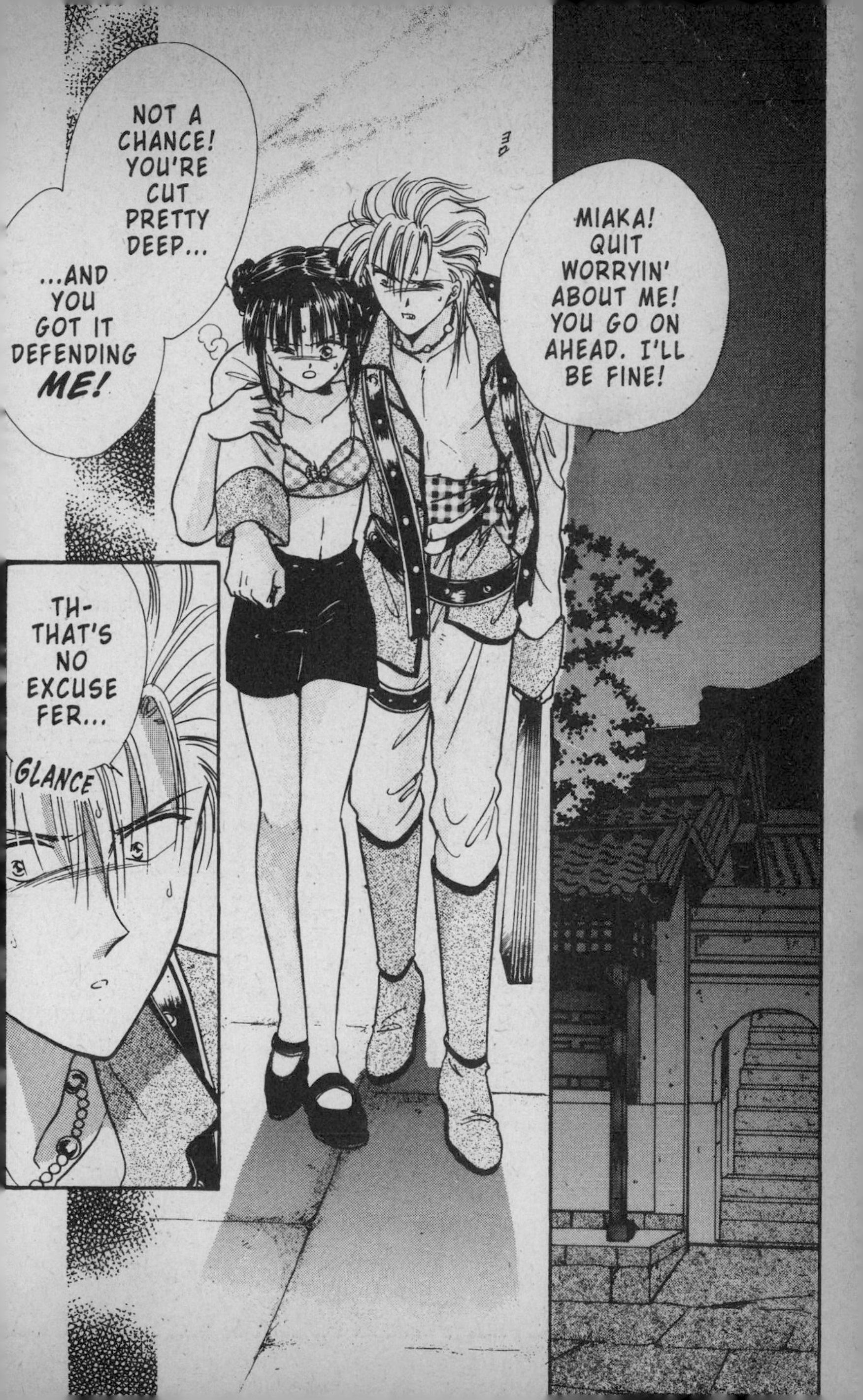
MIAKA! QUIT WORRYIN' ABOUT ME! YOU GO ON AHEAD. I'LL BE FINE!
NOT A CHANCE! YOU'RE CUT PRETTY DEEP...
...AND YOU GOT IT DEFENDING ME!
TH-THAT'S NO EXCUSE FER...
GLANCE

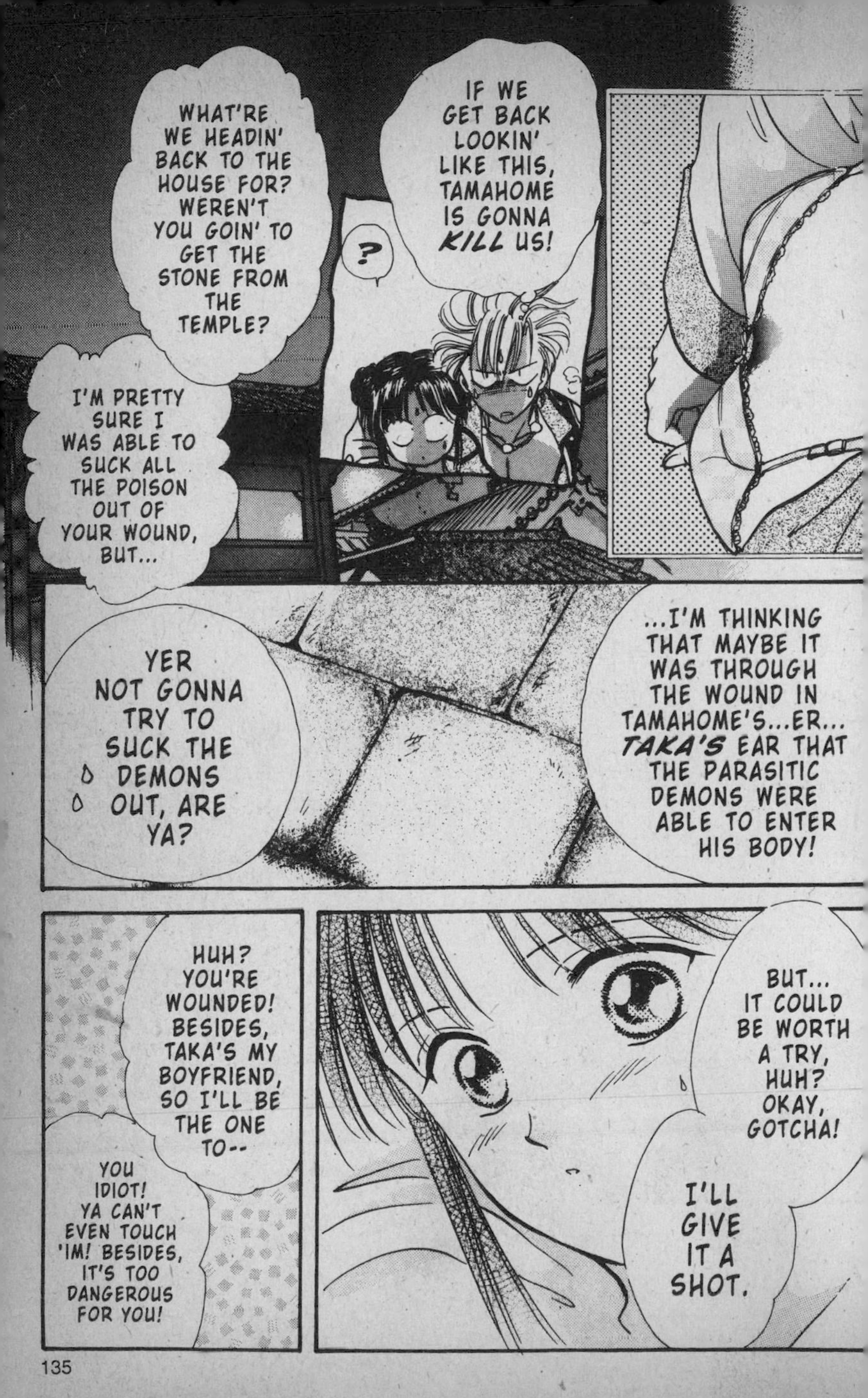
IF WE GET BACK LOOKIN' LIKE THIS, TAMAHOME IS GONNA KILL US!
?
WHAT'RE WE HEADIN' BACK TO THE HOUSE FOR? WEREN'T YOU GOIN' TO GET THE STONE FROM THE TEMPLE?
I'M PRETTY SURE I WAS ABLE TO SUCK ALL THE POISON OUT OF YOUR WOUND, BUT...
...I'M THINKING THAT MAYBE IT WAS THROUGH THE WOUND IN TAMAHOME'S...ER... TAKA'S EAR THAT THE PARASITIC DEMONS WERE ABLE TO ENTER HIS BODY!
YER NOT GONNA TRY TO SUCK THE DEMONS OUT, ARE YA?
BUT... IT COULD BE WORTH A TRY, HUH? OKAY, GOTCHA!
I'LL GIVE IT A SHOT.
HUH? YOU'RE WOUNDED! BESIDES, TAKA'S MY BOYFRIEND, SO I'LL BE THE ONE TO--
YOU IDIOT! YA CAN'T EVEN TOUCH 'IM! BESIDES, IT'S TOO DANGEROUS FOR YOU!

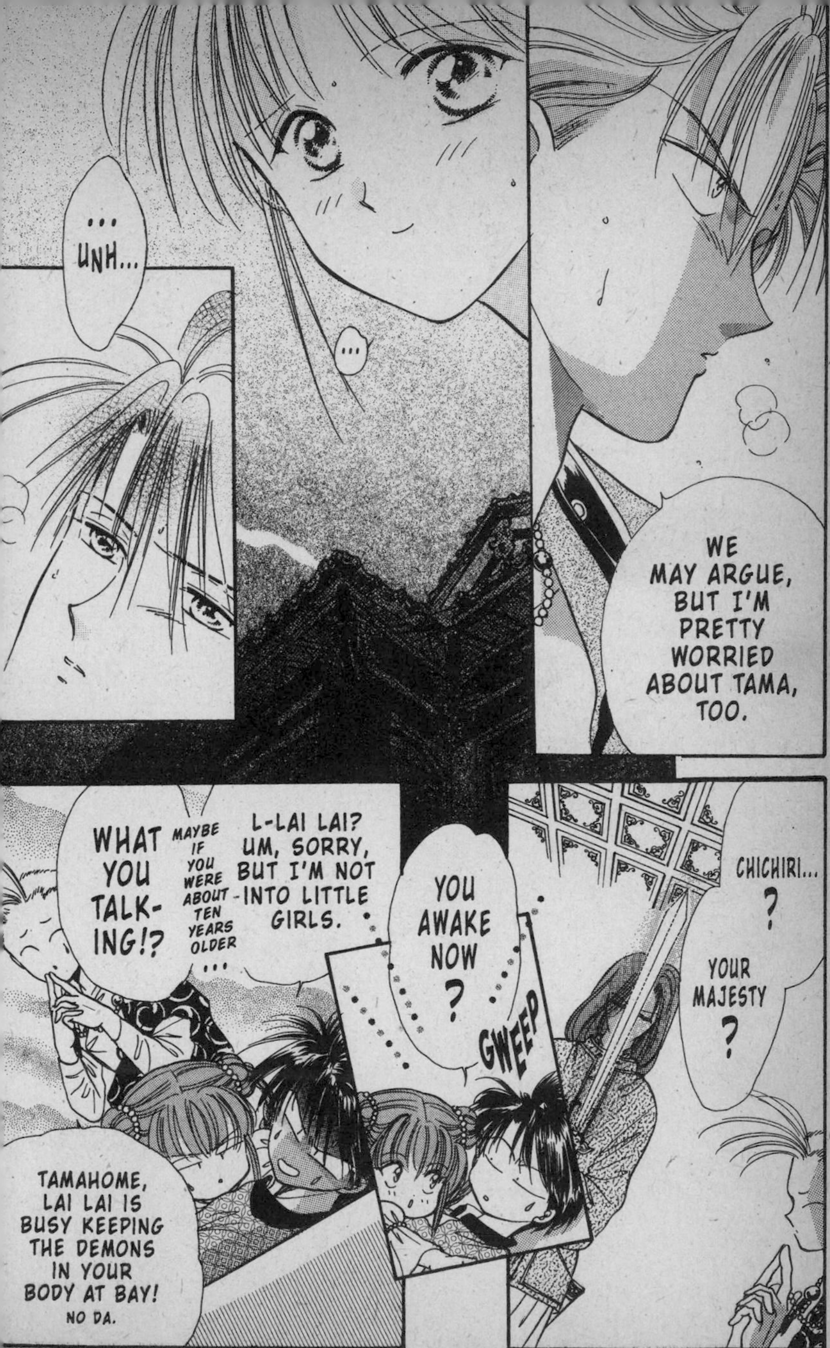
WE MAY ARGUE, BUT I'M PRETTY WORRIED ABOUT TAMA, TOO.
...
... UNH...
CHICHIRI... ?
YOUR MAJESTY ?
YOU AWAKE NOW ?
GWEEP
L-LAI LAI? UM, SORRY, BUT I'M NOT INTO LITTLE GIRLS.
MAYBE IF YOU WERE ABOUT TEN YEARS OLDER ...
WHAT YOU TALKING!?
TAMAHOME, LAI LAI IS BUSY KEEPING THE DEMONS IN YOUR BODY AT BAY! NO DA.

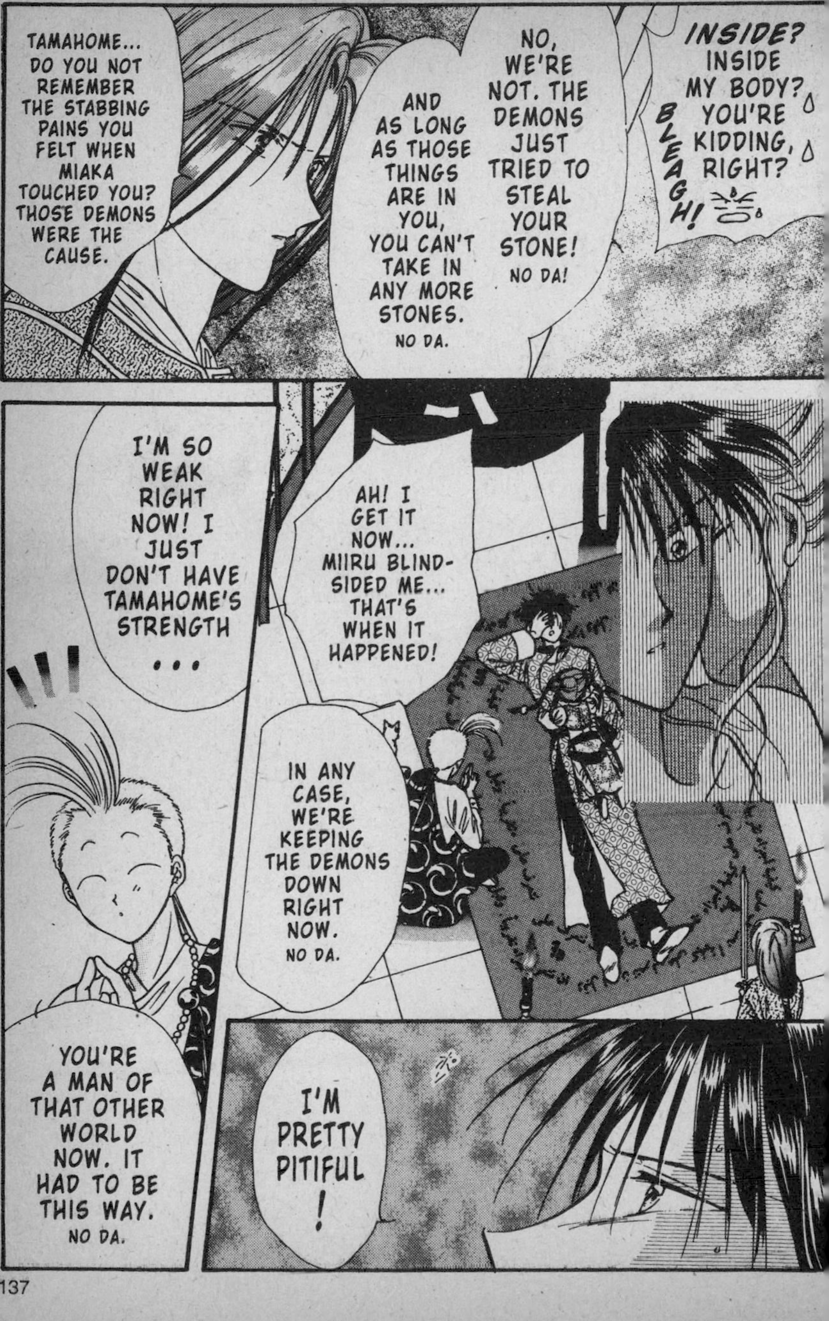
INSIDE? INSIDE MY BODY? YOU'RE KIDDING, RIGHT?
BLEAGH!
NO, WE'RE NOT. THE DEMONS JUST TRIED TO STEAL YOUR STONE! NO DA!
AND AS LONG AS THOSE THINGS ARE IN YOU, YOU CAN'T TAKE IN ANY MORE STONES. NO DA.
TAMAHOME... DO YOU NOT REMEMBER THE STABBING PAINS YOU FELT WHEN MIAKA TOUCHED YOU? THOSE DEMONS WERE THE CAUSE.
AH! I GET IT NOW... MIIRU BLIND-SIDED ME... THAT'S WHEN IT HAPPENED!
IN ANY CASE, WE'RE KEEPING THE DEMONS DOWN RIGHT NOW. NO DA.
I'M PRETTY PITIFUL!
I'M SO WEAK RIGHT NOW! I JUST DON'T HAVE TAMAHOME'S STRENGTH...
YOU'RE A MAN OF THAT OTHER WORLD NOW. IT HAD TO BE THIS WAY. NO DA.

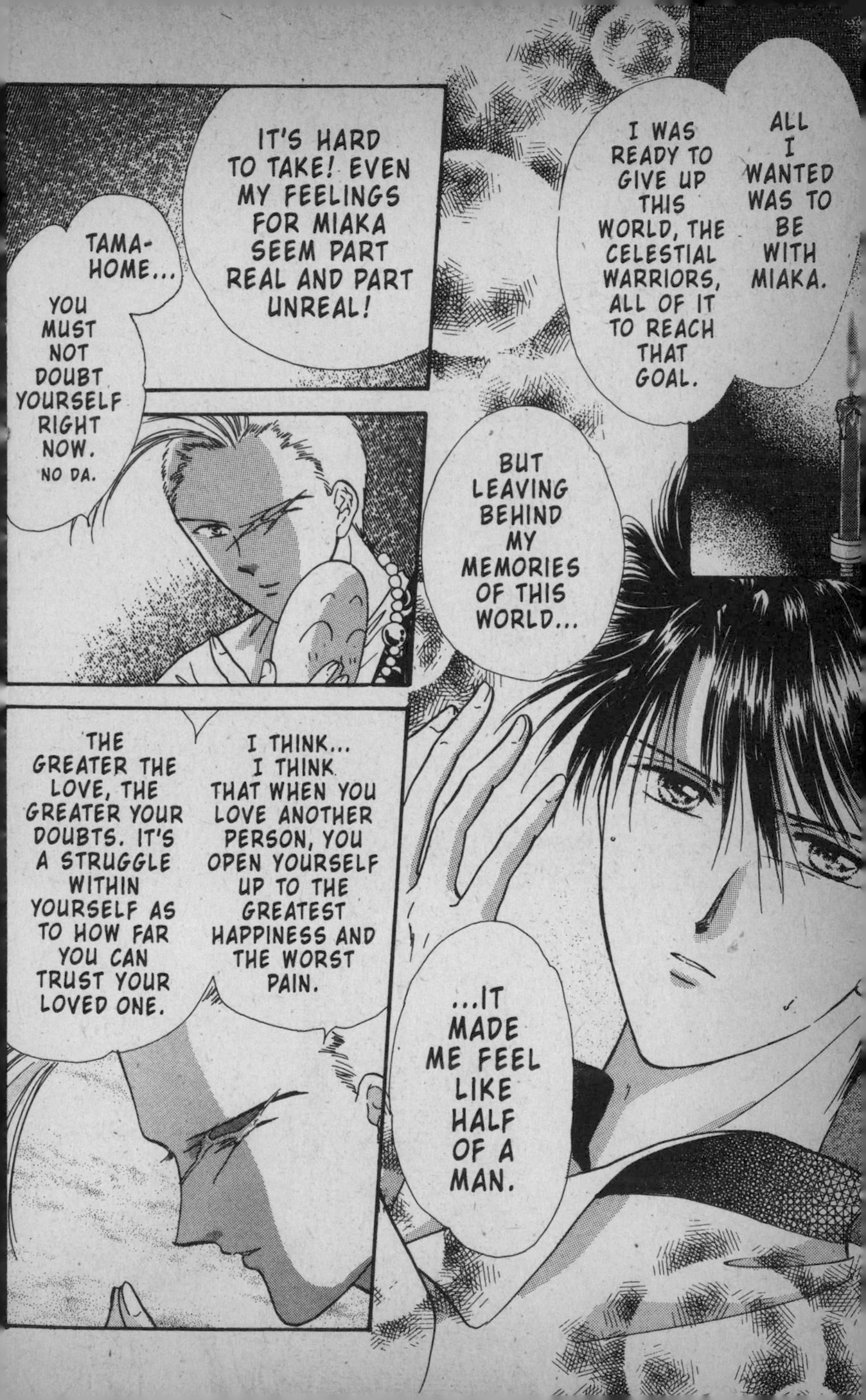
ALL I WANTED WAS TO BE WITH MIAKA.
I WAS READY TO GIVE UP THIS WORLD, THE CELESTIAL WARRIORS, ALL OF IT TO REACH THAT GOAL.
BUT LEAVING BEHIND MY MEMORIES OF THIS WORLD...
...IT MADE ME FEEL LIKE HALF OF A MAN.
IT'S HARD TO TAKE! EVEN MY FEELINGS FOR MIAKA SEEM PART REAL AND PART UNREAL!
TAMA-HOME... YOU MUST NOT DOUBT YOURSELF RIGHT NOW. NO DA.
I THINK... I THINK THAT WHEN YOU LOVE ANOTHER PERSON, YOU OPEN YOURSELF UP TO THE GREATEST HAPPINESS AND THE WORST PAIN.
THE GREATER THE LOVE, THE GREATER YOUR DOUBTS. IT'S A STRUGGLE WITHIN YOURSELF AS TO HOW FAR YOU CAN TRUST YOUR LOVED ONE.

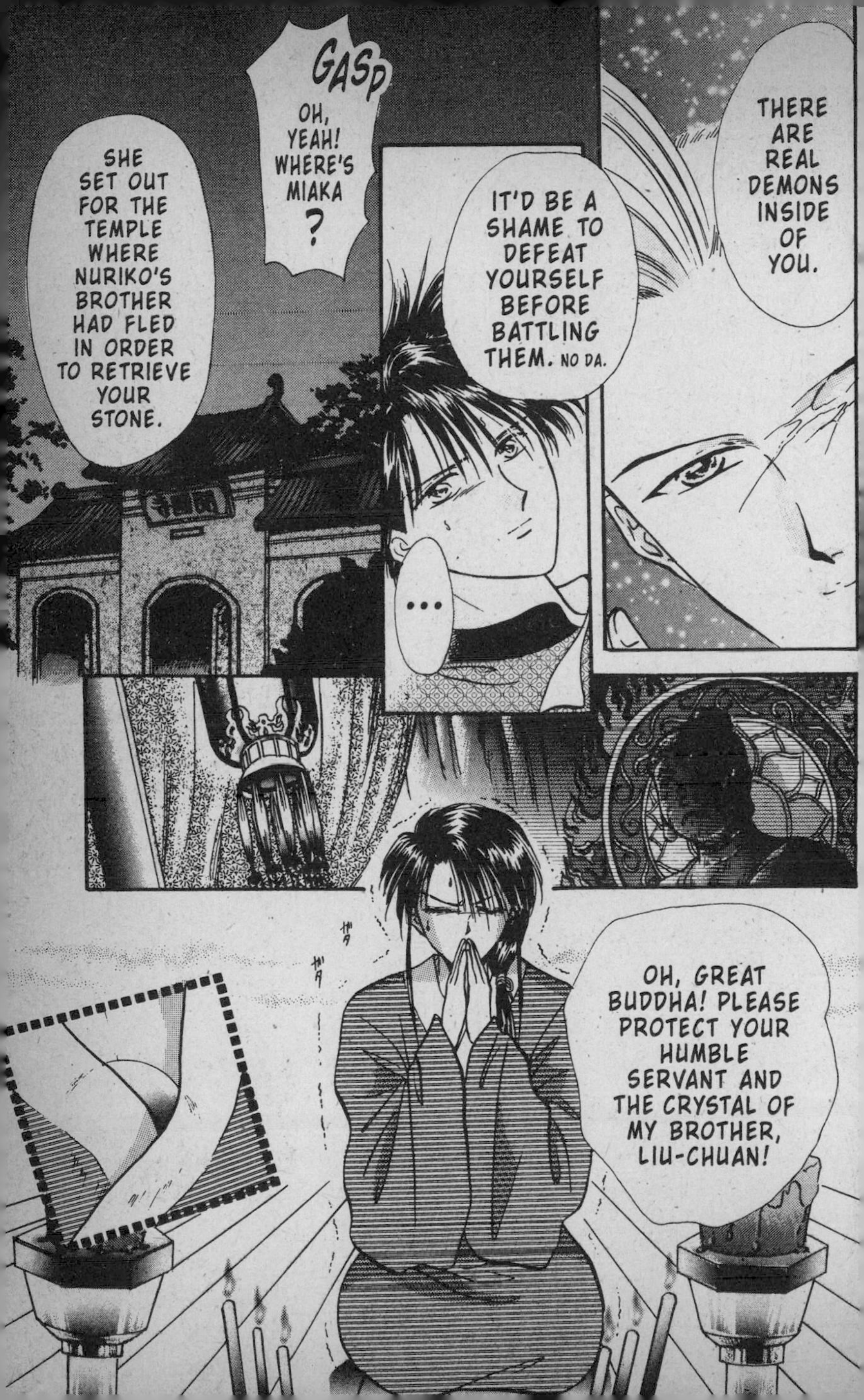
THERE ARE REAL DEMONS INSIDE OF YOU.
IT'D BE A SHAME TO DEFEAT YOURSELF BEFORE BATTLING THEM. NO DA.
...
GASP
OH, YEAH! WHERE'S MIAKA?
SHE SET OUT FOR THE TEMPLE WHERE NURIKO'S BROTHER HAD FLED IN ORDER TO RETRIEVE YOUR STONE.
OH, GREAT BUDDHA! PLEASE PROTECT YOUR HUMBLE SERVANT AND THE CRYSTAL OF MY BROTHER, LIU-CHUAN!

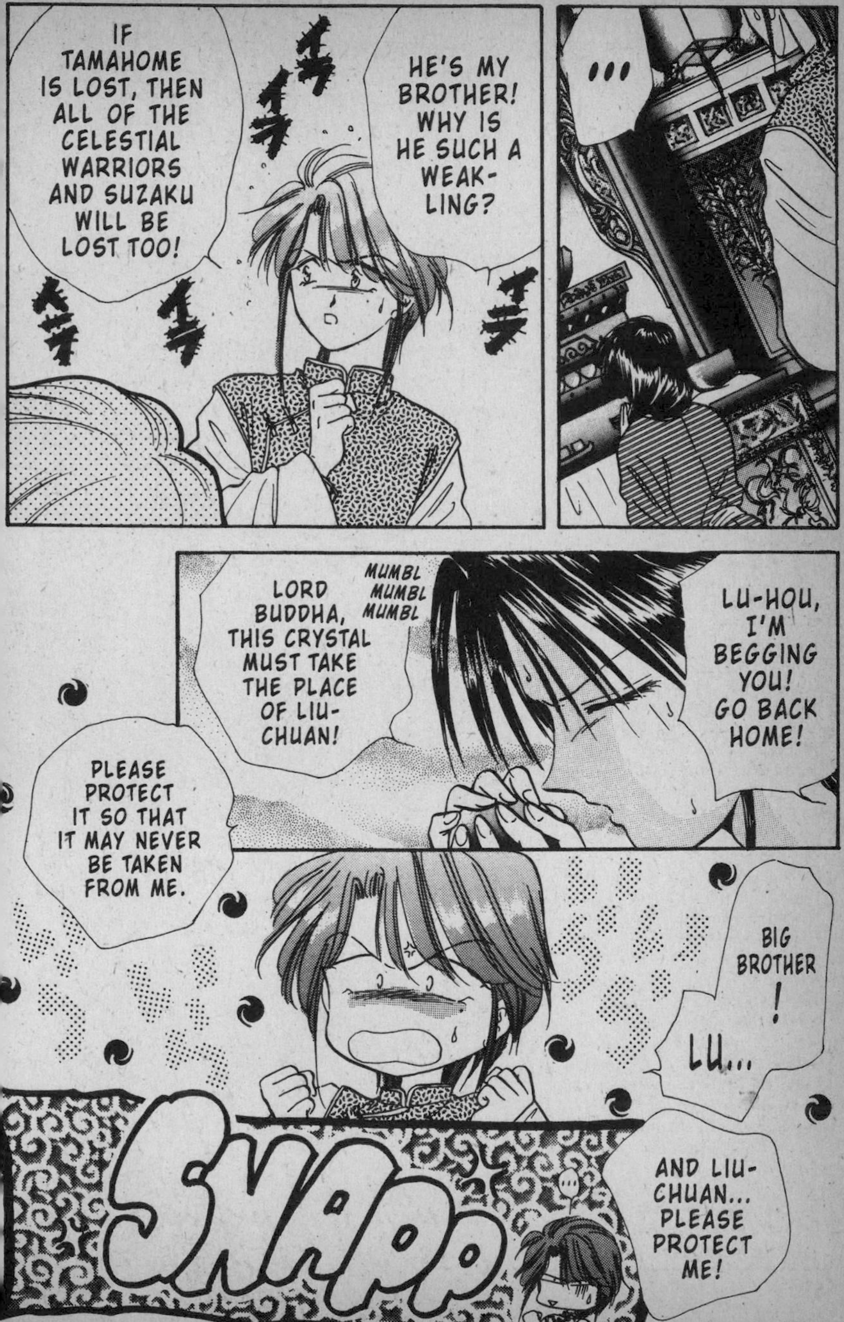
...
HE'S MY BROTHER! WHY IS HE SUCH A WEAK-LING?
IF TAMAHOME IS LOST, THEN ALL OF THE CELESTIAL WARRIORS AND SUZAKU WILL BE LOST TOO!
LU-HOU, I'M BEGGING YOU! GO BACK HOME!
MUMBL MUMBL MUMBL
LORD BUDDHA, THIS CRYSTAL MUST TAKE THE PLACE OF LIU-CHUAN!
PLEASE PROTECT IT SO THAT IT MAY NEVER BE TAKEN FROM ME.
BIG BROTHER!
LU...
SNAPP
AND LIU-CHUAN... PLEASE PROTECT ME!

(Continued...)
But since my professional manga debut, it seems like I've come to know the complexities of shôjo manga. Never underestimate it! It explores the details of how we express our feelings... It just has some wonderful attributes that shônen manga lacks! It's strongest with stories involving romantic love, but since that wasn't my personal interest early on, I'd say, "Oh, god!" and throw it away. But recently, I've come to like the romance more and more. ☺ The ones I like are the "couple fated to be together" stories... the ones where they're hanging all over each other! I can't get enough of them! ☺
When I see a real-life couple walking in the street (not the ones that make you sick! Let's forget those for now), I get this pleasant feeling. I think in the past when I used to say "ugh!" I was just jealous. ☺ One of my assistants is in the habit of saying, "Ahh, that's amore!"
Before my debut, everything I wrote was sort of all-over-the-place. (Really! My settings and situations were really detailed then, but when I go back and read them now, I don't understand what's going on. I had the mistaken impression that throwing people into wild situation after wild situation was interesting, but it isn't.) But no matter what the story, if there is no love in it, it can be pretty dull. When one person is thinking of another, don't you think that's pretty wonderful? ☺
I never intended to be a "shôjo manga artist." (I did some shôjo manga-style stories, but that's because the magazines were shôjo magazines.) But "shôjo manga" wasn't what I wanted to draw. I wanted children, adults, everybody to enjoy my manga! (Well... *Fushigi Yûgi* was meant for people in the 3rd year of middle school and up, and that's how I drew it.) I think that this obsession (in the manga world) with aiming stories at a particular segment of the population is extremely strange! Personally I like the general "middle school" feel of my manga, and I want to keep it in my work, ideally. But there are times when I worry about the feel of my manga... ☺

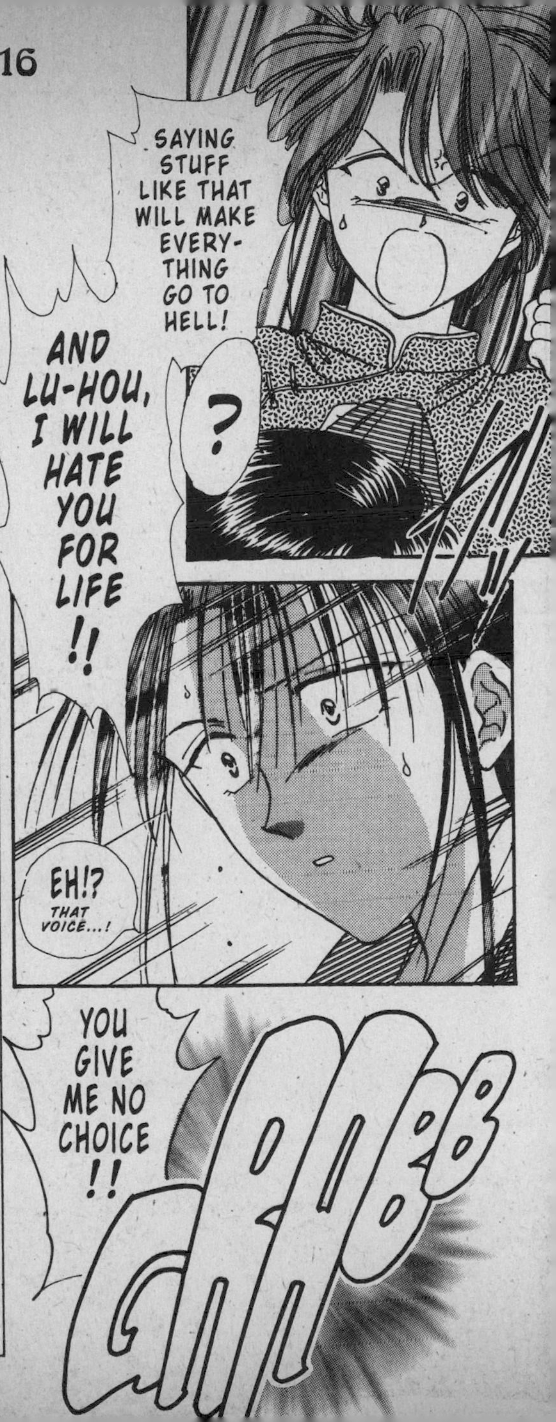
SAYING STUFF LIKE THAT WILL MAKE EVERYTHING GO TO HELL!
AND LU-HOU, I WILL HATE YOU FOR LIFE!!
?
EH!? THAT VOICE...!
YOU GIVE ME NO CHOICE!!

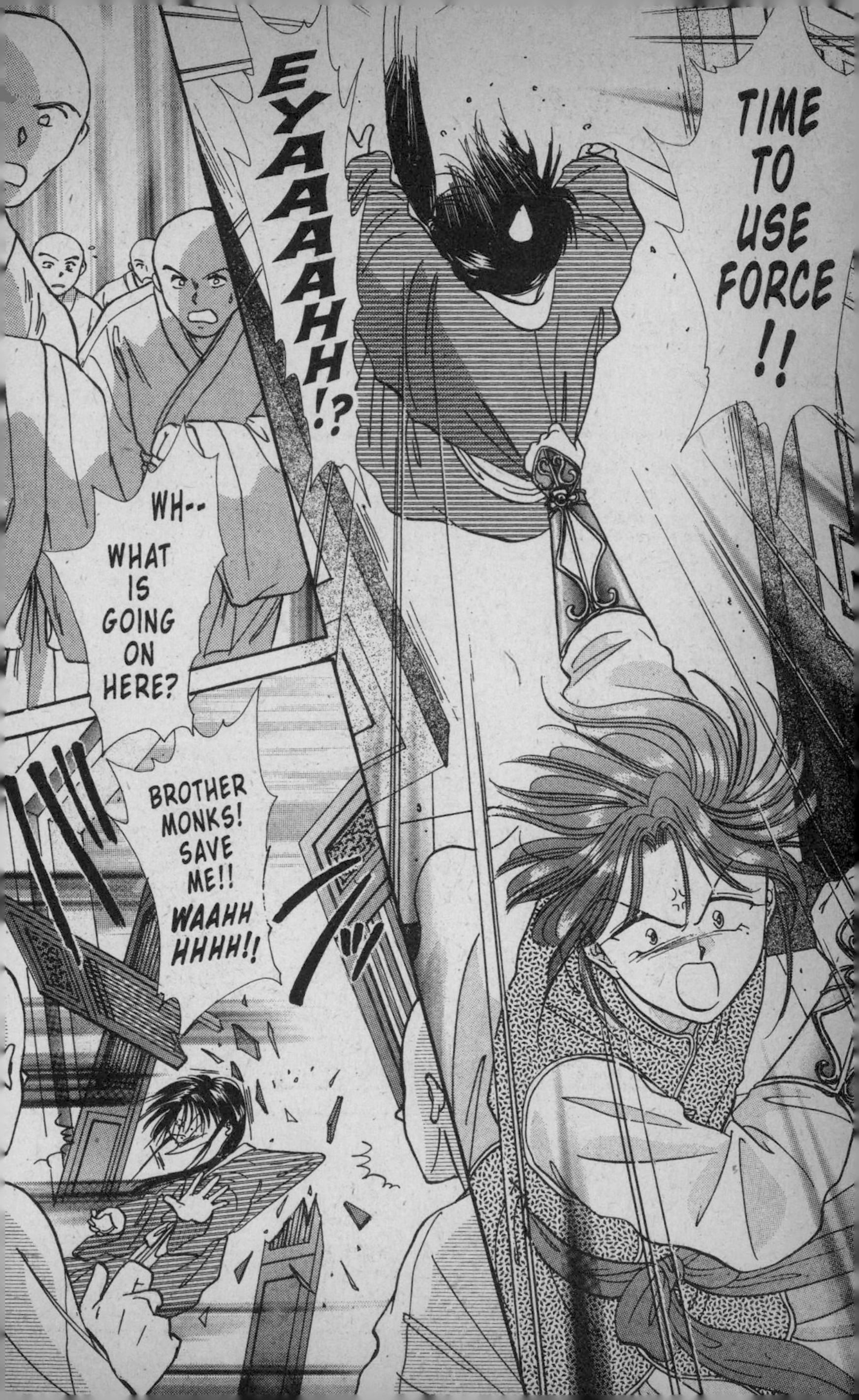
TIME TO USE FORCE!!
EYAAAHH!?
WH-- WHAT IS GOING ON HERE?
BROTHER MONKS! SAVE ME!! WAAHH HHHH!!

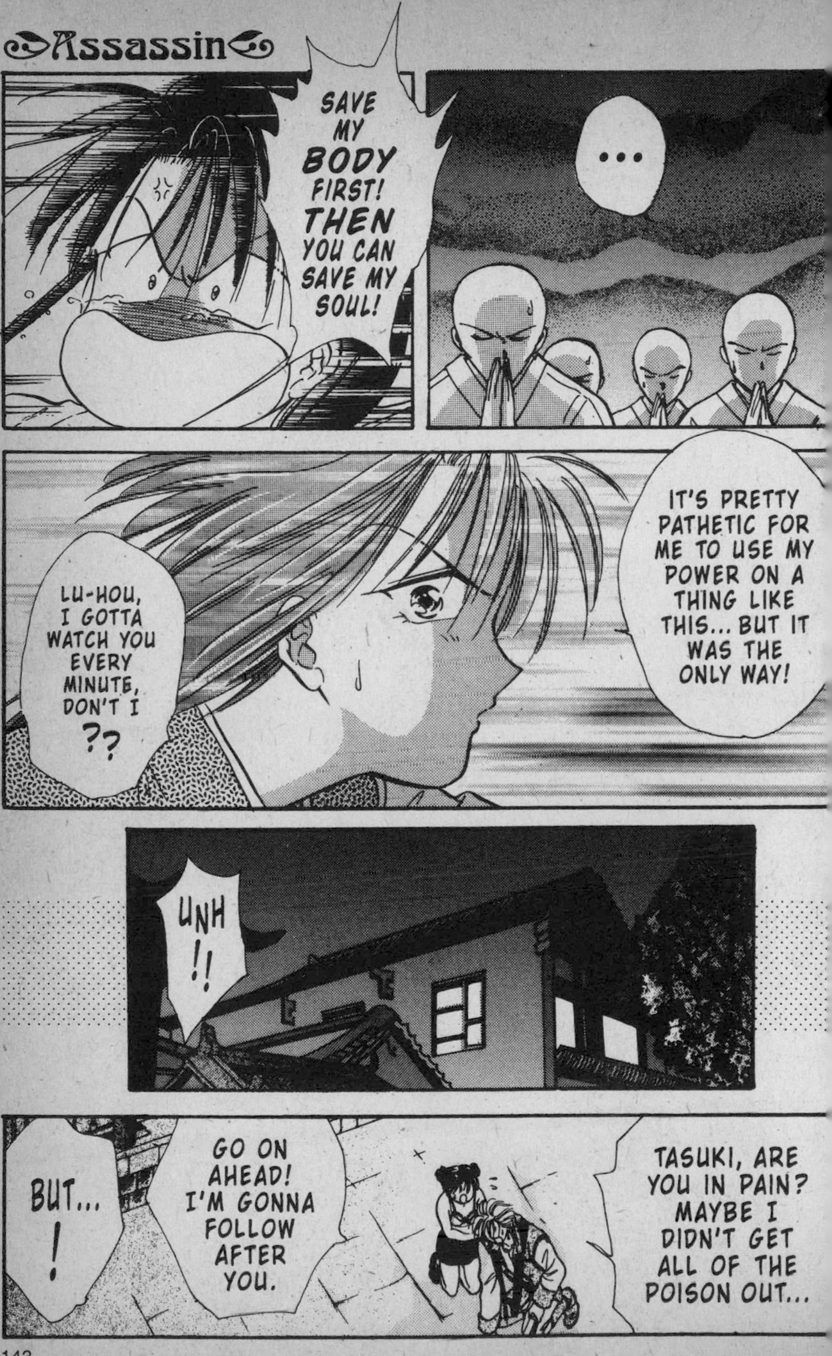
...
SAVE MY BODY FIRST! THEN YOU CAN SAVE MY SOUL!
IT'S PRETTY PATHETIC FOR ME TO USE MY POWER ON A THING LIKE THIS... BUT IT WAS THE ONLY WAY!
LU-HOU, I GOTTA WATCH YOU EVERY MINUTE, DON'T I ??
UNH !!
TASUKI, ARE YOU IN PAIN? MAYBE I DIDN'T GET ALL OF THE POISON OUT...
GO ON AHEAD! I'M GONNA FOLLOW AFTER YOU.
BUT... !

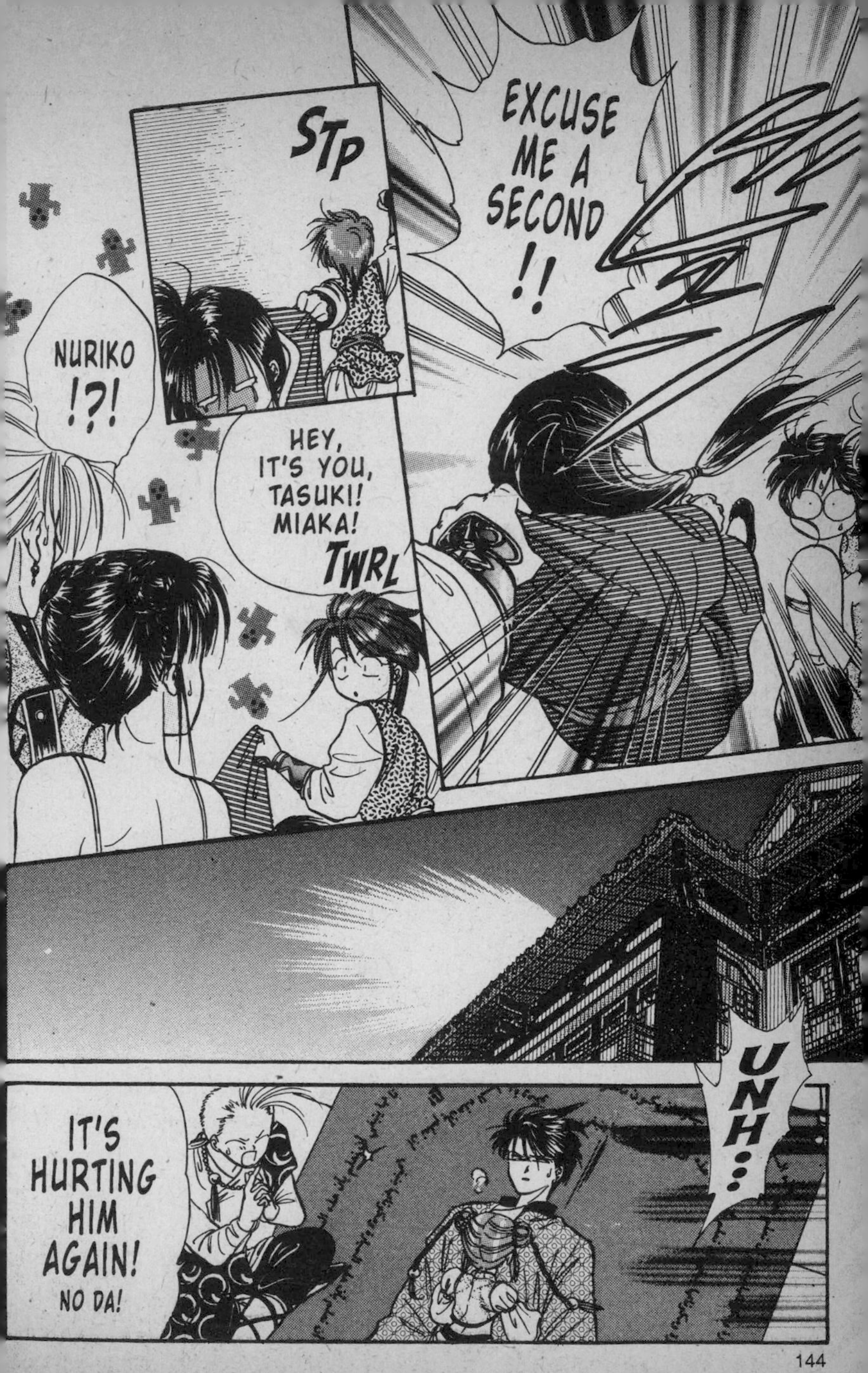
EXCUSE ME A SECOND !!
STP
HEY, IT'S YOU, TASUKI! MIAKA!
TWRL
NURIKO !?!
UNH...
IT'S HURTING HIM AGAIN! NO DA!

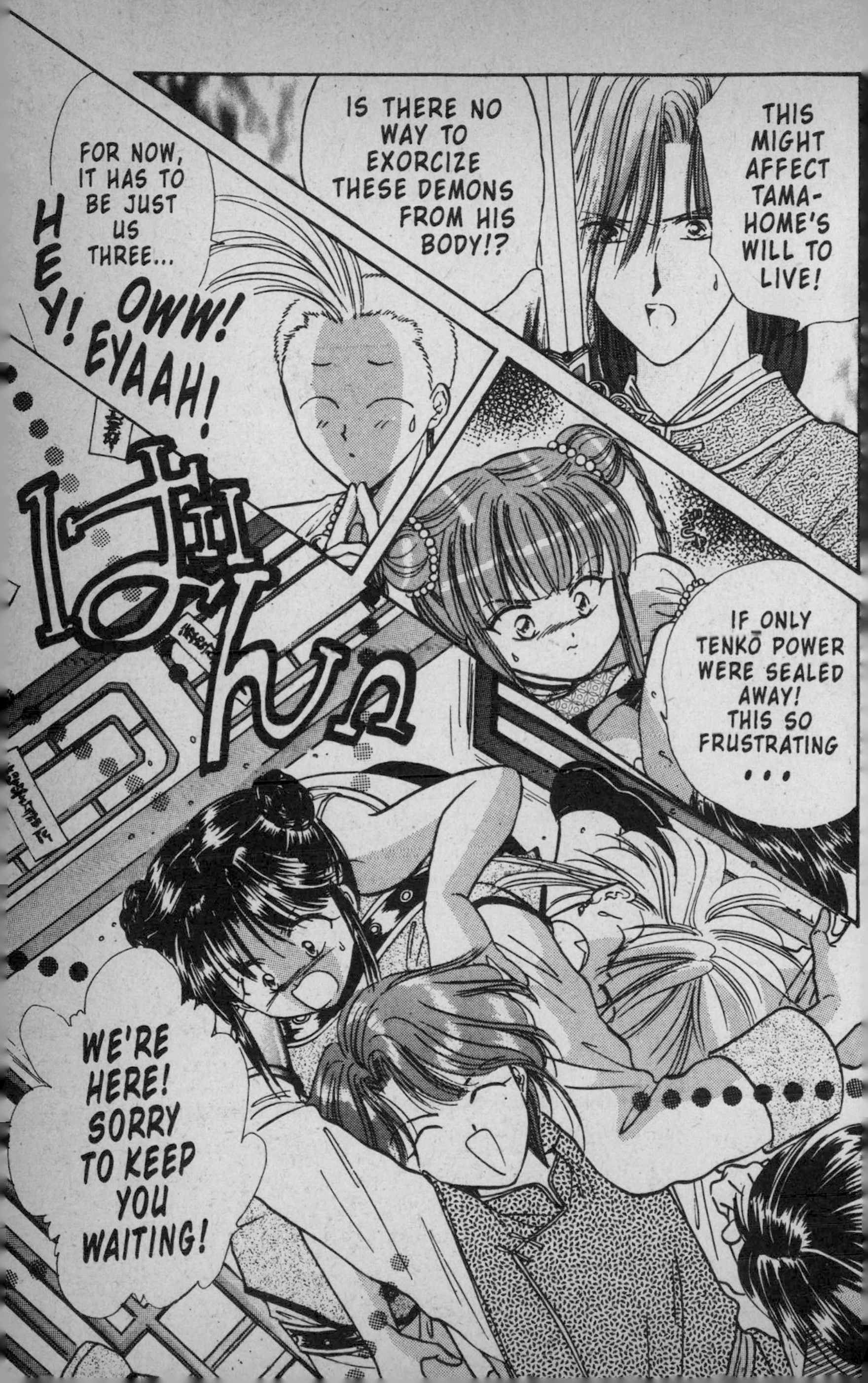
THIS MIGHT AFFECT TAMA-HOME'S WILL TO LIVE!
IS THERE NO WAY TO EXORCIZE THESE DEMONS FROM HIS BODY!?
FOR NOW, IT HAS TO BE JUST US THREE...
IF ONLY TENKŌ POWER WERE SEALED AWAY! THIS SO FRUSTRATING...
HEY!
OWW! EYAAH!
WE'RE HERE! SORRY TO KEEP YOU WAITING!

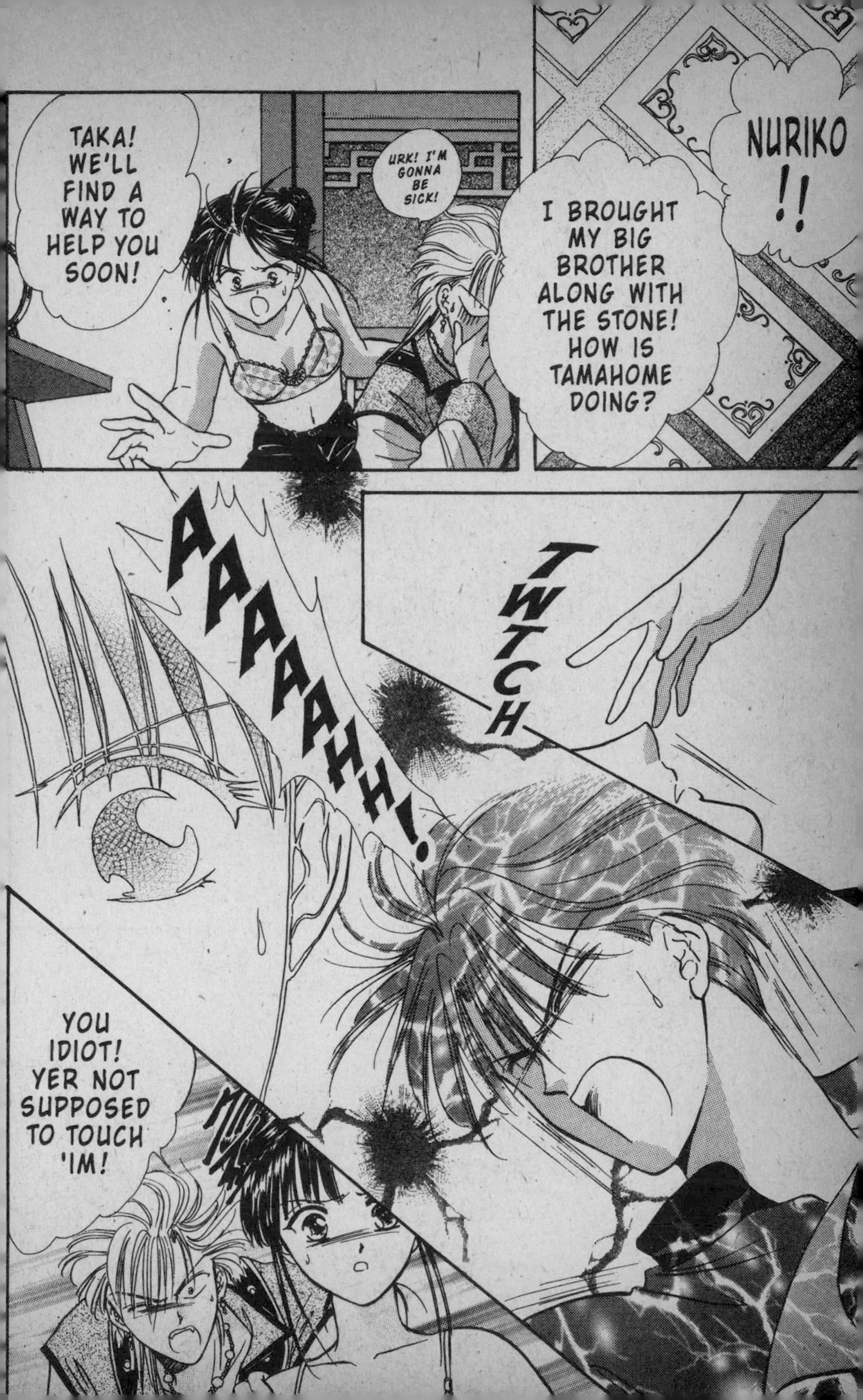
NURIKO !!
I BROUGHT MY BIG BROTHER ALONG WITH THE STONE! HOW IS TAMAHOME DOING?
URK! I'M GONNA BE SICK!
TAKA! WE'LL FIND A WAY TO HELP YOU SOON!
TWTCH
AAAAAHH!
YOU IDIOT! YER NOT SUPPOSED TO TOUCH 'IM!

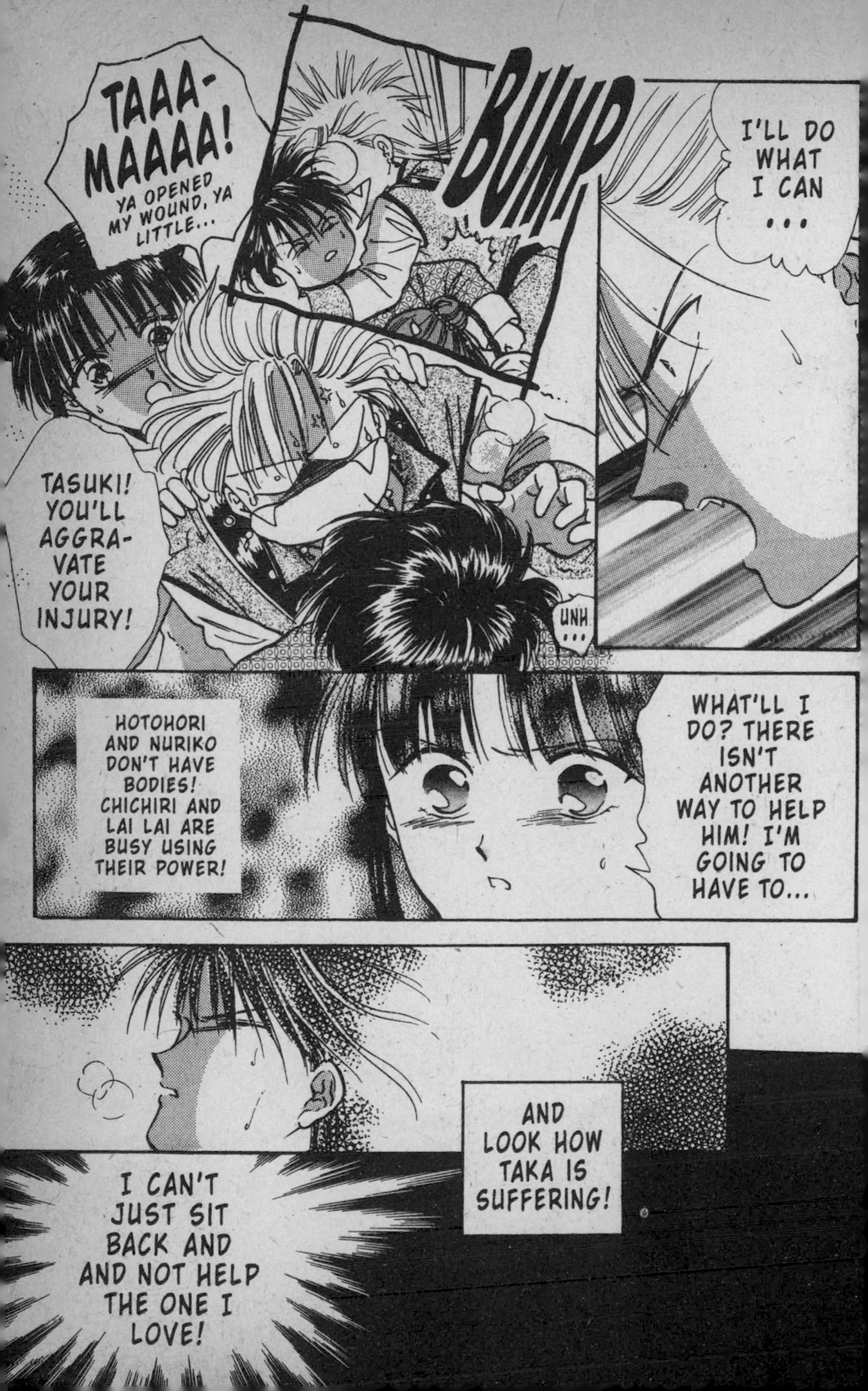
I'LL DO WHAT I CAN...
BUMP
TAAA-MAAAA!
YA OPENED MY WOUND, YA LITTLE...
UNH...
TASUKI! YOU'LL AGGRAVATE YOUR INJURY!
WHAT'LL I DO? THERE ISN'T ANOTHER WAY TO HELP HIM! I'M GOING TO HAVE TO...
HOTOHORI AND NURIKO DON'T HAVE BODIES! CHICHIRI AND LAI LAI ARE BUSY USING THEIR POWER!
AND LOOK HOW TAKA IS SUFFERING!
I CAN'T JUST SIT BACK AND AND NOT HELP THE ONE I LOVE!

... MI... AKA...
MIAKA ...
I DON'T KNOW... WHAT PLAN YOU HAVE IN MIND... BUT...
I... CAN TAKE IT! I'LL BE... ALL RIGHT!
TAKA ...
I WAS... CARELESS! THAT'S WHY... THAT WOMAN...
BUT... BECAUSE YOU STILL TRUST ME...

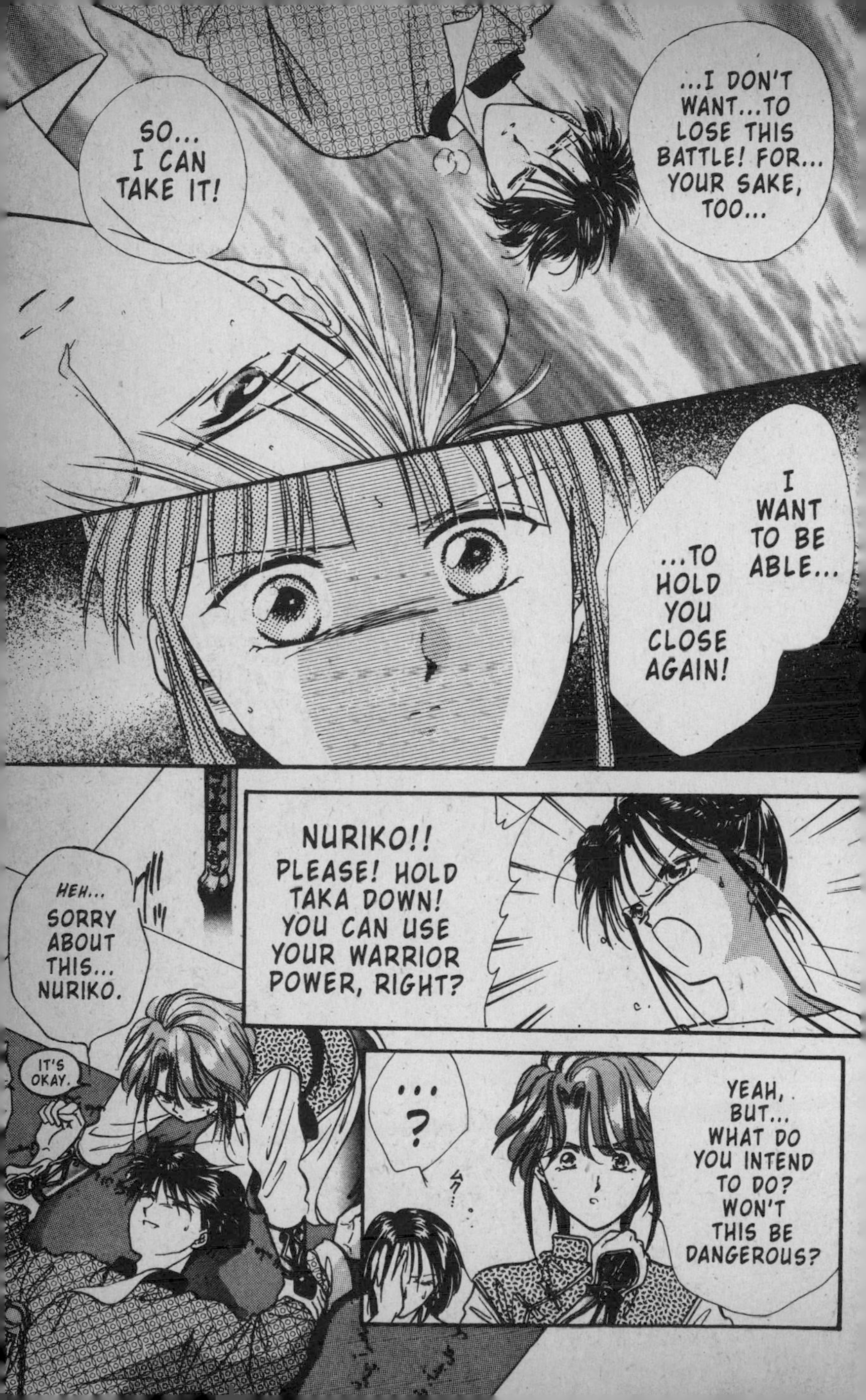
...I DON'T WANT...TO LOSE THIS BATTLE! FOR... YOUR SAKE, TOO...
SO... I CAN TAKE IT!
I WANT TO BE ABLE...
...TO HOLD YOU CLOSE AGAIN!
NURIKO!! PLEASE! HOLD TAKA DOWN! YOU CAN USE YOUR WARRIOR POWER, RIGHT?
YEAH, BUT... WHAT DO YOU INTEND TO DO? WON'T THIS BE DANGEROUS?
...?
HEH... SORRY ABOUT THIS... NURIKO.
IT'S OKAY.

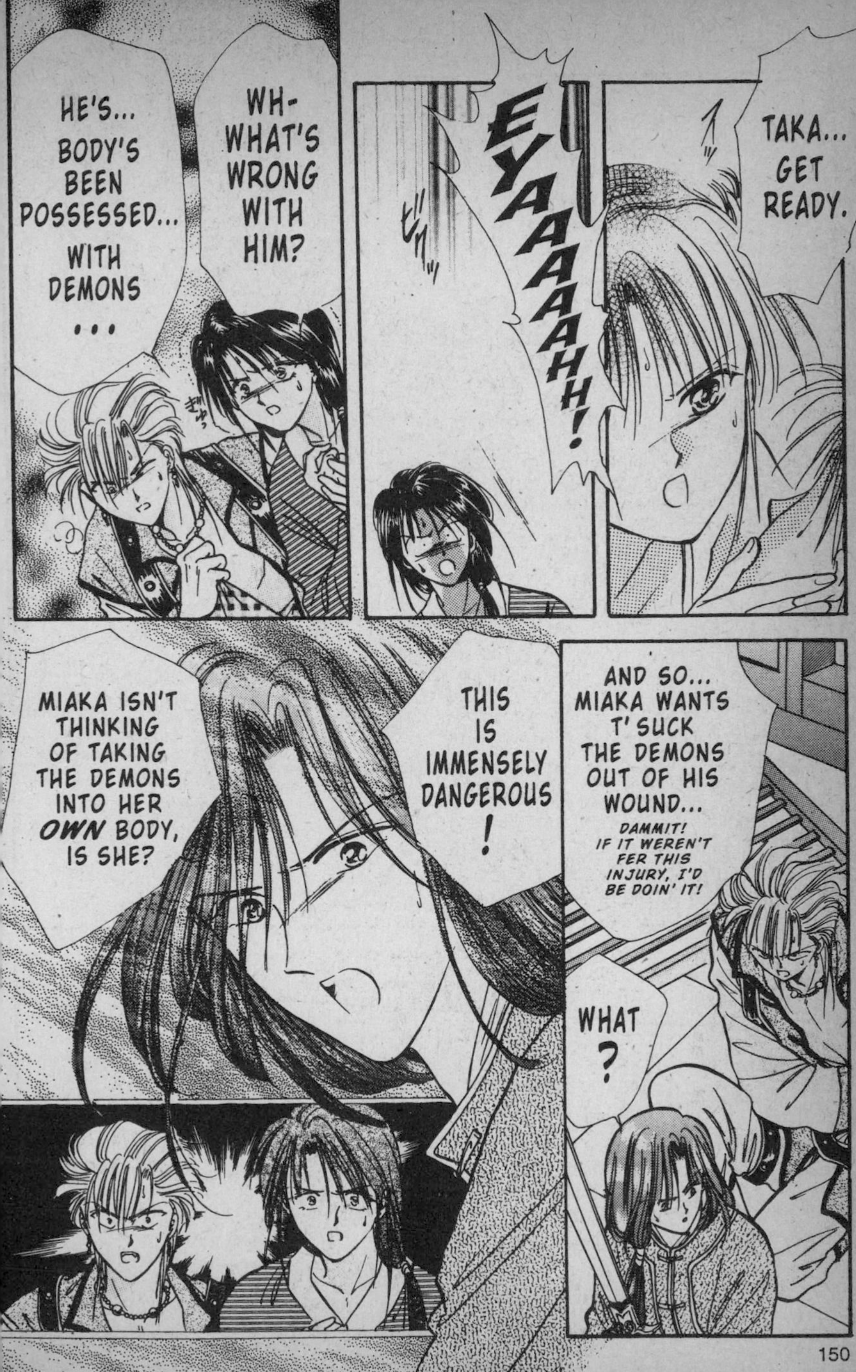
TAKA... GET READY.
EYAAAAAHH!
WH- WHAT'S WRONG WITH HIM?
HE'S... BODY'S BEEN POSSESSED... WITH DEMONS...
AND SO... MIAKA WANTS T' SUCK THE DEMONS OUT OF HIS WOUND...
DAMMIT! IF IT WEREN'T FER THIS INJURY, I'D BE DOIN' IT!
WHAT?
THIS IS IMMENSELY DANGEROUS!
MIAKA ISN'T THINKING OF TAKING THE DEMONS INTO HER *OWN* BODY, IS SHE?

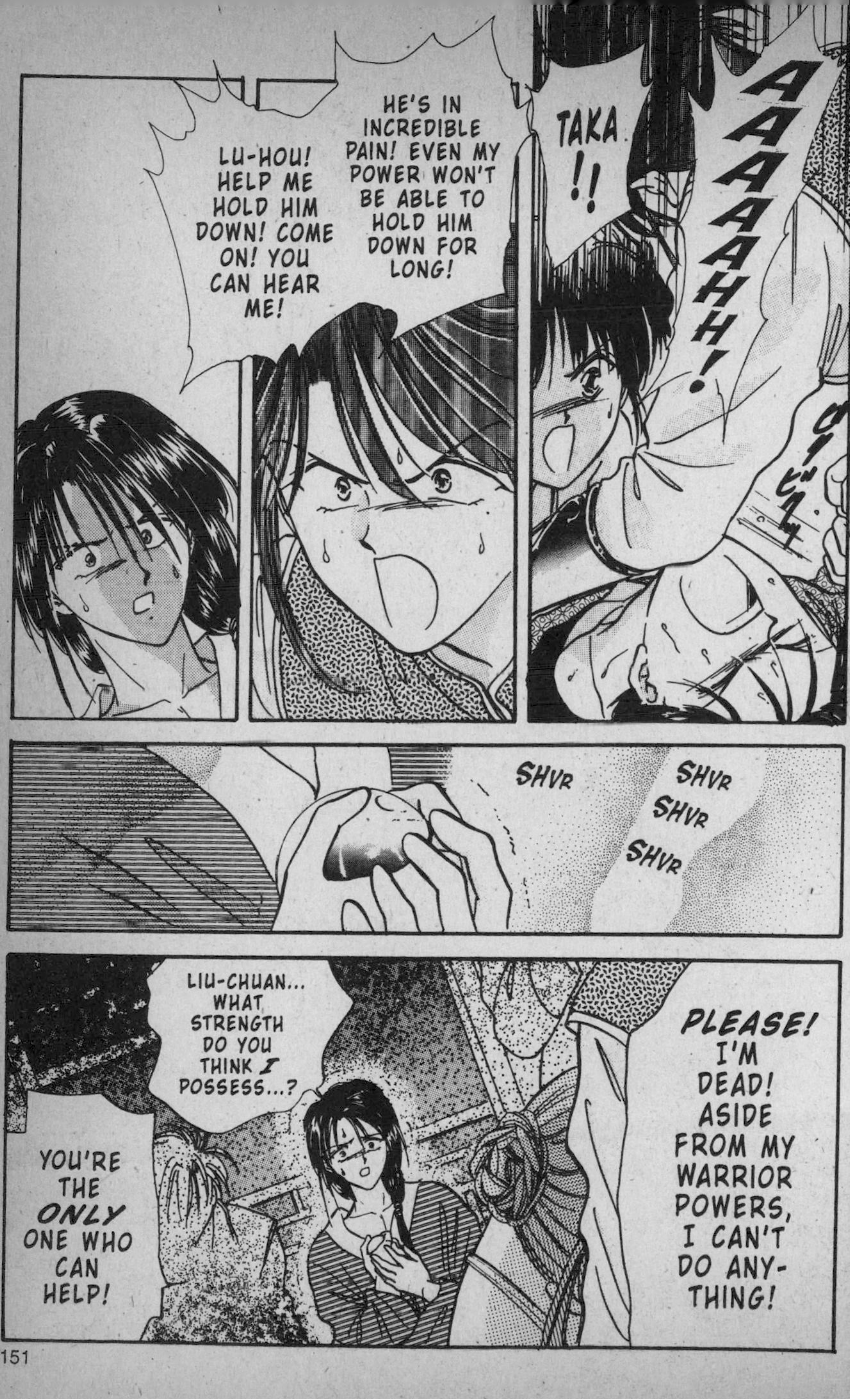
TAKA!!
AAAAAAHH!
HE'S IN INCREDIBLE PAIN! EVEN MY POWER WON'T BE ABLE TO HOLD HIM DOWN FOR LONG!
LU-HOU! HELP ME HOLD HIM DOWN! COME ON! YOU CAN HEAR ME!
SHVR
SHVR
SHVR
SHVR
LIU-CHUAN... WHAT STRENGTH DO YOU THINK *I* POSSESS...?
PLEASE! I'M DEAD! ASIDE FROM MY WARRIOR POWERS, I CAN'T DO ANYTHING!
YOU'RE THE *ONLY* ONE WHO CAN HELP!

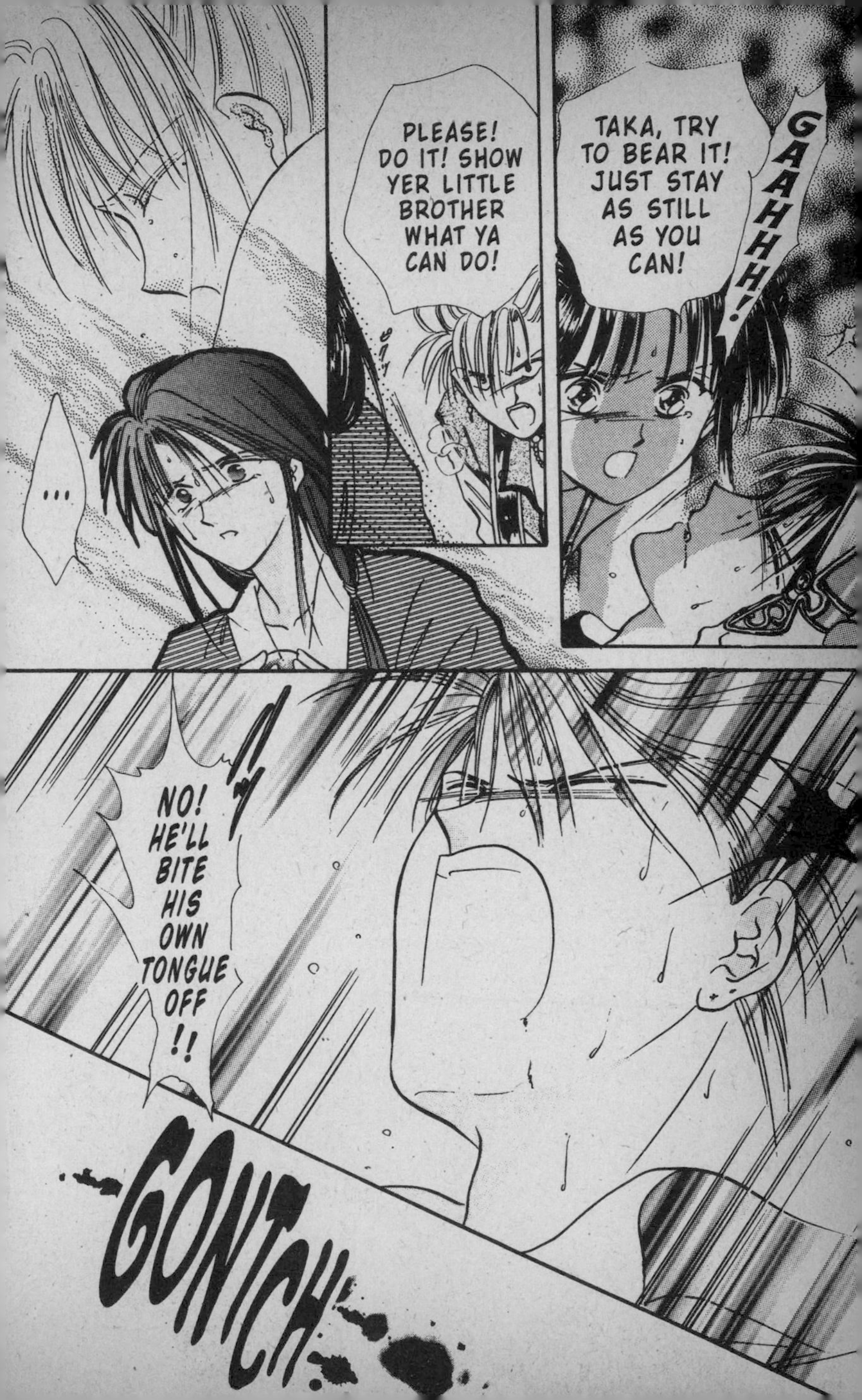
TAKA, TRY TO BEAR IT! JUST STAY AS STILL AS YOU CAN!
GAAHHHH!
PLEASE! DO IT! SHOW YER LITTLE BROTHER WHAT YA CAN DO!
...
NO! HE'LL BITE HIS OWN TONGUE OFF !!
GONTCH

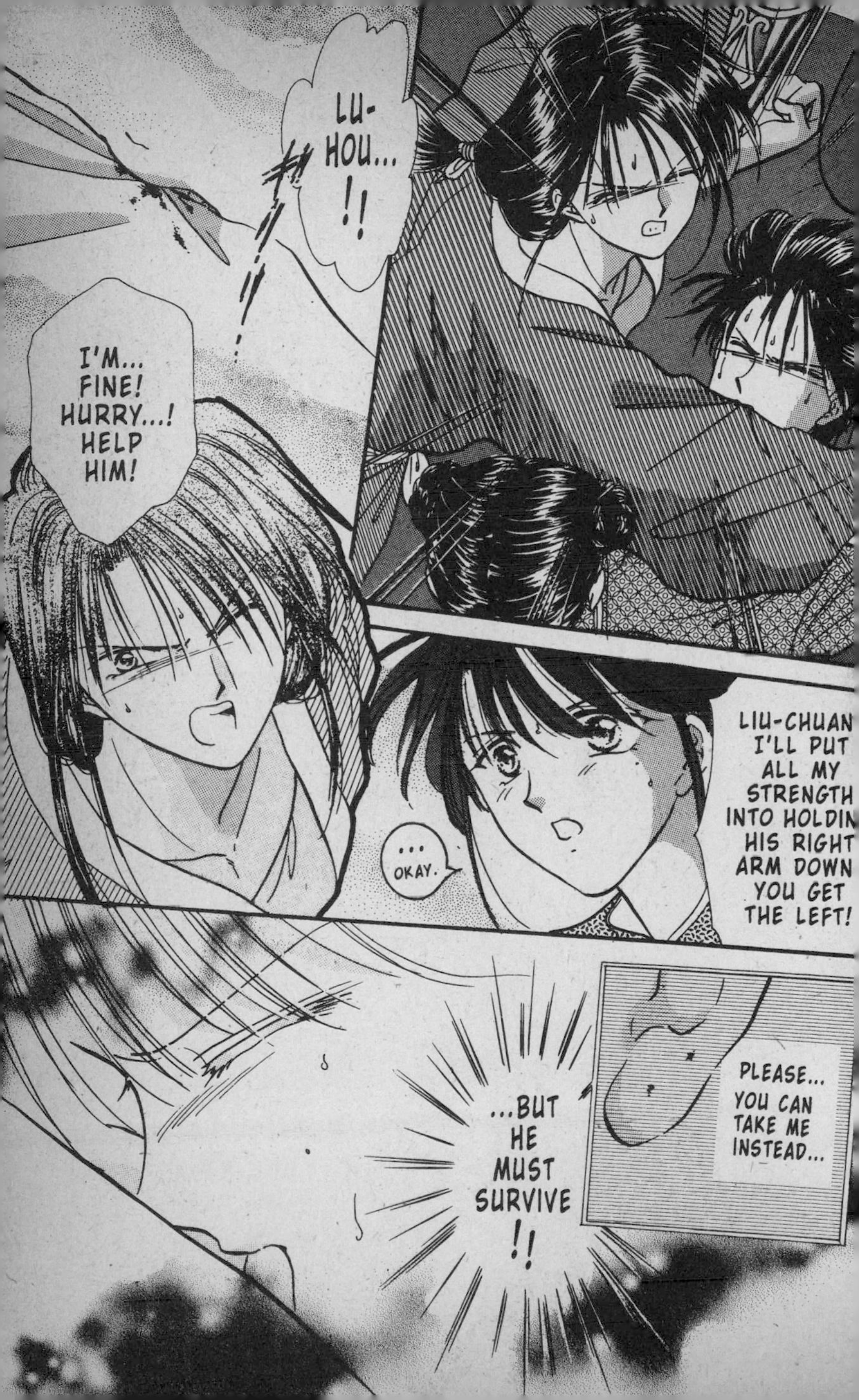
LU-HOU...!!
I'M... FINE! HURRY...! HELP HIM!
LIU-CHUAN I'LL PUT ALL MY STRENGTH INTO HOLDIN HIS RIGHT ARM DOWN YOU GET THE LEFT!
...OKAY.
PLEASE... YOU CAN TAKE ME INSTEAD...
...BUT HE MUST SURVIVE!!

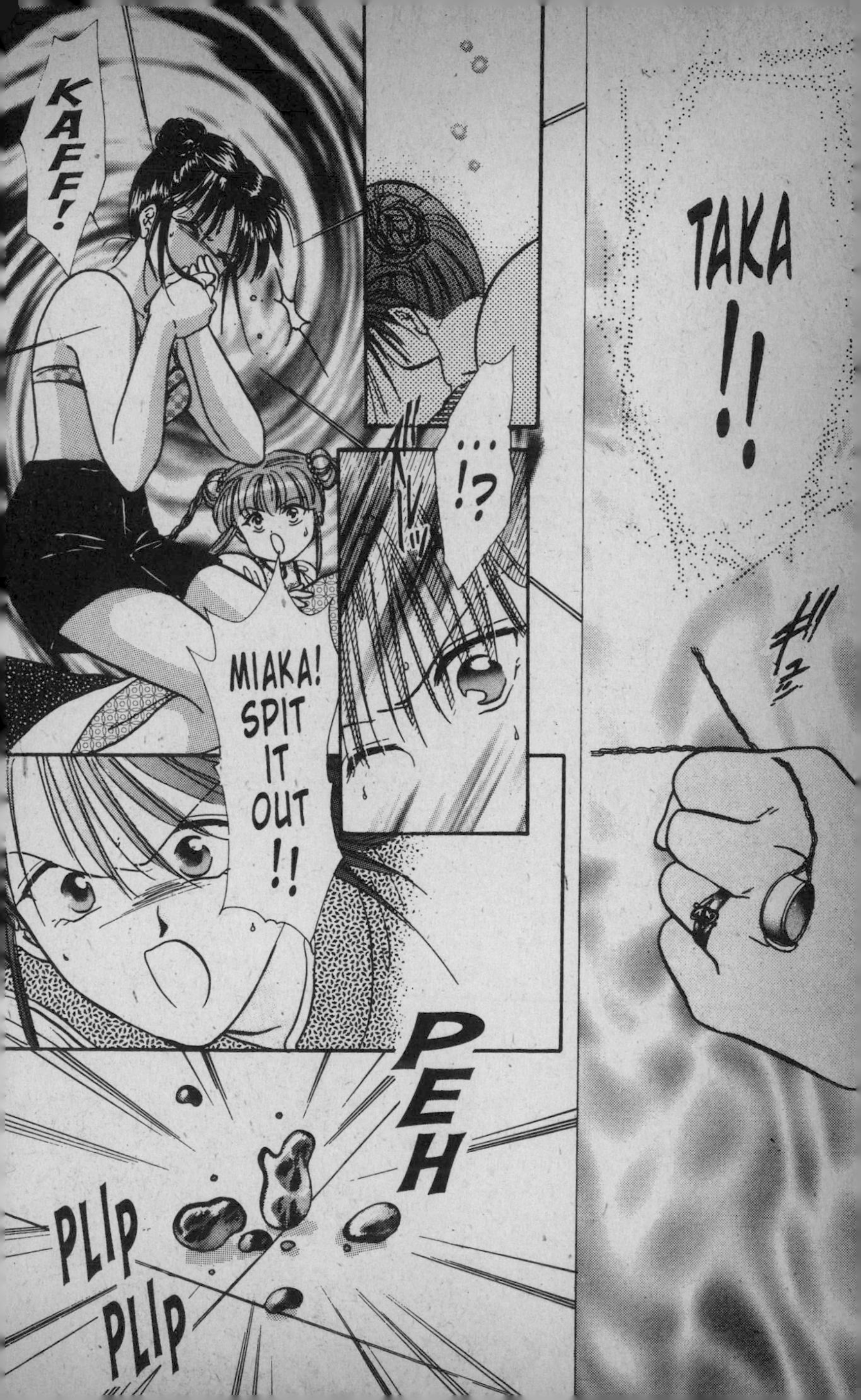
TAKA!!
KAFF!
...!?
MIAKA! SPIT IT OUT!!
PEH
PLIP
PLIP

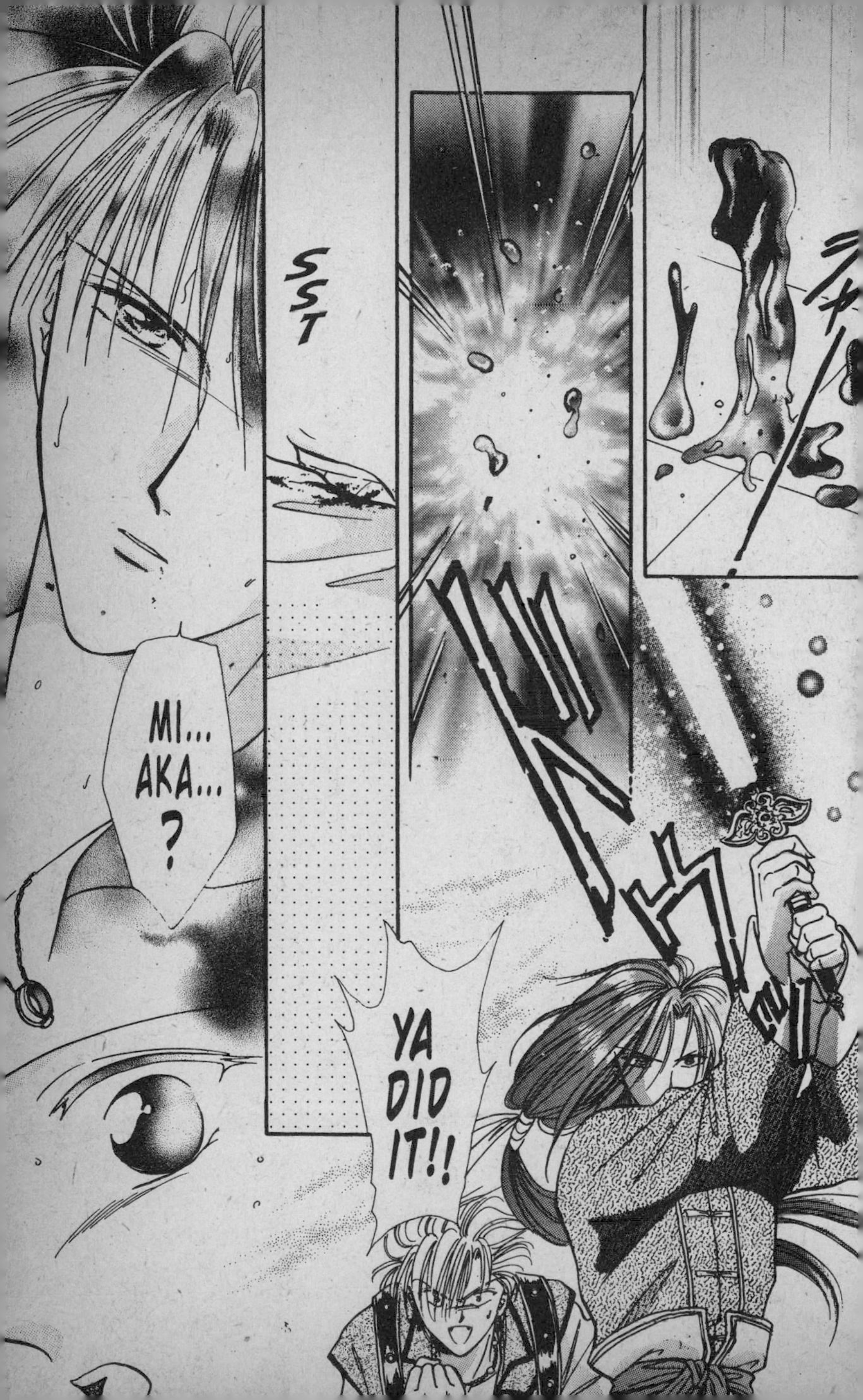
SST
YA DID IT!!
MI... AKA... ?

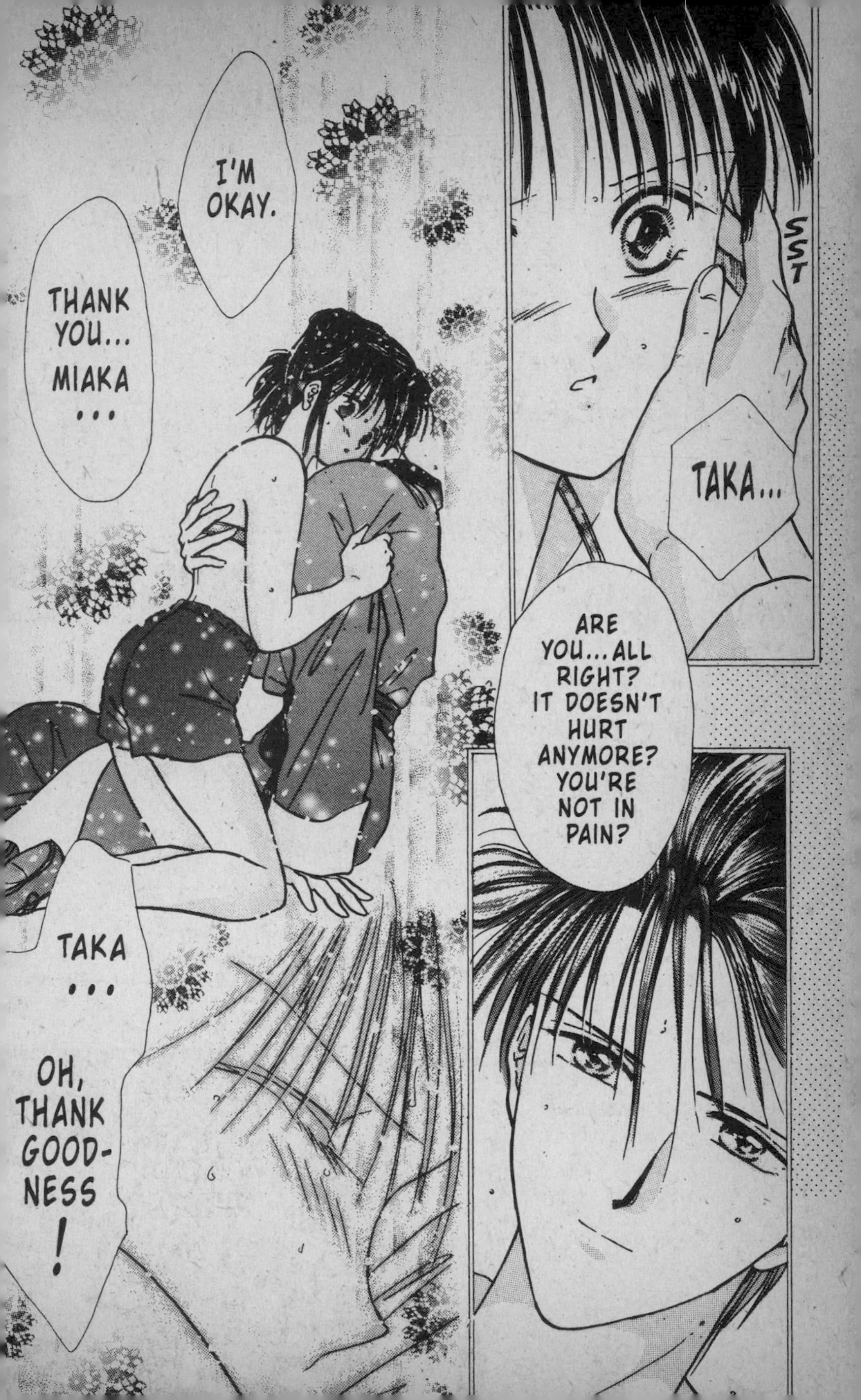
SST
TAKA...
ARE YOU...ALL RIGHT? IT DOESN'T HURT ANYMORE? YOU'RE NOT IN PAIN?
I'M OKAY.
THANK YOU... MIAKA...
TAKA...
OH, THANK GOODNESS!

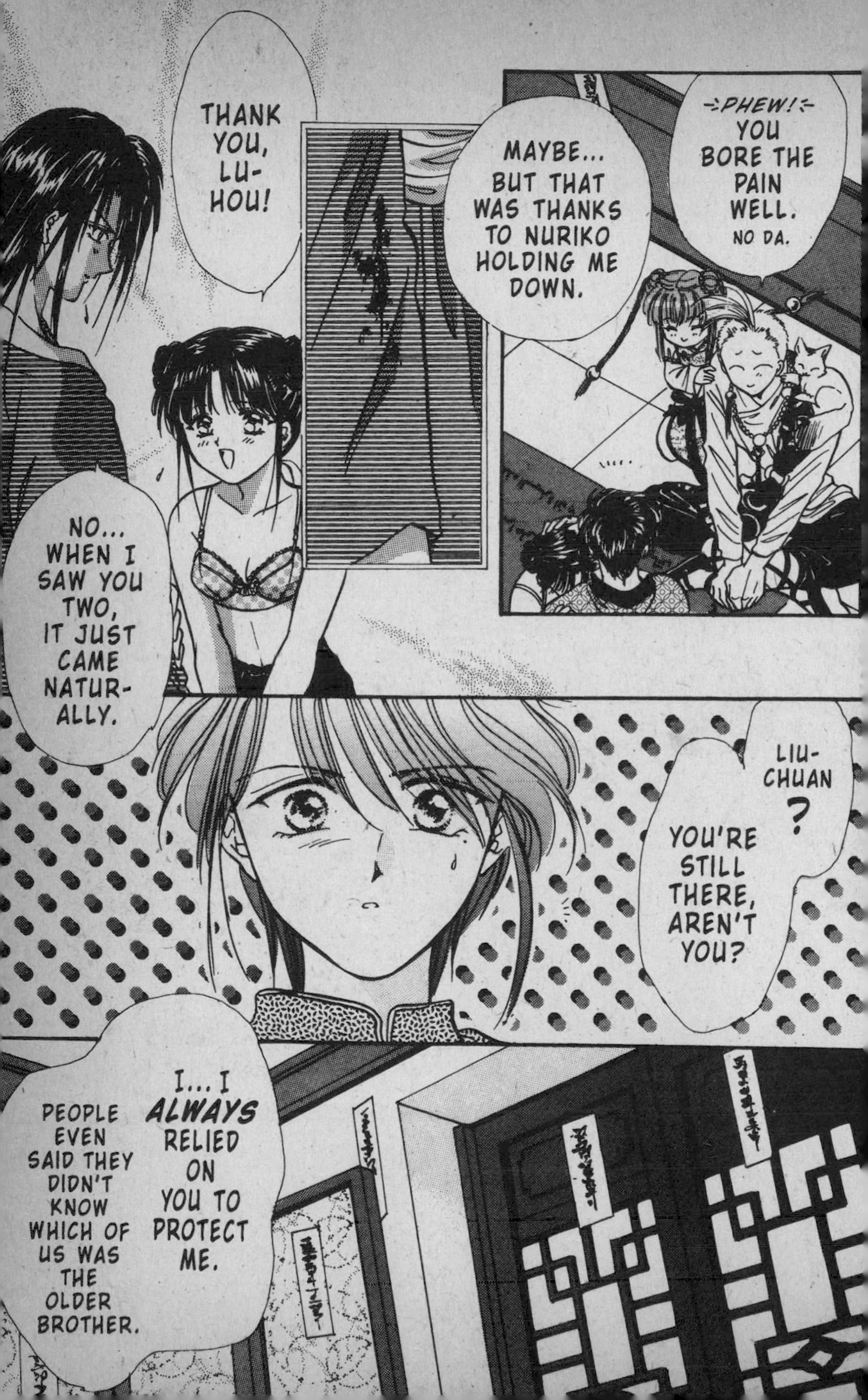
–PHEW!– YOU BORE THE PAIN WELL. NO DA.
MAYBE... BUT THAT WAS THANKS TO NURIKO HOLDING ME DOWN.
....
THANK YOU, LU-HOU!
NO... WHEN I SAW YOU TWO, IT JUST CAME NATURALLY.
LIU-CHUAN? YOU'RE STILL THERE, AREN'T YOU?
I... I ALWAYS RELIED ON YOU TO PROTECT ME.
PEOPLE EVEN SAID THEY DIDN'T KNOW WHICH OF US WAS THE OLDER BROTHER.

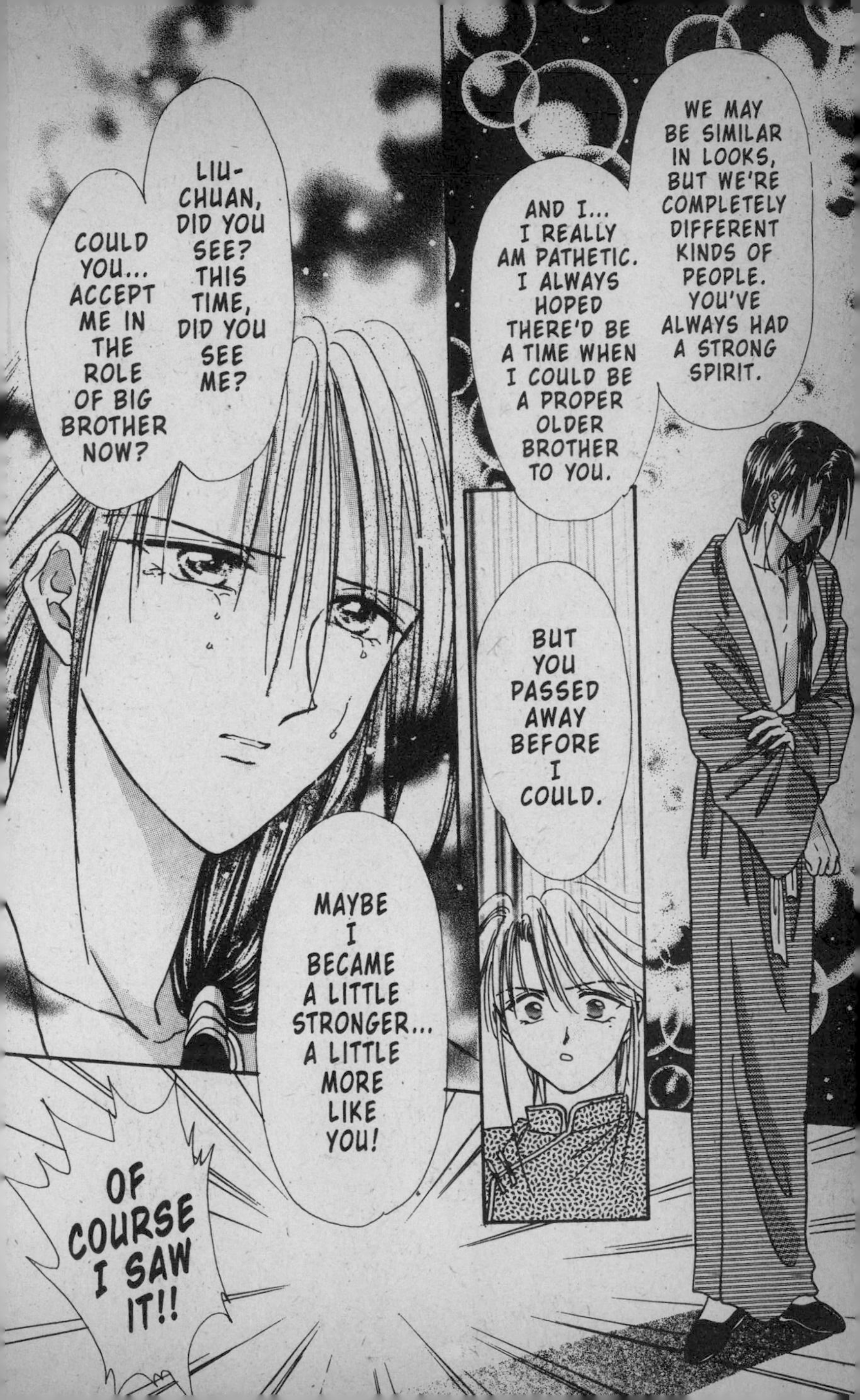
WE MAY BE SIMILAR IN LOOKS, BUT WE'RE COMPLETELY DIFFERENT KINDS OF PEOPLE. YOU'VE ALWAYS HAD A STRONG SPIRIT.
AND I... I REALLY AM PATHETIC. I ALWAYS HOPED THERE'D BE A TIME WHEN I COULD BE A PROPER OLDER BROTHER TO YOU.
BUT YOU PASSED AWAY BEFORE I COULD.
LIU-CHUAN, DID YOU SEE? THIS TIME, DID YOU SEE ME?
COULD YOU... ACCEPT ME IN THE ROLE OF BIG BROTHER NOW?
MAYBE I BECAME A LITTLE STRONGER... A LITTLE MORE LIKE YOU!
OF COURSE I SAW IT!!

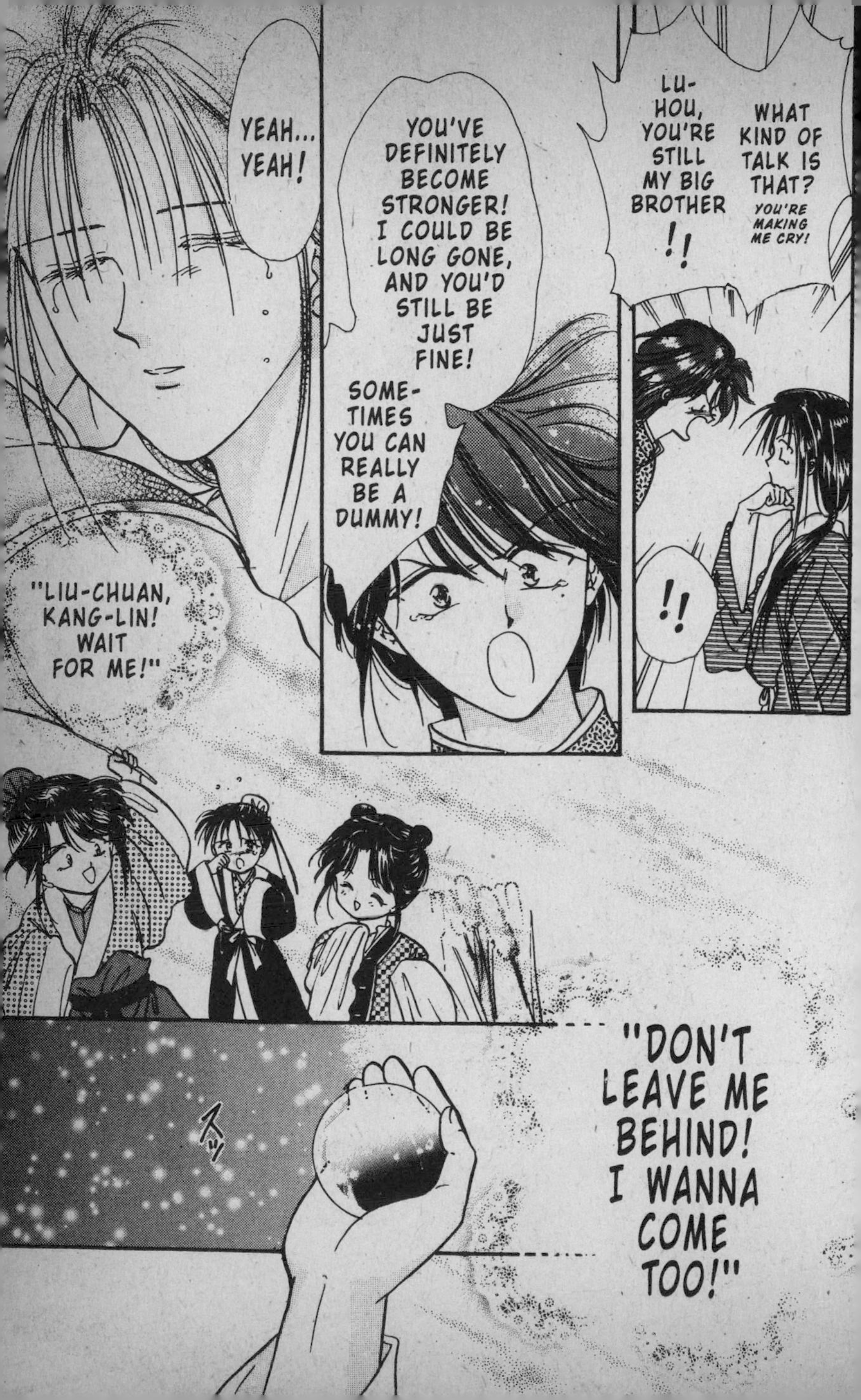
WHAT KIND OF TALK IS THAT? YOU'RE MAKING ME CRY!
LU-HOU, YOU'RE STILL MY BIG BROTHER !!
!!
YOU'VE DEFINITELY BECOME STRONGER! I COULD BE LONG GONE, AND YOU'D STILL BE JUST FINE!
SOME-TIMES YOU CAN REALLY BE A DUMMY!
YEAH... YEAH!
"LIU-CHUAN, KANG-LIN! WAIT FOR ME!"
"DON'T LEAVE ME BEHIND! I WANNA COME TOO!"
スッ

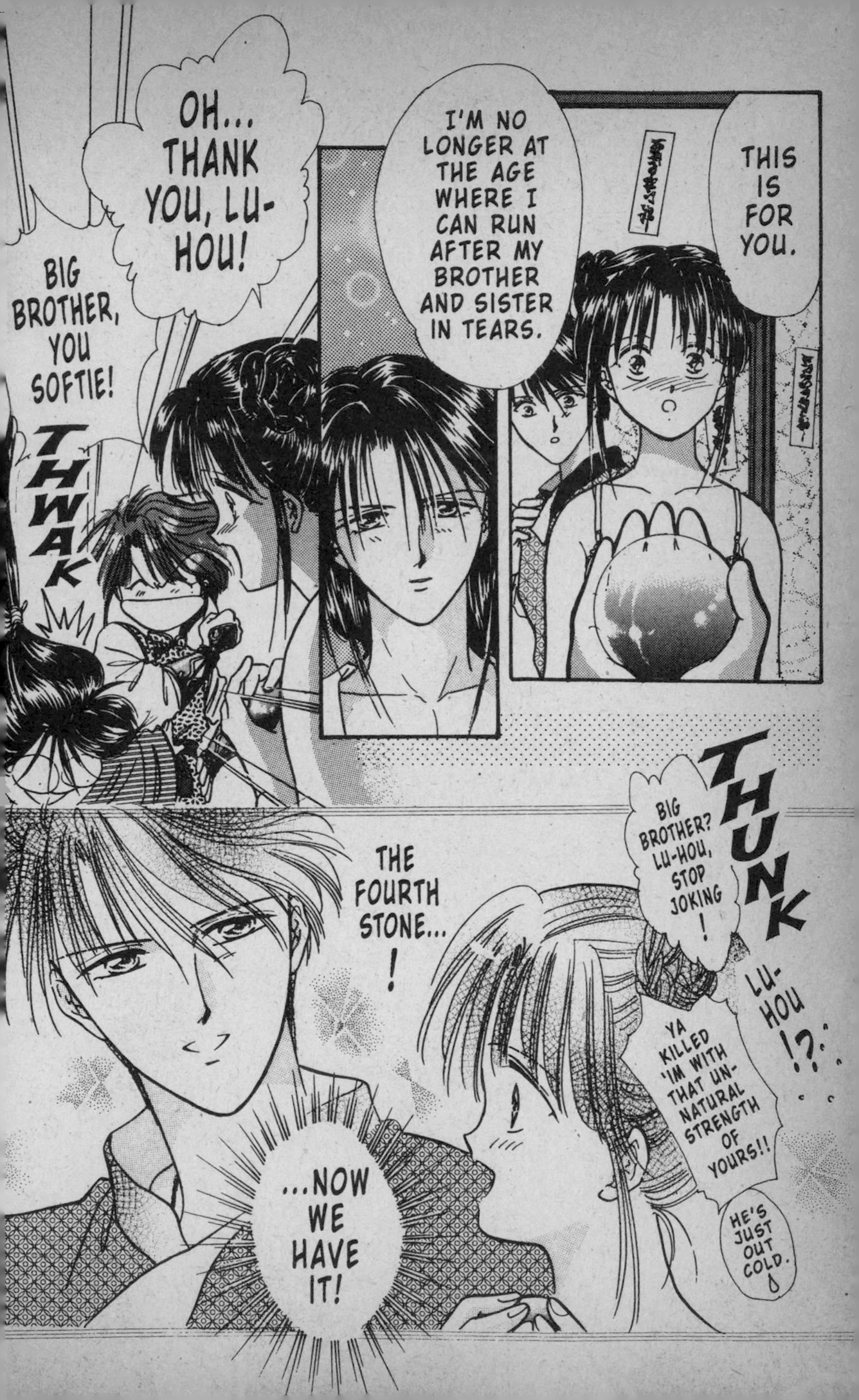
THIS IS FOR YOU.
I'M NO LONGER AT THE AGE WHERE I CAN RUN AFTER MY BROTHER AND SISTER IN TEARS.
OH... THANK YOU, LU-HOU!
BIG BROTHER, YOU SOFTIE!
THWAK
THUNK
BIG BROTHER? LU-HOU, STOP JOKING!
LU-HOU!?
YA KILLED 'IM WITH THAT UN-NATURAL STRENGTH OF YOURS!!
HE'S JUST OUT COLD.
THE FOURTH STONE...!
...NOW WE HAVE IT!

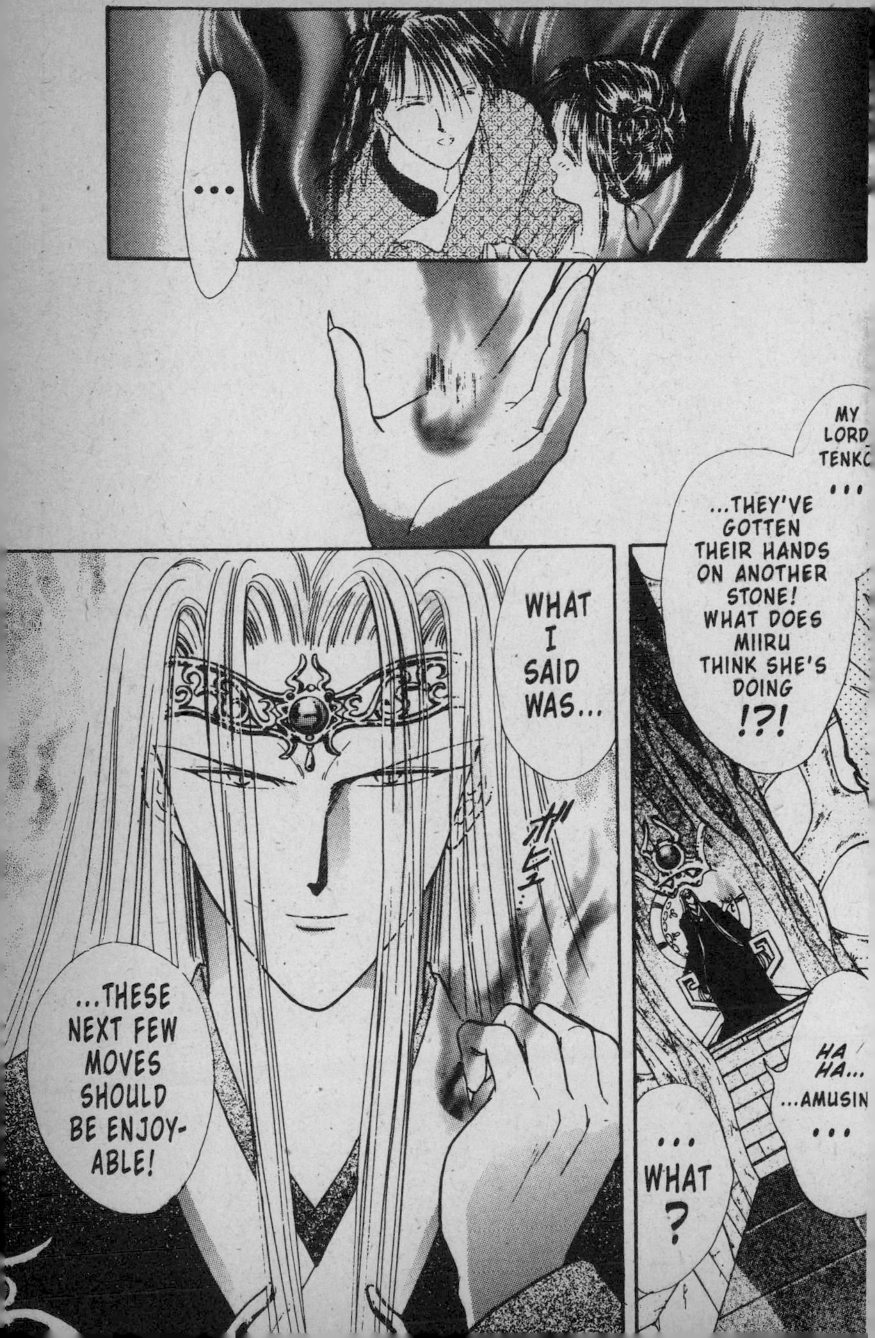
...
MY LORD TENKO...
...THEY'VE GOTTEN THEIR HANDS ON ANOTHER STONE! WHAT DOES MIIRU THINK SHE'S DOING !?!
HA HA... ...AMUSIN...
... WHAT?
WHAT I SAID WAS...
...THESE NEXT FEW MOVES SHOULD BE ENJOY-ABLE!

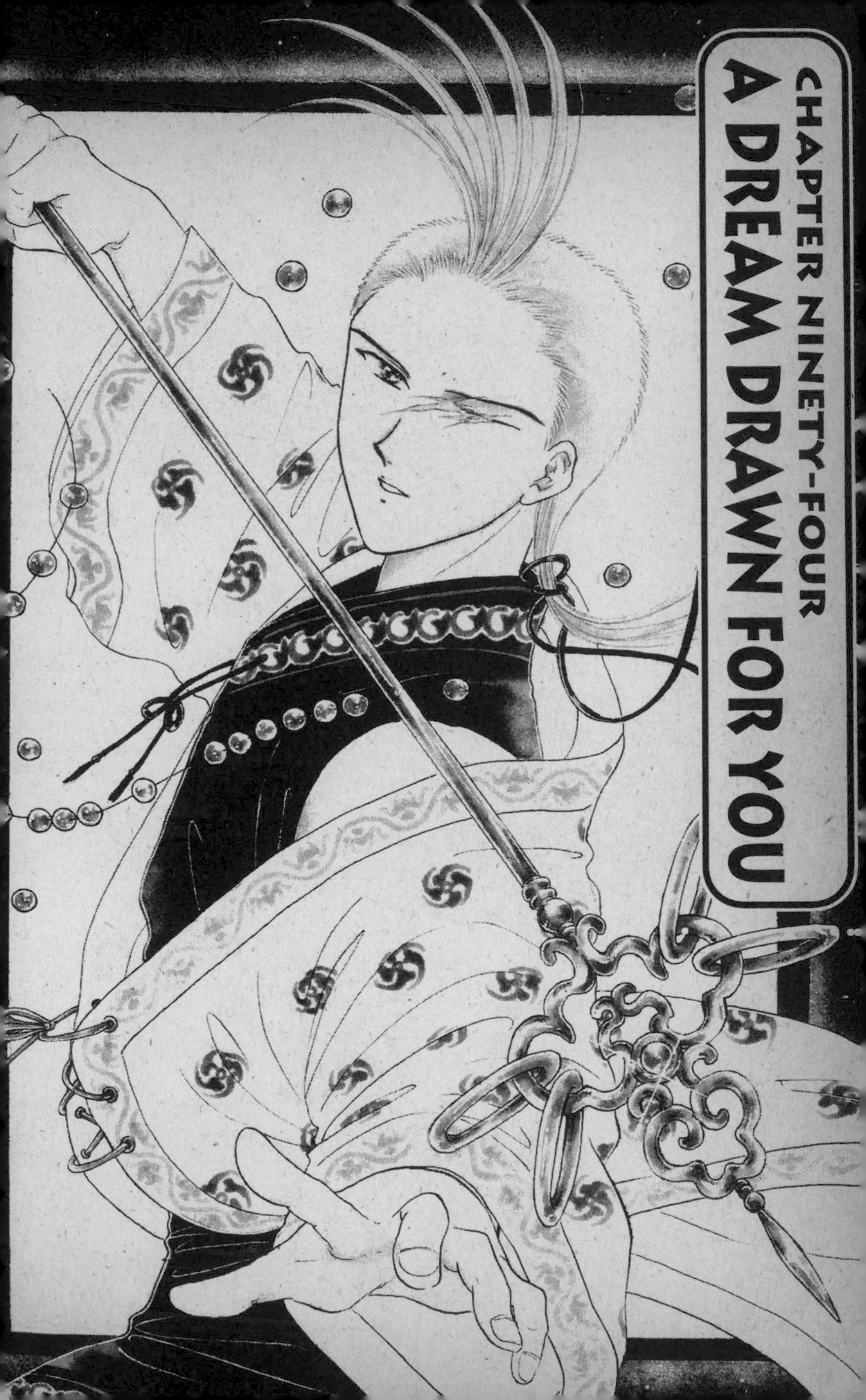
CHAPTER NINETY-FOUR
A DREAM DRAWN FOR YOU

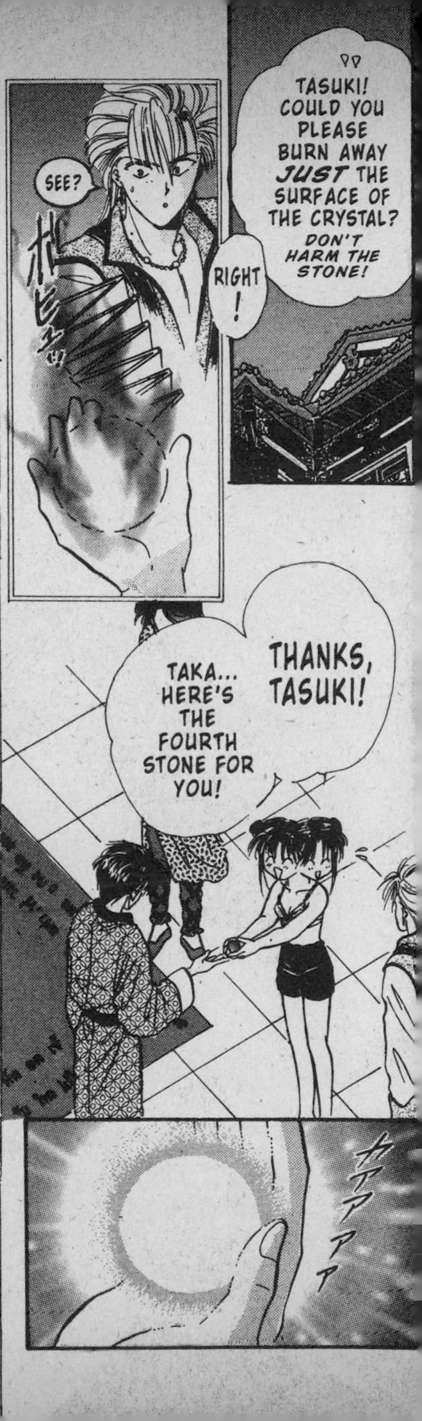
TASUKI! COULD YOU PLEASE BURN AWAY *JUST* THE SURFACE OF THE CRYSTAL? *DON'T HARM THE STONE!*
RIGHT!
SEE?
THANKS, TASUKI!
TAKA... HERE'S THE FOURTH STONE FOR YOU!

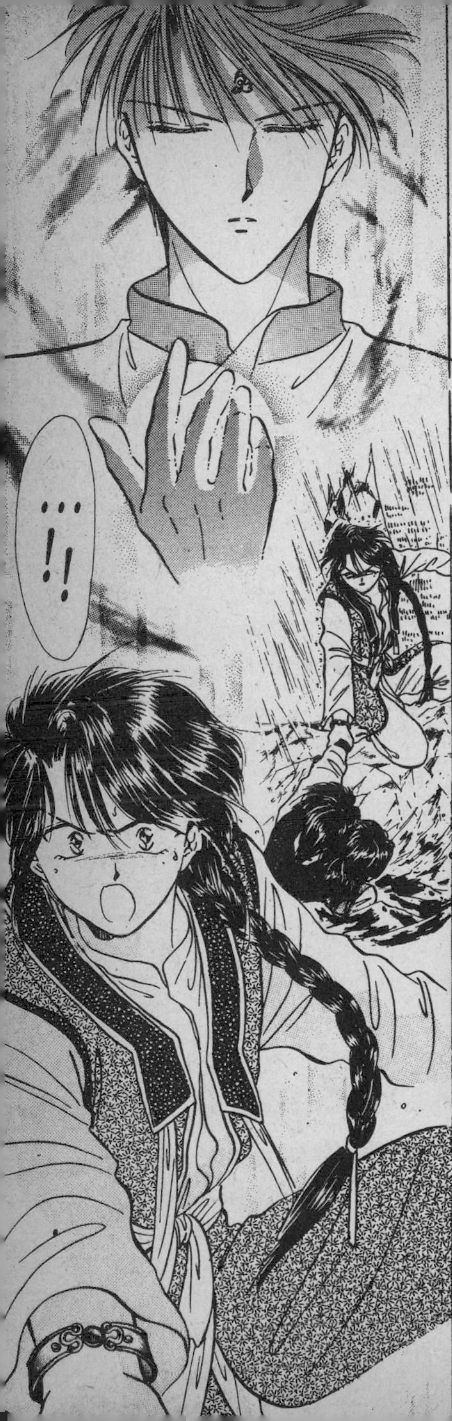
...!!

WHAT YOU SAID BACK THEN..., THAT WE HAD TO STAY ALIVE, BECAUSE ONE DAY WE'D LOOK BACK ON IT AND LAUGH...
...YOU TURNED OUT TO BE RIGHT, NURIKO.
TAMA-HOME, ARE YOU BEING SARCASTIC?
WE *ARE* DEAD, AFTER ALL.
NO! THAT'S NOT WHAT I MEANT!
IT TURNED OUT GOOD. ALL THAT WORK PAID OFF!
YUP!
TASUKI!
YEAH? WHATCHA WANT, TAMA?
WHAT IS THE MEANING OF *THAT!?*
WAAAAAAAAAH!
HEY, IT'S A LONG STORY!
I LIKE LONG STORIES! TELL ME ALL ABOUT IT!
THIS IS GREAT! NOW WE ONLY HAVE THREE STONES LEFT TO FIND!
I FOR-GOT!
ANCIENT HISTORY!
WHAT'S PAST IS PAST!

Fushigi Yûgi 16

Waaa! The last one!
With all of the new readers these days, I've been, on occasion, receiving some... *difficult* letters! When experts in Chinese history write all these detailed critiques... All I can say is "What? Huh? I don't understand!" ☺ It doesn't matter what history books or other specialty books I've studied... when I read these letters, it's like my mind is a blank! At the beginning, I was so intent on doing exhaustive research, but when I submitted my thoroughly researched stories to the publishers, they were all turned down! ☺ While on the job, I've learned that letters like these (complaining about accuracy) have nothing to do with whether the manga is interesting or not. I did read a bunch of books about the four gods (I don't understand them!), but as time went on, I stopped worrying so much about it. There are so many different stories that use the four gods! Every now and again I came across references to the 28 constellations, but there wasn't enough information there to write a story.
I got a letter from a male fan saying, "It's important to build a sense of a wide world, but the overall quality of the book depends on whether you can captivate the reader. A manga or novel or movie must appeal not so much to the knowledge centers but instead to the emotional centers." That was his opinion. I agree. ☺ I've adopted quite a few of my readers' opinions, and it's been a real education! I'm thankful for that. Although I'm sure that since *Fushigi Yûgi* is based on MY sense of a worldview, it must be distracting for some people...

Oh! Thanks for sending me your dōjinshi! They were so much fun! (I wonder if there'll be a lot more coming in...?) Hm... Why don't more of you guys send yours in? It's no fair to hog them all to yourselves! ☺ If you think, "The creator will get mad," well... there are a lot of different types of artists out there. And I'm not the type to get angry! I've seen racy books, and I'm fine with them! ☺ So just screw up your courage and send them!! Even just one, send them in! I want to see the-- Ah! I'm going too far! Farewell everyone! *stomp, stomp, stomp, slam!*

What a weird manga-ka! 95. 11. 17.

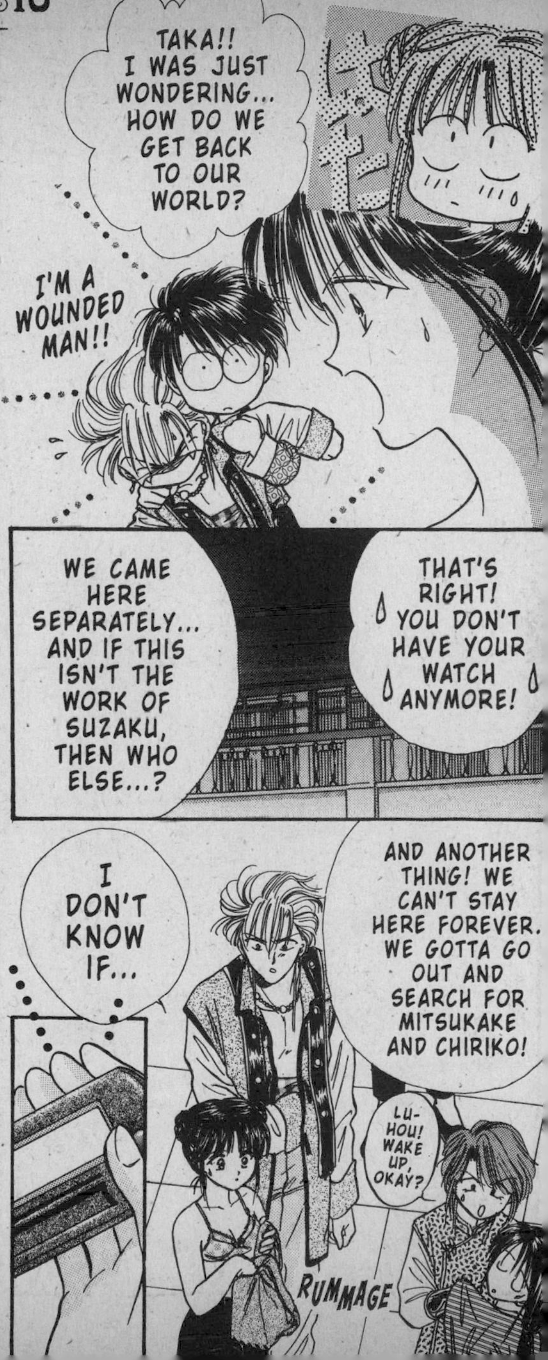

TAKA!! I WAS JUST WONDERING... HOW DO WE GET BACK TO OUR WORLD?
I'M A WOUNDED MAN!!
THAT'S RIGHT! YOU DON'T HAVE YOUR WATCH ANYMORE!
WE CAME HERE SEPARATELY... AND IF THIS ISN'T THE WORK OF SUZAKU, THEN WHO ELSE...?
AND ANOTHER THING! WE CAN'T STAY HERE FOREVER. WE GOTTA GO OUT AND SEARCH FOR MITSUKAKE AND CHIRIKO!
I DON'T KNOW IF...
LU-HOU! WAKE UP, OKAY?
RUMMAGE

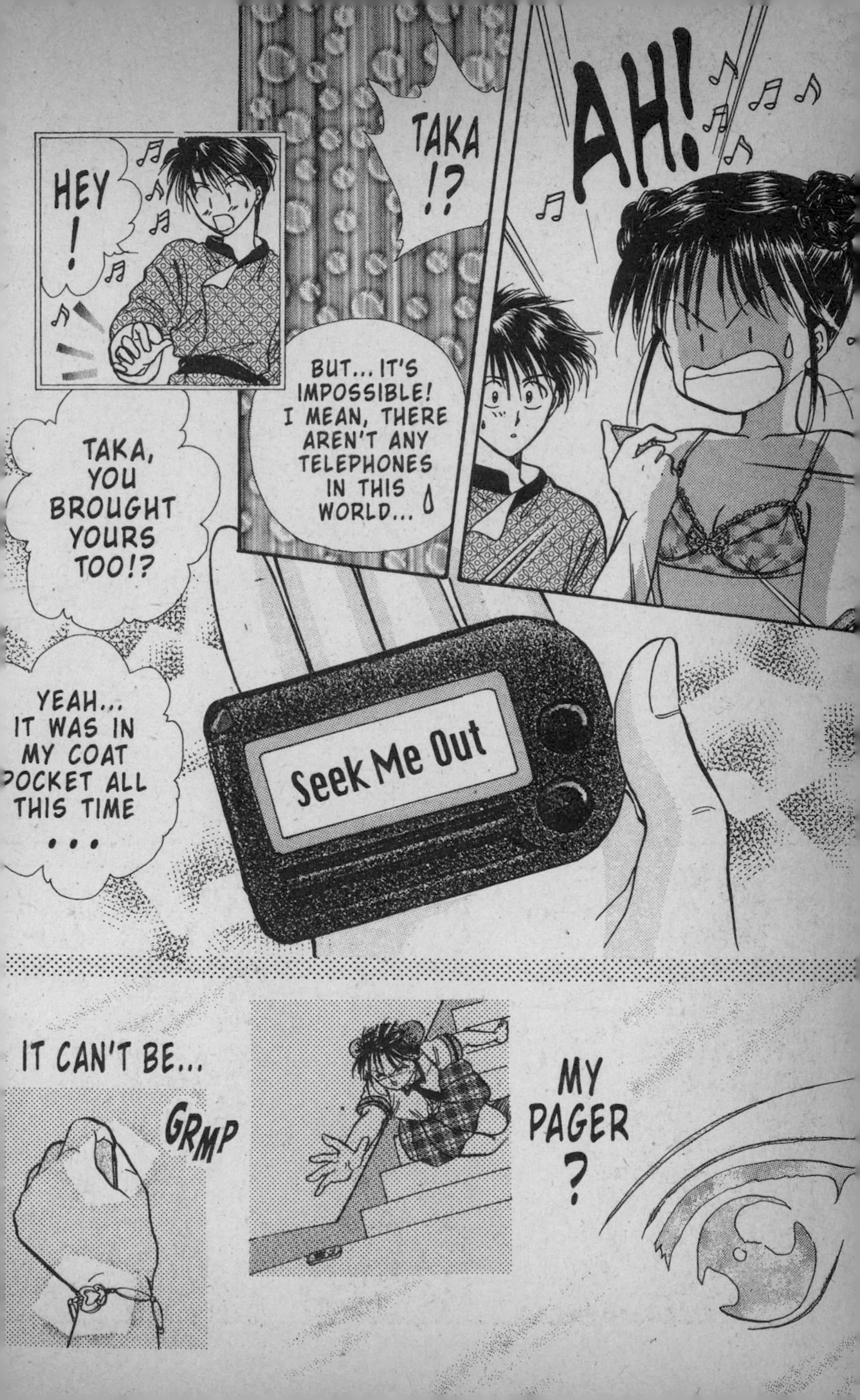
AH!
TAKA !?
BUT... IT'S IMPOSSIBLE! I MEAN, THERE AREN'T ANY TELEPHONES IN THIS WORLD...
HEY !
Seek Me Out
TAKA, YOU BROUGHT YOURS TOO!?
YEAH... IT WAS IN MY COAT POCKET ALL THIS TIME ...
MY PAGER ?
IT CAN'T BE...
GRMP

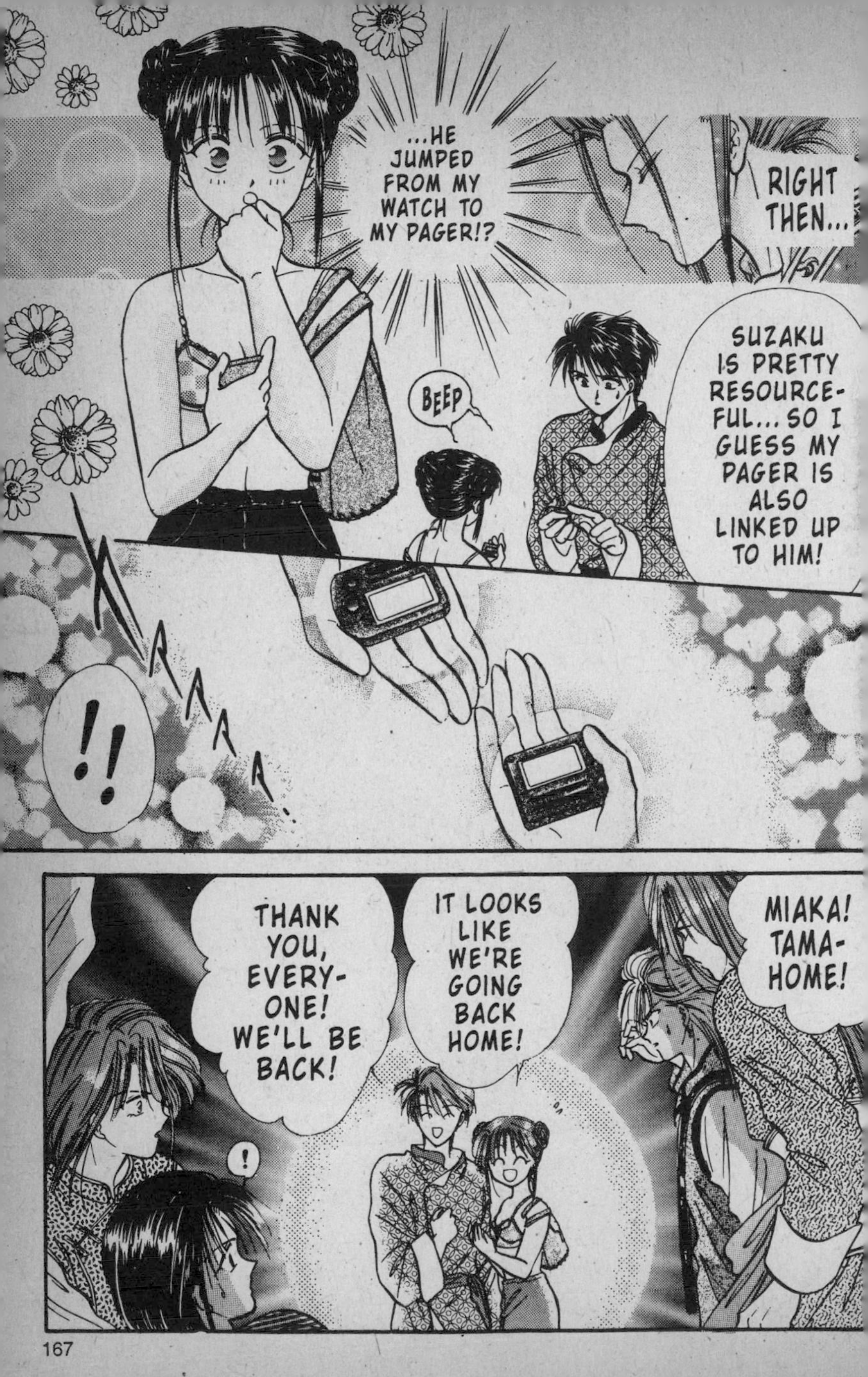
RIGHT THEN...
...HE JUMPED FROM MY WATCH TO MY PAGER!?
SUZAKU IS PRETTY RESOURCE-FUL... SO I GUESS MY PAGER IS ALSO LINKED UP TO HIM!
BEEP
!!
MIAKA! TAMA-HOME!
IT LOOKS LIKE WE'RE GOING BACK HOME!
THANK YOU, EVERY-ONE! WE'LL BE BACK!
!

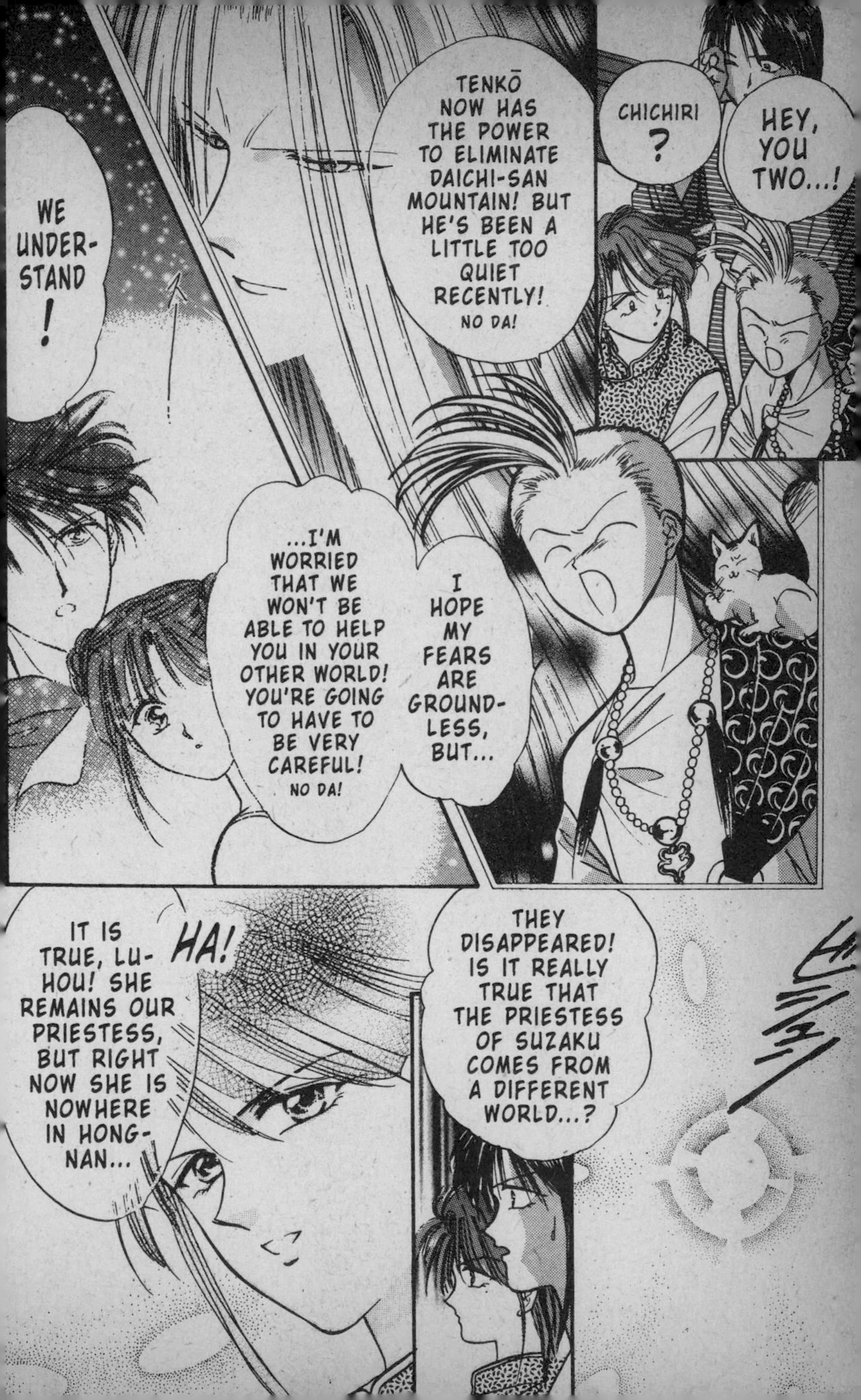
HEY, YOU TWO...!
CHICHIRI?
TENKŌ NOW HAS THE POWER TO ELIMINATE DAICHI-SAN MOUNTAIN! BUT HE'S BEEN A LITTLE TOO QUIET RECENTLY! NO DA!
I HOPE MY FEARS ARE GROUNDLESS, BUT...
...I'M WORRIED THAT WE WON'T BE ABLE TO HELP YOU IN YOUR OTHER WORLD! YOU'RE GOING TO HAVE TO BE VERY CAREFUL! NO DA!
WE UNDERSTAND!
THEY DISAPPEARED! IS IT REALLY TRUE THAT THE PRIESTESS OF SUZAKU COMES FROM A DIFFERENT WORLD...?
HA!
IT IS TRUE, LU-HOU! SHE REMAINS OUR PRIESTESS, BUT RIGHT NOW SHE IS NOWHERE IN HONG-NAN...

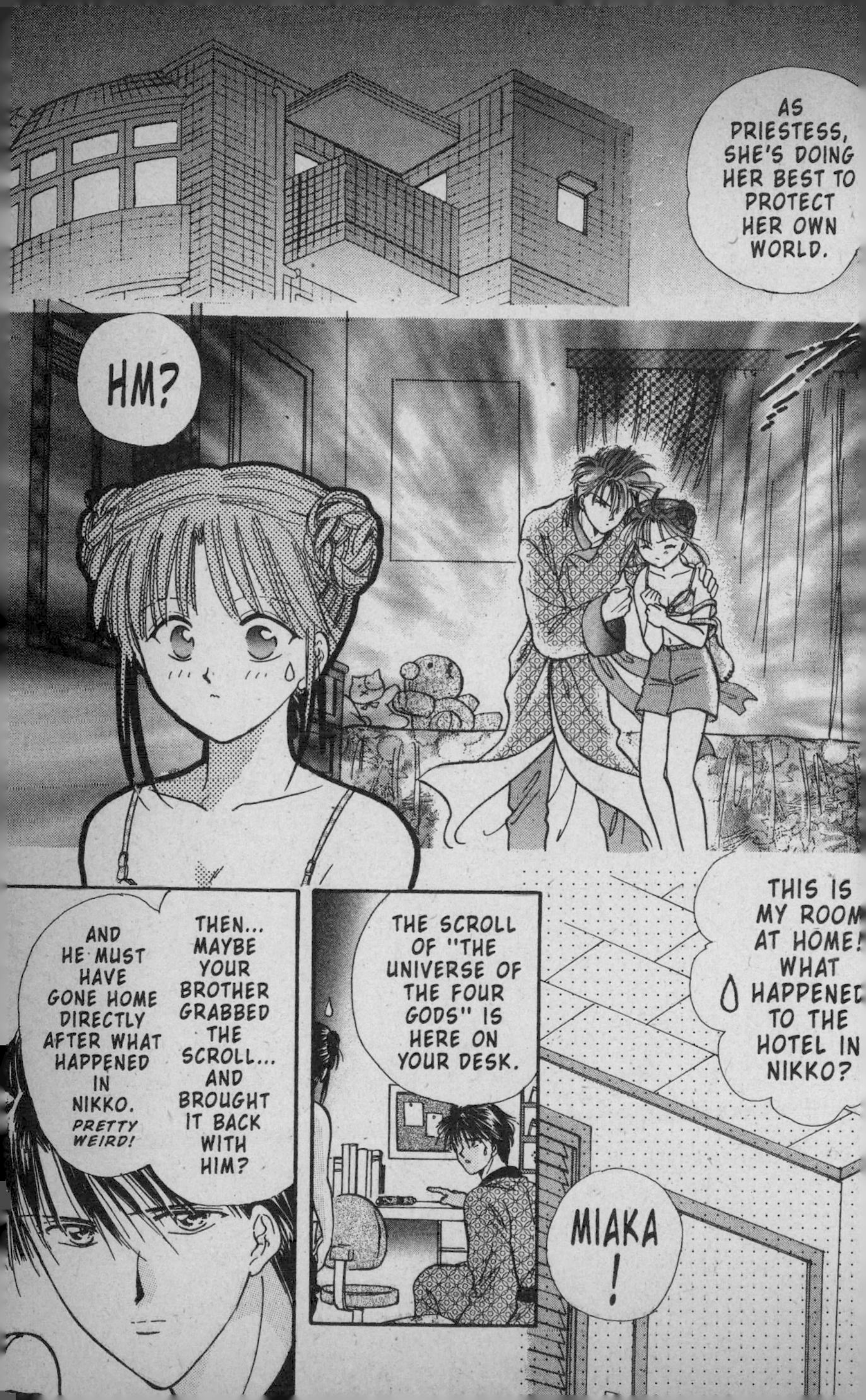
AS PRIESTESS, SHE'S DOING HER BEST TO PROTECT HER OWN WORLD.
HM?
THIS IS MY ROOM AT HOME! WHAT HAPPENED TO THE HOTEL IN NIKKO?
MIAKA!
THE SCROLL OF "THE UNIVERSE OF THE FOUR GODS" IS HERE ON YOUR DESK.
THEN... MAYBE YOUR BROTHER GRABBED THE SCROLL... AND BROUGHT IT BACK WITH HIM?
AND HE MUST HAVE GONE HOME DIRECTLY AFTER WHAT HAPPENED IN NIKKO. PRETTY WEIRD!

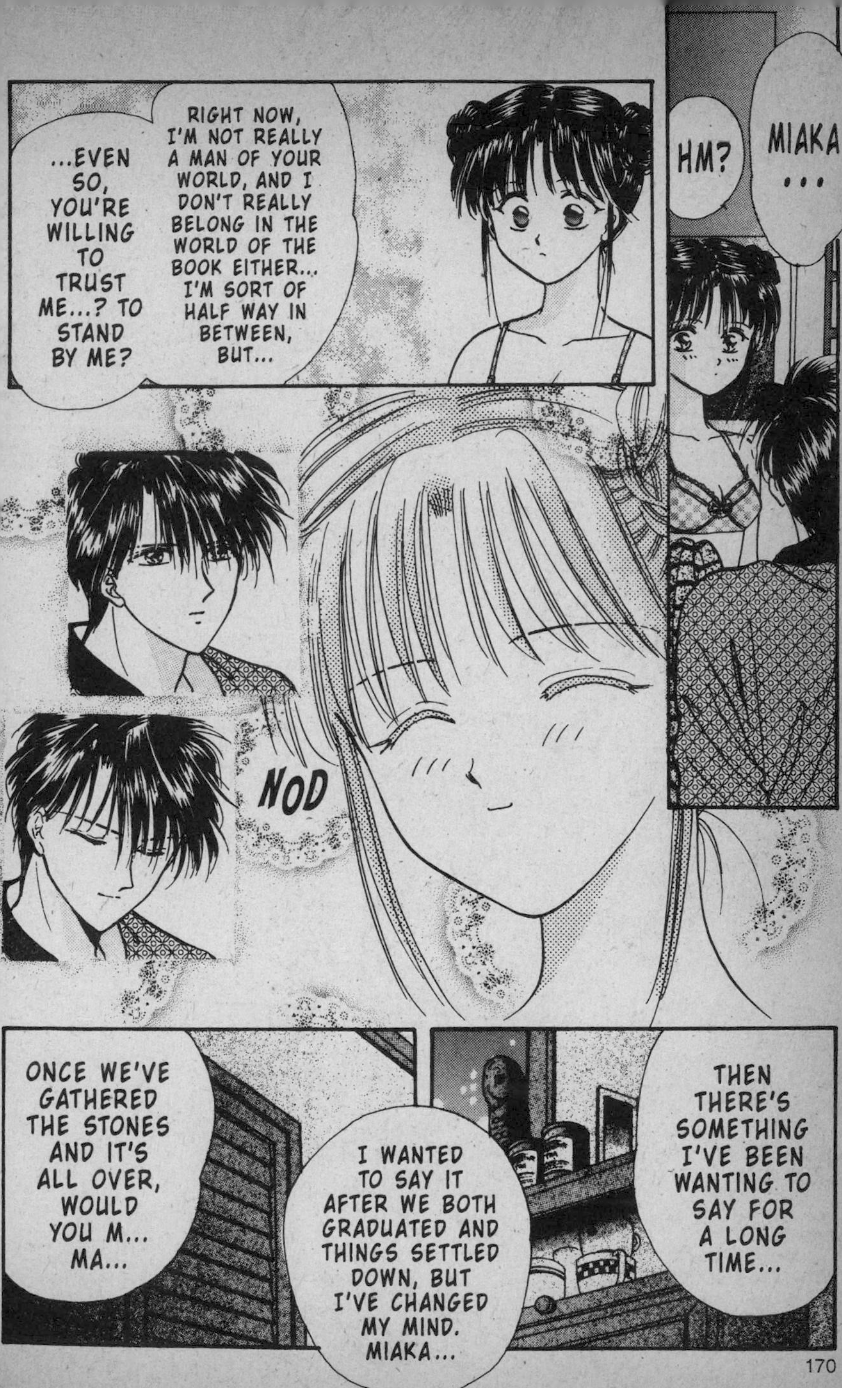
MIAKA...
HM?
RIGHT NOW, I'M NOT REALLY A MAN OF YOUR WORLD, AND I DON'T REALLY BELONG IN THE WORLD OF THE BOOK EITHER... I'M SORT OF HALF WAY IN BETWEEN, BUT...
...EVEN SO, YOU'RE WILLING TO TRUST ME...? TO STAND BY ME?
NOD
THEN THERE'S SOMETHING I'VE BEEN WANTING TO SAY FOR A LONG TIME...
I WANTED TO SAY IT AFTER WE BOTH GRADUATED AND THINGS SETTLED DOWN, BUT I'VE CHANGED MY MIND. MIAKA...
ONCE WE'VE GATHERED THE STONES AND IT'S ALL OVER, WOULD YOU M... MA...

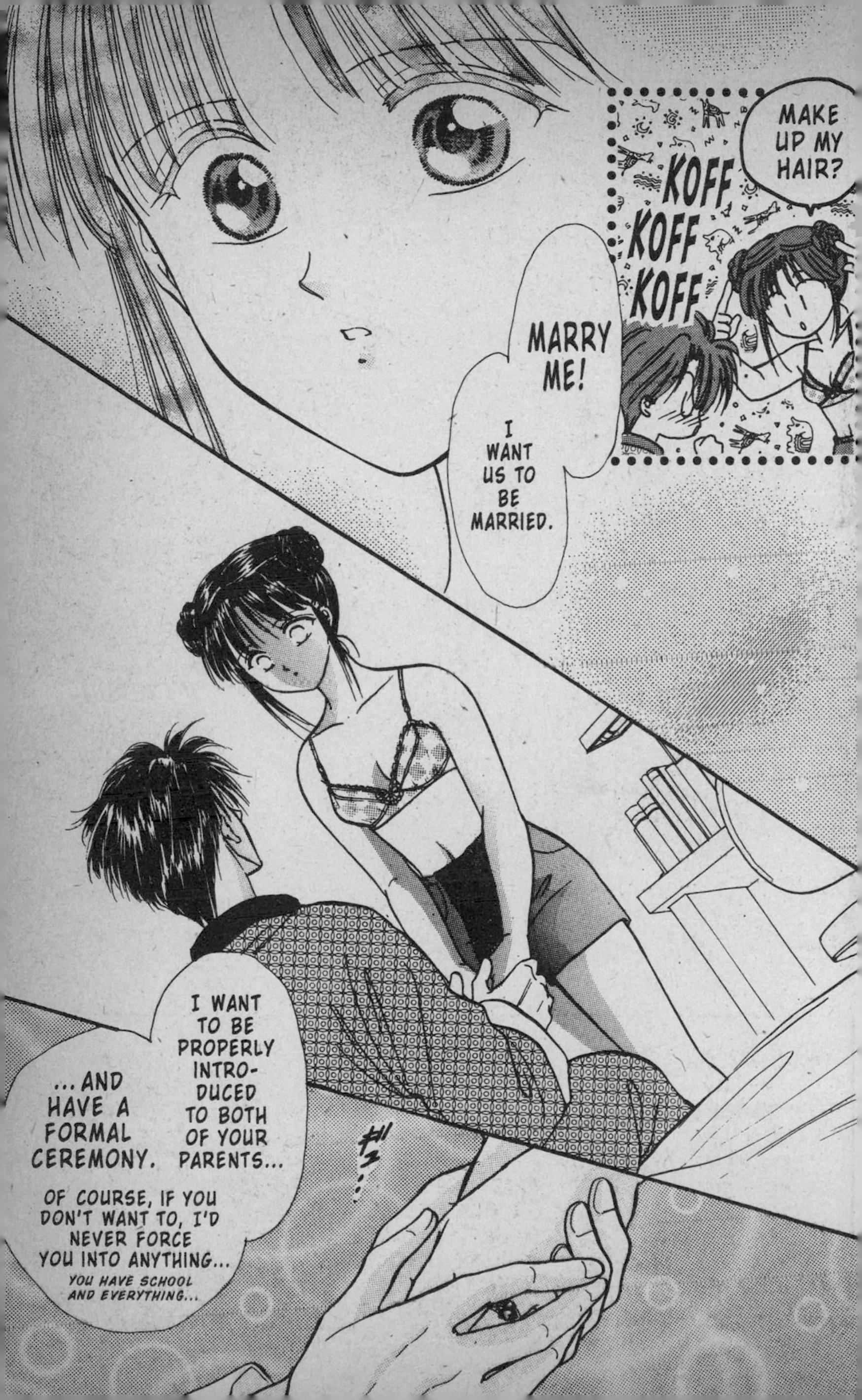
MAKE UP MY HAIR?
KOFF KOFF KOFF
MARRY ME!
I WANT US TO BE MARRIED.
I WANT TO BE PROPERLY INTRO-DUCED TO BOTH OF YOUR PARENTS...
...AND HAVE A FORMAL CEREMONY.
OF COURSE, IF YOU DON'T WANT TO, I'D NEVER FORCE YOU INTO ANYTHING...
YOU HAVE SCHOOL AND EVERYTHING...

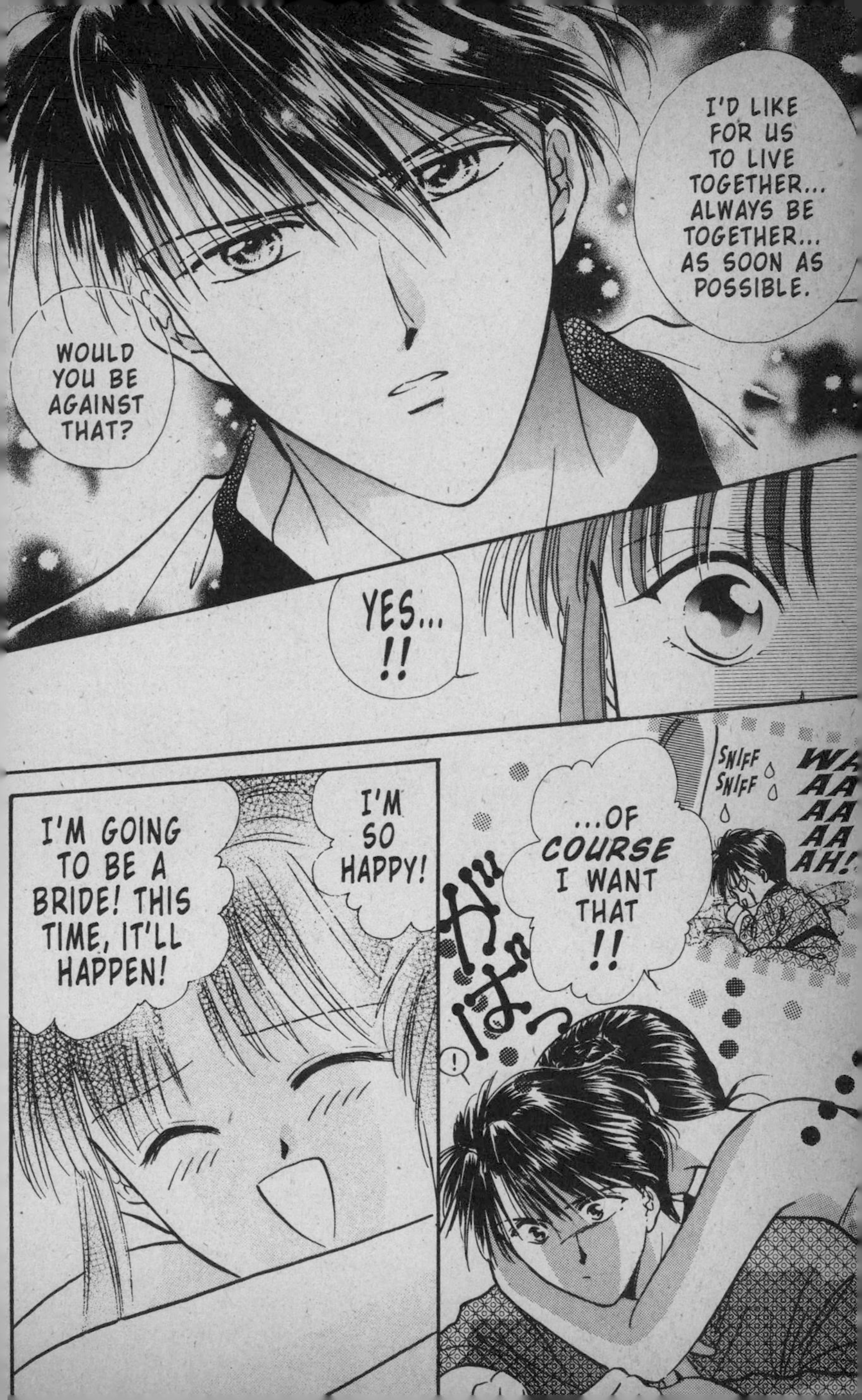
I'D LIKE FOR US TO LIVE TOGETHER... ALWAYS BE TOGETHER... AS SOON AS POSSIBLE.
WOULD YOU BE AGAINST THAT?
YES... !!
WAAAAAAAAH!
SNIFF SNIFF
...OF COURSE I WANT THAT!!
がばっ
!
I'M SO HAPPY!
I'M GOING TO BE A BRIDE! THIS TIME, IT'LL HAPPEN!

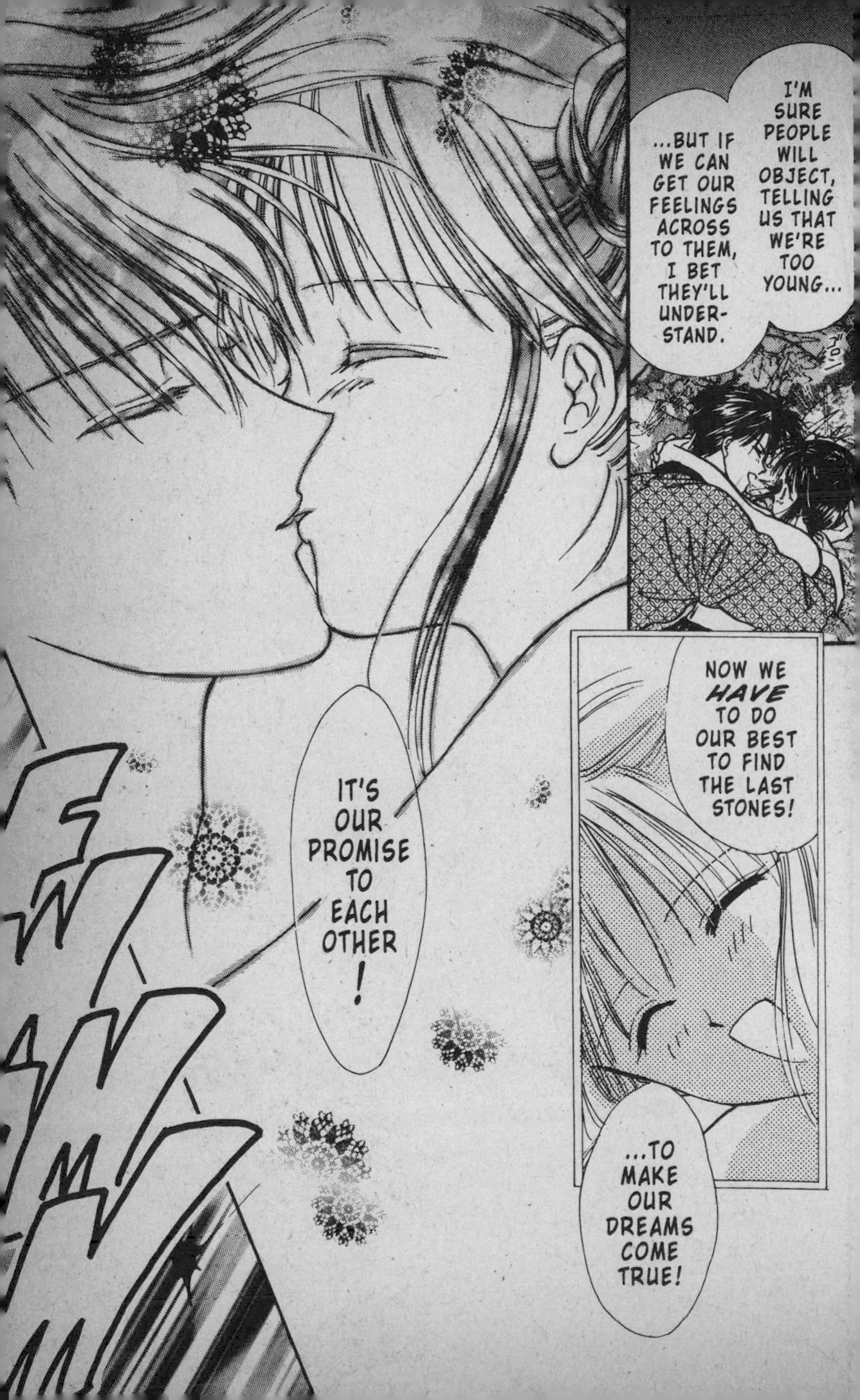
I'M SURE PEOPLE WILL OBJECT, TELLING US THAT WE'RE TOO YOUNG...
...BUT IF WE CAN GET OUR FEELINGS ACROSS TO THEM, I BET THEY'LL UNDER-STAND.
NOW WE HAVE TO DO OUR BEST TO FIND THE LAST STONES!
...TO MAKE OUR DREAMS COME TRUE!
IT'S OUR PROMISE TO EACH OTHER!

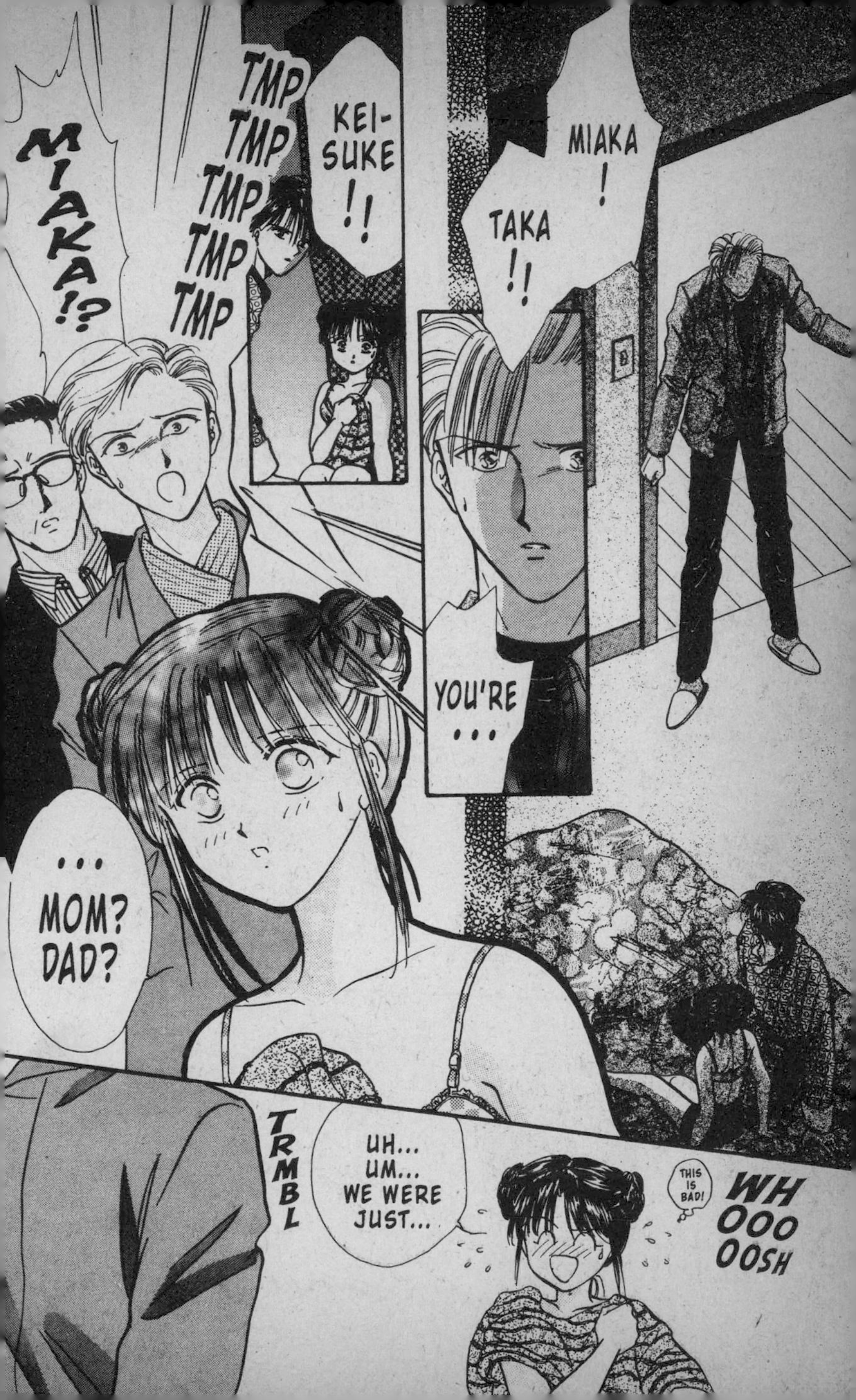
MIAKA!
TAKA!!
KEI-SUKE!!
TMP TMP TMP TMP TMP
MIAKA!?
YOU'RE...
...MOM? DAD?
WHOOOOOSH
THIS IS BAD!
UH... UM... WE WERE JUST...
TRMBL

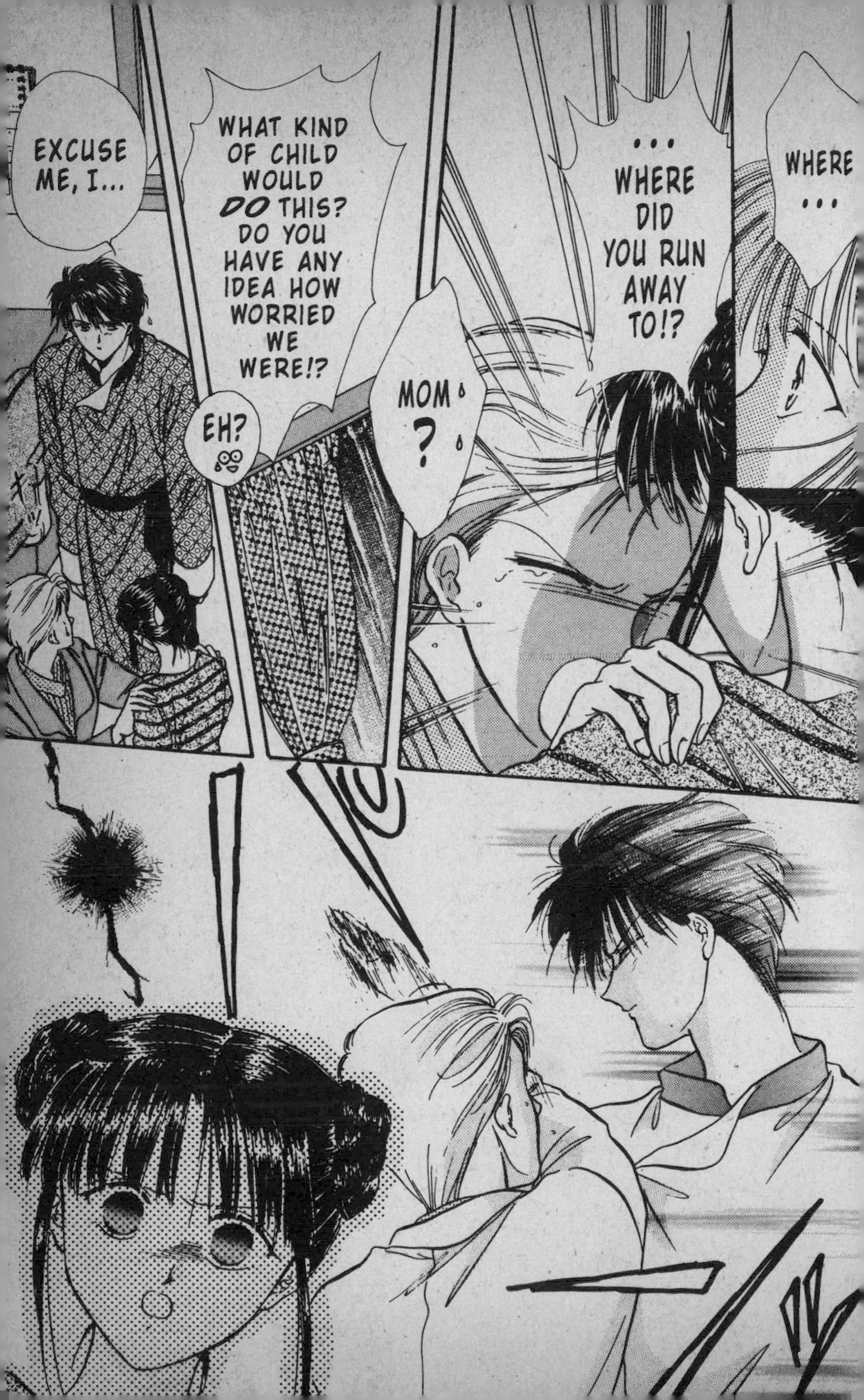
WHERE...
...WHERE DID YOU RUN AWAY TO!?
MOM?
WHAT KIND OF CHILD WOULD DO THIS? DO YOU HAVE ANY IDEA HOW WORRIED WE WERE!?
EH?
EXCUSE ME, I...

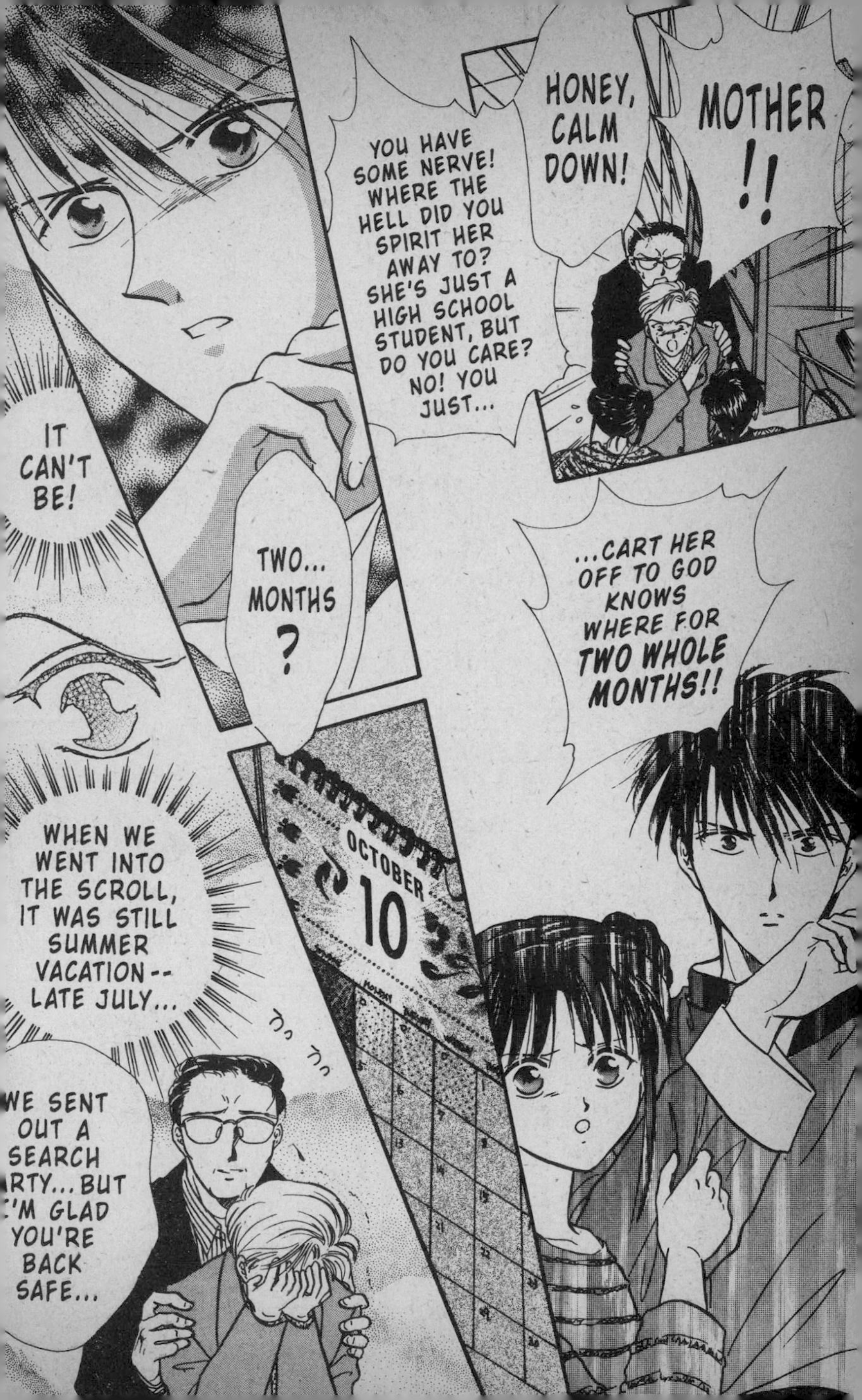
MOTHER!!
HONEY, CALM DOWN!
YOU HAVE SOME NERVE! WHERE THE HELL DID YOU SPIRIT HER AWAY TO? SHE'S JUST A HIGH SCHOOL STUDENT, BUT DO YOU CARE? NO! YOU JUST...
...CART HER OFF TO GOD KNOWS WHERE FOR TWO WHOLE MONTHS!!
TWO... MONTHS?
IT CAN'T BE!
OCTOBER
10
WHEN WE WENT INTO THE SCROLL, IT WAS STILL SUMMER VACATION-- LATE JULY...
WE SENT OUT A SEARCH RTY... BUT 'M GLAD YOU'RE BACK SAFE...

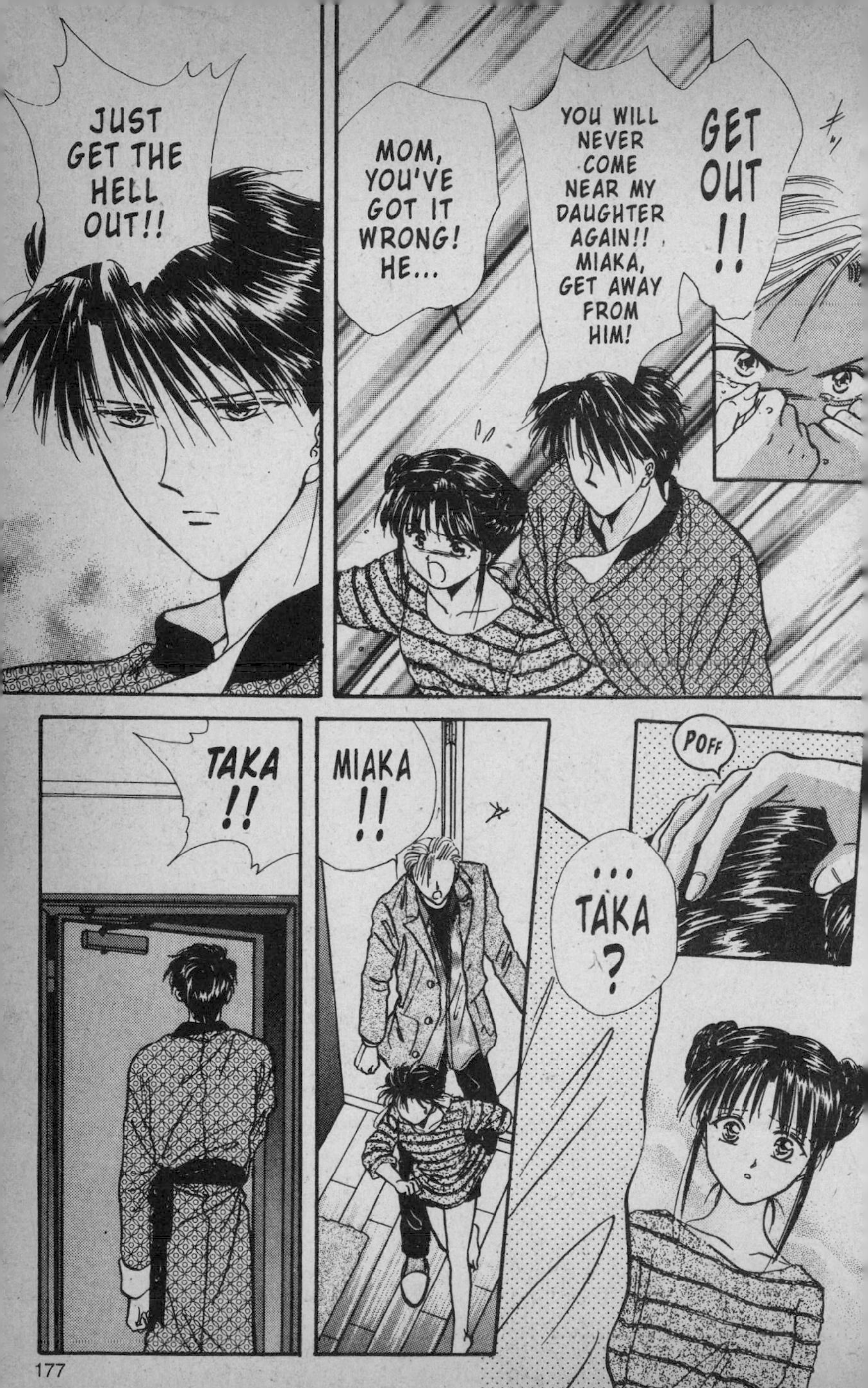
GET OUT!!
YOU WILL NEVER COME NEAR MY DAUGHTER AGAIN!! MIAKA, GET AWAY FROM HIM!
MOM, YOU'VE GOT IT WRONG! HE...
JUST GET THE HELL OUT!!
POFF
... TAKA?
MIAKA!!
TAKA!!

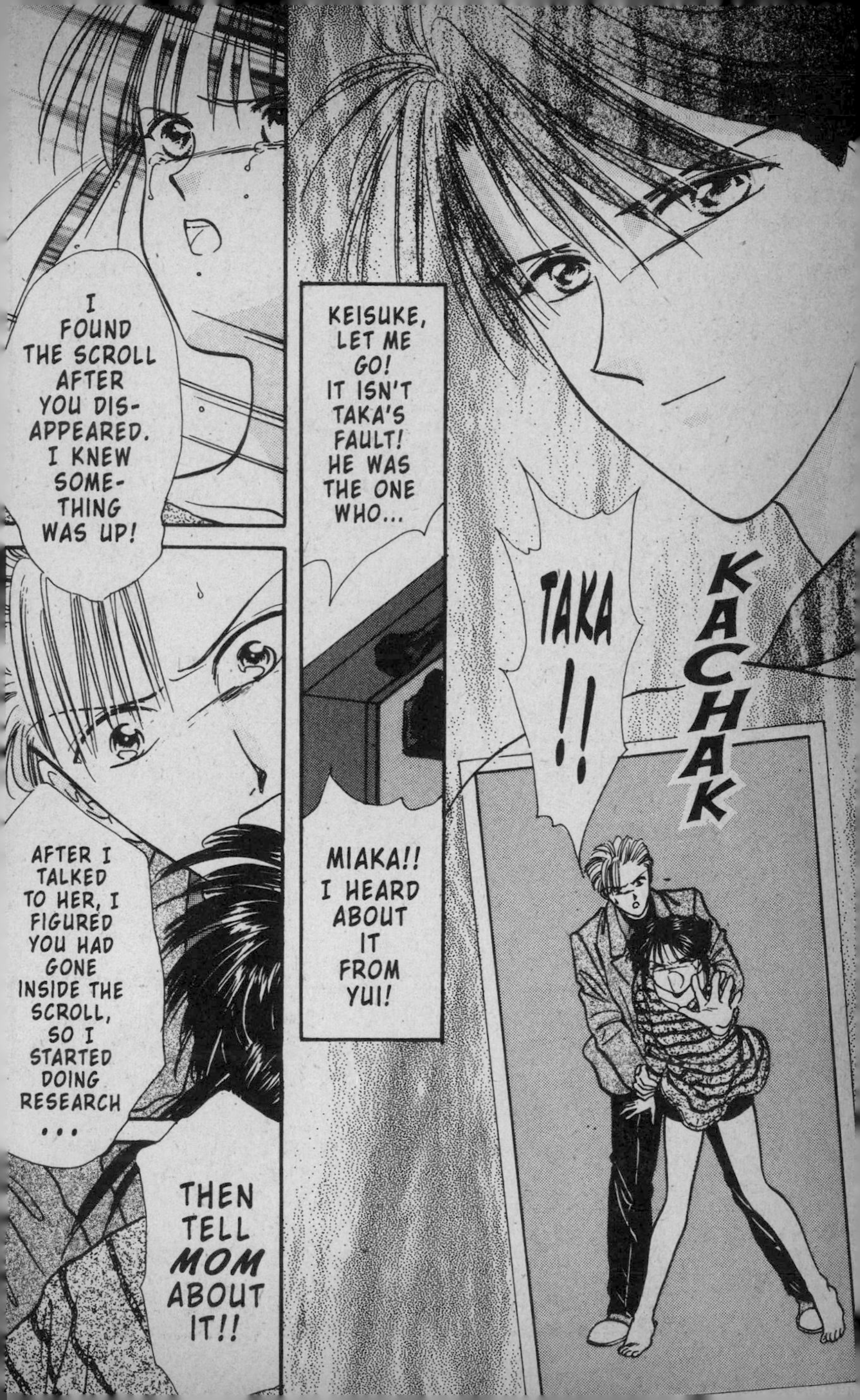
KACHAK
TAKA!!
KEISUKE, LET ME GO! IT ISN'T TAKA'S FAULT! HE WAS THE ONE WHO...
MIAKA!! I HEARD ABOUT IT FROM YUI!
I FOUND THE SCROLL AFTER YOU DIS-APPEARED. I KNEW SOME-THING WAS UP!
AFTER I TALKED TO HER, I FIGURED YOU HAD GONE INSIDE THE SCROLL, SO I STARTED DOING RESEARCH...
THEN TELL MOM ABOUT IT!!

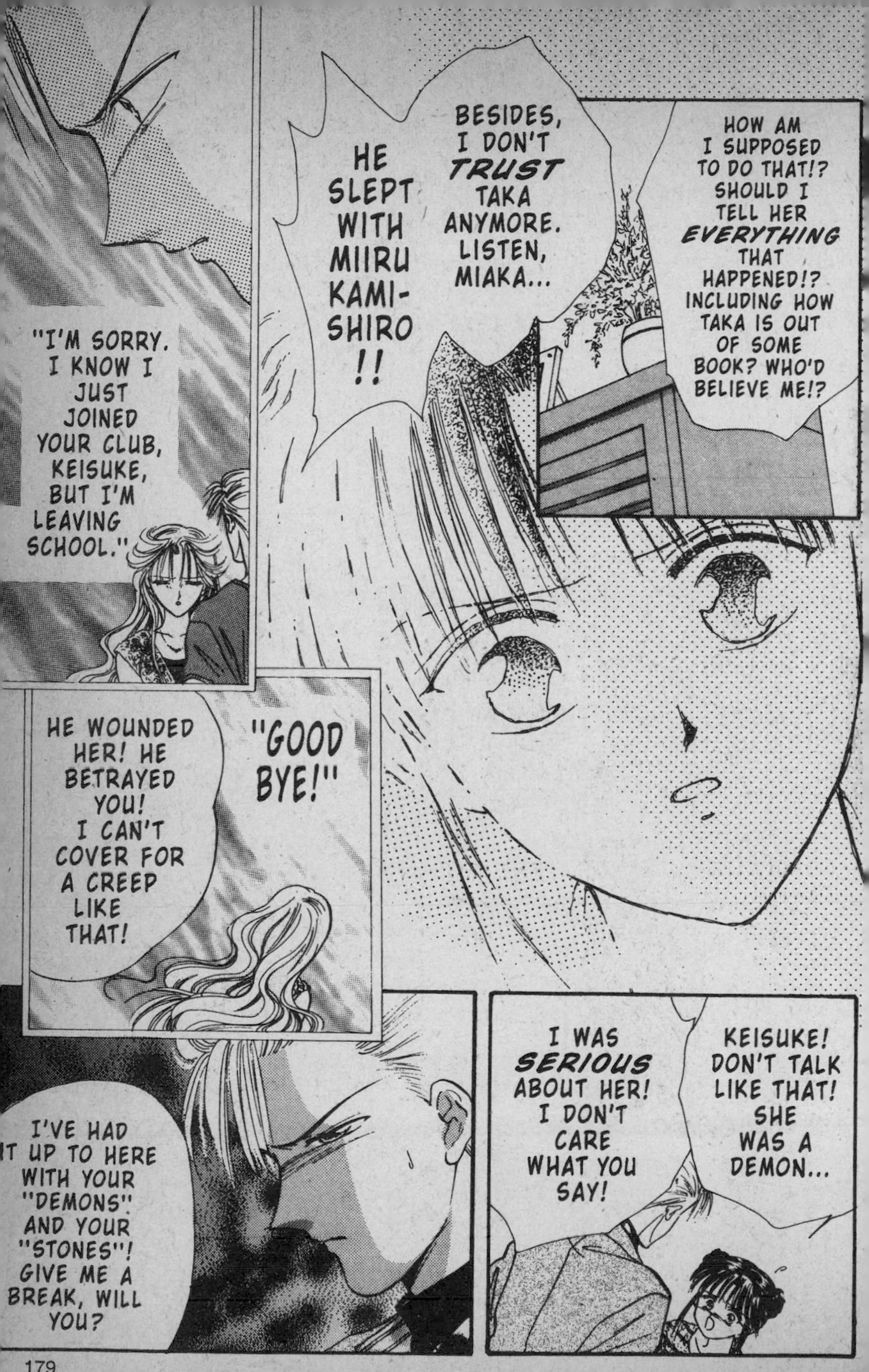
HOW AM I SUPPOSED TO DO THAT!? SHOULD I TELL HER *EVERYTHING* THAT HAPPENED!? INCLUDING HOW TAKA IS OUT OF SOME BOOK? WHO'D BELIEVE ME!?
BESIDES, I DON'T *TRUST* TAKA ANYMORE. LISTEN, MIAKA...
HE SLEPT WITH MIIRU KAMI-SHIRO !!
"I'M SORRY. I KNOW I JUST JOINED YOUR CLUB, KEISUKE, BUT I'M LEAVING SCHOOL."
"GOOD BYE!"
HE WOUNDED HER! HE BETRAYED YOU! I CAN'T COVER FOR A CREEP LIKE THAT!
KEISUKE! DON'T TALK LIKE THAT! SHE WAS A DEMON...
I WAS *SERIOUS* ABOUT HER! I DON'T CARE WHAT YOU SAY!
I'VE HAD IT UP TO HERE WITH YOUR "DEMONS" AND YOUR "STONES"! GIVE ME A BREAK, WILL YOU?

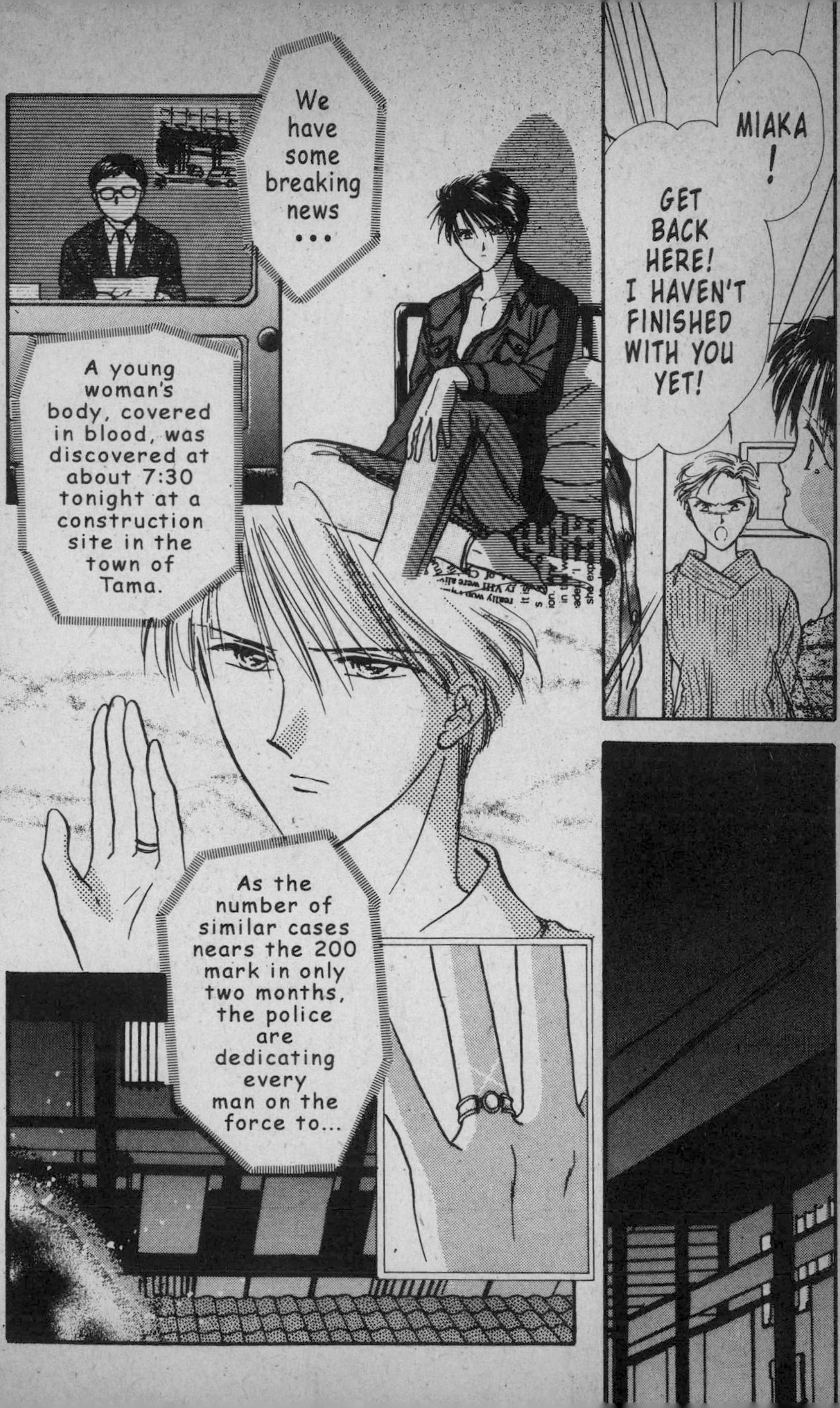
MIAKA!
GET BACK HERE! I HAVEN'T FINISHED WITH YOU YET!
We have some breaking news...
A young woman's body, covered in blood, was discovered at about 7:30 tonight at a construction site in the town of Tama.
As the number of similar cases nears the 200 mark in only two months, the police are dedicating every man on the force to...

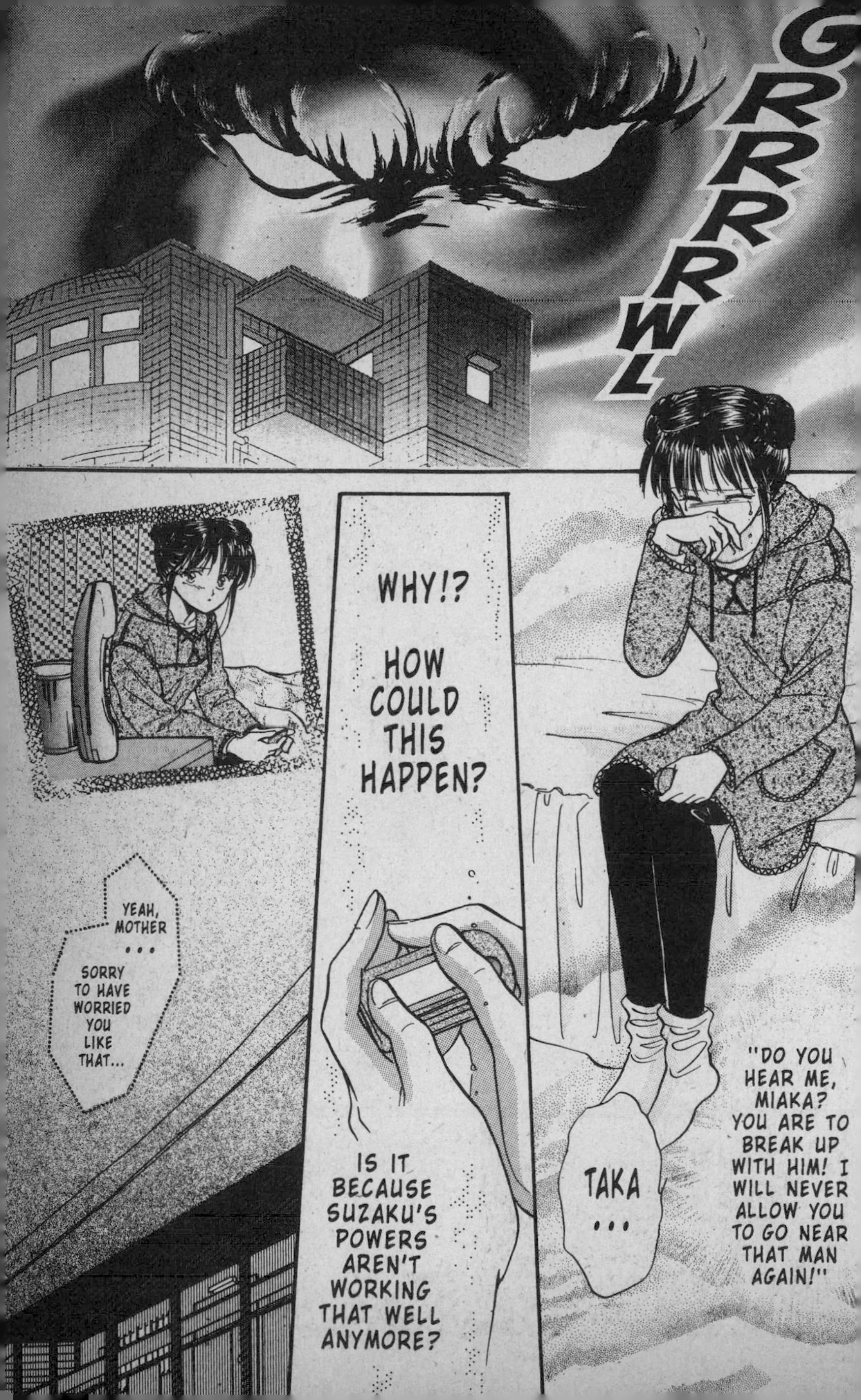
GRRRRWL
"DO YOU HEAR ME, MIAKA? YOU ARE TO BREAK UP WITH HIM! I WILL NEVER ALLOW YOU TO GO NEAR THAT MAN AGAIN!"
TAKA ...
WHY!?
HOW COULD THIS HAPPEN?
IS IT BECAUSE SUZAKU'S POWERS AREN'T WORKING THAT WELL ANYMORE?
YEAH, MOTHER ...
SORRY TO HAVE WORRIED YOU LIKE THAT...

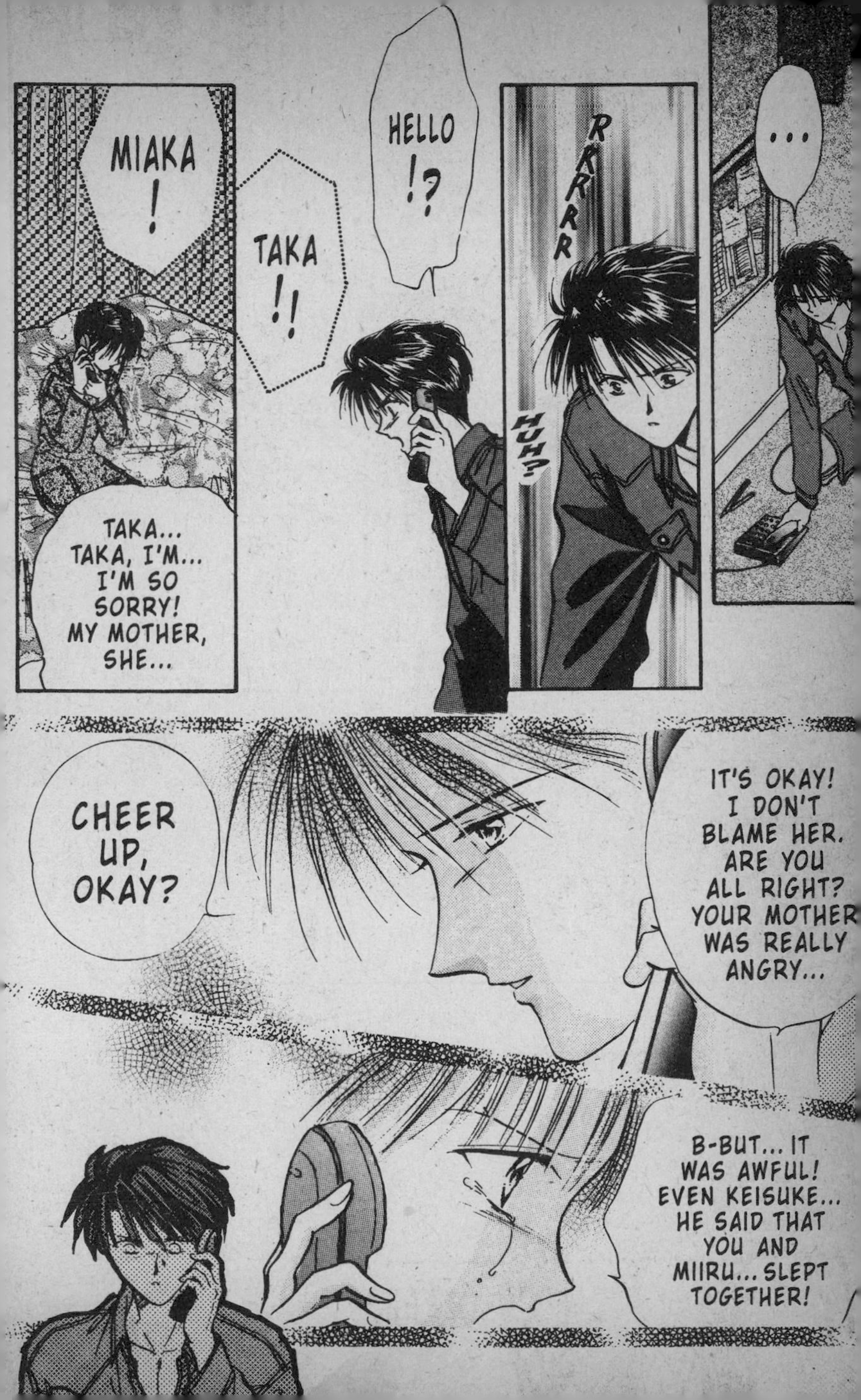
...
RRRRR
HUH?
HELLO !?
TAKA !!
MIAKA !
TAKA... TAKA, I'M... I'M SO SORRY! MY MOTHER, SHE...
IT'S OKAY! I DON'T BLAME HER. ARE YOU ALL RIGHT? YOUR MOTHER WAS REALLY ANGRY...
CHEER UP, OKAY?
B-BUT... IT WAS AWFUL! EVEN KEISUKE... HE SAID THAT YOU AND MIIRU... SLEPT TOGETHER!

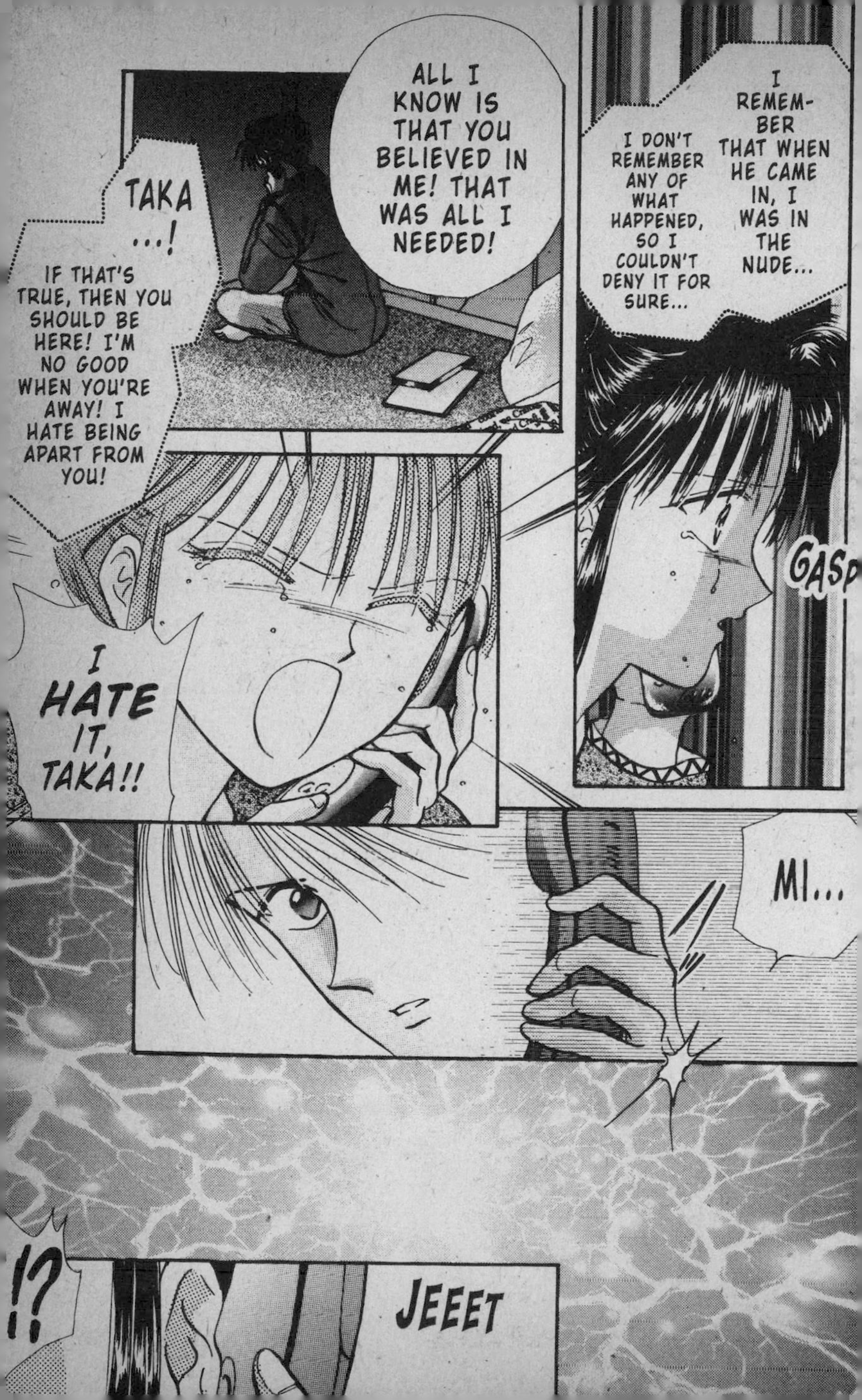
I REMEMBER THAT WHEN HE CAME IN, I WAS IN THE NUDE...
I DON'T REMEMBER ANY OF WHAT HAPPENED, SO I COULDN'T DENY IT FOR SURE...
GASP
ALL I KNOW IS THAT YOU BELIEVED IN ME! THAT WAS ALL I NEEDED!
TAKA ...!
IF THAT'S TRUE, THEN YOU SHOULD BE HERE! I'M NO GOOD WHEN YOU'RE AWAY! I HATE BEING APART FROM YOU!
I HATE IT, TAKA!!
MI...
!?
JEEET

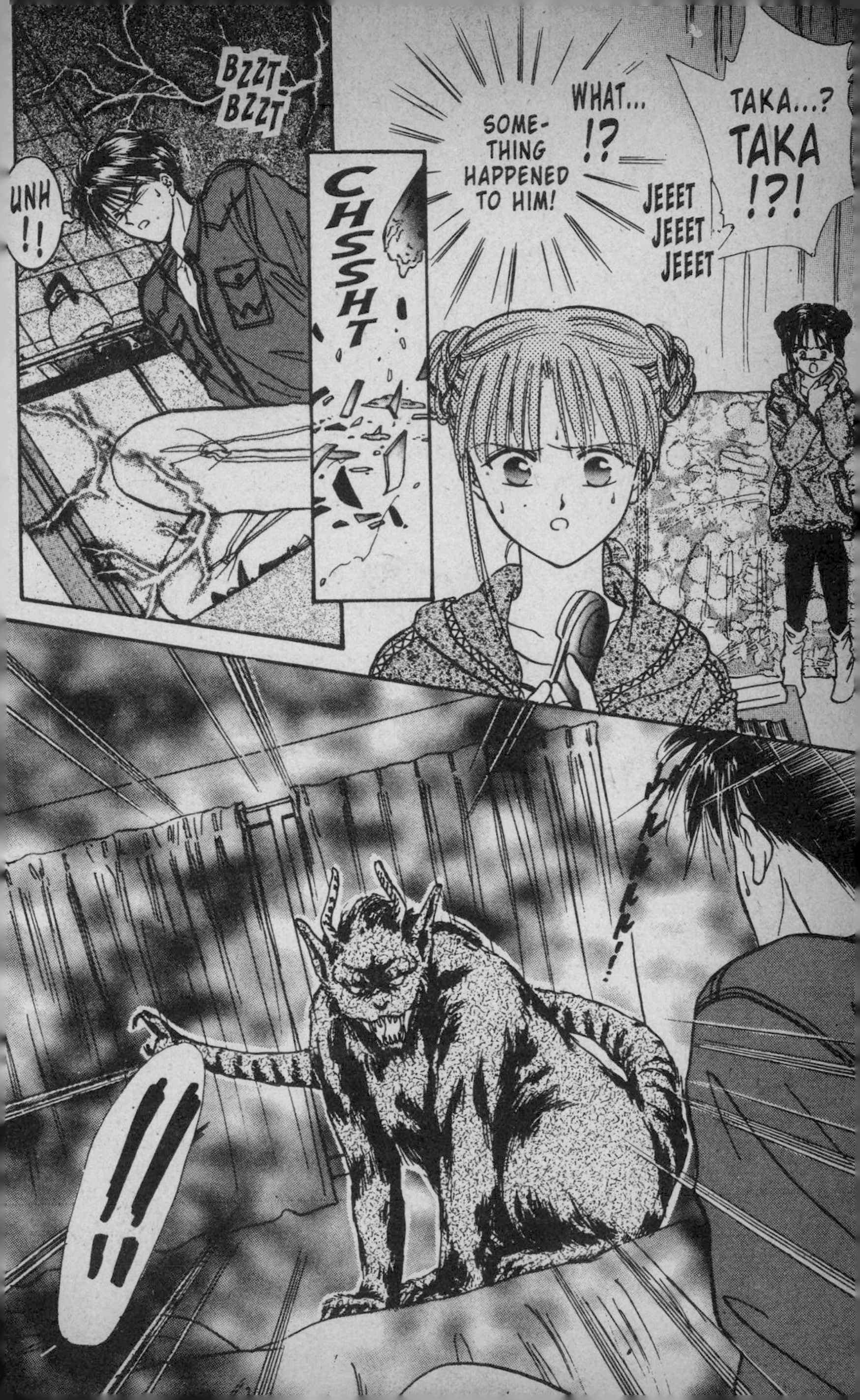
TAKA...? TAKA !?!
JEEET JEEET JEEET
WHAT... !?
SOME-THING HAPPENED TO HIM!
BZZT BZZT
CHSSHT
UNH !!
!!

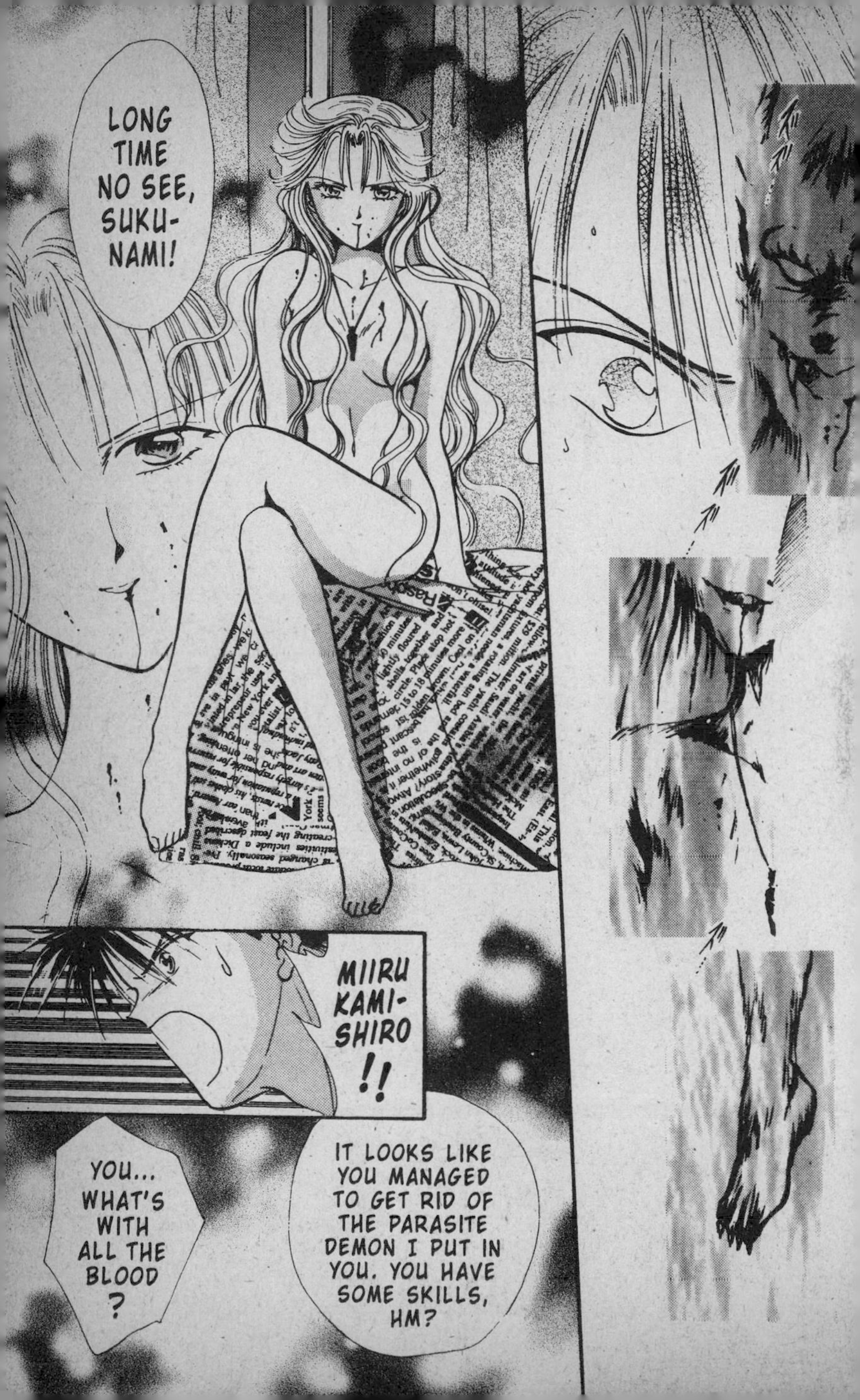
LONG TIME NO SEE, SUKU-NAMI!
MIIRU KAMI-SHIRO!!
IT LOOKS LIKE YOU MANAGED TO GET RID OF THE PARASITE DEMON I PUT IN YOU. YOU HAVE SOME SKILLS, HM?
YOU... WHAT'S WITH ALL THE BLOOD?

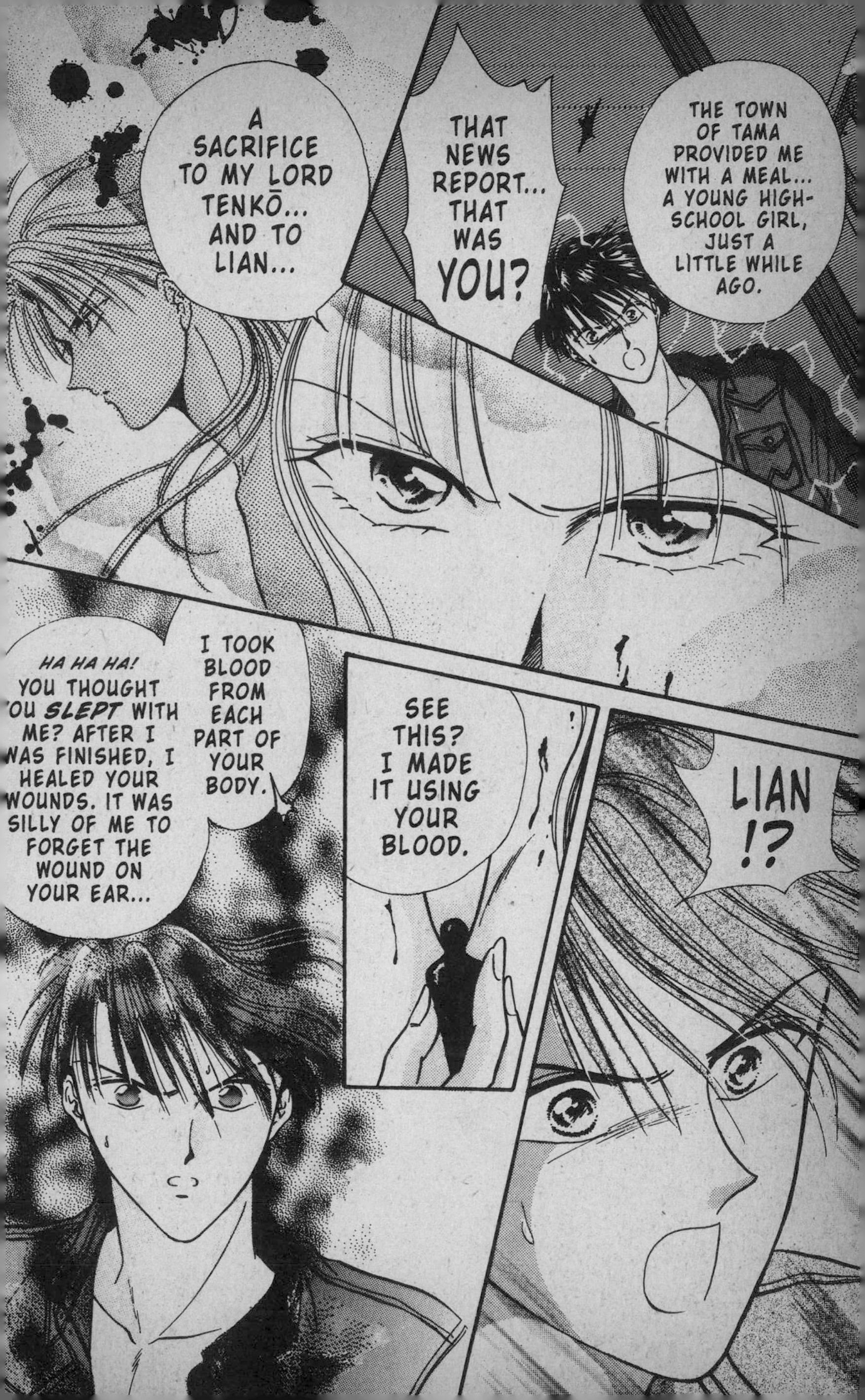
THE TOWN OF TAMA PROVIDED ME WITH A MEAL... A YOUNG HIGH-SCHOOL GIRL, JUST A LITTLE WHILE AGO.
THAT NEWS REPORT... THAT WAS YOU?
A SACRIFICE TO MY LORD TENKŌ... AND TO LIAN...
LIAN!?
SEE THIS? I MADE IT USING YOUR BLOOD.
I TOOK BLOOD FROM EACH PART OF YOUR BODY.
HA HA HA! YOU THOUGHT YOU SLEPT WITH ME? AFTER I WAS FINISHED, I HEALED YOUR WOUNDS. IT WAS SILLY OF ME TO FORGET THE WOUND ON YOUR EAR...

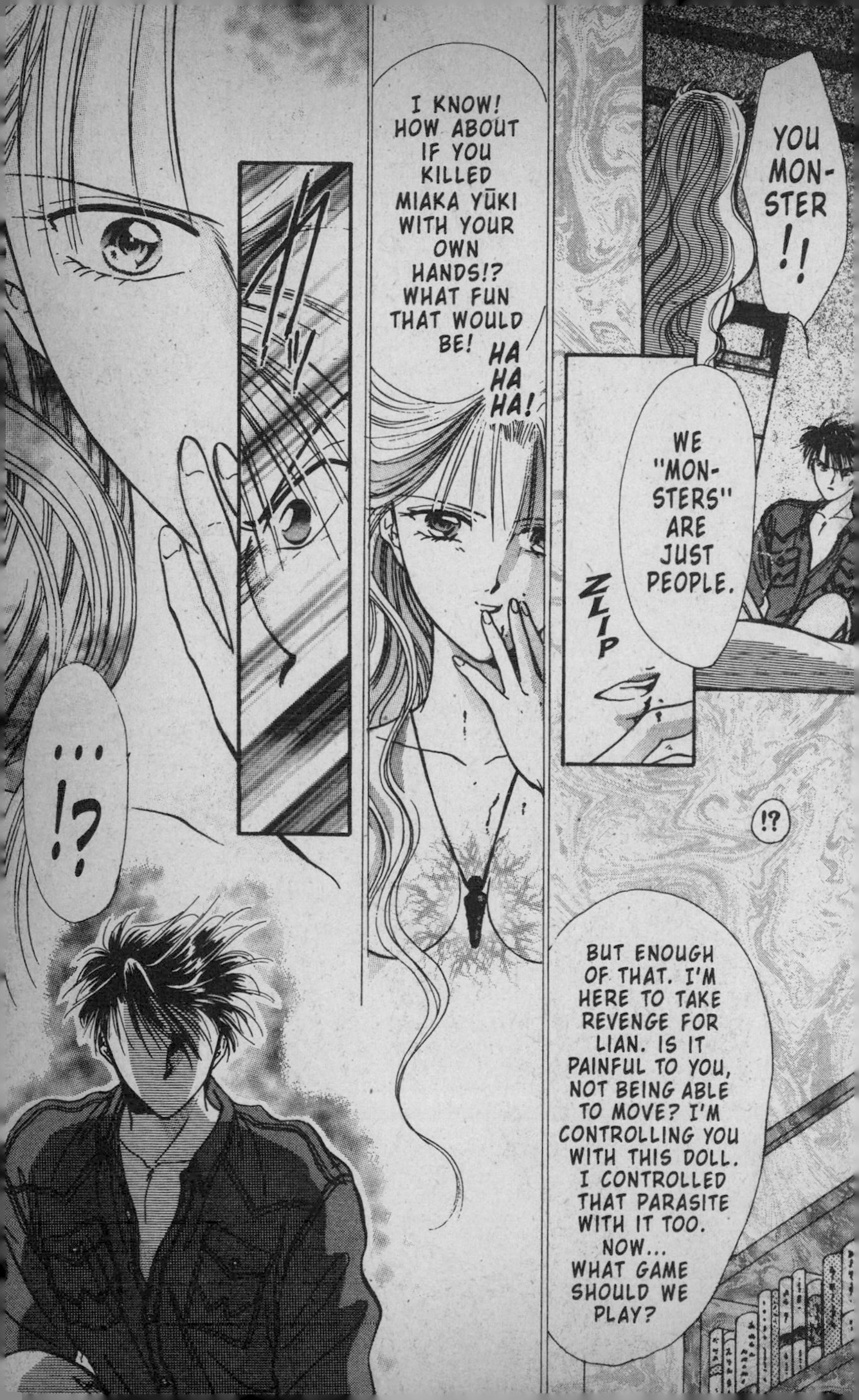
YOU MONSTER!!
WE "MONSTERS" ARE JUST PEOPLE.
ZLIP
!?
BUT ENOUGH OF THAT. I'M HERE TO TAKE REVENGE FOR LIAN. IS IT PAINFUL TO YOU, NOT BEING ABLE TO MOVE? I'M CONTROLLING YOU WITH THIS DOLL. I CONTROLLED THAT PARASITE WITH IT TOO. NOW... WHAT GAME SHOULD WE PLAY?
I KNOW! HOW ABOUT IF YOU KILLED MIAKA YŪKI WITH YOUR OWN HANDS!? WHAT FUN THAT WOULD BE!
HA HA HA!
...!?

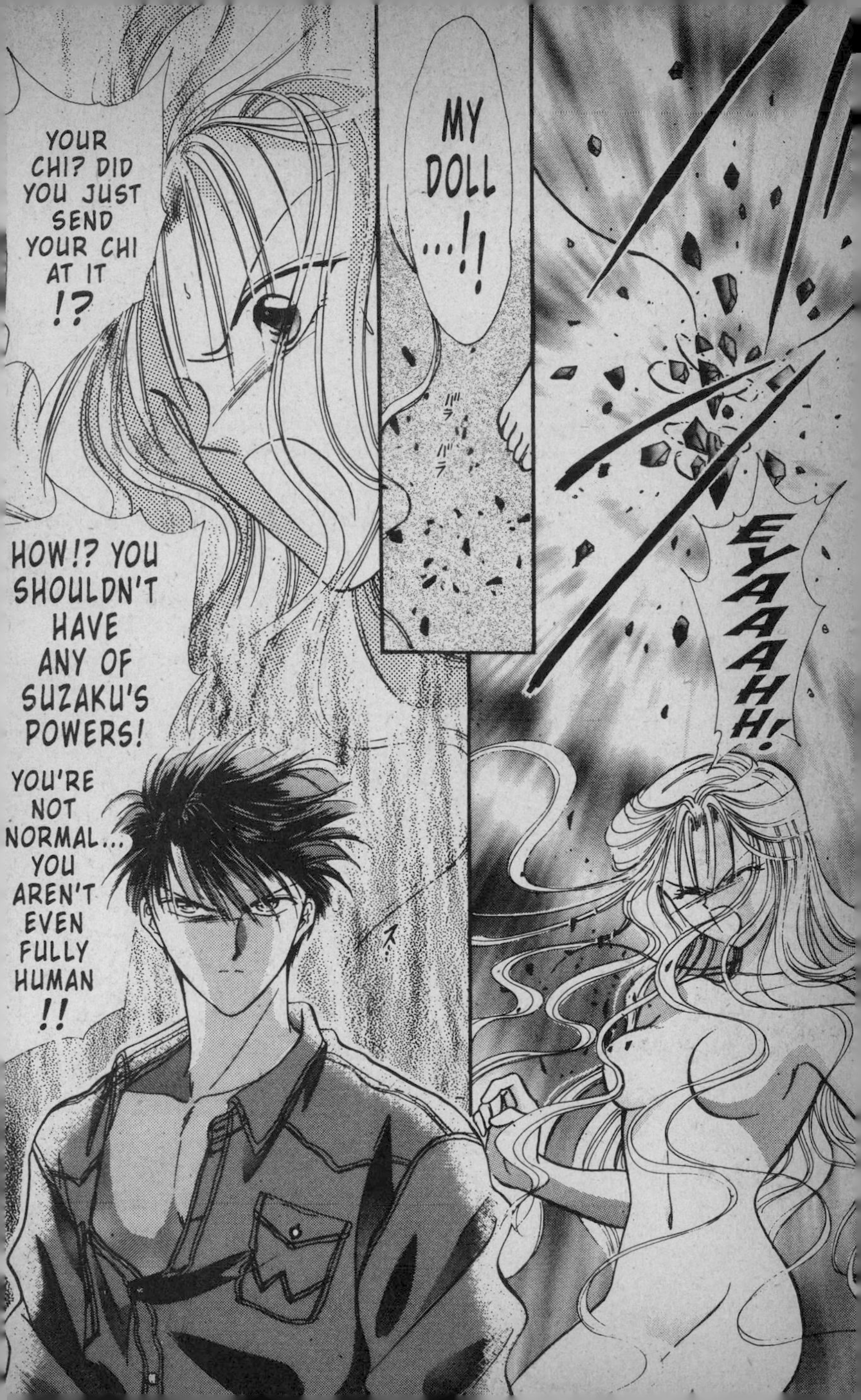
EYAAAAHH!
MY DOLL ...!!
バラバラ
YOUR CHI? DID YOU JUST SEND YOUR CHI AT IT !?
HOW!? YOU SHOULDN'T HAVE ANY OF SUZAKU'S POWERS!
YOU'RE NOT NORMAL... YOU AREN'T EVEN FULLY HUMAN !!
ス…

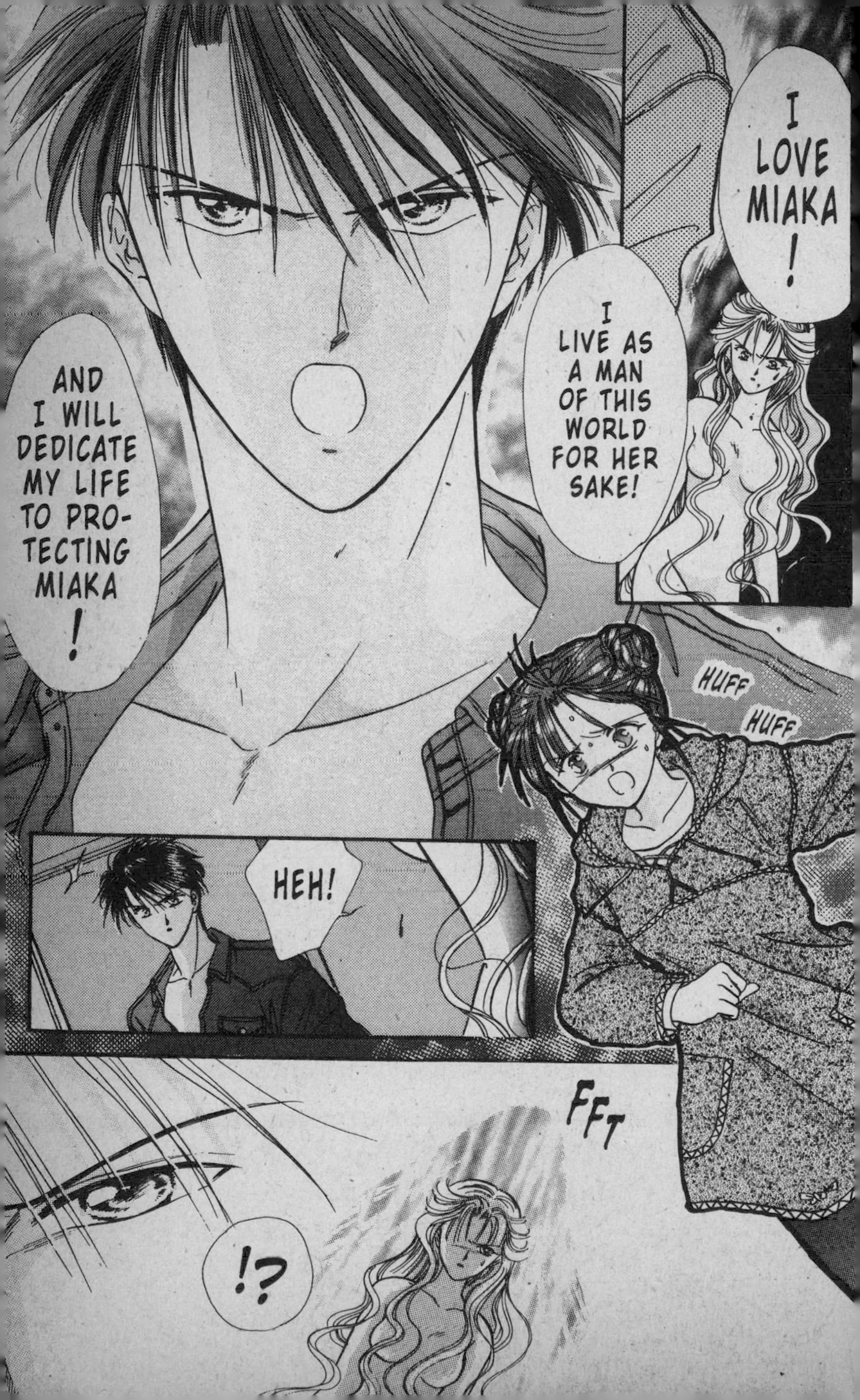
I LOVE MIAKA!
I LIVE AS A MAN OF THIS WORLD FOR HER SAKE!
AND I WILL DEDICATE MY LIFE TO PROTECTING MIAKA!
HUFF HUFF
HEH!
FFT
!?

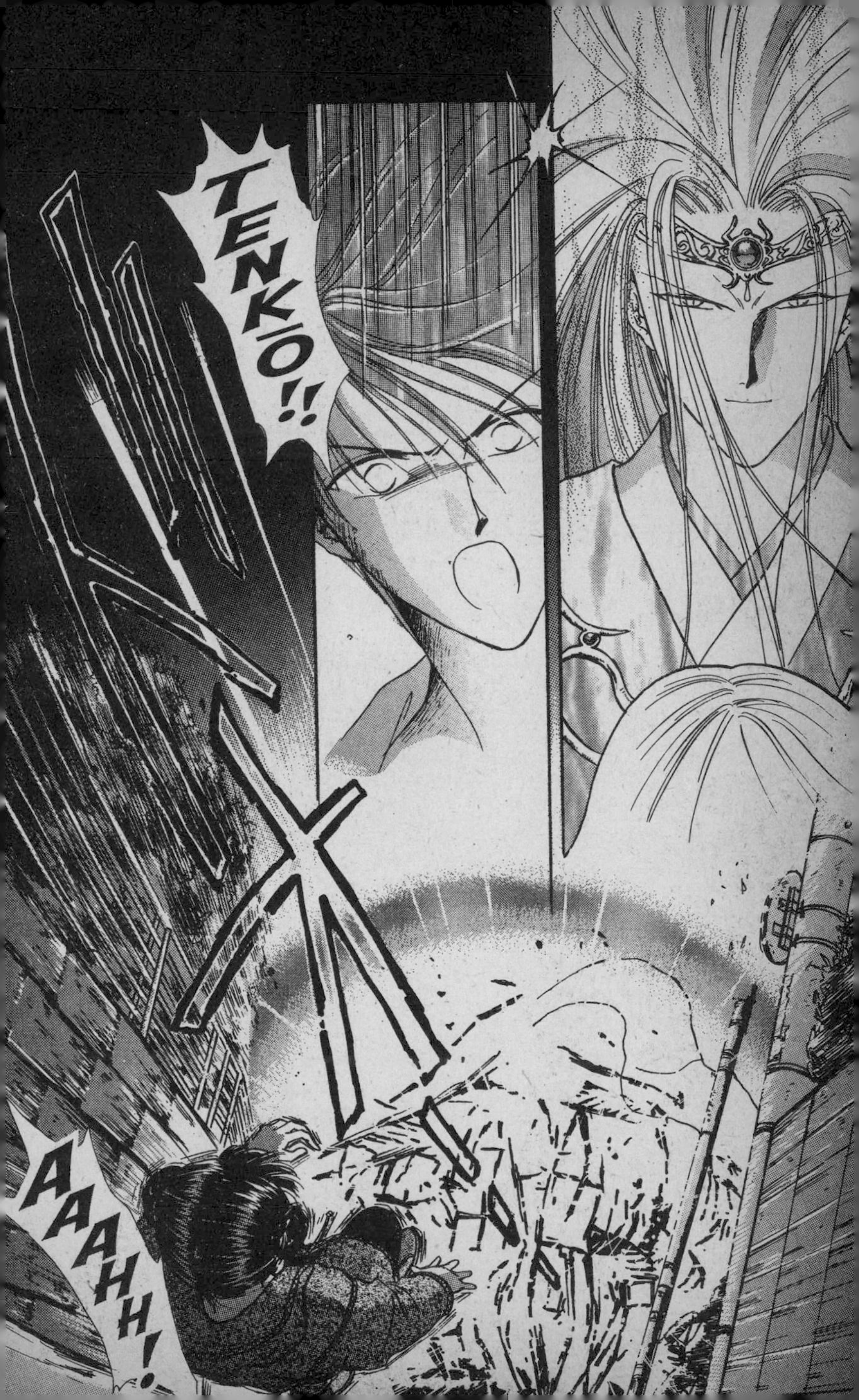
TENKŌ!!
AAAHH!

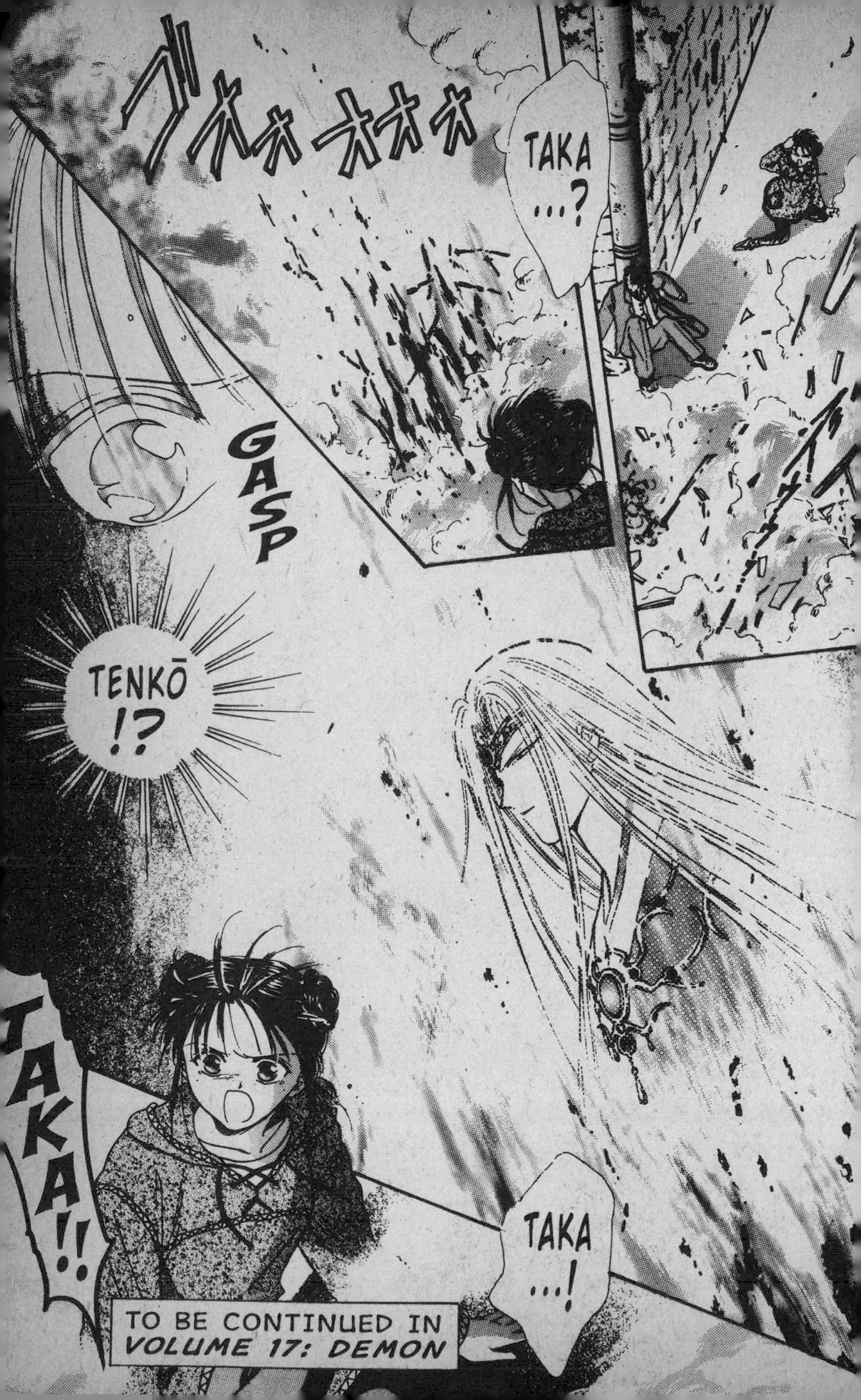
ゴォォォォオオオ
TAKA ...?
GASP
TENKŌ !?
TAKA ...!
TAKA!!
TO BE CONTINUED IN VOLUME 17: DEMON

ABOUT THE AUTHOR

Yuu Watase was born on March 5 in a town near Osaka, Japan, and she was raised there before moving to Tokyo to follow her dream of creating manga. In the decade since her debut short story, *PAJAMA DE OJAMA* ("An Intrusion in Pajamas"), she has produced more than 50 compiled volumes of short stories and continuing series. Her latest work, *ZETTAI KARESHI* ("Absolute Boyfriend"), has recently completed its run in Japan in the anthology magazine *SHÔJO COMIC*. Watase's other beloved series *CERES: CELESTIAL LEGEND*, *IMADOKI! (NOWADAYS)*, and *ALICE 19TH* are now available in North America in English editions published by VIZ Media.

The Fushigi Yûgi Guide to Sound Effects

Most of the sound effects in FUSHIGI YÛGI are the way Yuu Watase created them, in their original Japanese.

We created this glossary for a page-by-page, panel-by-panel explanation of the action and background noises. By using this guide, you may even learn some Japanese.

The glossary lists page and panel number. For example, page 1, panel 3, would be listed as 1.3.

31.3 FX: ZA ZA (stomping)
31.5 FX: MUKI (clothing being peeled away)
32.1 FX: JIIIIN (glaring)
32.5 FX: DAN (jumping)
33.4 FX: HYUUUUUU (wind)
34.2 FX: HA (sudden realization)
34.3 FX: SHULULULU (unrolling)
36.4 FX: ZAWA ZAWA (background chatter)
37.4 FX: HYUUU (wind)
37.6 FX: SUUU (disappearing)
38.1 FX: SUUU (disappearing)
40.1 FX: DOKUN (heavy heartbeat)
40.2 FX: GYU (holding tight)
47.3 FX: NIKO (grin)

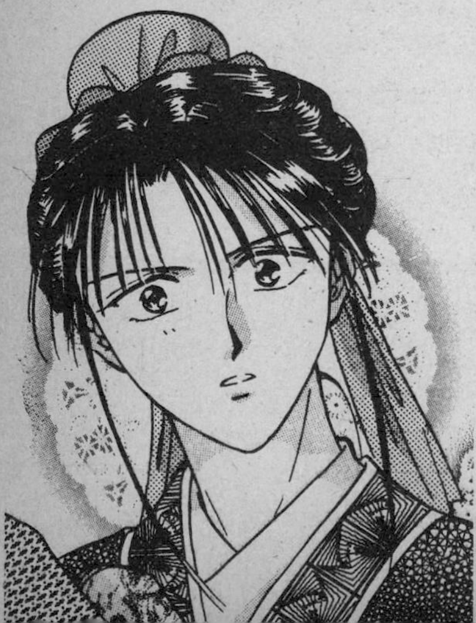

7.1 FX: KA (flash)
7.4 FX: SUUUU (build up of energy)
7.5 FX: KA (flash of light)
8.2 FX: KA (flash)
11.1 FX: NUUUUN (intense disapproving stare)
14.2 FX: ZAWA (background chatter)
14.3 FX: ZAWA (background chatter)
14.4 FX: ZAWA (background chatter)
19.3 FX: DA (running)
19.5 FX: BAN (opening the door)
20.2 FX: BAN (crashing through the door)
21.4 FX: HA (sudden realization)
22.5 FX: ZUDADA (falling)
23.2 FX: GUSHA (crunching sound)
23.3 FX: GA (pulling hair)
24.1 FX: ZA (stepping)
24.2 FX: DOKUN DOKUN DOKUN DOKUN (heavy heartbeats)
24.6 FX: SU (movement)
25.3 FX: TO (landing)
25.4 FX: SHARA (jingle)
26.1 FX: GRASHA (crunching)
26.2 FX: PARA (clatter)
26.4 FX: GUGU (grinding)
28.3 FX: KI (anger)
30.1 FX: DOKA (breaking in)
30.2 FX: DOSA (sudden movement)
30.3 FX: HA (breaking the spell)

47.6 FX: ZAAAA (shower sounds)
48.3 FX: BURU BURU BURU (shaking head)
49.1 FX: GISHI (drying with towel)
49.2 FX: PIKU PIKU (veins popping out)
53.2 FX: BASA (flap)
53.3 FX: FUU (vanishing)
53.4 FX: BASA (flap)
56.3 FX: BASA (flap)
56.4 FX: SU (vanishing)
57.1 FX: SHUWA SHUWA SHUWA (leaves fluttering)
58.1 FX: HAA HAA (panting)
58.5 FX: PAMU (plopping into his hand)
59.1 FX: BURU BURU (trembling)
60.5 FX: SAWA (wind through his hair)
60.6 FX: SAWA SAWA (wind rustling)
63.4 FX: DOKI DOKI (heartbeats)
64.1 FX: ZAAA (unscrolling)
65.1 FX: GASHI (grabbing)
66.1 FX: DOSA (hitting the floor)
67.3 FX: TSU (sucking)
68.2 FX: PASHA PASHA (splashing sounds)
68.3 FX: KACHA (door latch)
69.1 FX: KACHA (picking up receiver)
69.6 FX: DA (running)
70.3 FX: HAA HAA HAA (panting)
71.1 FX: YORO (wobble)
71.3 FX: TOSA (hitting the ground)
71.6 FX: BAN (pounding)
72.1 FX: KA (flash)
72.2 FX: SUUU (disappearing)
72.4 FX: NYA (smile)
72.5 FX: FU (vanished)
74.1 FX: FU (vanishing)
74.3 FX: KAPPO KAPPO (hoof sounds)
75.2 FX: KAPPO KAPPO (hoof sounds)
76.4 FX: PACHI (blink)
76.5 FX: GABA (rising suddenly)
77.2 FX: ZAWA ZAWA (rustling)
79.3 FX: ZAWA ZAWA (wind rustling)
79.5 FX: BAN (slamming the table)
80.3 FX: SU (sudden appearance)
80.6 FX: BAN (slam)
81.2 FX: ZAWA ZAWA (crowd noises)
82.1 Note: Tasuki's joke was, "A crab (kani) who apologizes gets forgiveness (kannin)." Not the best of puns.
84.2 Small Sign: Chao ("Cho" in Japanese. It means "ultra" but is most likely a family name)
84.2 Large Sign: Nanpandaichao ("Nanbandaicho" in Japanese. It means "south, platter, large, and ultra" but is most likely just fortuitous Chinese characters strung together to make a shop name.)
85.3 FX: FU (lit incense)
85.5 FX: SHIIIIIN (silence)
87.1 FX: KYAA KYAA (happy squeals)

87.3 FX: U U (sniffles)
89.3 FX: NI (smile)
89.4 FX: SU (slight movement)
89.5 FX: KIII (door creaking)
91.1 FX: BASHI (a hit)
92.4 FX: BATAN (door slamming)
94.3 FX: SHARA (fidgeting)
94.5 FX: HA (sudden realization)
95.2 FX: GU (gripping)
95.4 FX: KA (flash of light)
96.4 FX: HA (sudden realization)
97.2 FX: KYU (clench)
100.1 FX: GI GI GI (electricity)
101.1 FX: PIN (stretching taught)
106.4 FX: ZAWA ZAWA (background noise)
107.1 FX: SO (placing the stone)
108.2 FX: TON TON (footsteps on the stairs)
108.3 FX: KYU (tightening)
108.4 FX: DOKI (heartbeat)
109.2 FX: GAKUN (powerful flinch)
110.1 FX: HOO (shining)
110.3 FX: SU (appearing)
112.1 FX: NYA (smiling)
112.2 FX: KIII (door creaking open)
113.1 FX: DOOOO (dramatic appearance)
113.2 FX: DOKAN (falling down)
115.3 FX: DO (explosive movement)
116.2 FX: ZUBA (slashing)
116.3 FX: SHAAA (hissing)
116.4 FX: BATA BATA BATA (footsteps)
117.1 FX: SHU (fast movement)
117.2 FX: DO (sudden stop)
118.2 FX: GATA GATA (trembling)
119.4 FX: FOOOOON (howling)
119.4 FX: ON ON ON (howling)
120.5 FX: DA (running)

125.1 FX: ZAZA (violent rustling)
125.2 FX: SHA (hissing)
126.2 FX: HIHIIIN (whinnying)
128.2 FX: BA (gushing)
130.2 FX: GABA (pulling off)
132.4 Note: Tasuki's joke in Japanese was, "The bedding (futon) flew away (futtonda)."
134.2 FX: YORO (wobble)
137.4 FX: PON (sweat appearing)
139.5 FX: KATA KATA (shivering)
140.2 FX: IRA IRA IRA (worry)
141.1 FX: KA (rushing)
142.3 FX: BAN (bang)
144.1 FX: BYUN (zooming past)
145.2 FX: GYU (gripping)
145.4 FX: BAN (bam)
146.5 FX: GUI (grabbing)
149.4 FX: MUKU (lifting his head)
149.5 FX: GU (holding)
150.1 FX: SU (movement)

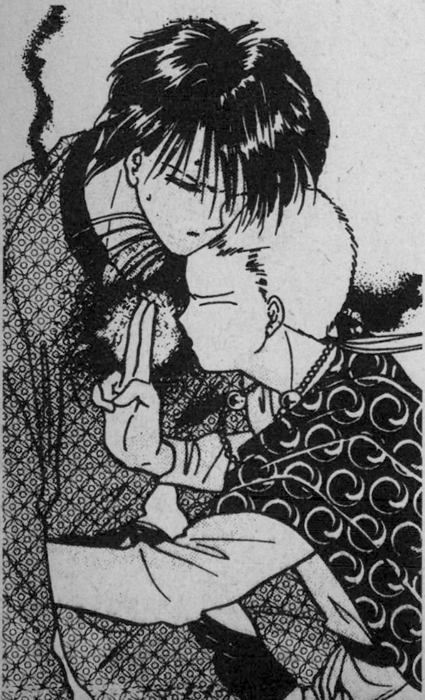

150.2 FX: BIKU (surprise)
150.3 FX: GYU (clenching)
151.1 FX: BI-BIKU (flinching back)
152.2 FX: BIKU (flinch)
152.4 FX: HA (gasp)
152.2 FX: GIRIRI (grinding)
154.1 FX: GYU (holding tight)
154.3 FX: ZURU (something slurped in)
155.1 FX: SHAAA
(rising up, taking shape)
155.2 FX: DOO (explosive movement)
159.4 FX: SU (movement)
161.4 FX: BOHYU (flames)
163.2 FX: BOHYUU (flames)
163.4 FX: KAAAAA (light shining)
164.3 FX: PON (clap)
165.1 FX: HATA (sudden realization)
167.3 FX: KAAAAA (light)
168.3 FX: SUUU (vanishing)
168.4 FX: BISHUN (vanishing in light)
169.2 FX: KA (flash of light)
171.4 FX: GYU (gripping)
172.4 FX: GABA (hugging)
173.1 FX: GORON (twirl)
175.4 FX: KI (anger)
175.5 FX: PAN (a slap)
176.5 FX: UU UU (crying)
177.1 FX: KI (anger)
183.4 FX: HA (realization)
184.4 FX: ULULULULU (growling)
185.1 FX: ZUZU ZUZU ZU…
(shape shifting)
187.5 FX: KA (concentration)
188.1 FX: BAN (bang)
188.2 FX: BARA BARA
(breaking into pieces)
188.3 FX: SU (flowing)
190.3 FX: DOO (explosion)
191.1 FX: ZUUUU (burning)
191.2 FX: GOOOO (roaring fire)

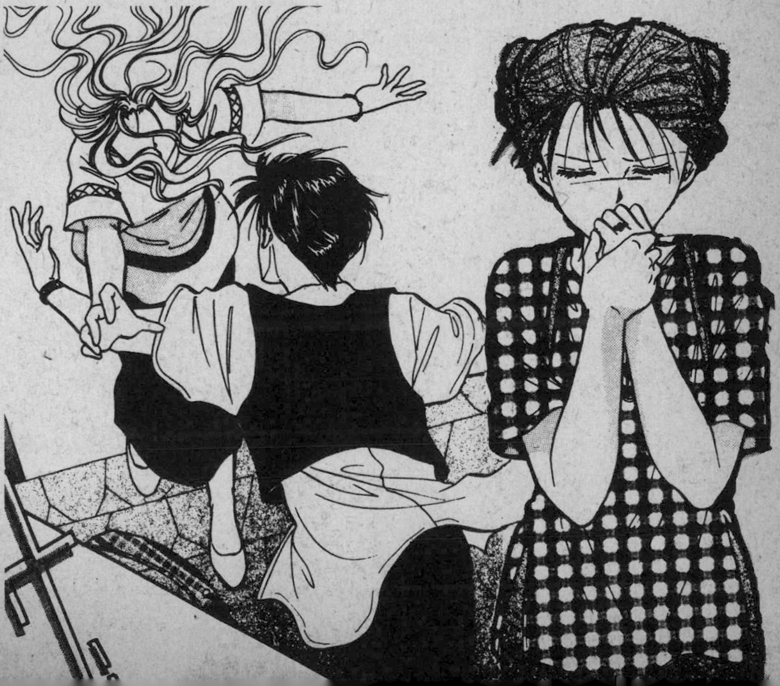

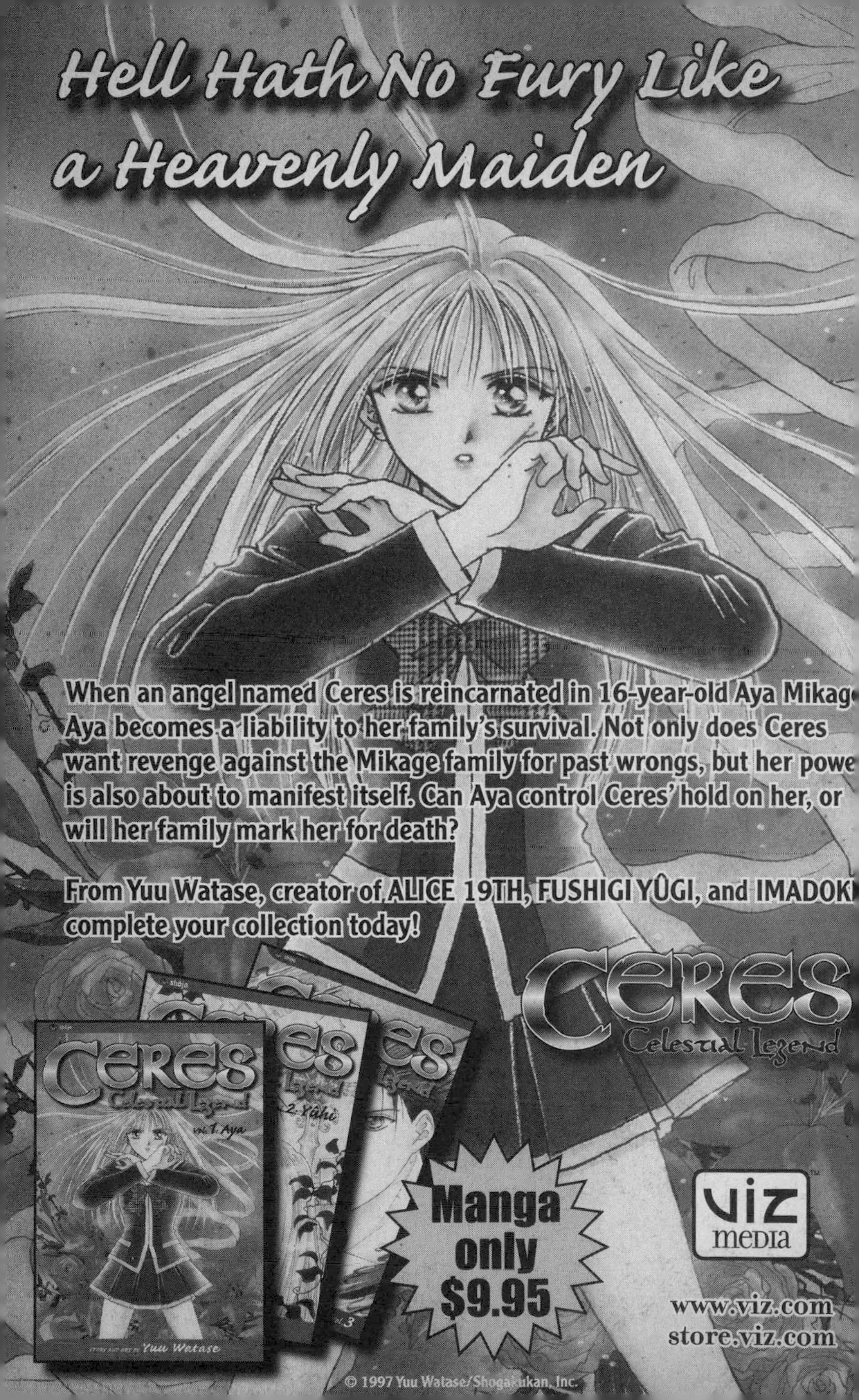
Hell Hath No Fury Like a Heavenly Maiden
When an angel named Ceres is reincarnated in 16-year-old Aya Mikag Aya becomes a liability to her family's survival. Not only does Ceres want revenge against the Mikage family for past wrongs, but her powe is also about to manifest itself. Can Aya control Ceres' hold on her, or will her family mark her for death?
From Yuu Watase, creator of ALICE 19TH, FUSHIGI YÛGI, and IMADOKI complete your collection today!
CERES Celestial Legend
Manga only $9.95
VIZ MEDIA
www.viz.com
store.viz.com
© 1997 Yuu Watase/Shogakukan, Inc.

LOVE SHOJO? LET US KNOW!

☐ Please do NOT send me information about VIZ Media products, news and events, special offers, or other information.

☐ Please do NOT send me information from VIZ' trusted business partners.

Name: _____

Address: _____

City: _____ State: _____ Zip: _____

E-mail: _____

☐ Male ☐ Female Date of Birth (mm/dd/yyyy): ___ / ___ / ___ (Under 13? Parental consent required)

What race/ethnicity do you consider yourself? (check all that apply)

☐ White/Caucasian ☐ Black/African American ☐ Hispanic/Latino

☐ Asian/Pacific Islander ☐ Native American/Alaskan Native ☐ Other: _____

What VIZ shojo title(s) did you purchase? (indicate title(s) purchased)

_____

What other shojo titles from other publishers do you own? _____

_____

Reason for purchase: (check all that apply)

☐ Special offer ☐ Favorite title / author / artist / genre

☐ Gift ☐ Recommendation ☐ Collection

☐ Read excerpt in VIZ manga sampler ☐ Other _____

Where did you make your purchase? (please check one)

☐ Comic store ☐ Bookstore ☐ Mass/Grocery Store

☐ Newsstand ☐ Video/Video Game Store

☐ Online (site: _____) ☐ Other _____

CLAYTON

How many shojo titles have you purchased in the last year? How many were VIZ shojo titles?
(please check one from each column)

SHOJO MANGA
- ☐ None
- ☐ 1 – 4
- ☐ 5 – 10
- ☐ 11+

VIZ SHOJO MANGA
- ☐ None
- ☐ 1 – 4
- ☐ 5 – 10
- ☐ 11+

What do you like most about shojo graphic novels? (check all that apply)

- ☐ Romance
- ☐ Drama / conflict
- ☐ Fantasy
- ☐ Comedy
- ☐ Real-life storylines
- ☐ Relatable characters
- ☐ Other ____________________

Do you purchase every volume of your favorite shojo series?

- ☐ Yes! Gotta have 'em as my own
- ☐ No. Please explain: ____________________

Who are your favorite shojo authors / artists? ____________________

____

What shojo titles would like you translated and sold in English? ____________________

____

THANK YOU! Please send the completed form to:

NJW Research
ATTN: VIZ Media Shojo Survey
42 Catharine Street
Poughkeepsie, NY 12601

Your privacy is very important to us. All information provided will be used for internal purposes only and will not be sold or otherwise divulged.

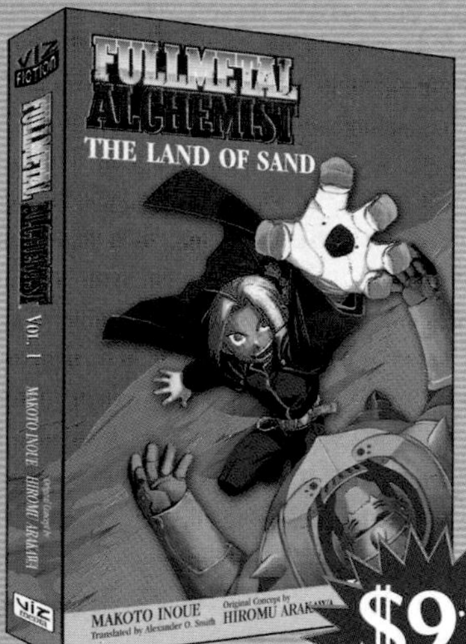
VIZ FICTION
FULLMETAL ALCHEMIST
THE LAND OF SAND
VOL. 1
MAKOTO INOUE
Translated by Alexander O. Smith
Original Concept by
HIROMU ARAKAWA

FULLMETAL ALCHEMIST™

The Land of Sand

by Makoto Inoue
Original Concept by
Hiromu Arakawa

Ever since an accident trapped his brother's soul in a suit of armor, Edward has spent his life searching for a way to turn Alphonse back to normal. Legend tells of an alchemical artifact, known as the Philosopher's Stone, with ties to a former gold-mining town called Xenotime. Will they find the miracle they need? Or discover that this once-rich town's treasures are long gone?

Continue the adventure in *Fullmetal Alchemist: Captured Alchemist*, in stores January 2006!

$9.99
paperback

GHOST IN THE SHELL 2: *INNOCENCE*

After The Long Goodbye

by Masaki Yamada

In 2032, cyborg counterterrorist and black ops veteran Batou is carving out a miserable existence, with only his job and beloved Basset Hound, Gabriel, to live for. But when Gabriel goes missing, Batou's life becomes even more desperate and his search hopeless, forcing him to weigh his strengths and recognize his weaknesses...

$19.99
hardcover

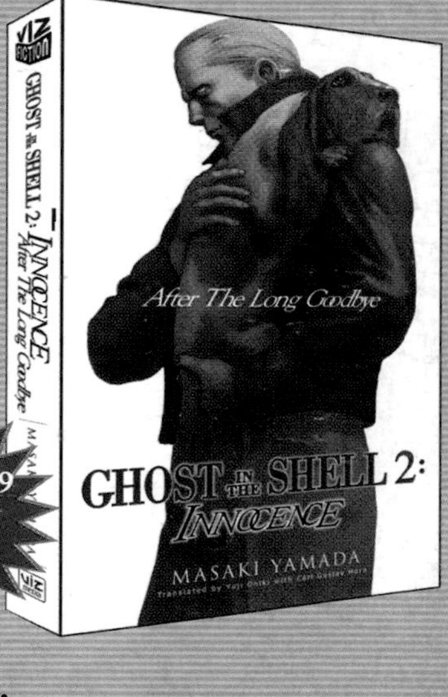
VIZ FICTION
After The Long Goodbye
GHOST IN THE SHELL 2:
INNOCENCE
MASAKI YAMADA

Other novels available from VIZ Media:

Battle Royale	In stores now
Steamboy	In stores December 2005
Fullmetal Alchemist:	
Captured Alchemist	In stores January 2006
Kamikaze Girls	In stores February 2006

VIZ media™

www.viz.com
store.viz.com

Printed in Canada